AF623364

# Coalition Politics and the Iraq War

# Coalition Politics and the Iraq War

## Determinants of Choice

Daniel F. Baltrusaitis

Viva Books

New Delhi | Mumbai | Chennai | Kolkata | Bengaluru | Hyderabad | Kochi | Guwahati

*The views expressed in this book are those of the author and do not reflect the official policy or position of the U.S. Air Force the U.S. Department of Defense, or the U.S. Government*

Copyright © FirstForumPress

**First Indian Edition 2011**

**VIVA BOOKS PRIVATE LIMITED**

- 4737/23 Ansari Road, Daryaganj, New Delhi 110 002
  E-mail: vivadelhi@vivagroupindia.net, Tel. 42242200
- 76, Service Industries, Shirvane, Sector 1, Nerul, Navi Mumbai 400 706
  E-mail: vivamumbai@vivagroupindia.net, Tel. 27721273, 27721274
- Jamals Fazal Chambers, 26 Greams Road, Chennai 600 006
  E-mail: vivachennai@vivagroupindia.net, Tel. 28290304, 28294241
- B-103, Jindal Towers, 21/1A/3 Darga Road, Kolkata 700 017
  E-mail: vivakolkata@vivagroupindia.net, Tel. 22836381, 22816713
- 7, Sovereign Park Apartments, 56-58, K. R. Road, Basavanagudi, Bengaluru 560 004
  E-mail: vivabangalore@vivagroupindia.net, Tel. 26607409, 26607410
- 101-102 Mughal Marc Apartments, 3-4-637 to 641, Narayanguda, Hyderabad 500 029
  E-mail: vivahyderabad@vivagroupindia.net, Tel. 27564481, 27564482
- Beevi Towers, First Floor, SRM Road, Kaloor, Kochi 682 018, Kerala
  E-mail: vivakochi@vivagroupindia.net, Tel: 0484-2403055, 2403056
- 232, GNB Road, Beside UCO Bank, Silpukhuri, Guwahati 781 003
  E-mail: vivaguwahati@vivagroupindia.net, Tel: 0361-2666386

***www.vivagroupindia.com***

*Published by arrangement with*

Lynne Rienner Publishers, Inc.
1800 30th Street, Suite 314
Boulder, Colorado 80301
USA

All rights reserved. No part of this book may be reproduced or utilized in any form or by any means, electronic or mechanical, including photocopying, recording or by any information storage or retrieval systems, without permission in writing from the publisher.

*This edition is for sale in the Indian subcontinent only. Not for export elsewhere.*

ISBN : 978-81-309-1524-1

Published by Vinod Vasishtha for Viva Books Private Limited, 4737/23, Ansari Road, Daryaganj, New Delhi - 110 002. Printed and bound by Raj Press, R-3, Inderpuri, New Delhi - 110 012.

S0000 / S0800 / S0810

# Contents

# Tables and Figures

## Tables



## Figures

# Acknowledgments

Any book requires a great amount of burden sharing to accomplish, and this book was no exception. I can easily say that this work is the culmination of a long effort during which I was able to "stand on the backs of others" to explain the decisions of states to join military coalitions. Many people contributed in this work and made it a much finer book than it would have been otherwise. I owe a profound debt of gratitude to colleagues at Georgetown University, who refined my analysis of coalition burden sharing. I am especially grateful to Andrew Bennett, who inspired the idea to work on burden sharing and constantly refined my effort; Robert Lieber, who sharpened my analysis of foreign policy; and Jay Parker, who provided excellent guidance on the influence of public opinion on policy, as well as on the ability of elites to influence public opinion. I am especially grateful to Liz Grimm, who endured numerous edits of my manuscript and always cheerfully provided insightful comments. I would also like to thank Sarah Cross, Tricia Bacon, John Sawyer, Hamutal Bernstein, Paul Fritz, and the anonymous reviewer who read and commented on the manuscript. I am deeply indebted for their support and guidance, which made this project possible.

Last, and certainly not least, I would like to give special thanks to those who suffered most during the research process. I am grateful to my parents, William and Marian, who inspired me to always do my best and gave me a thirst for learning. To my children, Becky and Melissa, who saw only the back of my head while I was writing and editing, and who missed numerous fun weekends so that I could finish another chapter, I am sorry for the time I missed with you. I am immensely proud of the women you have become and your drive to be the best that you can be. I finally want to thank the love of my life, Janset, who showed amazing patience and always ensured that I did not take myself too seriously. This work is more representative of my family's love and support than my effort. Of course, any faults are entirely my own.

# 1
# Untangling the Puzzle of Coalition Burden Sharing

I was first attracted to the issue of coalition burden sharing, especially within the context of the Iraq War, while living in South Korea. I observed several anti-American protests due to the American military presence, and saw a liberal Korean president elected on a platform that argued for a reduced U.S. presence on the peninsula, along with greater decision role for Korea within the alliance. Given this high level of domestic and political resistance to the U.S., I was surprised when the newly elected Korean President, Roh Moo-hyun, announced that the Republic of Korea (ROK) would support the U.S. led "coalition of the willing" in Iraq. Korea eventually provided the third largest contingent to the stability operations even though it had no direct stake in the intervention. I was puzzled by this outcome. Why would a state that was not directly affected by the Iraq crisis join the coalition, especially considering the strong anti-American rhetoric of the elections only months prior? Additionally, why would Korea provide such a large military contribution when that contribution was very unpopular domestically?

In addition to the ROK's behavior, I was further intrigued by the different levels of support provided by other coalition partners in the two U.S.-Iraq conflicts. The Turkish parliament's failure to grant U.S. ground forces the necessary access to launch a direct land assault against northern Iraq, after months of negotiations in late 2002-early 2003, struck a critical blow to the Bush administration's military plan, and added an additional political disappointment to the "coalition of the willing." This diminished level of support contrasts sharply with Turkey's assistance to the 1991 Gulf War coalition. In that conflict, Turkish President Turgut Özal pursued active regional diplomacy to mobilize Middle Eastern support and allowed use of Turkish airbases for U.S. strikes into Iraq. Given Turkey's robust support of past U.S. military efforts, and its economic incentives to work with the United

States to protect its interests in northern Iraq, why did the Turkish government refuse a substantial aid package to remain on the sidelines of the Iraq war and consequently risk U.S. censure? Why was the usually centrally controlled government unable to garner the support in the legislature for the memorandum of understanding negotiated with the United States, especially after the United States had significantly improved Turkish infrastructure to support the war in 2003?

Finally, Germany's position concerning Iraq was also puzzling. First, why did Germany adopt an extreme foreign policy position in 2003 regarding the coalition when it could have quietly withheld support? The Schröder government not only declined to make a direct German contribution to the war, but also engaged in active counter-coalition-building by lobbying France and Russia to support Germany's resistance to what Gerhard Schröder called an "adventure."[1] Germany abandoned its traditional policy of balancing between Washington and Paris and instead created a counter-coalition with Russia and France against the United States. Germany's refusal to support the U.S.-led coalition—even under a UN mandate—seriously undermined the diplomatic position of the Bush administration in building an effective coalition against Iraq. In addition, why did Germany cooperate with the United States in a variety of other aspects of the war effort while at the same time thwarting U.S. efforts diplomatically? Germany put no limitations on the use of U.S. military bases and actually supplied German soldiers to guard U.S. bases so that U.S. military forces could deploy to Iraq. This level of coalition participation is in contrast with the robust German financial support of *Operation Desert Storm* through "checkbook diplomacy."

Pundits, commentators, journalists, and some international relations scholars simply attribute the lack of vigorous participation to the Bush administration's "unilateralism" and the lack of international legitimacy surrounding the 2003 effort. Unfortunately, this explanation is not only incomplete, but flawed: it does not adequately explain why states such as South Korea supported the coalition robustly in the face of international and domestic criticism while others such as Germany opposed any intervention even under a UN mandate.

These initial observations motivated me to more broadly question why states assume burdens within security coalitions. This book seeks to answer the questions of why states contribute to ad hoc security coalitions and what factors influence their level and composition of support? Through an examination of the 2003 Iraq War coalition, this book presents a burden sharing decision model that provides a framework for explaining—and perhaps even predicting—how states will choose whether to participate in future military conflicts.

## The Coalition of the Willing

Twelve years after *Operation Desert Storm*, events in Iraq again precipitated an international crisis and a U.S.-led military coalition. The coalition composition for the 2003 Iraq War differed significantly from the 1991 Persian Gulf War. In 2003, the international community was unified in its assessment that Iraq had violated its Security Council mandate to disarm, but was divided on the appropriate course of action. The United Kingdom and Spain were strong advocates in the Security Council for military intervention in Iraq. In particular, British Prime Minister Tony Blair significantly influenced U.S. war deliberations, convincing the Bush administration on the need for a Security Council Resolution in order to garner domestic and international legitimacy for the use of force. British and U.S. efforts were critical in garnering a unanimous consensus for Security Council Resolution 1441 (November 8, 2002), which labeled Iraq in "material breach" of the of the ceasefire terms presented under the terms of Resolution 687. This resolution put the onus on Iraq to prove that it did not have Weapons of Mass Destruction (WMD) and warned Iraq that it would face "serious consequences" as a result of its continued violations of its obligations.[2] This resolution solidified international support to engage Iraq, but left doubt on the meaning of "serious consequences." The unanimous vote on Resolution 1441 disguised a number of fundamental policy differences among the Security Council Members.

While the United States saw Resolution 1441 as a stepping-stone for military action, France and Germany interpreted the resolution as a pretext for more aggressive weapons inspections. In early March 2003, the governments of France, Russia, and Germany informally rejected a second U.S.-British draft resolution advocating the use of force. Germany initially led international efforts against a war. The second resolution became a "trial of strength" between Paris and the United States. France went to great lengths to dissuade the United States and the United Kingdom from presenting a second resolution to the Council.[3] In the end, the diplomatic efforts of France and Germany—and to a lesser extent Russia and China—assured that the second resolution was not brought to a vote. German Chancellor Gerhard Schröder won reelection in national elections the previous September, partly based on his rejection of a U.S. military intervention in Iraq. He undermined U.S. efforts to build a military coalition by rejecting German participation in a war even with a Security Council Resolution.[4] France supported diplomatic action and weapons inspections, but eventually joined with Germany in a diplomatic blocking effort in the Security Council, once it was clear that war was likely.[5] In the diplomatic buildup to the second resolution, Germany and France applied significant pressure on the former Soviet states of Eastern Europe to repel U.S. advances to participate in a coalition.

In a late January 2003 rebuke of the assertion that Germany and France were speaking for Europe, eight NATO members issued an open letter of support for U.S. policy towards Iraq. The eight included Great Britain, Spain, Italy, the Netherlands, Poland, the Czech Republic, Hungary, and Portugal. The letter from the NATO-Eight was followed by another endorsement from Eastern European nations aspiring to NATO and EU membership. The group, known as the Vilnius 10, included Albania, Bulgaria, Estonia, Croatia, Latvia, Lithuania, Macedonia, Romania, Slovakia, and Slovenia. In an open letter, dated February 5, 2003, the group declared, "Our countries understand the dangers posed by tyranny and the special responsibility of democracies to defend our shared values."[6] They claimed that it was already clear Iraq was in breach of U.N. Security Council Resolution 1441. The Vilnius group gave the Bush administration a diplomatic boost by stating, "In the event of non-compliance, we are prepared to contribute to an international coalition to enforce its provisions and the disarmament of Iraq."[7]

Japan was very supportive of the second draft resolution authorizing the use of force against Iraq and launched a diplomatic effort to persuade undecided members of the Security Council to support the resolution. Tokyo warned France on the dangers of splitting the international community and the Security Council over the resolution. In an official statement Japan warned, "[i]f the international community divides, it will not only benefit Iraq, but also place in doubt the authority and effectiveness of the United Nations."[8] Japan also offered financial assistance to states bordering Iraq, including $1.3 billion to Egypt, Syria, Turkey, and Jordan.[9]

The Iraq War coalition formed without a UN mandate for the use of force to disarm Iraq. The U.S. legitimized the invasion under Chapter VII of the United Nations Charter, referencing in particular Resolutions 678, 687 and 1441.[10] President Bush argued that these resolutions provided clear authority for the use of force against Iraq, even without the authority granted from additional resolutions.

The United States commenced combat operations in Iraq on March 19, 2003, with a "coalition of the willing" comprised of 40 countries that publicly committed to the war effort. This coalition provided a variety of support, including logistical and intelligence support, over-flight rights, and humanitarian and reconstruction aid, but did not necessarily provide direct military assistance for combat operations. Table 1.1 illustrates military contribution to the coalition for combat operations. The table depicts troop strength for the initial coalition and percent of that nation's total armed forces. Only six coalition members (besides the United States) provided military support to conventional combat operations, and only four coalition members committed troops to combat.

**Table 1.1 Military Contribution to Initial Combat Operations**

| Country | Troop Strength | % Total Active Armed Forces |
|---|---|---|
| United States | 250,000 | 17.5% |
| United Kingdom | 45,000 | 21.2% |
| Australia | 2,000 | 3.7% |
| Spain | 900* | 0.6% |
| Denmark | 300* | 1.3% |
| Poland | 180 | 0.1% |
| Bulgaria | 150* | 0.3% |

**Provided non-combat mission support outside Iraq such as chemical decontamination and logistic support units.*

Data Sources: Cordesman, *The Iraq War: Strategy, Tactics, and Military Lessons*, (Washington DC, 2003),16, 37-40; Katzmann, *Economic and Military Support for the U.S. Efforts in Iraq*, (Washington DC, 2007), 9-10; International Institute for Strategic Studies, *The Military Balance*, (London, 2004), 353-358.

As the Iraq war progressed, the composition of the coalition evolved from predominately a U.S., U.K., Australian coalition to a multinational coalition of many small to medium-sized contributors; however, the United States still provided the bulk of military forces. Figure 1.1 shows aggregate troop levels during the Iraq War. U.S. participation is shown in white and multinational partner participation is in black.

**Figure 1.1 Coalition Strength for Stabilization Operations**

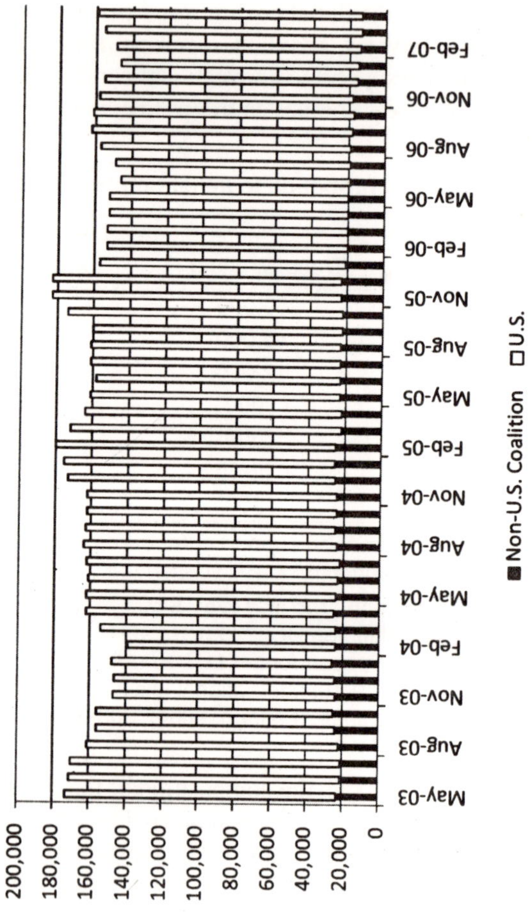


Data Source: The Brookings Institution, *Iraq Index*, September 10, 2007.

These data show that while U.S. forces responded to changing security conditions in Iraq, non-U.S. coalition contributions remained relatively steady from 2003 to 2005, and then steadily declined thereafter. These data are puzzling in that the coalition seemed to lose multinational support even after the United States gained international legitimacy from a successful Iraqi election in January 2005 and a succession of UN Resolutions authorizing support of stability operations. U.S. burdens fluctuated to the security situation, while coalition partners were insulated from these changes and maintained a rather steady—if not declining—level of burden. These data seem to show that legitimacy based on UN authorization did not significantly affect the collective effort; one would expect the international presence to increase as the coalition gained legitimacy through successful elections and UN sanction.

Throughout the operation, the United States continued to pursue UN Security Council support in an attempt to gain support for the military effort. In the wake of the U.S.-led invasion, the UN Security Council passed Resolution 1472 on March 28, which called on, "the international community also to provide immediate humanitarian assistance to the people of Iraq."[11] This resolution authorized the use of "Oil-for-Food" funds to be used in the humanitarian effort. It also marked the U.S.-led coalition as an occupying power.[12] Resolution 1483, on May 22, established the Iraq Development Fund. This resolution was significant in that it was the first UN Resolution that provided a measure of international legitimacy to states, other than the United States and Britain, for participating in the military coalition. By late May 2003, the United Kingdom and the United States had begun redeploying significant combat strength home on the assumption of a pacific occupation combined with the anticipation of international support for post-war administration. The security situation in Iraq, however, continued to decline throughout the summer of 2003; by October, the Bush administration pressed the UN for an additional resolution to garner support for the Iraq coalition. Resolution 1511 on October 16 provided legitimacy to the Iraqi Governing Council, which was the provisional government of Iraq, established by the U.S. led Coalition Provisional Authority. More importantly for the Bush administration, the resolution provided a mandate for member states to contribute to the multinational force in Iraq to maintain security under a unified command until Iraq established a representative government.[13] The UN continued to provide a mandate for the multinational coalition under Resolutions 1546 (2004), 1637 (2005), 1723 (2006) and 1790 (2007). Finally, the UN mandate for providing security assistance to Iraq expired December 31, 2008. This review of UN Security Council actions shows that the military coalition, although initially lacking UN authority, had gained UN Security Council approval beginning in the fall of 2003.

Unfortunately for the Bush administration, coalition partner presence declined throughout the duration of the war. Although the UN—and to a lesser extent the Iraqi government—provided a level of legitimacy to the U.S.-led occupation, international participation actually declined as resolutions supporting the effort mounted. Figure 1.2 presents the level of coalition partner participation as a percentage of the total military effort.

**Figure 1.2 Percentage of Non-U.S. Participation in Iraq Coalition**

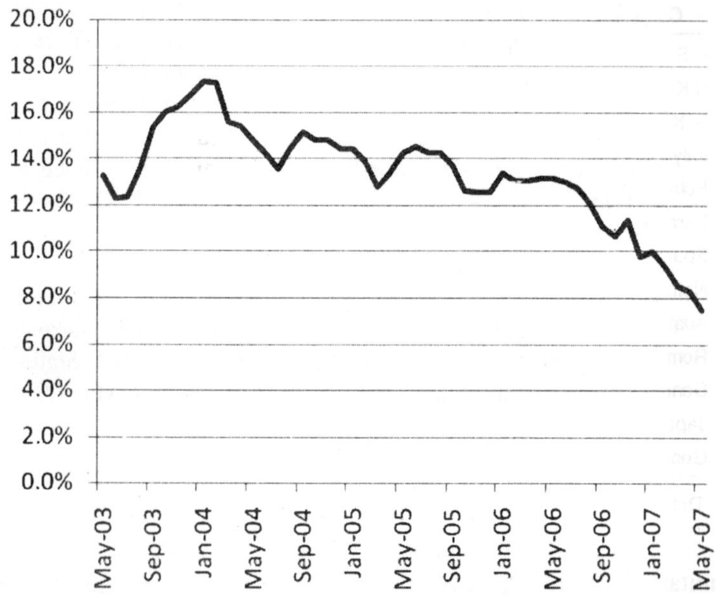


Data Source: The Brookings Institution, *Iraq Index*, September 10, 2007

These data reflect coalition military support to Iraq stability operations after the conclusion of conventional combat operations in May 2003. Non-U.S. coalition contributions peaked at 17.3 percent of the total effort in February 2004; four months after the coalition gained full UN support, and steadily declined to 7.5 percent by May 2007. This seems to indicate that the mild support for nation building operations was suffering under the weight of an ongoing military operation and increasingly violent insurgent attacks. The United States was suffering from the classic collective action predicament; because it had significant military forces in Iraq, it was expected to maintain a disproportional amount of military burden.

Coalition support not only decreased over the duration of the conflict, but coalition composition significantly changed throughout. Table 1.2 illustrates the level military support, by year, of the top contributors to the Iraq coalition. As evidenced by these data, the

**Table 1.2 Military Contribution to Stability Operations March 2003-March 2007**

| | Coalition Military Contribution | | | | |
|---|---|---|---|---|---|
| Country | 2003 | 2004 | 2005 | 2006 | 2007 |
| U.S. | 250,000 | 138,000 | 150,000 | 133,000 | 142,000 |
| U.K. | 45,000 | 8,220 | 8,000 | 8,000 | 7,100 |
| S. Korea | | 675 | 3,600 | 3,270 | 2,300 |
| Italy | | 3,000 | 3,000 | 2,900 | 0 |
| Poland | 180 | 2,500 | 1,700 | 900 | 900 |
| Ukraine | | 1,650 | 1,500 | 0 | 0 |
| Spain | 900 | 1,300 | 0 | 0 | 0 |
| Netherlands | | 1,307 | 0 | 0 | 0 |
| Australia | 2000 | 850 | 900 | 900 | 550 |
| Romania | | 500 | 800 | 860 | 600 |
| Denmark | 300 | 500 | 530 | 530 | 460 |
| Japan | | 200 | 500 | 600 | 0 |
| Georgia | | | 800 | 900 | 900 |

Data Source: The Brookings Institution, *Iraq Index*, Multiple March Issues

military coalition evolved over the life of the Iraq War. The United Kingdom rapidly downsized its 45,000 strong invasion force and installed a significantly smaller contingent of peacekeepers in the south. Poland robustly supported peacekeeping operations initially—even leading coalition operations south of Baghdad—but reduced its support to providing a battalion sized combat element and a divisional headquarters. Spain also initially provided robust support to the reconstruction effort, but terminated that support following the March 2004 Madrid train bombing and the election of Prime Minister José Luis Rodríguez Zapatero, who campaigned on Spanish troop withdrawal.

South Korea remained a firm supporter of military operations for several years; however, its support waned due to domestic pressure resulting in a complete withdrawal in December 2008.

Although military support to the coalition is a significant indicator of burden sharing, financial support is also an essential element of coalition participation. States typically substitute financial support for military support when they are domestically unable or unwilling to contribute military forces. During the 1991 Gulf War, Japan and Germany—constitutionally limited from deploying military personnel—were the third and fourth largest financial contributors to the coalition, underwriting many U.S. military expenses. In that conflict, the United States was reimbursed almost entirely for its military expenses as it collected approximately $74 billion in 2007 dollars from coalition partners. The limited financial support the United States received for its 2003 operations in Iraq stand in stark contrast to the 1991 Gulf War. The United States not only funded its own operations, but also directly funded several coalition partners' participation. Table 1.3 presents a list

**Table 1.3 U.S. Financial Support to Non-U.S. Coalition Partners**

| Country | Total (Millions) | Percent |
|---|---|---|
| Poland* | $988.4 | 66.2% |
| Jordan | $295.0 | 19.7% |
| Georgia | $63.1 | 4.2% |
| Ukraine | $12.5 | 0.8% |
| United Kingdom | $5.6 | 0.4% |
| Romania | $3.0 | 0.2% |
| Bosnia | $2.0 | 0.1% |
| Mongolia | $1.3 | 0.1% |
| Other Nations | $123.3 | 8.3% |
| **Total** | **$1,494.2** | **100%** |

* *Funding to Poland included funding for troops operating under its command.*

Data Source: GAO-07-827T, *Stabilizing and Rebuilding Iraq*, (Washington DC, 2007) of countries that received U.S. assistance to participate in the military coalition. These countries provided personnel, or other material military support,to themultinational force in Iraq, but were not financially able to support their troops in the field for extended periods and therefore required financial assistance to prepare their troops for the operation. Between 2003 and 2007, the United States provided approximately $1.5 billion to 20 countries to support their military contribution to the Iraq coalition.

U.S. objectives in Iraq also required a significant financial investment for the reconstruction of the Iraqi government and infrastructure. In October 2003, A UN-sponsored donors' conference was held in Madrid, shortly after passage of Security Council Resolution 1511. Foreign donors pledged approximately $20 billion in grants and loans for Iraq reconstruction, but grants and loans for reconstruction were only a small portion of the international commitment.[14] According to the Special Inspector General for Iraq Reconstruction, more than $139 billion has been raised for Iraq reconstruction through three main sources: Iraqi funding of $71.01 billion, U.S. funding of $51.00 billion, and international funding of $17.79 billion.[15] International assistance includes $6.04 billion in grants and $11.75 billion in pledged loans. Figure 1.3 shows the distribution of international donor grants by country. The white bars display pledges to Iraqi reconstruction and the black bars show funds committed. The largest non-American contributors are Japan, the European Commission, the United Kingdom, Australia, Canada, Denmark, Italy, Spain, and South Korea. This $6 billion in international grant assistance pales in comparison to the $51 billion appropriated by the United States.[16]

This short summary of military, economic, and diplomatic engagement underscores the variety, scope, and duration of contributions that states make to participate in multinational coalitions. Each method of contribution requires negotiation on the international level regarding the composition and timing of contributions. At the same time, however, state executives must make the case for action—or inaction—with their domestic publics.[17] State executives must continually reassess their contributions in light of the domestic and international costs and benefits inherent in a coalition action.

Because of this tension between the international environment and domestic politics, a multi-level model is ideal to untangle the puzzle of constraints placed on decision-makers by the international environment and domestic politics. The burden sharing model presented here reflects the choices state executives must make to balance state imperatives when called to participate in a coalition.

**Figure 1.3 International Donor Grants by Country**

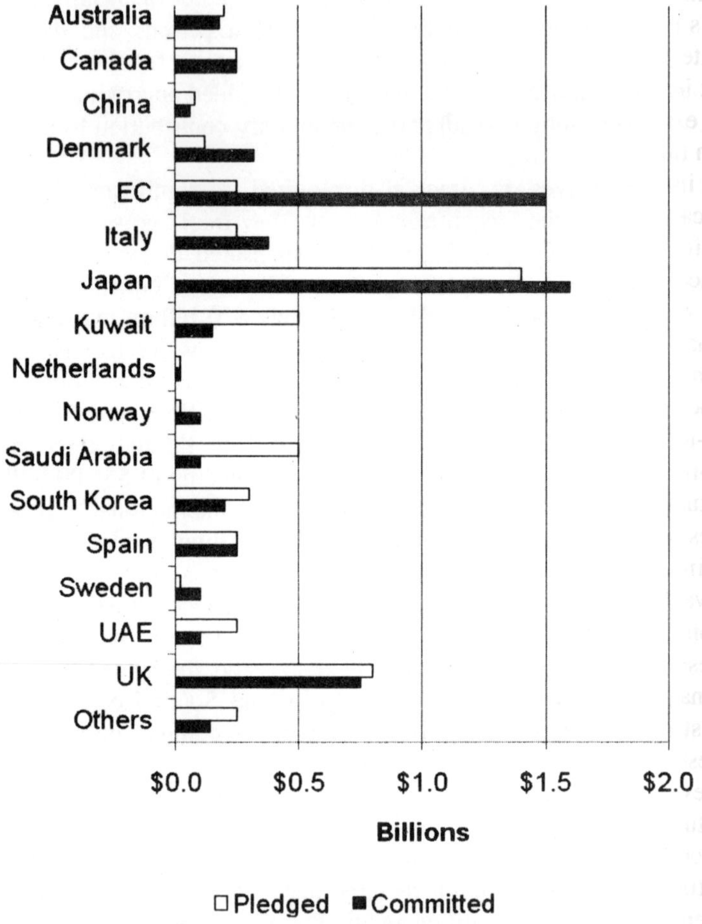


Source: Special Inspector General for Iraq Reconstruction, *Iraq Reconstruction: Funding Sources and Uses, Section 2 Report*, April 2009

## Burden Sharing Decision Model

Due to the complex nature of burden sharing decisions, no single analytical outlook can adequately explain state burden sharing behavior. Systemic theories such as collective action or realist theories describe the systemic forces that influence state chief executives, but these theories do not explain decision outcomes. Systemic theories are unable to explain the foreign policies of individual states because they do not examine the sources of state level variation. For instance, Stephen Walt's balance of threat theory predicts that states will balance against an external threat, but it cannot explain why a state is perceived as a threat in the first place. Balance of threat theory treats threat perception as an exogenous variable rather than as a social construction. Collective action theory explains the problems initiating and executing a collective event in pursuit of a public good. However, this approach is agnostic to political motivations for allying in the first place. It fails to explain coalition contributions as a result of side-payments, bargaining, or alliance dependence. For coalitions, burden sharing decisions take the form of a two-level game where the state executive must balance international and domestic interests.[18]

In most coalition burden sharing situations, states have choices that can be explained in terms of domestic politics and goals of key actors. State-level analytical approaches are necessary to explain the influence of domestic politics and society on foreign policy decisions. Domestic structure research convincingly demonstrates the influence of differing domestic structure on state foreign policy. States' foreign policies are not simply the result of international constraints defined by power, but also vary according to the executive's willingness and political ability to respond to systemic necessities. The research demonstrates that domestic political processes help to shape a state's definition of the national interest and its ability to implement it.[19] Content and consistency of foreign policy result as much from the constraints of domestic structures as from international systemic influences.[20] However, one cannot understand a state's foreign policy merely through structures. Scholars must also understand the biases and influences of key constituencies in the foreign policy process to determine how structure translates these influences into policy. A theory of individual influence is necessary to complete the picture since foreign policy is the culmination of many individual lessons from history that form decision maker's beliefs.

Individual and cognitive theoretical approaches explain the influence of individuals' beliefs on foreign policy. Cognitive theory provides a methodology for exploring the influence of decision maker experience and beliefs the formulation of effective foreign policy strategies. John Lewis Gaddis maintains that every U.S. presidential administration has "certain assumptions about American interests in the world, potential threats to them and feasible responses, which tend to be formed before or just after an administration takes office."[21] This statement highlights the influence of past experience on future policy choices; decision makers may be predisposed to certain coalition choices regardless of systemic pressures. Common ideologies, perceptions of threat, domestic and societal influences, and individual motivations all affect foreign policy outcomes in some respect.

Since burden sharing decisions lie at the intersection of domestic and international politics, only a multi-level model may explain the spectrum of constraints and opportunities defined by the dynamics of the international system and each state's domestic political structures. When domestic political considerations are not included in the study of foreign policy, researchers are limited to developing a set of necessary, but not sufficient, conditions for foreign policy decision making.[22] The foreign policy decision maker must answer to an international audience that includes other political leaders, international organizations, and regional institutions while keeping an eye on maintaining office. The international arena establishes the attributes of the executives' menu of available choices for a particular foreign policy decision. Systemic theories, based only on the international environment, are incomplete because they do not explain domestic constraints on choices and ignore domestic forces that motivate state executives. Domestically, the executive must answer to an audience that includes supporters, critics, constituents, agents responsible for execution of policy, and most importantly, challengers for the leadership position.[23] However, domestic models alone do not explain national motivations for foreign policy choices. The domestic audience shapes and is shaped by the international environment, but each alone only partially explains why states make the foreign policy decisions that they make.[24] Integrated models provide an attractive choice for explaining multifaceted decisions, particularly when simpler, existing theories have an uneven track record in explaining complex outcomes.

The burden sharing decision model presented in Figure 1.4 is a multi-level model of foreign policy decision making that accounts for the international, domestic, and cognitive influences on state burden sharing decisions.[25] This model is a reformulation of the security decision model originally developed by Andrew Bennett, Danny Unger, and Joseph Lepgold to explain the contributions to the 1991 Persian Gulf War.[26] The model accounts for the interactions between the cognitive, international, and domestic domains and provides multiple causal paths to outcomes.

**Figure 1.4 Burden Sharing Decision Model**

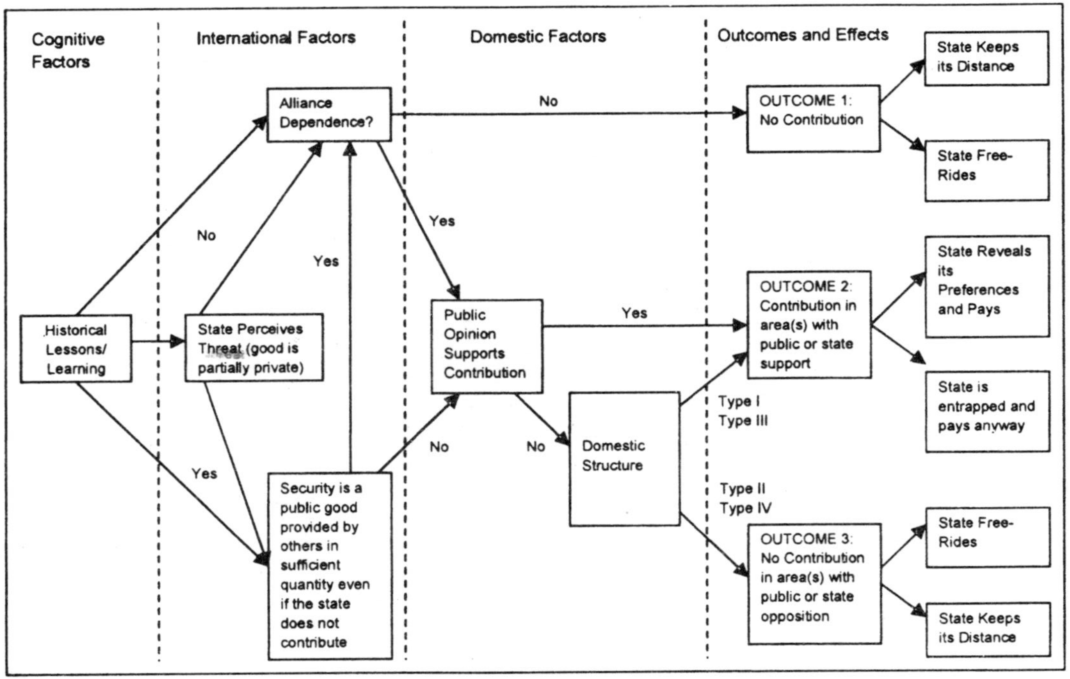

## Independent Variables

The blocks depicted in the first three columns of the burden sharing decision model represent the independent variables affecting foreign policy outcomes.

### *Cognitive Factors*

*Historical Learning.* Studies employing a cognitive approach that focus on beliefs and images held by political elites provide a powerful source for understanding foreign policy behavior.[27] Policy makers rely heavily on historical analogy to simplify and understand complex situations. A historical analogy provides a comparison of some past experience with a current decision, so that some important aspect of the past experience can provide an insight into the current problem. Analogy helps decision makers define the nature of the situation, assess the stakes, and provide policy prescriptions. Unfortunately, this use of analogy often results in poor policy choices. Policy makers tend to oversimplify complex lessons, neglecting important historical details, which leads to inappropriate analogizing and misguided policy choices. Additionally, vivid personal events are more likely to guide decision makers than other more relevant events. Decision makers tend to "learn" from events in which they were personally involved, rather than from others' experiences.[28] Historical learning through analogy can explain foreign policy outcomes that seem irrational when considered merely through systemic paradigms.

Learning is the application of historical analogy from past experience to facilitate understanding of a particular policy question.[29] Given the complexity of measuring cognitive beliefs and values, I incorporate a simplified cognitive model that can offer useful predictions of state beliefs concerning coalition burden sharing. This analysis makes four assumptions on the influence of beliefs and choice heuristics on actors in their use of analogies to make decisions.[30] First, a key component of beliefs consists of the lessons or analogies drawn from the past. Second, individuals rely on their particular society's experiences as sources of lessons and analogies. Third, lessons and analogies are more likely to be influential if they involve events that are recent, vivid, evocative, personal, or of significant historical importance. Finally, decision makers who undergo similar experiences will tend to share dominant sets of analogies and lessons.

With these assumptions in mind, the case study analysis considers the following beliefs in the historical lessons and learning module. First, the study will assess the motivation for collective action. Beliefs about the threat of Saddam Hussein to regional stability, and his capability to proliferate nuclear, chemical, or biological weapons to terrorist organizations should affect perceptions of the public good of collective action. Beliefs about the likelihood of free riding should matter as well since state burden sharing decisions are influenced by expectations of the collective effort. Secondly, coalition contributions should be shaped by beliefs about the influence of force and diplomacy on external threats. Each state decision has the potential to be affected by whether each state's most important and recent experiences of using force was successful. Thirdly, decisions should be influenced by perceptions of alliance dependence. States that recently experienced entrapment by an ally should be reluctant to contribute to the Iraq coalition. Conversely, states that experienced abandonment should be more likely to contribute if they believed that a failure to support an ally in an earlier case led to their abandonment. Additionally, states that suffered abandonment after supporting an ally should be even less likely to support another coalition without extreme guarantees. Finally, leaders should be more likely to contribute if they believed a failure to do so in an earlier instance led to a domestic backlash. Conversely, if recent military intervention led to domestic backlash leaders should be wary of making major contributions to another coalition.

According to the learning hypothesis, leaders will be more likely to contribute to an effort if they gained full participation rights, influenced decision making, and received compensation in the form of increased influence with the coalition leader, or material benefits, for their participation in previous efforts. Leaders will be less likely to contribute if they recently experienced alliance entrapment or abandonment. Leaders should be more likely to contribute if they believed a failure to do so in an earlier instance led to a domestic backlash, conversely, they would be less likely if participation generated domestic backlash.

Historical learning is expected to not only influence whether a state supports a coalition, but it is likely to affect the method and timing of support. Past "mistakes" or "successes" influence the makeup, duration, and timing of support. One lesson is the influence of timing on past coalition efforts. Early or late support to a coalition can influence the ingrained lessons learned. Early support runs the risk of entrapment in an action that grows well beyond the initial level of commitment. Additionally, joining a coalition too early runs the risk that a state's effort is taken for granted because it did hold out in bargaining for a larger share of the coalition benefits. Late support, on the other hand, can be seen by the coalition leader as a lack of support, thereby running the risk of abandonment. On the other hand, late support may have saved a state from entrapment in a failed intervention.

### International Factors

International, or systemic factors, are those broad factors that define and shape the international environment and explain the interaction of external inducements and constraints on states foreign policy behavior. Systemic theory allows the understanding of the context of action before explaining unit level variation.

*Balance of Threat.* Since private versus collective incentives significantly influence the motivation for burden sharing, the balance of threat block in the burden sharing decision model seeks to explain whether an ally considers the action a "war of choice," or a necessary intervention to counter an existential threat. This block of the model aims to identify state motives for action. If a collective action, one can expect to see states attempt to free ride. On the other hand, if states consider the coalition as countering a significant threat, one can expect to see states robustly supporting the effort. Since collective action problems can be overcome when states have private incentives, the balance of threat block aims to explain contributions that cannot be explained by the collective action proposition.[31]

States will generally balance by forming alliances against a perceived threat. Stephen Walt, in *The Origins of Alliances*, outlines four factors—military capability, geographic proximity, offensive power, and aggressive intentions—which affect states' perceptions of threat.[32] However, the question of how states identify threats is relevant. Walt takes threat as given; a composite of the four factors outlined above. In this formulation, there is an implicit assumption that the source of greatest threat is obvious to decision makers. Yet the question of how states actually identify threats is much more complex.[33] Walt provides no guidance to how states prioritize among the four elements of threat: "One cannot determine a priori which sources of threat will be most important in any given case; one can say only that all of them are likely to play a role."[34] When analyzing an environment of multiple potential threats to a state, it is essential to unpack the bundle of independent variables Walt designates as encompassing threat. The differentiation of threat better defines the environmental conditions in which policy is formulated. The type of threat and adversary will have an obvious impact on policy choices.[35]

Threat perception is a function of the ordering of multiple sources of threat to a given state. Identity and ideas are as important as material power in determining the influence of threat. States overwhelmingly identify ideological and political threats to internal stability, emanating from abroad, as more salient than threats based upon aggregate power, geographic proximity and offensive capabilities. Internal unrest threatening the existing government is perceived as dangerous as a direct invasion.[36] Therefore, for many Persian Gulf states, a resurgent Iraq was not seen as threatening as Iran, ideologically bent on causing domestic disturbance to further its political agenda. Similarly, a weakened Iraq that does not check Iranian influence may be more threatening to Gulf States than an Iraq under Saddam Hussein. This argument does not discount the typical material based depictions of threat, but rather emphasizes the influence of domestic and transnational political identity factors in explaining threat perceptions. It looks to additional factors to help explain state choices in an indeterminate structural environment.

This study operationalizes threat as a factor of material capability and intentions to influence a state internally and externally. If military defeat is seen as the most serious threat to regime security, then state decision makers should seek to balance against the state that is geographically closest and whose aggregate military power capabilities is the greatest. Even if that state's intentions are not immediately hostile, its power presents the most serious threat to state security because intentions can change drastically and rapidly. Since the first Gulf War diminished Iraq's power projection capability, the balance of threat effect should be most visible in states where Iraq could potentially threaten with offensive WMD.[37] If, on the other hand, ideational factors are seen as the most serious threat to security, then state leaders should balance against the state that manifests the most hostility toward their regimes, regardless of that state's aggregate power and geographic proximity. Hostile intent is defined as public attempts by one state to destabilize another state's ruling regime through propaganda, or support by one state for domestic or exile political groups opposed to another state's ruling regime, or threatening with military or economic sanctions.[38] In this instance, leaders do not see military capabilities by themselves as threatening, but rather view external threatening challenges to their domestic legitimacy and security as being more serious than threats based simply upon a preponderance of military capabilities.

*Collective Action.* Lacking private incentives—such as threat—collective action theory aims to explain how groups unite to fulfill a common action. Collective action involves group benefits that are inherently shared and therefore they cannot be privatized for individual benefit. Since the benefits are shared, everyone has an incentive to "free ride" on the contributions of others; to let others pay the price of the good.[39] The reason for the smaller expectation is due to how size affects marginal gains calculations. A state acting rationally is expected to increase the supply of a good until its marginal cost equals its marginal gain. However, when such reasoning leads a powerful state to contribute, less powerful states will be tempted to ride free because their efforts cannot be expected to secure much more of the collective good than what will be already supplied by the larger states. Because of this tendency to "free ride," a collective action usually needs a powerful organizer that can overcome the resistance of states to contribute to an action.[40]

The value of the collective good should influence state participation in a collective coalition. Those states that highly value a public good are expected to contribute significantly towards obtaining that good. Much of the political disagreement with the United States in the buildup to the Iraq War concerned the value or worth of the "public goods" for potential coalition allies. States clearly did not value the collective action equally. This observation conflicts with most of the existing literature on collective burden sharing. The majority of collective action studies of NATO, for example, assume that states equally value the "collective good." In the Iraq War, however this assumption did not hold. To determine the collective benefits of the Iraq War, this study identifies three collective goods: the disarmament of Iraqi offensive WMD; the stability of global oil markets; and lastly, the stabilization of the region through the removal of the Hussein regime.

Based on defense expenditures, the United States dwarfed all coalition and potential coalition nations in military spending, comprising 111percent of the next nine spenders combined and nearly seven times the second largest spender (China).[41] This fact should encourage a coalition partners to free ride, or keep their distance altogether, since the United States possessed more than enough military power to provide the public good.

The collective action hypothesis predicts that the United States and United Kingdom would provide a majority of coalition forces while other partners would provide a minimum. Since the U.S./U.K. bloc was willing and capable for a near-unilateral action, other states had a motivation to ride free. The United States alone was militarily capable of disarming Iraq unilaterally. Since the United States held the capability for unilateral action, other states had a diminished collective action motivation to participate.

*Alliance Dependence.* Another external dynamic that affects coalition formation and burden sharing is the concept of the alliance security dilemma. Potential allies face a security-autonomy tradeoff when entering into a defense pact; if an excess of "security" exists, a state may opt to trade some of the excess for more autonomy by loosening alliance bonds or by reducing support to the ally on some issues, potentially risking the ally's support on future security issues.[42] However, the security-autonomy trade-off creates a tension between two fears, the fear of abandonment and the fear of entrapment.[43] This "alliance security dilemma" recognizes that each ally has alternative alliance choices and may opt for one of them if it becomes dissatisfied with the present allies. Therefore, a pervasive aspect of alliances is the constant fear about being deserted by one's ally. Exercising too much autonomy runs the risk of abandonment, or defection, by allies. Abandonment can range from realigning with one's adversary, withdrawing from the standing alliance, failing to make good on explicit commitments, or failing to provide support in contingencies where support is expected.[44] The most common form of abandonment is the failure to support the ally diplomatically in a dispute with its adversary, when support was expected.[45] The trade-off also creates another fear: being too dependent on an ally and risking entrapment. Entrapment occurs when a state becomes entangled in a conflict central to an ally's interests but peripheral to its own, in the hope that the gains of preserving the alliance will outweigh the risks and costs of future war. Entrapment occurs when one state values the preservation of the alliance over the cost of fighting for its ally's interests.[46]

The risks of abandonment and entrapment tend to vary inversely. A possible hedge against abandonment is to increase one's commitment to an ally, thus increasing the ally's security and reducing its temptation to defect. However, this increases the likelihood that one will be entrapped by the ally. Concerns about possible entrapment may be reduced by limiting commitment to the ally or by withdrawing support in specific crises. However, this strategy risks devaluing the alliance for the ally and causing its defection. Acting to reduce one's own alliance concerns tends to increase the ally's concerns.

The alliance security dilemma arises because reducing the risk of entrapment tends to increase the risk of abandonment: the greater one's dependence on the alliance and the stronger one's commitment to the ally, the higher the risk of entrapment.[47] These pressures apply even without a formal alliance if weaker coalitional partners are vulnerable to security threats that they cannot deal with alone.[48] Weaker states, dependent on a dominant ally for security, are significantly influenced by future promises as much as threats of abandonment. Future promises provide the motivation to participate in peripheral security coalitions.[49]

Dependence is not limited to the security realm; states may also be dependent economically or politically. States will be more likely to support an ally that can impose costly adjustments to existing relationships. Additionally, allies may also support an effort in response to incentives, such as military aid or debt forgiveness. Hence, alliance dependence refers to a state's susceptibility to arm twisting and the conditioning of incentives by coalition leaders.

The alliance security dilemma also influences inter-coalition bargaining considerations. A strategy of strong commitment and support will have the undesired effect of reducing bargaining leverage over the ally. Conversely, bargaining power over the ally is enhanced when support is doubtful because one can make credible threats of nonsupport. Alliance bargaining thus favors the strategy of weak or ambiguous commitment.[50]

The severity of the alliance security dilemma, and the intensity of fears of abandonment and entrapment, is determined largely by commonality of interests, level of dependence, and commitment to the ally. Thus, the dilemma will be mild when the allies have a high proportion of common interest. The allies will have little fear of abandonment because of shared interests, and since the threat of abandonment has little credibility, they will have little bargaining advantage over each other. In contrast, the alliance security dilemma will be most severe if the allies do not share common interest in the conflict, or if they face the same adversary but have different conflicts with that adversary. Then both the likelihood of abandonment and the cost of entrapment will be high. The allies will simultaneously be skeptical of the other's commitment and anxious against being trapped into a widening conflict.[51]

The burden sharing decision model operationalizes alliance dependence by analyzing a state's susceptibility to demands and incentives from the coalition leaders. The most important determinant is the relative dependence of a potential coalition partner on U.S.-provided security. Additionally, trade and economic dependence on the United States should also factor into state burden sharing decisions. The more dependent a state is the more likely the costs and risks of abandonment will outweigh the costs and risks of abandonment.[52] In the Iraq War case, the greater a state's dependence on the United States relative to entrapment concerns, the more it should have contributed to the anti-Hussein coalition. I measure coalition member's dependence in terms of military and economic ties or other assistance that would be hard to replace with other partners. Britain would be expected to strongly support America because of the shared interests and close diplomatic, economic, and military ties between them. Japan and South Korea are also likely to strongly support due to the U.S. balancing role against China and North Korea in East Asia. Due to the diminished threat of Russia to Western Europe, France, Germany, Spain, Italy, and Canada should show a reluctance to be entrapped in a U.S. incursion into Iraq. Finally, according to this theory, Iranian, Chinese, and Russian participation should be zero. The effects of alliance dependence are clearest when states make contributions unrelated to any collective action pressures or immediate Iraqi threat.[53] Evidence of alliance dependence is most likely to be seen in bargaining considerations and U.S. pressure to generate support.

U.S. pressure is expected to be highly visible when it becomes part of a "two-level" bargaining game between an ally's leadership and domestic constituency.[54] As part of a "two-level" bargaining situation, the leadership of an ally will use international pressure to gain concessions from domestic constituencies. Conversely, potential allies will use domestic pressure to gain leverage with the coalition lead in the alliance or coalition bargaining situation. An ally's negotiators may invoke domestic pressure concerns to soften the coalition lead's demands, or might use international pressure to garner domestic support.

### *Internal Factors*

*Public Opinion.* Public opinion plays an important role in the formation of state preferences and the introduction of those preferences into policy choices. Most of the available literature on the interaction between mass public opinion and elites in the foreign policy-making process of liberal democracies can be categorized into to three broad concepts, a "bottom-up" approach, a "top-down" approach, and a "structural" approach where public opinion influence is shaped by issues, domestic structure, elite coalitions, and cleavages.

The first concept, the "bottom-up" approach, assumes that public opinion is often a proximate cause of policy.[55] In this mode, leaders follow mass beliefs. This approach assumes the Kantian notion of democracy in which domestic opinion has a great impact on foreign policy. The public has a strong influence on foreign policy because the people bear the costs of a given foreign policy decision.[56] However, the empirical record for the "bottom-up" thesis shows mixed results. Numerous cases exist where elites have made crucial foreign policy decisions in the absence of public consensus. Examples include the U.S. decisions favoring an active international role post World War II, the West German decision to rearm and join NATO in the early 1950s, the French decision to build an independent nuclear force and leave NATO military structure, and more recently the military surge in Iraq.[57]

A second approach, the "top-down" approach of public opinion, posits an orientation where public consensus is more a function of elite consent that trickles down to the mass public. This approach assumes a state-centered approach to foreign policy. It presumes the public is easily manipulated by political leaders in the foreign policy realm because of the low salience of international issues compared to domestic issues, combined with the low degree of public knowledge on foreign policy issues.[58] In this view, public officials tend to respect their constituents' preferences on domestic issues, but feel unconstrained on issues pertaining to foreign affairs.[59] However, scholars have reported a high degree of consistency between U.S. public opinion and foreign policy, including a high degree of congruence between shifts in public opinion and changes in foreign policy. Additionally, researchers have also shown public opinion shifting before policy changes, suggesting the weakness of the "top-down" hypothesis.[60]

Lastly, the third approach argues that the role of public opinion varies across issue area, domestic institutional structure, and coalition-building process among elites.[61] This approach assumes that "bottom-up" or "top-down" theories ignore the rich diversity in the ways that public opinion influences policy decisions. Simplistic theories tend to ignore that public opinion and societal groups may influence the policy-making process in several ways and at different stages. The public can directly affect decision making by changing policy goals or how those goals are prioritized or by narrowing the range of policy options. Moreover, the public may also indirectly affect policies by influencing the coalition building processes among the elites. It can influence the positions of bureaucracies or single actors within the government.[62] Lawrence Jacobs and Robert Shapiro, in their review of the state of the discipline with regards to studying public opinion, suggest that domestic structure and societal interaction with the government influence foreign policy. According to their hypothesis, public and elite opinion interact with each other and are transformed into policy decisions differently depending on the issue area, domestic structure, leadership preferences, and elite coalition building processes.[63] Thomas Risse-Kappen and Ole Holsti, in their studies of public opinion on foreign policy, have demonstrated that understanding domestic structures and coalition-building processes is essential to explain the impact of public opinion on the foreign policy. With these developments in mind, the next section discusses the interaction of public opinion with domestic institutions and politics and their effect on burden sharing outcomes.

*Domestic Structure.* Domestic structure theory provides simplifying assumptions concerning the interaction of the state and society, which in turn allow the prediction of likely foreign policy outcomes. Domestic structure approaches seek to explain the role of the interaction of state political institutions with a given state's society. They determine the selectivity of political systems to societal demands.

The burden sharing decision model incorporates a structural approach to understanding domestic influence of foreign policy decisions.[64] Table 1.4 shows the typology of executive influence based on state structure. This

**Table 1.4 Executive Influence Based on State Structure**

| | **Degree of Executive Autonomy from the Legislature** | |
|---|---|---|
| | Autonomous | Non-autonomous |
| **State Executive Structure**<br>Centralized | **Type I**<br>***Cognitive Explanation:***<br>The beliefs of a chief executive determines the burden sharing strategy. | **Type II**<br>***Societal Constraints:***<br>Burden sharing strategy is formulated by a chief executive whose preferences reflect public and legislative pressures. |
| Decentralized | **Type III**<br>***Elite Coalition Building:***<br>The state's policy is determined by intra-elite bargaining | **Type IV**<br>***Elite Coalition Building Subject to Societal Constraints:***<br>Policy is the outcome of compromise and coalition building among elites whose preferences reflect societal pressures |

Adapted From: Susan Peterson, *Crisis Bargaining and the State* typology of state-societal relations provides a framework for predicting outcomes based on domestic structure theory. The organization of decision making authority varies along a continuum from *centralized* to *decentralized* based on the number of bureaucratic agencies, ministries, and other governmental offices that have authority over a given issue. A centralized configuration exists when foreign policy decision making is restricted to relatively few government officials. The second element, degree of executive autonomy from the legislature, defines the executive autonomy vis-à-vis society. The greater the executive autonomy, the less control the legislature can exert over the content of a state's foreign policy. The legislature exerts control through two possible causal paths. First, the legislature may possess the authority to make policy for a specific issue area. For instance, the Turkish parliament must approve the stationing of foreign troops on its soil. Second, the executive may be responsible to and dependent on the legislature for tenure in office. A foreign policy executive that is not constrained by the legislature is considered *autonomous*, while an executive constrained by the legislature is considered *non-autonomous*.[65]

In a Type I structure, decision making authority is restricted to relatively few government officials and the chief executive enjoys near total autonomy from legislative scrutiny. In a Type I environment, foreign policy depends on cognitive explanations, or the strategic beliefs of the chief executive.[66] Cognitive explanations distinguish between those who view the international system as conflictual and those who see a more harmonious world.[67] While the structure of decision making authority determines that the chief executive is responsible for decision making, the content and rigidity of the leader's own beliefs explains how the state responds to burden-sharing requests.[68]

In a Type IV state, domestic political factors have the greatest influence on foreign policy decisions. A Type IV structure exists when the foreign policy decision process is composed of a number of different offices that share responsibility for foreign policy decision making, and when the legislature performs a significant oversight function. In this type of state, domestic pressures shape national leaders' preferences, and the state's policy response is the result of internal bureaucratic bargaining. Unable to act alone, individual policy makers must recognize domestic opponents who may appeal directly to the public. Interest groups, political parties, the media, and public opinion shape the policy-making process because the foreign policy executive is responsible to the legislature and, indirectly, to the public. Because of the many hands formulating policy, even the most powerful leaders must build a coalition of support for their preferred policy. State institutions shape national policy preferences by allowing societal actors a voice in the process. State structure determines that policy will be the outcome of domestic bargaining and coalition building.[69]

Decision making in a Type III state resembles that of the Type IV state with one exception. An internal process of coalition building and compromise among bureaucratic agencies exists, however, the executive branch benefits from significant autonomy from the legislature. Therefore, societal constraints do not enter the decision-making process. Foreign policy elite actors appeal to various bureaucratic or institutional constituencies, since a direct appeal to the public or interest groups would be ineffective. No representative element exists to channel public opinion into the policy-making process. Coalition politics prevail in a state where foreign policy is created by a multitude of actors.[70]

Finally, Type II states are characterized by need for the large-scale coalition building by the chief executive. The chief executive cannot ignore domestic considerations created by the executive-legislative relationship. Thus while a centralized cadre formulates foreign policy, the existence of administrative, regulatory, or legislative procedures enable societal influences to assume a legitimate role in the government's policy process.[71] Policy preferences will reflect not only the executive beliefs, but will also reflect the pressures exerted by political parties, interest groups, public opinion, and the legislature. One would expect the executive to give attention to societal groups' interests in this configuration.[72]

These two components of state structure—structure of the foreign policy executive and degree of executive autonomy from other societal actors—determine the avenues through which foreign policy is made, but do not determine outcomes. These components determine the contingent conditions where cognitive, bureaucratic, or domestic bargaining theories dominate. In all cases, it still remains necessary to determine the preferences of the decision making elite and society to determine the executive influence on outcomes.

The domestic structure typology provides a predictive framework of the influence of domestic politics on foreign policy. Type I states are expected to make contributions in response to pressure from the alliance leader unless preexisting beliefs, or a threat to key national interests exist. Conversely, Type IV states are likely to keep their distance or ride free due to the influence of societal pressure and the need to build an elite consensus for coalition participation. Type III states are expected to support the coalition to the level of support determined by elite consensus, while Type II states are expected to be support to the limit of public and legislature support. The domestic structure typology formalizes the link between public opinion and foreign policy and explicitly stipulates the causal mechanisms in which public opinion becomes expressed in foreign policy decisions.

## Dependent Variable

The dependent variable is a state's relative contribution to the Iraq War coalition. Coalition contributions are measured as military, economic, and diplomatic contributions to the Iraq coalition, and post war stability operations. Coalition contributions are ranked according to the level of commitment to the coalition. This book operationalizes the level of commitment in the following manner. States that provided combat forces in Iraq demonstrate the highest level of commitment: stationing troops within Iraq could generate the largest domestic backlash and therefore these states incur the greatest amount of political risk. The next highest level of support would go to those states that provided personnel into areas surrounding Iraq, significant financial contribution, allowed basing of coalition personnel, and/or diplomatically supported the U.S. position in the UN. The next level of support includes states that provided nominal military support such as over-flight rights or refueling privileges, provided a minimum level of economic support, or eventually diplomatically supported the Iraq coalition. Finally, the lowest level of commitment includes those states that provided no support, or were outspoken diplomatically in their opposition to the U.S.-led coalition.[73]

The security coalition model has three contribution outcomes indicating a state's contribution or lack thereof towards the coalition objective. The model accounts for equifinality; therefore, there may be more than one path to a given outcome. The outcomes include: (1) no contribution, or negative contribution; (2) the state contributes robustly in areas with public or state support; and (3) the state supports minimally and does not contribute in areas with public or state opposition. These three outcomes generate four possible explanatory effects that match a state's contribution, or lack thereof, to the coalition. States will either (1) keep their distance; (2) free ride; (3) show their preferences and pay; or (4) pay due to entrapment.

A state "keeps its distance" if it neither shares the public or private security "good," and does not contribute to the coalition. This situation is likely if a state does not benefit from the coalition and is not alliance dependent on coalition members. States that do not share the public good but are alliance dependent—such as on NATO—may also "keep its distance" due to domestic constraints, but they risk alliance abandonment in the future.

A state "free rides" if it perceives security to be a private or public good but does not contribute. Free riding is likely when a state believes other states will provide adequate security without its contribution and if the state is not dependent coalition members. Free riding also occurs when a state under-contributes to the coalition. States are likely to free ride when domestic pressures limit involvement. Similar to the "keep the distance" effect, alliance dependent states risk abandonment if they free ride.

Two effects occur when a state contributes robustly to a coalition, they "reveal their preferences" or are "entrapped and pay." States "reveal their preferences and pay" when they share in the public or private good and fear that it will be undersupplied by the coalition. In this instance, they will reveal their preferences for the public or private good and supply support appropriately. Conversely, states are "entrapped and force to pay," when they do not highly value the good but are highly dependent on a coalition partner. States seeking favor from a dominant power may be forced to support a coalition even if they have no direct stake security good.

Two additional burden sharing models currently seek to explain the complexity of coalition burden sharing decisions, but each is limited in its application. In "Wars of Choice: An Integrated Decision Model of NATO policy in Kosovo," David Auerswald presents an integrated model explaining state decisions for participation in the 1999 *Operation Allied Force.*[74] He examines the variation in burden sharing in NATO's intervention using four relatively sparse, existing approaches to foreign policy analysis: theories of collective action, balance of threat, public opinion, and government institutional structures. In his analysis, Auerswald developed a simple, integrated, decision making model that incorporates the core concepts from each existing explanation in a staged, conditional manner. Auerswald's research demonstrates that the integrated model is more explanatory than each theory individually. Although his model provides a parsimonious explanation for NATO burden sharing in Kosovo, it suffers from two significant weaknesses. First, Auerswald's analysis is limited to "wars of choice" where direct threat is insignificant. Although he accounts for threat in his theory, he limits its influence by stating, "I assume that no group member's survival is threatened, an assumption consistent with the vast majority of contemporary interventions of choice by western powers."[75] Although this restriction was valid for the Kosovo intervention, it limits the generalizability of the model. Since the model fails to account for threat, it does not account for the dynamics of burden sharing where the adversary directly threatens some members of the coalition. The second limitation of the model is that it assumes knowledge of the "K-Group," or collective action core group, in advance. Outcomes significantly change whether one is a member of the collective action core, but the designation of the group is tautological in Auerswald's analysis. K-Group membership is exogenous to the model, but determination of group membership is typically determined by level of support for a particular intervention. Determining K-Group members in advance is difficult if not impossible methodologically. Membership in the core of a collective action group is often the product of "strategic behavior" that Auerswald admits is missing from the model.[76] In total, Auerswald's model is a useful, but limited, analysis tool.

The second burden sharing model was proffered by Andrew Bennett, Joseph Lepgold, and Danny Unger to explain burden sharing decisions in the 1991 Persian Gulf War.[77] The Bennett, Lepgold, Unger model is a multi-causal theory that accounts for international, domestic, and cognitive influences. It incorporates the same international factors as the Auerswald model, but also accounts for threat in a state's decision calculus. The strength of the Bennett, Lepgold, and Unger model is that it accounts for a greater range of interventions than the Auerswald model. This model accounts for complex interactions between independent variables, and provides multiple causal paths to outcomes. It is not limited to a certain subset of interventions and therefore is generalizable to a wider range of security interventions. The weakness of the Bennett, Lepgold, and Unger model, however, is that its explanation of domestic influences on decision making is overly complicated making it difficult to employ for the foreign affairs specialist.

The domestic institutions and politics conceptualization, as presented in Bennet, Lepgold, and Unger security decision making model, provides a rich, nuanced approach to the influence of society on foreign policy decisions. However, the interaction of the theories is difficult to operationalize into a predictive framework. Due to the complex interactions of the domestic variables, predictions are indeterminate.[78] To improve the predictive capability of the model, these state-societal interactions may be simplified using assumptions developed recently in the area of domestic structure theory. The burden sharing model presented in this chapter preserves the external and cognitive theorizing of the Bennett model, but significantly improves its predictive and analytic capability by presenting a structural approach to explain the influence of domestic politics on foreign policy decisions.

## Methodology

I incorporate in-depth qualitative analysis on state burden sharing decisions—each case from a different domestic structure typology—to explore the influence of domestic politics on Iraq War burden sharing decisions. Cases were selected based on their importance to the U.S.-led coalition as well as their differing state-society relations. This methodology highlighted the influence of domestic structure under similar constraints. Additionally, the following three case studies demonstrate the influence of war duration on coalition participation. A coalition leader must expend significant effort to manage coalition participation when war duration is long and the costs of participation are high.

Chapter two presents an analysis of South Korea's support of the coalition. The ROK, representing a Type I domestic structure where decision making authority is restricted to relatively few government officials and the chief executive enjoys near autonomy from legislative scrutiny, was the third largest provider of military forces for a significant portion of the stabilization effort. Korea's economic participation was also significant. Korea's contribution of over $250 million to the Iraq reconstruction fund marked it as a significant donor, within the top ten states providing monetary support to Iraq. Korea's participation was significant theoretically considering it had no direct national interest in the Iraq War.

Chapter three analyzes the German decision to lobby against the U.S. position concerning Iraq. Within a year of declaring Germany's unqualified support to the U.S. global war on terrorism, Schröder became the first Western leader to issue a categorical "no" to the Bush administration for participation in the Iraq War. The Schröder government not only declined to make a direct German contribution to the war in 2003, but also engaged in active counter-coalition building by lobbying France and Russia to support Germany's resistance to the U.S. "adventure." Germany abandoned its traditional policy of balancing between Washington and Paris, and instead created a counter-coalition with Russia and France against the United States. Due to the influence of German national elections, incumbent Chancellor Gerhard Schröder's government reflected a Type II domestic structure. Schröder was able to commandeer the foreign policy process and imprint his preferences on German policy by appealing directly to public attitudes during his re-election campaign concerning the use of force in Iraq. Since Schröder's stance resonated well with the public, he was able to accomplish a policy coup and develop a policy position individually, rather than through the typical collaborative process. Germany's refusal to support the U.S.-led coalition, regardless of the Security Council's position, seriously undermined the diplomatic position of the Bush administration in building an effective coalition against Iraq.

Finally, chapter four explores the Turkish decision to remain on the sidelines for the invasion of Iraq, even under immense U.S. pressure. Historically, Turkish foreign policy was forged in a highly centralized manner that did not necessarily reflect societal interests, reflecting a Type I domestic structure. Due to national elections in November 2002—which prompted a change of the ruling party and a restructuring of the National Assembly—Turkey acted rather as a Type IV state in the domestic structure typology. During the approach to the Iraq War, Turkey showed decentralized decision making that was dominated by the influence of a newly elected National Assembly. This influence was not immediately recognized by the Bush administration and U.S. attempts to influence Turkey failed to account for the change in political dynamics. The Bush administration's inability to win Ankara's approval for a northern front in the Iraq War significantly affected U.S. war plans and dealt a serious blow to U.S.-Turkish relations.

I close with a discussion of the results of this research and implications for coalition participation. Several factors influence the proliferation of military action within coalitions rather than alliances. The United Nations Security Council has become more active in collective security and peacekeeping operations. Since the end of the Cold War, Russia and China have approved numerous operations that would have previously garnered a veto.[79] These UN authorized security missions are typically implemented through ad hoc coalitions since the UN maintains no standing security agreement. Secondly, the United States has fought only two military actions since World War II as a member of a standing military alliance. It rather chooses to engage in military action unilaterally or as a member of a coalition.[80] The termination of Cold War alignments and alliances will continue to contribute to a less rigid and more dynamic structure of international security favoring coalitions over alliance military action. "Coalitions of the willing" will need to be formed to answer to security dilemmas not anticipated by formal alliance structures. When a sense of urgency combines with sufficient international support for undertaking joint military action, coalitions—rather than alliances—are more likely to distribute costs among military members and politically provide a sense of legitimacy and common purpose for a given action.[81] With this in mind, a more detailed understanding of coalition burden sharing is a significant and timely topic.

---

[1] Graham Timmins, "Germany: Solidarity without Adventures," in *The Iraq War: Causes and Consequences*, ed. Rick Fawn and Raymond A. Hinnebusch (Boulder, Colo.: Lynne Rienner Publishers, 2006).

[2] United Nations Security Council, *Resolution 1441* (United Nations, 2002 [cited October 12, 2007]); available from http://daccessdds.un.org/doc/UNDOC/GEN/N02/682/26/PDF/N0268226.pdf.

[3] Jolyon Howorth, "France: Defender of International Legitimacy," in *The Iraq War: Causes and Consequences*, ed. Rick Fawn and Raymond A. Hinnebusch (Boulder, Colo.: Lynne Rienner Publishers, 2006), 55.

[4] Robert J. Pauly and Tom Lansford, *Strategic Preemption: U.S. Foreign Policy and the Second Iraq War* (Burlington, VT: Ashgate Pub., 2004), 73-75.

[5] Rick Fawn, "The Iraq War: Unfolding and Unfinished," in *The Iraq War: Causes and Consequences*, ed. Rick Fawn and Raymond A. Hinnebusch (Boulder, Colo.: Lynne Rienner Publishers, 2006), 3-5. Pauly and Lansford, *Strategic Preemption: U.S. Foreign Policy and the Second Iraq War*, 98-99.

[6] Pauly and Lansford, *Strategic Preemption: U.S. Foreign Policy and the Second Iraq War*, 96.

[7] Ambrose Evans, *Ten Eastern European States to Join in War* (2003 [cited September 21, 2007]); available from http://www.telegraph.co.uk/news/main.jhtml?xml=/news/2003/02/06/weur06.xml&sSheet=/news/2003/02/06/ixnewstop.html.

[8] Quoted in Pauly and Lansford, *Strategic Preemption: U.S. Foreign Policy and the Second Iraq War*, 97.

[9] Ibid.

[10] Chapter VII of the United Nations Charter allows the Security Council to "determine the existence of any threat to the peace, breach of the peace, or act of aggression" and to take military and nonmilitary action to "restore international peace and security." United Nations, *Chapter VII: Action with Respect to Threats to the Peace, Breaches of the Peace, and Acts of Aggression* (United Nations, 1945 [cited June 4, 2009]); available from http://www.un.org/en/documents/charter/chapter7.shtml.

[11] United Nations Security Council, *Resolution 1472* (United Nations, 2003 [cited May 10, 2009]); available from http://daccessdds.un.org/doc/UNDOC/GEN/N03/563/91/PDF/N0330209.pdf.

[12] The opening paragraph of resolution 1472 notes, "Occupying Power has the duty of ensuring the food and medical supplies of the population; it should, in particular, bring in the necessary foodstuffs, medical stores and other articles if the resources of the occupied territory are inadequate." Ibid.

[13] United Nations Security Council, *Resolution 1511* (United Nations, 2003 [cited October 24, 2007]); available from http://daccessdds.un.org/doc/UNDOC/GEN/N03/563/91/PDF/N0356391.pdf.

[14] Jeremy M. Sharp and Christopher M. Blanchard, "Post-War Iraq: Foreign Contributions to Training, Peacekeeping, and Reconstruction," *CRS Report for Congress-RL32105* (Congressional Research Service, 2007), CRS-1.

[15] Special Inspector General for Iraq Reconstruction, "Section 2—Iraq Reconstruction: Funding Sources and Uses," (Arlington, Virginia: SIGIR, 2009).

[16] Ibid.

[17] See Robert D. Putnam, "Diplomacy and Domestic Politics: The Logic of Two-Level Games," *International Organization* 42, no. 3 (1988).

[18] Ibid.

[19] Joe D. Hagan, "Domestic Political Explanations in the Analysis of Foreign Policy," in *Foreign Policy Analysis: Continuity and Change in Its Second Generation*, ed. Laura Neack, Jeanne A. K. Hey, and Patrick Jude Haney (Englewood Cliffs, N.J.: Prentice Hall, 1995).

[20] Andrew P. Cortell and James W. Davis, "How Do International Institutions Matter? The Domestic Impact of International Rules and Norms," *International Studies Quarterly* 40, no. 4 (1996), Herbert P. Kitschelt, "Political Opportunity Structures and Political Protest: Anti-Nuclear Movements in Four Democracies," *British Journal of Political Science* 16, no. 1 (1986).

[21] John Lewis Gaddis, *Strategies of Containment: A Critical Appraisal of Postwar American National Security Policy* (New York: Oxford University Press, 1982), ix.

[22] Hagan, "Domestic Political Explanations in the Analysis of Foreign Policy," Douglas Van Belle, "Domestic Imperatives and Rational Models of Foreign Policy Decision Making," in *The Limits of State Autonomy: Societal Groups and Foreign Policy Formulation*, ed. David Skidmore and Valerie M. Hudson (Boulder: Westview Press, 1993).

[23] Bruce M. Russett and Harvey Starr, *World Politics: The Menu for Choice*, 3rd ed. (New York: W.H. Freeman, 1989), 21-25.

[24] See Putnam, "Diplomacy and Domestic Politics: The Logic of Two-Level Games."

[25] This model builds on the security decision model presented in Andrew Bennett, Joseph Lepgold, and Danny Unger, eds., *Friends in Need: Burden Sharing in the Persian Gulf War*, 1st ed. (New York: St. Martin's Press, 1997). The domestic politics module of the original security decision model was simplified using the domestic structure framework presented in Susan Peterson, *Crisis Bargaining and the State: The Domestic Politics of International Conflict* (Ann Arbor: University of Michigan Press, 1996).

[26] For a detailed description of the model see Bennett, Lepgold, and Unger, eds., *Friends in Need: Burden Sharing in the Persian Gulf War*. This model is limited in that the complexity of its Domestic Institutions and Politics module makes it very difficult to operationalize.

[27] Jerel A. Rosati, "A Cognitive Approach to the Study of Foreign Policy," in *Foreign Policy Analysis: Continuity and Change in Its Second Generation*, ed. Laura Neack, Jeanne A. K. Hey, and Patrick Jude Haney (Englewood Cliffs, N.J.: Prentice Hall, 1995), 55.

[28] Yuen Foong Khong, *Analogies at War: Korea, Munich, Dien Bien Phu, and the Vietnam Decisions of 1965* (Princeton, N.J.: Princeton

University Press, 1992), Richard E. Neustadt and Ernest R. May, *Thinking in Time: The Uses of History for Decision-Makers* (New York: Free Press; Collier Macmillan, 1986), Jeffrey Record, *The Specter of Munich: Reconsidering the Lessons of Appeasing Hitler*, 1st ed. (Washington, D.C.: Potomac Books, 2007), Dan Reiter, *Crucible of Beliefs: Learning, Alliances, and World Wars*, Cornell Studies in Security Affairs (Ithaca, N.Y.: Cornell University Press, 1996).

[29] This definition builds on the work of Khong and Reiter in that it recognizes that decision-makers use analogy to simplify complex cognitive problems and that lessons are "learned" from past experience. See Khong, *Analogies at War: Korea, Munich, Dien Bien Phu, and the Vietnam Decisions of 1965*, Reiter, *Crucible of Beliefs: Learning, Alliances, and World Wars.*

[30] These assumptions draw heavily on the methodology in Bennett, Lepgold, and Unger, eds., *Friends in Need: Burden Sharing in the Persian Gulf War*, 14-17.

[31] The determination of threat is critical to determining the amount of publicness of the security intervention. A non-threatened ally will likely display collective action motivations, while a threatened ally will more likely participate fully with a countering coalition. Ibid., 10.

[32] Stephen M. Walt, *The Origins of Alliances*, Cornell Studies in Security Affairs (Ithaca: Cornell University Press, 1987), 21.

[33] See David A. Baldwin, "Thinking About Threats," *The Journal of Conflict Resolution* 15, no. 1 (1971), Raymond Cohen, *Threat Perception in International Crisis* (Madison: University of Wisconsin Press, 1979), Robert Jervis, *Perception and Misperception in International Politics* (Princeton, N.J.: Princeton University Press, 1976), Klaus Knorr, "Threat Perception," in *Historical Dimensions of National Security Problems*, ed. Klaus Knorr (Lawrence: University Press of Kansas, 1976).

[34] Walt, *The Origins of Alliances*, 26.

[35] Reiter, *Crucible of Beliefs: Learning, Alliances, and World Wars*, 24.

[36] Michael N. Barnett and Jack S. Levy, "Domestic Sources of Alliances and Alignments: The Case of Egypt, 1962-73," *International Organization* 45, no. 3 (1991), Scott Cooper, "State-Centric Balance-of-Threat Theory: Explaining the Misunderstood Gulf Cooperation Council," *Security Studies* 13, no. 2 (2003/4), 310, F. Gregory Gause, III, "Balancing What? Threat Perception and Alliance Choice in the Gulf," *Security Studies* 13, no. 2 (2003/4), 274.

[37] Although it is now known that Iraq did not have WMD capability for some time, overtly Iraq maintained the threat of WMD that was seen as credible by many parties. This threat can be accounted for in balance of threat theory. Kevin Woods, James Lacey, and Williamson Murray, "Saddam's Delusions: The View from the Inside," *Foreign Affairs* 85, no. 3 (2006). For a detailed review of the delusion throughout Iraq's military regime see Kevin M. Woods and Joint Center for Operational Analysis (U.S.), *Iraqi Perspectives Project: A View of Operation Iraqi Freedom from Saddam's Senior Leadership* (United States Joint Forces Command, Joint

Center for Operational Analysis, 2006 [cited October 11, 2007]); available from http://purl.access.gpo.gov/GPO/
LPS68139

[38] This method of coding threat is seen in Gause, "Balancing What? Threat Perception and Alliance Choice in the Gulf."

[39] Mancur Olson, *The Logic of Collective Action; Public Goods and the Theory of Groups*, Harvard Economic Studies, V. 124 (Cambridge, Mass.,: Harvard University Press, 1965).

[40] Russell Hardin, *Collective Action* (Baltimore: Johns Hopkins University Press, 1982).

[41] International Institute for Strategic Studies, "The Military Balance," (London: Routledge, 2002).

[42] Glenn H. Snyder, *Alliance Politics*, Cornell Studies in Security Affairs (Ithaca, N.Y.: Cornell University Press, 1997), 181.

[43] Michael Mandelbaum, *The Nuclear Revolution: International Politics before and after Hiroshima* (New York: Cambridge University Press, 1981), 150-51.

[44] Glenn H. Snyder, "The Security Dilemma in Alliance Politics," *World Politics* 36, no. 4 (1984), 466.

[45] Snyder, *Alliance Politics*, 182.

[46] Bennett, Lepgold, and Unger, eds., *Friends in Need: Burden Sharing in the Persian Gulf War*, 12.

[47] Snyder, "The Security Dilemma in Alliance Politics," 466.

[48] Bennett, Lepgold, and Unger found that several states in the Desert Storm coalition were motivated not so much by *actual* dependence on the United States, but rather *expected* future dependence. Bennett, Lepgold, and Unger, eds., *Friends in Need: Burden Sharing in the Persian Gulf War*, 347-48. This behavior is consistent with a hedging strategy, see Patricia A. Weitsman, *Dangerous Alliances: Proponents of Peace, Weapons of War* (Stanford, Calif.: Stanford University Press, 2004).

[49] Victor D. Cha, "Abandonment, Entrapment, and Neoclassical Realism in Asia: The United States, Japan, and Korea," *International Studies Quarterly* 44, no. 2 (2000).

[50] Snyder, "The Security Dilemma in Alliance Politics," 467.

[51] For an excellent discussion on the intensity of the alliance dilemma see Snyder, *Alliance Politics*, 186-92.

[52] Snyder, "The Security Dilemma in Alliance Politics," 471-72.

[53] Bennett, Lepgold, and Unger, eds., *Friends in Need: Burden Sharing in the Persian Gulf War*, 13.

[54] Putnam, "Diplomacy and Domestic Politics: The Logic of Two-Level Games."

[55] Page and Shapiro statistically show public opinion leads policy outcomes, but fail to determine the mechanisms in which public opinion affects elite behavior, see Benjamin I. Page and Robert Y. Shapiro, "Effects of Public Opinion on Policy," *American Political Science Review* 77, no. 1 (1983).

[56] Ole R. Holsti, *Public Opinion and American Foreign Policy*, Analytical Perspectives on Politics (Ann Arbor: University of Michigan Press, 1996), 2-4.

[57] Thomas Risse-Kappen, "Public Opinion, Domestic Structure, and Foreign Policy in Liberal Democracies," *World Politics* 43, no. 4 (1991).

[58] Benjamin Ginsberg, *The Captive Public: How Mass Opinion Promotes State Power* (New York: Basic Books, 1986), Edward S. Herman and Noam Chomsky, *Manufacturing Consent: The Political Economy of the Mass Media* (New York: Pantheon Books, 2002), John E. Mueller, *War, Presidents, and Public Opinion* (Lanham, MD: University Press of America, 1985), James N. Rosenau, *Public Opinion and Foreign Policy; an Operational Formulation* (New York,: Random House, 1961).

[59] Warren E. Miller and Donald E. Stokes, "Constituency Influence in Congress," *American Political Science Review* 57, no. 1 (1963).

[60] Douglas C. Foyle, "Public Opinion and Foreign Policy: Elite Beliefs as a Mediating Variable," *International Studies Quarterly* 41, no. 1 (1997), 142.

[61] Holsti, *Public Opinion and American Foreign Policy*, Risse-Kappen, "Public Opinion, Domestic Structure, and Foreign Policy in Liberal Democracies."

[62] Risse-Kappen, "Public Opinion, Domestic Structure, and Foreign Policy in Liberal Democracies."

[63] Lawrence R. Jacobs and Robert Y. Shapiro, "Studying Substantive Democracy," *PS: Political Science and Politics* 27, no. 1 (1994). See also Tamar Hermann, "Grassroots Activism as a Factor in Foreign Policy-Making," in *The Limits of State Autonomy: Societal Groups and Foreign Policy Formulation*, ed. David Skidmore and Valerie M. Hudson (Boulder: Westview Press, 1993).

[64] In a methodology adapted from Susan Peterson's work to explain state strategies for crisis bargaining, the domestic structure block presents a typology of likely responses to a burden sharing situation based on the centralization of the executive branch of government in the influence of society through the legislature. See Peterson, *Crisis Bargaining and the State: The Domestic Politics of International Conflict*. See also Cortell and Davis, "How Do International Institutions Matter? The Domestic Impact of International Rules and Norms."

[65] Peterson, *Crisis Bargaining and the State: The Domestic Politics of International Conflict*, 24-30.

[66] Ibid., 31. See also Cortell and Davis, "How Do International Institutions Matter? The Domestic Impact of International Rules and Norms," 455-56.

[67] Jervis, *Perception and Misperception in International Politics*, chap. 3.

[68] Peterson, *Crisis Bargaining and the State: The Domestic Politics of International Conflict*, 31-36.

[69] Ibid., 36-38.

[70] Ibid., 38-40.

[71] Cortell and Davis, "How Do International Institutions Matter? The Domestic Impact of International Rules and Norms," 457.

[72] Peterson, *Crisis Bargaining and the State: The Domestic Politics of International Conflict*, 40-41.

[73] I rely on the typology of support developed in George Sprowls, "States and War Coalitions: A Study of the Gulf War" (Dissertation, West Virginia University, 1998).

[74] David P. Auerswald, "Explaining Wars of Choice: An Integrated Decision Model of NATO Policy in Kosovo," *International Studies Quarterly* 48, no. 3 (2004).

[75] Ibid., 643.

[76] Ibid., 658.

[77] For a full discussion of the security decision model, see Bennett, Lepgold, and Unger, eds., *Friends in Need: Burden Sharing in the Persian Gulf War*.

[78] David Auerswald notes that he had to simplify the complicated methodology in Auerswald, "Explaining Wars of Choice: An Integrated Decision Model of NATO Policy in Kosovo." Gerald Steinberg in a review of *Friends in Need* notes "the heavy weapons of social science were too powerful for the issues at hand" in Gerald Steinberg, *The American Political Science Review* 92, no. 3 (1998), 743-44.

[79] The number of United Nations (U.N.) peacekeeping operations has increased by more than 400% since the end of the Cold War. Since 1948 there have been 61 U.N. authorized peacekeeping operations, 47 have been authorized since 1998. United Nations Department of Peacekeeping Operations, *United Nations Peacekeeping Factsheet* (United Nations, 2007 [cited October 1, 2007]); available from http://www.un.org/Depts/dpko/factsheet.pdf. See also Bruce M. Russett, *What Price Vigilance? The Burdens of National Defense* (New Haven: Yale University Press, 1970), 322.

[80] The U.S. participated with alliance partners in Bosnia and Kosovo, however, even these actions were somewhat ad hoc since Article V of the North Atlantic Treaty was not activated. Participation by NATO states was voluntary for these military actions. Terry J. Pudas, "Preparing Future Coalition Commanders," *Joint Forces Quarterly*, no. 3 (1993/1994). In non-Article V operations no one can know with certainty the extent to which NATO members ultimately will contribute, see Auerswald, "Explaining Wars of Choice: An Integrated Decision Model of NATO Policy in Kosovo." U.S. participation in Afghanistan is separate from NATO stabilization operations.

[81] Andrew J. Pierre, *Coalitions Building and Maintenance: The Gulf War, Kosovo, Afghanistan, and the War on Terrorism* (Washington, DC: Georgetown University, Institute for the Study of Diplomacy, 2002), 13-14.

# 2
# South Korea: Between Iraq and a Nuclear Crisis

South Korean cooperation in the Iraq War coalition provides a compelling case for burden sharing analysis. The Republic of Korea (ROK) support for the Iraq War coalition is puzzling in two dimensions. First, the ROK had no direct stake in the Iraq War, yet it was the third largest provider of military forces to the post-conflict stability operations.[1] South Korea was not threatened by Saddam Hussein, possessed a reliable source of oil, and was not expected to contribute troops as a member of a collective security organization. Only 15 percent of South Koreans surveyed in the summer of 2002 considered terrorism to be a national priority, one of the lowest figures for major countries surveyed. Additionally, 72 percent of South Koreans opposed the U.S.-led war on terrorism.[2] Second, the newly elected liberal government campaigned on a pledge of assertiveness against the asymmetric alliance relationship with the United States, and exploited a wave of anti-Americanism. President Roh Moo-hyun was elected president over his pro-U.S. conservative opponent based on a platform that called for a Korea that would not "kowtow" to the United States.[3] Roh's victory reflected public anger towards the United States concerning President Bush's aggressive policy regarding North Korea and the acquittal of two U.S. servicemen in a traffic accident that killed two South Korean schoolgirls.[4] Unlike most South Korean political leaders, Roh had no ties to the United States and had not even visited before he assumed office. This is a rare occurance for politicians of national stature in Korea.[5] During the fall 2002 presidential campaign, Roh promised to be more assertive with the United States concerning alliance issues and resolved to solve the problem of North Korea's nuclear programs through dialogue rather than force.[6] Given the lack of threat, President Roh's stance in the election, and rampant anti-Americanism at the time, Korea's support to the Iraq War coalition is puzzling. Why would an administration, which was elected on an anti-

American platform, provide the third largest troop contingent to post-war stabilization operations and commit those forces during the combat phase of the conflict?

This chapter demonstrates that domestic structure and alliance dependence explain South Korea's policy towards the Iraq War coalition. The Republic of Korea represents a weak Type I domestic structure in the typology, where decision making authority is restricted to relatively few government officials and the chief executive enjoys near autonomy from legislative scrutiny. In a Type I environment, the chief executive has significant influence over foreign policy and is relatively free from legislative oversight.[7] The political culture of Korea, though substantially democratized in the past two decades, still favors strong executive leadership in which the President sets the tone and agenda for the National Assembly.[8] Although executive prerogatives usually gain traction in the National Assembly, the introduction of civic groups and an opposition legislature made the Roh government a weak Type I state.[9]

The Roh Moo-hyun government defied strong opposition from its core political constituencies and committed non-combat troops during the invasion of Iraq as a method to gain leverage over U.S. nuclear policy towards the North. However, Roh was able to overcome public discontent by linking the troop deployment to U.S. policy towards North Korea. By making a timely promise of his "active support" of the unpopular Iraq War, Roh attempted to repair damage that had been done by anti-American protests in an effort to soften the U.S. stance towards North Korean nuclearization.[10] South Korea's alliance dependence, combined with a strong executive allowed the government to support the coalition with an outcome of "State is Entrapped and Pays" in the burden sharing decision model.

## The Timing, Size, and Mix of South Korea's Contributions

Korea walked a diplomatic tightrope with the United States in the approach to the Iraq War. The ROK government did not want to commit to a costly military intervention with the potential to alienate Arab oil suppliers.[11] At the same time, the Kim and Roh governments attempted to balance U.S. requests for military support against their need for U.S. cooperation in the North Korean nuclear standoff. To obtain U.S. consent to the "Policy for Peace and Prosperity," the Korean NSC encouraged the government to join the Iraq War effort with the eventual dispatch of 3,600 troops by summer 2004. South Korea provided a significant number of military personnel supporting the Iraq War coalition in two phases. The first phase involved the dispatch of approximately 650 medical and engineering personnel in the immediate aftermath of declared combat operations. The second dispatch of an additional 3,000 troops occurred in response to the U.S. request for forces to support stabilization and reconstruction operations in Iraq. Korea's diplomatic support was less noteworthy. Politically, South Korea remained on the sidelines in 2002 and early 2003 while the Bush administration attempted to forge a coalition of the willing against Iraq. However, once military intervention was inevitable, Seoul provided political support to the intervention. Economically, Seoul's contributions were significant. Seoul provided approximately $275 million in assistance, soft loans, and grants through UN organizations and bilaterally.[12] The following sections describe the timing and composition of ROK political, economic, and military contributions to the coalition of the willing.

### *Political Contributions*

Seoul's political strategy in the approach to the Iraq War was to walk the fine line between supporting U.S. efforts to condemn the Hussein regime while not angering Arab oil suppliers. Korea imports the bulk of its oil from the Middle East, and the region is an important export market for Korean goods as well. Seoul's political strategy hinged on encouraging a UN mandate until it was inevitable that the U.S. would implement a military strategy in Iraq.

Under the administration of President Kim Dae-jung, Korea maintained a strategy of ambivalence towards the U.S. efforts aimed at Iraq. This ambivalence mirrored the South Korean attitude towards contributing to the 1991 Gulf War coalition; the ROK government maintained a diplomatically neutral stance until asked by the United States to support the coalition.[13] The Blue House (Korean White House) refrained from either endorsing or disapproving U.S. policy and offered no reaction to President Bush's September 12 speech to the UN General Assembly accusing the Hussein regime of developing weapons of mass destruction (WMD). According to a ROK government official, Seoul's strategy was to not publicly reveal its stance on Iraq until necessary.[14] Considering the anti-American climate in South Korea, and the lack of international consensus regarding Iraq, Seoul maintained diplomatic neutrality in an effort to not inflame its domestic or international constituencies.

President Kim encouraged a UN mandate in private conversations with President Bush. In a September 2002 phone conversation, Kim expressed his support for U.S. intentions to gain a UN resolution on Iraq before resorting to the use of force. Seoul's stance was articulated publicly at the Asia-Europe Meeting (ASEM), September 22-24, 2002, when President Kim and leaders of 24 ASEM member countries called on Washington to work within the UN framework regarding military action in Iraq.[15] According to a presidential aide, "Kim's support doesn't cover a unilateral U.S. move."[16] However, Seoul had to maintain a moderately pro-U.S. diplomatic stance so that it could coordinate North Korean policy.[17] The same aide declined to answer whether Korea would support the U.S. if it eventually pursued unilateral action against Iraq.

In late November 2002, the Bush administration allegedly requested military support from Seoul for the Iraq coalition; however, the government did not publicly acknowledge this request until February 2003. According to an anonymous senior Korean government official, "There has been a US request for a 'usual level of support' in case a war breaks out in Iraq." The official added, "We have not yet decided our position regarding this."[18] In anticipation of a visit to Seoul by Deputy Secretary of State Richard Armitage in December, the ROK government continued to announce that it had not yet received a specific request from the United States for assistance in the event of military action.[19] Regional experts stated that with the current anti-American mood in Seoul, combined with North Korea's nuclear declaration, a direct request from Armitage would put the Kim administration in a tough position.[20]

By early February 2003, alliance dependence concerns seemed to overcome Korean reluctance to support the coalition of the willing. In late January, in a response to President-elect Roh's markedly anti-American campaign and Korean demands for a change of the Status of Forces agreement, James Baker reputedly gave a disturbing assessment for a delegation of South Korean National Assembly members visiting the United States:

> When Corazon Aquino asked U.S. troops to leave we left without any second thought...When China seized some Filipino islands by force, she telephoned to ask whether we will let China get away with this. I said there were no U.S. soldiers in her country to prevent any such Chinese aggression...The same applies to Korea were she to opt for U.S. military pullout.[21]

Within two weeks of this visit, the ROK government openly announced its support for the coalition of the willing, although its commitment was limited to non-combat forces.[22] On February 10, the outgoing Kim government declared that Seoul would likely provide support to the impending U.S. military action if requested. Prime Minister Kim Suk-soo stated to the National Assembly that Seoul could send troops to the Middle East to show support for the U.S. military action.[23] Brig. General Hwang Young-soo, from the Defense Ministry, added, "If the U.S. asks for soldiers [in non-combat areas], we will consider it by following the precedents set during the Gulf War and the war in Afghanistan."[24]

Finally, at the urging of the United States, the newly seated Roh government pledged its support to the coalition of the willing. On March 11, nine days before the start of the war and two days before the U.S. and United Kingdom withdrew demands for a new U.N. Security Council vote on war with Iraq, South Korea officially accepted the U.S. request to assist in its war effort against Iraq. A Chong Wa Dae (Office of the President of the Republic of Korea, or Blue House) spokesman said that Washington conveyed a request that Seoul express its support of the coalition by providing it with medical assistance to deal with the anticipated refugee flow.[25] Another official stated, "We are not in a position to sit idle, when our ally is sending a desperate call," however he cautioned that, "We will first issue a statement pledging our support but in a way that will minimize misunderstanding in the Arab world."[26] In a March 13 telephone conversation with President Roh, President Bush affirmed that he needed Seoul's outspoken support for its possible war on Iraq.[27] In return, Roh gained Washington's confirmation that the United States would seek a peaceful solution to its nuclear standoff with North Korea.[28]

Diplomatically, South Korea remained on the sidelines until compelled by the Bush administration to support the war effort. The Kim Dae-jung administration attempted to maintain a position of neutrality by maintaining that it would not get involved in the Iraq issue. The only stance that the administration took was that it encouraged the United States to seek a UN mandate for a military mission. The successor Roh administration attempted to maintain its distance, but increasing tensions on the peninsula, combined with U.S. pressure to participate, influenced Seoul's decision making.

During the approach to the Iraq War, Seoul was considerably more concerned with tensions emanating from North Korea's declaration that it would restart its nuclear program rather than the implications of U.S. action in the Middle East. Initially, the Roh administration aimed for de-escalation of the North Korean nuclear crisis through a continuation of sorts of President Kim Dae-jung's "Sunshine Policy" as the "Policy for Peace and Prosperity." Roh unveiled his "Policy for Peace and

Prosperity" in his February 25, 2003 inauguration address. The Policy for Peace and Prosperity advocated the normalization of relations between North Korea and the international community as a means of developing a durable peace regime on the Korean peninsula.[29] Roh stressed that a peaceful resolution through dialogue was the only solution, and that heightened military tension must be avoided at all costs, undermining the U.S. strategy of confrontation.[30] Roh's continuation of the "sunshine" approach was in direct conflict with the Bush strategy of confrontation. The ROK's continued engagement with North Korea made it appear to be a "spoiler" of the U.S. nonproliferation policy, making up for North Korea's lack of resources with aid, regardless of DPRK actions.[31]

Until February 2003, Seoul declined to give clear-cut answers on whether the government would support a possible U.S. action without UN approval; however, the fledgling Roh administration realized that non-cooperation could lend a fatal blow to South Korean efforts to defuse the tension catalyzed by North Korea's nuclear declaration.

### *Economic Contributions*

In terms of economic assistance, Korea's economic pledges have earned it a position as a major donor for Iraq Reconstruction, but its $260 million of support pales in comparison to the $4.9 billion pledged by Japan. The Republic of Korea's initial pledge of $10 million in economic assistance earned it a position on the Donor Committee of the International Reconstruction Fund Facility for Iraq (IRFFI). The UN sponsored IRFFI has been one of the principal vehicles for delivering international donor assistance to Iraq. IRFFI is a multilateral mechanism made up of two Iraq trust funds, one managed by the UN Development Group and the other by the World Bank. The Donor Committee consists of countries that have committed at least $10 million to the fund facility and also includes two rotating representatives from countries that have committed less than $10 million.[32]

Korea's initial pledge of $10 million in April 2003 towards humanitarian assistance for Iraqi refugees was increased to $60 million by the time of the Madrid Donor Conference in October 2003.[33] This aid was distributed through international organizations such as the UN High Commissioner for Refugees, UNICEF, and the World Food Program.[34] Seoul eventually pledged an additional $200 million over five years at the Madrid conference.[35] Washington acknowledged South Korea's contribution at the 2003 Security Consultation Meeting. According to ROK Defense Minister Cho Young-kil, "Secretary Rumsfeld expressed his appreciation for President Roh Moo-hyun's decision to provide both additional forces in Iraq and $260 million in reconstruction funds from 2003 to 2007."[36]

These contributions were seen as a means to display to the Arab community that Korea was supporting the coalition of the willing as a means to reconstruct Iraq rather than as part of an occupying force. The Roh administration underscored these financial contributions to Arab leaders as a means to foster an atmosphere favorable to Korean troop deployments to Iraq. On February 17, 2004, President Roh hosted a group of envoys from 13 Arab nations to seek their support for South Korea's plan to send 3,000 troops to Iraq. During the meeting, Roh urged the envoys to play a role in persuading their constituencies that Korean military efforts were geared towards gaining security and rehabilitating Iraq.[37] Since most Arab nations opposed any additional troop deployment that was not led by the United Nations Seoul felt that Korea needed to explain their contributions directly to the Arab public. In that effort, President Roh provided interviews to Al Jazeera, Egypt's Middle East News Agency, and Iran's Islamic Republic News Agency

In addition to Madrid pledges, a number of countries made new pledges to help Iraq at Sharm El-Sheikh, Egypt, at the launching of the International Compact with Iraq (ICI or Compact) in May 2007. South Korea's pledge included a $200 million soft loan provided by Korea's Economic Development and Cooperation Fund to help rebuild and develop Iraq's oil industry.[39] Finally, the ROK and Iraq also reached agreements to strengthen economic ties through construction, energy, and information technology sharing. South Korea's contribution to Iraq reconstruction marks it as one of the six major donors of foreign aid.[40]

Korea's economic assistance compares favorably with its economic role in 1991. In that effort, South Korea was forced through U.S. pressure to contribute $115 million to international assistance efforts and $45 million to the United Kingdom, Egypt, and Morocco for their military forces. In both the 1991 and 2003 efforts, Korean assistance was provided after U.S. pressure.[41]

### *Military Contributions*

The ROK government deployed military personnel to Iraq in two phases, both in response to pressure from the Bush administration. The first deployment of troops was in response to a February 2003 request to Seoul to assist militarily with post-war reconstruction, combat operations, and humanitarian assistance. Seoul initially hesitated, in light of domestic opposition to the U.S. action. However, considering the importance of the ROK-U.S. alliance and increasing tensions between the United States and North Korea, Seoul finally decided to send troops in levels similar to the assistance given to Operations *Desert Storm* and *Enduring Freedom* (Afghanistan). During the 1991Gulf War, Seoul deployed a 150-member medical team, five C-130 transport aircraft, and 150 transportation personnel. Similarly, the ROK government sent 150 medical personnel, 350 transportation personnel, and a team of 150 military engineers to Afghanistan.[42] In April 2003, Seoul dispatched 670 military engineers and medical personnel to Iraq supporting the U.S. military mission.[43] Significantly, these troops were pledged to the U.S. war effort in March 2003—before combat operations began—and they arrived in theater in April, while the U.S. was still engaged in combat against the Hussein regime. After the end of the conventional combat phase of the war, these units moved to Nasiriyah to assist the reconstruction of Iraq.[44]

In an effort to put a more "international face" on the American led occupation, the Bush administration aggressively solicited for additional coalition troops in an effort to replace some American forces.[45] This request resulted in the eventual deployment of an additional 3,000 ROK military personnel in August 2004. U.S. requests for assistance were reported in the Korean press throughout July and August 2003 provoking rumors across Korea that additional ROK forces might soon be sent to Iraq to assist the American forces already there.[46] At the fourth Future of Alliance (FOTA) talks in Seoul on September 3 and 4, and in a meeting with U.S. Deputy Secretary of Defense Wolfowitz and ROK Foreign Minister Yoon Young-kwan in Washington September 5, the U.S. requested that Korea deploy a sizable military contingent to Iraq.[47] In response, Minister Yoon hinted that his government would comply with the U.S. request.[48] On October 17, 2003, the UN Security Council unanimously passed Resolution 1511, which urged UN members to assist in the reconstruction of Iraq. The Roh government quickly took advantage of this event and on October 18, Roh announced that he would send additional troops to Iraq.[49] The U.S. requested 5,000 ROK combat troops to be deployed to Mosul to replace the 101st Airborne Division; the Roh administration, however, opted to send a contingent consisting primarily of support troops to provide reconstruction aid rather than the security that was desperately needed.[50] Although the government committed itself to the additional deployment in October, the deployment was repeatedly delayed due to the increased violence in Iraq and domestic resistance at home.[51] The Korean deployment was conditioned that the ROK send mostly a peacekeeping force rather than a combat force, and that the U.S. find a safe location for the ROK area of operations. The ROK government, already concerned about domestic unrest, cited security concerns in Mosul and U.S. pressure to participate in "offensive operations" for its delay.[52] The U.S. complied with Seoul's requests and the ROK dispatched the Zaytun unit to the Arbil province in August 2004. This unit was composed of 1,400 combat Marines and Special Forces commandos and 1,600 military engineers and medics responsible for security and reconstruction of the Kurdish Autonomous Region centered in Arbil.[53] The Zaytun deployment was South Korea's largest troop dispatch since the Vietnam War, when it deployed over 300,000 personnel over a twelve-year period. In fact, Korea's presence was the third largest military contingent in the coalition of the willing until late 2007.[54] The Zaytun division's mission was to reconstruct roads and infrastructure, offer vocational training assistance, provide medical treatment to local residents, and provide training to Iraqi Security Forces.[55] Later, in March 2006, the unit assumed guard and escort missions for UN officials in the region, but was constrained by its parliamentary mandate from participating in offensive military operations throughout the deployment.[56]

Though the ROK National Assembly has repeatedly extended the Zaytun unit's mandate, the number of Korean troops in Iraq has steadily decreased to approximately 650, as of May 2008.[57] The Korean National Assembly voted for the first significant troop reduction December 20, 2005 in reaction to anticipated domestic pressure to withdraw from the Iraq coalition and the planned drawdown of U.S. and British forces. Seoul unilaterally scaled back its force level by 1,000 personnel as part of their plan for extending deployments in Iraq, which require parliamentary approval each year to gain approval.[58] In a blow to the Bush administration, the first indication of the troop reduction was from the Korean media.[59] The next force reduction was bundled into the approval bill the next year. The government gained parliamentary approval for extending the deployment for another year by reducing the size of the contingent from 2,300 to 1,200. Additionally, in a concession to the ruling Uri party, the government agreed to present a plan for a complete withdrawal of all Korean troops by the end of 2007 in order to gain approval of the National Assembly.[60] The Assembly did not specify any specific timetable for troop pullout, and the Roh administration extended the troop mandate for an additional year with a reduced troop level, hoping to gain economic benefits and strengthening ties with the United States for continuing support.[61]

## Explaining South Korean Contributions

The Republic of Korea's contribution to the Iraq coalition is noteworthy, since the country provided the third largest military contingent from 2003 through 2006. This level of support was initiated, and maintained, in the face of significant criticism from the public, who elected the Roh administration on a platform of independence and greater autonomy within the ROK-U.S. bilateral relationship. Shortly after his inauguration, the Roh administration made an abrupt policy reversal and acquiesced to U.S. requests to assist the Iraq coalition. At the same time, Roh's policy towards North Korea hardened to a policy contingent on North Korean concessions. Why would an administration striving for greater autonomy and independence from the United States become such a willing participant in the coalition of the willing?

The alliance dependence and domestic political structure hypotheses of the burden sharing decision model best explain the ROK's contribution to the Iraq coalition. President Roh himself aptly describes the forces that converged to encourage participation by Korean military forces, "Cooperation from the U.S. is essential to the security of Northeast Asia and the denuclearization of the Korean Peninsula. Amid the unpredictability surrounding the North Korean nuclear weapons issue, the importance of a closer South Korea-U.S. alliance cannot be overemphasized."[62] Alliance dependence influenced Korean decision making towards the Iraq coalition. Seoul felt obliged to submit to U.S. requests in order to gain influence over U.S. policy towards North Korea. President Roh attempted to link deployment of ROK troops to progress on defusing tensions on the Korean Peninsula over the Democratic People's Republic of Korea (DPRK) nuclear ambitions. While alliance dependence pressures motivated Seoul to participate in the coalition, the influence of public opinion on the government explains the timing, composition, and level of military support in both the dispatch of troops and the eventual drawdown. Public discontentment with the troop deployment influenced government decision making in a very indirect manner after the U.S. request for a substantial troop deployment in the fall of 2003. The Blue House and the NSC were concerned that putting troops at risk would have a negative impact on President Roh's public ratings. To manage public opinion concerning the deployment, the NSC advised President Roh to limit the troop deployment to 3,000 consisting of primarily non-combat troops.[63] Accordingly, the Blue House considered it necessary to offer troop reductions in order for the National Assembly to continue the Iraq troop mandate. The troop reductions were preventive in nature in anticipation of domestic backlash concerning the deployment to Iraq.

The following sections analyze the influence of external and domestic factors using the burden sharing decision model.

### *Historical Learning*

According to the learning hypothesis, leaders are more likely to contribute to a military effort if they gained full participation rights with the coalition leader, influenced decision making, and received compensation in the form of increased influence with the coalition leader or material benefits, for their participation in previous efforts. The South Korean case demonstrates a shift in attitude in the decision making elite, learned not from combat operations, but "unlearned" in the ROK government attempt to have a more favorable relationship with the DPRK.

Since the United States defended the Republic of Korea in the Korean War and the ROK provided the second largest contingent of soldiers that supported the United States in Vietnam, one might assume that these previous wars would shape decision making towards the Iraq intervention. However, scant evidence exists that these experiences influenced elite decision making. Rather, with the introduction of the Roh Administration, a new generation of political leaders, known as the "386 generation" has risen to power with little if any direct recollection of the Korean conflict and no allegiance to the virtually uncontested acceptance of the Korean-American alliance by previous generations.[64] Unlike their parents who held the United States in high regard due to its role in the Korean War and the ensuing Cold War, this group views the United States as a supporter of the authoritarian governments in South Korea from the 1960s to 1980s and therefore complicit in numerous military crackdowns, including the massacre at Kwangju in 1980.[65] These formative experiences provide a frame of reference significantly altered from the Korean War generation. While the political agenda for the Korean War generation was economic sustenance, security, and survival, the younger, more affluent, and higher-educated generation is more concerned with quality-of-life issues including labor rights, environmental issues, urban congestion, and the status of U.S. forces in the Korean legal system.[66] Overall, the 386 generation regards the United States less as the country that fought for Korean independence than as the country that backed past military dictators. Although more conservative policy makers were integral to Roh's foreign policy apparatus, the 386 influence significantly altered the view of U.S. policy in high government circles.

The election of President Roh Moo-hyun marked the ascendency of the 386 generation into Korean national politics. Roh entered politics in 1988 with an activist agenda, grilling the government over corruption allegations and the 1980 Kwangju Massacre. His election as President in 2002 marked the most liberal government to be voted into office since the ROK's inception in 1948.[67] The Roh administration policy preferences reflect Roh's 386 influences, such as the desire for a more even footing in the ROK-U.S. bilateral alliance and independence in policy concerning the DPRK. First, the administration reflected a "post-Cold War mindset" that framed North Korea as a Korean problem rather than a continuing confrontation, moving away from conventional notions of threat toward an affirmation of North Korean vulnerabilities as Pyongyang sought to balance regime survival with domestic reform. Second, the administration advocated a parallel need to foster a more equal partnership with the United States. Throughout his race for the presidency in 2002, Roh portrayed himself as a leader who would be able to send a strong message to Washington that "business as usual" would no longer be considered to be the norm in the ROK-U.S. relationship. Roh stressed the need for an alliance relationship that would mature into a more reciprocal and equitable relationship. Lastly, the influence of the 386 generation is significant considering that the Roh administration tended to formulate policy based on the advice of 386 generation progressives rather than from those with significant domestic and foreign policy experience.[68]

Based on the experiences of the 386 generation, the learning hypothesis predicts that the ROK would not be an active participant in the Iraq coalition. Seoul would be expected to distance itself from the Bush administration in order to gain a greater degree of independence from the United States. According to University professor Kim Il Young, "The younger generation believes more in self-reliance and independence. It feels that in the long term, South Korea should strike a balance between the United States and China and adopt a more neutral position toward the United States."[69] The Iraq War provided an excellent opportunity for the Korean government to demonstrate independence from the United States and to court potential regional allies. Participation in the coalition would not be predicted unless the Korean government was afforded an influential role in Iraq policy, or unless the ROK could significantly influence U.S. policy bilaterally in regards to the DPRK.

### Balance of Threat

Since private versus collective incentives significantly influence the degree of burden sharing, the balance of threat block in the burden sharing decision model seeks to explain whether an ally considers the action a "war of choice" or a necessary intervention to counter an existential threat. This book operationalizes threat as a factor of material capability and intentions to influence a state internally and externally. If military defeat is seen as the most serious threat to regime security, then state decision makers should seek to balance against the state that is geographically closest and whose aggregate military power capabilities are greatest. Given South Korea's distance from Iraq and the lack of any threatening intentions from Saddam Hussein towards the ROK, the balance of threat hypothesis fails to directly explain Korean participation in the Iraq War coalition. However, when the scope of threat is enlarged to include proximate threats to South Korea, balance of threat theory provides some explanatory power for Korean motivation to join the coalition of the willing. The U.S. war on terrorism—including the inclusion of North Korea in the "axis of evil" and the Bush doctrine of preemptive war—raised serious concerns in the ROK government that hard-line U.S. policy towards North Korea could easily catalyze an all-out war on the Korean peninsula.[70] The Roh administration considered this U.S. policy stance threatening to ROK security interests and sought to influence U.S. policy by deploying military forces in the Iraq coalition.[71]

South Korean perceptions of threat, and attitudes toward North Korea and the U.S., have changed substantially as a result of President Kim Dae-jung's "sunshine policy" and his subsequent summit in Pyongyang in June 2000.[72] As a part of this engagement strategy, the ROK government engaged in a campaign to convince the South Korean public that the North was a country to be pitied rather than feared. This campaign included removing remarks of North Korea as a threat in military documents and framing the North Korean famine as an economic problem rather than an issue of authoritarian control.[73] As a result, the public and much of the decision making elite—especially the 386 generation—appeared much less concerned with the threat from the North than reason would otherwise dictate.[74] Kim Dae-jung's sunshine policy fostered a psychological metamorphosis in the South by framing North Korea as an underprivileged sibling rather than existential threat. In a national survey, 75 percent of South Koreans regard citizens of the North as "brothers."[75] Ignoring Korean War history, many in the South see the North as incapable of starting a war against its "brothers" in the

South.[76] At the same time, an increasing number of South Koreans came to perceive the U.S. as a bully, a threat to peace, and an obstacle to inter-Korean reconciliation and unification.

President Bush's hard-line policy toward North Korea, combined with President Kim's sunshine policy, created tension and friction in ROK-U.S. relations. The first ROK-U.S. summit between Bush and Kim Dae-jung, held in Washington, D.C. in March 2001, highlighted the great separation of policy preferences between the two leaders. Instead of endorsing his partner's sunshine policy, Bush lectured Kim about Kim Jong-il's untrustworthiness.[77] After the 9/11 terrorist attacks, and the subsequent attention to the threat of nuclear terrorism, Bush's stance further hardened toward North Korea. As the U.S. foreign policy goals focused on curtailing WMD and preempting potential terrorist acts against the United States, President Bush designated North Korea as part of the "axis of evil" and displayed a personal distaste against dangerous autocratic regimes. During his February 2002 visit to South Korea Bush revealed to Kim that he would not let the world's "most dangerous regimes" acquire its "most dangerous weapons."[78] South Korean reaction to this position was largely negative. The majority of South Koreans felt the Bush administration's hard-line policy towards the North effectively encouraged its nuclear weapons development.[79] The Bush administration's perceived proclivity for unilateralism, regime change policy, and preference for military rather than diplomatic solutions, was considered threatening to peace on the Korean peninsula.[80] These fears were all ignited when the U.S. confronted the DPRK over its covert nuclear development program.

The fall 2002 nuclear crisis brought ROK-U.S. relations and the ROK public trust in U.S. intentions to a new low. In a visit to North Korea, arranged by Seoul to re-engage U.S. bilateral relations with the DPRK, Assistant Secretary of State James Kelly accused North Korea of developing uranium enrichment capabilities (a potential building block for nuclear weapons) in violation of the 1991 Joint Denuclearization Declaration and the 1994 Agreed Framework.[81] According to news accounts, DPRK Vice Foreign Minister Kang Sok-joo acknowledged the program and responded that North Korea had been "compelled" to begin a uranium enrichment program for self defense after being branded a member of the "axis of evil" by President Bush.[82] Thus, what began as a fact-finding mission to resume long-stalled talks with the reclusive Stalinist North Korea turned into unproductive and failed diplomacy. Suspicions regarding U.S. motives in confronting Pyongyang on its nuclear weapons program and the continued U.S. refusal to yield to North Korean demands, helped raise anti-American sentiments to new heights in the South.[83] North Korean motives seemed to be accepted as legitimate, while U.S. motives in confronting the DPRK were questioned less frequently.[84] They feared that Bush would not have the patience to engage in dialogue with the North, and that a tough U.S. reaction would cause crisis on the peninsula.[85] These views were expressed by President Roh when he stated that "success or failure of a U.S. policy toward North Korea isn't too big a deal to the American people, but it is a life-or-death matter for South Korea" and "therefore, any U.S. move should fully consider South Korea's opinion."[86] In general, South Koreans feared a preemptive war against North Korea by the United States to resolve the nuclear crisis.[87]

South Korea judged its primary threat to be the possibility of a military confrontation or regime collapse, not Pyongyang's WMD capabilities.[88] For this reason, easing tension between the U.S. and the DPRK and preventing any potential crisis that could threaten South Korean prosperity became the first priority of the government.[89] The economic consequences of a North Korean regime change, or collapse, caused much concern in Seoul. Seoul's lessons from German reunification were hardly positive.[90]

Balance of threat theory does not directly explain the ROK assistance in Iraq; however, when viewed from the perspective of South Korea's security priorities, the theory provides explanatory power to the ROK contribution. President Roh used a contribution to the Iraq coalition to gain influence over U.S. policy towards the DPRK and lessen the threat of direct confrontation on the Korean peninsula. By the time of Roh's inauguration in February 2003, the U.S. invasion of Iraq was imminent and there was a widespread concern among South Koreans that North Korea would be the next target for U.S. attack.[91] To gain U.S. acquiescence to a more measured strategy with the DPRK, President Roh and the National Security Council accommodated global U.S. security policy by joining the Iraq War coalition and maintaining the peacekeeping operations even after the other U.S. allies began disengagement.[92]

### *Collective Action*

States are more likely to fully participate in a coalition if it perceives a threat from an adversary state. If collective action motivations dominate, however, states are less likely to contribute to the collective good. This book identifies one collective good for the second Iraq War case: the disarmament of Iraqi WMD. This research demonstrates that South Korean decision makers were not concerned with Iraq as a proliferator of WMD and regional instability, but rather were motivated by private concerns with U.S. policy towards North Korea. If Seoul had been motivated by collective action concerns, it would be predicted to limit its effort to a token contribution.[93] Instead, the ROK government submitted to U.S. requests for significant participation in the larger stabilization operations. Threat and alliance dependence concerns motivated the Roh administration to support the war coalition as a means to gain leverage over U.S. policy. Though Korea provided the third largest contingent to the Iraq coalition in an effort to be marked as a major contributor to U.S. counterterrorism efforts, its contribution reflected alliance dependence concerns rather than a desire to be an integral element of a collective action.

### *Alliance Dependence*

Allies face a security-autonomy tradeoff when entering into a defense pact; if an excess of "security" exists, a state may opt to trade some of the excess for more autonomy, by loosening alliance bonds or by reducing support to the ally on some issues, potentially risking the ally's support on future security issues. Conversely if "security" is needed, a state may tighten alliance bonds or support an ally on an issue important to that ally.[94] This security-autonomy tradeoff creates a tension between two fears, the fear of abandonment and the fear of entrapment. This "alliance security dilemma" recognizes that each ally has alternative alliance choices and may opt for one of them if it becomes dissatisfied with the present allies.[95] The Roh administration's support for the Iraq War coalition reflected alliance pressures on foreign policy decisions. Domestically, Roh's "386" backers assessed that the ROK was strong enough to allow for more autonomy in the ROK-U.S. alliance.[96] Roh campaigned for the presidency on a platform that argued for increased independence in the alliance. In addition, he portrayed himself as a leader who would be able to send a strong message to Washington that "business as usual" would no longer be considered the norm in the ROK-U.S. relationship.[97] However, the 2002-2003 North Korean nuclear crisis highlighted the need for Seoul to maintain strong alliance ties with the United States in order to influence U.S. policy on Iraq.[98] Instead of loosening the alliance in an effort to gain more autonomy, Seoul was entrapped into supporting the Iraq War coalition in an effort to gain U.S. concessions towards North Korea.

The liberal leadership under Roh reflected Korea's increased national confidence. Roh's 386 generation led transition team posited that the ROK's economic status as twelfth worldwide, combined with an armed force that numbered over 600,000 soldiers, should allow Korea significant influence over U.S. policy towards the DPRK. They believed that South Korea was indispensable for U.S. global security strategy, while at the same time more capable in dealing with threats emanating from the North. Moreover, indoctrinated into radical leftist ideologies during college years, the transition team dismissed conservative warnings that increased independence from U.S. policy would lead to alliance problems as Cold War paranoia.[99] During the fall 2002 presidential campaign, the Roh camp capitalized on the fear among the South Korean public and many in the government that South Korea would be entrapped in a military conflict precipitated, at least in part, by U.S. unwillingness to pursue a more flexible policy toward Pyongyang.[100] Against the backdrop of the developing nuclear crisis with the DPRK and the accidental death of two Korean schoolchildren by a U.S. armored vehicle, Roh leveraged nationalistic themes to bring ROK-U.S. alliance politics to the forefront of the December presidential election. Roh secured the election by a 2.3 percent margin, emphasizing alliance reform as one of the main themes of the election.[101] Once elected, however, the Roh administration realized that it was trapped by U.S. policy towards the North, which necessitated a strategy of concessions concerning the alliance relationship in an effort to gain leverage over U.S.-DPRK policy.

Roh's Policy for Peace and Prosperity was in direct conflict with the Bush strategy of confrontation. While Roh was promoting a policy of engagement with the North, Secretary of Defense Rumsfeld used the most provocative language toward North Korea since President Bush included it in his "axis of evil." Rumsfeld, at a committee hearing in the House of Representatives, called the North Korean government a "terrorist regime."[102] U.S. and ROK policy differences were highlighted when Roh's transition team was hosted by U.S. government leaders in early February. One of President Roh's personal advisors, at a private dinner with U.S. policy makers, was quoted as saying that "the incoming government would prefer that North Korea had nuclear weapons to seeing it collapse."[103] This statement reflected that the Roh administration's willingness to tolerate a nuclear North in exchange for stability on the Korean peninsula.

Unfortunately for the Roh's Policy of Peace and Prosperity, the DPRK engaged in a series of escalatory measures that ensured that the U.S. would remain engaged on the Korean peninsula. First, Pyongyang announced that it would withdraw from the Nuclear Non-Proliferation Treaty. Second, it reactivated its nuclear facilities and announced that operations were proceeding "on a normal footing." Third, a North

Korean jet violated South Korean airspace over the Yellow Sea. Finally, on the eve of Roh's inauguration, North Korea test fired an anti-ship missile that landed in the sea between the Korean Peninsula and Japan.[104]

Seoul's efforts to mediate the crisis resulted in growing distrust between the U.S. and the ROK on the value of the alliance. These efforts at mediation confirmed the perception of many in Washington that their South Korean allies were flirting with the enemy, betraying the spirit of the alliance by acting as mediators rather than taking sides with the United States.[105] Richard V. Allen, president of a U.S. consulting firm that serves U.S., European, and Asian-based companies seeking access to South Korean markets, spoke for many Americans when he said that South Korea's option was either to side with its U.S. ally or to take "another path."[106] Reacting to highly visible anti-U.S. demonstrations in South Korea, many Americans voiced displeasure in the alliance and some even demanded a possible reduction and relocation of American troops stationed in South Korea. As described earlier, former Secretary of State James Baker warned a visiting delegation from the National Assembly in February that a pull out of U.S. troops would reflect less U.S. commitment towards ROK concerns on the peninsula. Secretary of Defense Rumsfeld stated in Congressional testimony that he was ready to discuss issues of restructuring and relocating U.S. forces in Korea and floated the idea of moving forces off the Korean peninsula.[107] Shortly after Roh's inauguration, the U.S. ambassador in Seoul, Thomas Hubbard, suggested that the U.S. was considering reducing the number of American combat troops in Korea, an unusual move in a time of crisis.[108] The diplomatic onslaught by the Bush administration conveyed the message that the United States was prepared to disengage from the ROK-U.S. alliance at a time of significant importance for South Korea.

Roh's change in attitude appears to be in reaction to spiraling tensions between the DPRK and United States, combined with U.S. threats to withdraw U.S. Forces Korea (USFK) personnel away from the demilitarized zone. On March 1, 2003, North Korean fighter aircraft intercepted an American reconnaissance aircraft in international waters, reportedly "locking on" to the American aircraft with its fire-control radar, which is considered a hostile act.[109] In response, U.S. repositioned 24 long-range B-52 and B-1 bombers near North Korea and hinted that it may send fighter escorts with surveillance planes.[110] In this way, the U.S. signaled that it would not be distracted by Iraq and still retained enough military capability in the theater to pressure the Kim Jong-il regime against their nuclear ambitions.

The ROK reaction to the spiraling tensions, especially Roh's defense of the DPRK intercept caused significant tension in the ROK-U.S. relationship. U.S. military and defense officials were upset by the failure of South Korea to offer firm support for U.S. surveillance flights near North Korea or to condemn the interception of a U.S. spy plane. Instead, South Korea's Defense Ministry said nothing, while President Roh exacerbated U.S. sensitivities in an interview with *The Times of London*, saying that the spy plane episode was part of "a very predictable chain of events."[111] In response, the Bush administration signaled that it was willing to disengage militarily from the peninsula. Defense Secretary Rumsfeld remarked that South Korea "has all the capability in the world of providing the kind of upfront deterrent that's needed to events on the peninsula."[112] The U.S. response to events on the peninsula illustrated to the Roh government that by playing a neutral role, it risked degrading the bilateral relationship and any subsequent means to influence U.S. policy.

Roh's advisers recognized that by allowing a rift to develop with the United States, South Korea may have encouraged the North to believe that its aggressive tactics were successful. Roh's advisors consequently determined that a change of policy was necessary to defuse tensions.[113] Within two weeks of gaining office, South Korea's fledgling administration executed a political about face as it called on Washington not to withdraw its troops, while at the same time pledging support to the Iraq War coalition. Senior figures surrounding President Roh were concerned that the U.S. moves were the initial steps towards a U.S. pre-emptive strike on North Korean nuclear facilities.[114] The timing of Rumsfeld's comments, combined with the bomber deployment, generated speculation in South Korea that the purpose of the USFK redeployment below the Han River was to place U.S. forces out of range of North Korean artillery fire.[115] In response, at the March 6 NSC meeting, Roh charted a new course for his administration stating, "The international standoff over the North's nuclear programs should be resolved peacefully. The top priority of our government policy dealing with this issue should be placed on the reduction of the chance of war on the Korean peninsula."[116]

With the nuclear standoff as a backdrop, the United States requested that the South Korean government no longer remain neutral towards Iraq. This request was forwarded by U.S. Secretary of State Colin Powell at Roh's inauguration February 25, and reportedly presented to the senior presidential staff sometime before March 10.[117] National Security Adviser Ra Jong-yil reported the U.S. request on March 10 during a meeting of advisers and senior presidential staff at the Blue House.[118]

The Roh administration responded with what they thought was a strategy of asymmetrical exchange with the United States. In order to obtain U.S. acceptance to Roh's engagement strategy towards the DPRK Seoul accepted a significant role in the Iraq War coalition.[119] Local news reports indicated that the NSC principals discussed assistance options for a possible U.S. war in Iraq in the period between March 6 and March 13. Blue House spokeswoman Song Kyoung-hee stated in a press briefing March 12 that four Iraq support plans were discussed at the last NSC meeting and that South Korea was considering sending non-combat troops to help the U.S. in the event of war with Iraq. She continued by emphasizing that no decision had yet been made concerning the size of the force.[120] At the same time, Foreign Minister Yoon Young-kwan acknowledged on a local radio program that the ROK government intended to dispatch a contingent of non-combat troops to Iraq in support of the coalition of the willing.[121]

The Roh administration defended its support of the Iraq coalition in alliance dependence terms. The administration argued that, for the purpose of national security, it was imperative to maintain a close alliance relationship with the United States, whose cooperation was essential to resolve the tension in the Korean peninsula.[122] Ryu In-tae, a top political aide of President Roh, framed the deployment as a means to gain influence with the U.S. in a meeting with opposition civic leaders, "The troop dispatch plan is unavoidable, in order to influence U.S. to settle the North Korean nuclear crisis peacefully through dialogue."[123] Pointing out Korea's "alliance duty to help the United State when it is in difficulty," President Roh affirmed, "by fulfilling such a duty rather than by directly confronting the U.S. on the question of the war's legitimacy, we can better serve our national security objective of the peaceful resolution of the North Korean problem."[124] Roh acknowledged in his first speech to the National Assembly that the troop dispatch was a *quid pro quo* to repair damaged ROK-U.S. relations, "I decided to dispatch troops, despite ongoing antiwar protests, because of the fate of our country and the people...In order to resolve the North Korean nuclear issue peacefully, it is important to maintain strong cooperation with the United States."[125] South Korean political analysts described President Roh's decision to push for the troop deployment—despite his own antiwar views and public opposition to the war—as part of a shrewd but risky bid to preserve the alliance with the United States.[126] By making a timely promise of his "active support" of the unpopular war, Roh was betting on the chance to rescue the damaged U.S.-Korea alliance that he regarded as indispensable not only to deter a potentially devastating war on the peninsula, but also to pursue inter-Korean reconciliation.[127]

While Roh's linkage strategy did appear to influence the Bush administration's North Korean policy, it was also seen as an early domestic defeat for Roh.[128] In their first summit meeting in May 2003, President's Roh gained Bush's agreement that a peaceful resolution of the North Korean nuclear crisis was achievable. However, Bush highlighted that further inter-Korean exchanges and cooperation should depend on North Korean behavior and increased threats to peace and stability on the peninsula would require "consideration of further steps."[129] Roh accepted this position, making engagement contingent on North Korean nuclear concessions rather than the "sunshine" position of unconditional support. This abrupt change in policy, combined with ROK support of the Iraq coalition, was criticized as a renunciation of Roh's campaign pledge to forge a foreign policy independent of the U.S.[130] The fact that public opinion was decidedly against the Iraq War, damaged Roh's populist image. As a populist head of state who had a weak partisan power base in the National Assembly, he had to be at least aware of public opinion so that his party could gain a majority in the 2004 general election. Even more critical for Roh was that the nation's anti-war movement was spearheaded by the same reform-minded lawmakers and civic groups that supported his presidential campaign only months prior. Those citizens most active against the Iraq war aid were the same ones who voted him into office the previous December.

Although Roh sought to extract concessions on U.S. policy towards North Korea, Roh's linkage strategy failed to resonate with U.S. policy makers. As seen by many U.S. strategists, South Korea's dispatch of peacekeeping forces to Iraq was an act of duty expected of military allies in times of crisis, not a concession on the part of South Korea to be repaid by the United States in the form of support for the Peace and Prosperity Policy. The 1954 Mutual Defense Treaty had reciprocity as its central organizing principle, and according to the interpretation of that treaty by U.S. policy makers, South Korea's assistance to U.S. war efforts in Iraq was a payment in kind for U.S. guarantees of South Korean security.[131] Rather than moderating its Korean policy, the Bush administration announced plans to redeploy U.S. troops from the Korean demilitarized zone to south of Seoul. The plan to reduce force levels and shift troops south on the peninsula was unilaterally accelerated by the U.S. in the spring 2003, even after Seoul announced its support to the Iraq coalition. U.S. officials announced a reduction of the U.S. military presence in Korea as part of the U.S. Global Posture Review while at the same time continuing its strategy of confrontation with the DPRK.[132] In a May 2003 interview, Undersecretary of Defense for Policy Doug Feith stated that nearly all U.S. forces deployed in East Asia could be reassigned to new locations for operations very different from their traditional missions.[133] Deputy Secretary of Defense Wolfowitz quickly disavowed these remarks, but the U.S. accelerated discussions with the ROK government concerning the movement of USFK troops.[134] The U.S. adopted a take-it-or-leave-it attitude, presenting USFK troop relocation as nonnegotiable on the principle that it was only the U.S. president, as commander in chief, who could determine the deployment of US military troops. Consequently, many South Koreans viewed the Pentagon decision to reposition and reduce U.S. forces on the peninsula as "punishment" for their recent protests against the U.S. troops and foreign policy.[135] The realignments were initiated despite the continued military confrontation with the North and without weighing the implications of a nuclear North Korea, potential instability on the peninsula, or the prospect of unification.[136]

The threat of troop withdrawal again gave the U.S. leverage in alliance matters and highlighted Seoul's dependent position in ROK-U.S. bilateral relations when, in the fall of 2003, the U.S. again asked for additional troops to assist in quelling the developing insurgency in Iraq. Seoul accommodated the request, again framing the deployment in terms of alliance dependence. The ROK government deployed an additional 3,000 soldiers, mostly non-combat personnel in August 2004, to meet with the Bush administration approval. Korean contributions were unprecedented and were acknowledged as such by the United States. In a major policy address on terrorism by President Bush on the one-year anniversary of the war against Iraq, the U.S. president singled out both Japan and South Korea for their "historic commitments" of troops and materiel to the war on terrorism.[137] Korea subsequently also gained a reprieve from the threatened drawdown of USFK forces. In the immediate aftermath of the decision to augment troop deployments to Iraq, the U.S. agreed to extend the U.S. withdrawal from the peninsula by another three years.[138]

Overall, in the wake of the North Korean nuclear crisis, the ROK decision to support the Iraq coalition was formulated based on alliance dependence concerns. Although President Roh campaigned on a stance reflecting a more equal relationship in the alliance, when confronted with escalating tensions and a potential U.S. troop withdrawal, Seoul was trapped. Seoul provided numerous alliance concessions with the aim of influencing the Bush administration's stand on North Korea. Seoul committed troops to the Iraq war and subsequently expanded that commitment in response to U.S. requests for a larger role for Korea. At the same time, Seoul conceded to a repositioning and eventual drawdown of U.S. forces on the peninsula.[139] Seoul's commitment to Iraq did not reflect commitment to U.S. global counter-terrorism policy, but rather a linkage strategy to gain influence over a senior alliance partner. According to Korean policy expert Victor Cha, Seoul's support can be viewed as a bargaining chip to gain favors from the U.S. rather than a commitment to U.S. objectives in the global war on terrorism.[140] Seoul's support for the Iraq War reflects alliance dependence since the government continues to justify it as an alliance obligation rather than an international obligation. Ironically, alliance dependence concerns caused President Roh, initially skeptical of the justification for the ROK-U.S. alliance, to provide the third highest level of support to the Iraq War coalition, while at the same time accommodating a major troop reduction and realignment of USFK forces on the peninsula.[141]

### *Domestic Structure and Politics*

Although alliance dependence issues motivated Seoul to support the U.S. led coalition in Iraq, domestic structure and politics highly influenced the timing and composition of the Korean effort.

The Republic of Korea is a presidential democratic republic where the president maintains significant control over the executive branch and unicameral legislature. Korean government reflects a state-centered approach where a powerful state was required for economic development and defense against the Communist North and politics has been dominated by a string of dominate presidents that sought to exert total control over all aspects of the political process.[142] South Korea's president maintains a considerable amount of power and authority compared to the other branches of government. The president—directly elected for a single five-year term—serves as the head of state, chief executive, and the commander-in-chief of the armed forces. The president is assisted by a prime minister who acts as the chief operating officer, overseeing day to day operations of the executive branch. The prime minister is a political confidant appointed by the president and is not required to be a member of parliament, effectively consolidating the power of the president in the executive branch. Government policy is formulated by the State Council, or cabinet, which is also directly appointed by and includes the president. Members of the State Council are collectively and individually responsible to the president only.[143] The National Assembly, or legislature, is unicameral and is directly elected every four years for a four year term.[144] Local governments, though gaining autonomy, are highly influenced by the executive branch and thus are often indistinguishable from the central government.[145] The three branches of government are interwoven into a hierarchical relationship in which the executive branch and the president form the center pillar of Korean government.[146] The weak legislature and the unstable party system contribute to the president's substantial influence on Korean government and politics.[147] This strong presidential leadership and control of the bureaucracy, combined with a weak legislature, marks South Korea as a Type I state in the domestic structure typology.

In the burden sharing decision model, a Type I government under alliance dependence pressure is expected to contribute substantially to the coalition because the chief executive is likely to respond to external pressure without being significantly influenced by the legislature or public. This section will articulate that Roh did exert significant influence over the ROK burden sharing strategy, but that domestic reforms implemented by the Kim Dae-jung and Roh Moo-hyun administrations weakened executive influence, allowing some consideration towards legislative support and public opinion on the composition and timing of Korea's contribution. Ultimately, however, once President Roh determined the size and disposition of the Korean troop dispatch, public opinion and the legislature had little effect on decisions to deploy soldiers to Iraq. Roh was able to deploy and maintain a sizable military contingent to Iraq while public opinion was, at least initially, significantly opposed to the conflict.

President Roh Moo-hyun—the most liberal President in the republic's history—stunned his supporters by brokering the deployment of 670 military personnel to Iraq within two month of assuming office. His troop dispatch plan was a very politically risky move as he was elected on a promise to devolve Seoul from the U.S.-oriented foreign policy orbit. Additionally, South Korean public opinion data consistently showed ambivalence towards U.S. intervention in Iraq. In the summer of 2002, polling data shows that only 15 percent of South Koreans surveyed considered terrorism to be a national priority—one of the lowest figures for major countries surveyed—and 72 percent of South Koreans opposed the U.S.-led war on terrorism. During the run-up to the war in Iraq, 81 percent of the general public in South Korea opposed U.S.-led military action against Iraq and only 10 percent supported it. Additionally, 76 percent opposed the deployment of ROK combat troops to Iraq and only 16 percent supported it. [148] Clearly, Roh's decision to deploy troops would meet with public opposition.

The first deployment decision was the result of the influence of conservative elements on Roh's national security team and Roh's weak position for influencing the conservative National Assembly. Roh presided over a *yoso yadae* government in which the governing party was the minority in the assembly.[149] Party distribution in the National Assembly at the time of Roh's election was 111 seats for the Millennium Democratic Party (MDP), 129 seats for the conservative Grand National Party (GNP), and 14 seats divided between the conservative United Liberal Democratic Party (ULD) and Independents. This situation of a "divided" government between the executive and legislative branches necessitated a brand of politics and presidential leadership in which Roh had to court the conservative GNP with skill and tact to overcome political stalemate in national politics.[150] The GNP was very supportive of the ROK-U.S. alliance and concerned that the liberal Roh government would damage relations by not supporting the Iraq coalition.[151] Additionally, an influential number of Roh's key foreign policy advisors reflected the conservative agenda of the GNP. National Security Advisor Ra Jong-yil was a strong advocate of a closer South Korea-U.S. alliance.[152] National Defense Adviser Kim Hui-sang maintained a critical stand on the sunshine policy and had strong U.S. connections. Lastly, Foreign Policy Advisor Ban Ki-mun was a career diplomat who has spent more than 30 years in the Foreign Ministry, 70 percent of whose priorities lie with the United States.[153] A pragmatic politician, Roh navigated a middle course politically that reflected the need for the ROK to address the crisis on the peninsula by pursuing a more conservative agenda with the United States. According to a political observer, "Roh realized that the North Korean nuclear crisis is his most pressing task whose outcome can make or break his presidency."[154]

In a response to a U.S. request for military support in Iraq, senior advisors on the NSC recommended a moderately sized deployment of non-combat troops to demonstrate support for the U.S.-led coalition. Additionally, they formulated a public campaign that stressed that the deployment was in the national interest of the ROK-U.S. alliance. Foreign Minister Yoon Young-kwan expressed the deployment as an alliance "duty" expected of an ally on a Korean radio program.[155] National Security Advisor Ra Jong-yil, together with Roh's top defense advisor Kim Hee-sang, explained to the press that, "The U.S. war on Iraq is justifiable. Besides, helping an ally in need is what the South Korea-U.S. alliance is all about."[156] In public statements, Roh stressed the importance of the South Korea-U.S. alliance as a means to justify the deployments. He emphasized that Seoul had accepted the U.S. request to resolve the North Korean issue. Meanwhile, the administration immediately framed the scope of the deployment as consistent with previous ROK efforts. Roh immediately pledged that, "The scale of the assistance is not expected to surpass that of our support made during the Gulf War in the early 1990s."[157]

On the recommendation of MDP chairman Chyung Dai-chu, Roh formed a supra-partisan committee of party leaders in the National Assembly to aid policy coordination and to suppress opposition within the Assembly. Roh personally assured them that the Cabinet approved of the deployment measure, and he met with lawmakers from the Assembly's National Defense Committee to coordinate legislation for the Iraq deployment.[158] Roh acknowledged the domestic anti-war sentiment and, with statements of support from political leaders of the two major political parties, he expected the authorization bill to face little opposition.[159]

Though Roh fast-tracked the deployment legislation, a vocal opposition within his own party emerged to impede administration efforts to pass the mandate. Roh's public relations efforts failed to impress liberal members of the MDP, who saw the deployment as supporting the "inhumane invasion of Iraq."[160] A group of reformist lawmakers from the ruling and opposition parties issued a statement opposing the government plan to dispatch troops to Iraq. A statement by a group of 18 ruling and opposition lawmakers stated, "There is[are] no grounds to participate in the war of aggression, which lacks a UN resolution, in the name of (the US-Korea) alliance."[161] The authorization vote was delayed while the MDP attempted to consolidate support for the assembly vote. Public protests mounted outside the National Assembly and civic action groups threatened to take retribution against lawmakers in the next general election.[162] Nosamo, an internet based group that had supported Roh's presidential bid, announced that it would mount opposition campaigns against lawmakers in the next general election if they voted for the deployment.[163] In response, civic groups supporting the alliance with the United States spearheaded a drive to block lawmakers from seeking re-election if they voted against the bill proposed by the government.[164] In light of this domestic turmoil and in an effort to relieve legislator's concerns against retribution, the MDP allowed its lawmakers to cast a vote "free" from the party endorsement, an unusual move in Korean politics.[165] Each MDP lawmaker could thus cast his or her vote based on local concerns rather than party recommendation.

While MDP support for the resolution began to falter, the GNP grew concerned that it would be held politically responsible for the authorization bill. To gain support for the measure, Roh courted the conservative opposition to approve the troop deployment. At a dinner with ruling and opposition party leaders, Roh asked floor leaders to, "deal with the motion as soon as possible." The opposition GNP floor leader Rhee Q-taek responded that the president had to make tangible efforts directly to the public first.[166] The GNP leadership promised a positive vote only after President Roh, "reaches out to the public himself and his persuasion efforts show results."[167] GNP members did not oppose the deployment *per se*, but were concerned with being blamed for an unpopular resolution.[168] Conservatives generally backed the decision to send troops to Iraq on the grounds of national interest and strengthening the ROK-U.S. alliance. Since the MDP had authorized a free vote, the GNP grew concerned that an approval of the deployment would be seen a GNP policy rather than a Roh administration decision.[169]

Roh resisted efforts to make a public appeal for the dispatch, relying instead on administration officials to make public statements for the troop deployment. Advisors to Roh urged civic organizations to exercise restraint in their attempts to pressure lawmakers over the Iraq deployment issue.[170] After a second delay for the authorization vote, amid rising opposition, Roh directed his aides to intervene to ensure the bill's passage. Presidential Chief of Staff Moon Hee-sang and political advisor Ryu In-tae contacted dissenting lawmakers and pressured them to support the bill. The MDP leadership intensified efforts to persuade lawmakers opposed to the presidential motion. Party chairman Chyung Dai-chul held a news conference at the party headquarters to call for cooperation to pass the bill.[171] Finally, Roh appealed to his own and opposition party members in his first speech to the National Assembly. Roh's public campaign seemed to convince the public that the troop deployment reflected ROK national interests. By April 1, public opinion polls showed that 55 percent of the public supported the government's troop deployment decision while approximately 43 percent did not.[172]

Roh's speech to the National Assembly gave the GNP the necessary political cover, while at the same time convincing a portion of the MDP that the authorization bill was necessary to defuse the nuclear crisis and restore Korean economic stability. Roh's acceptance of responsibility for the deployment decision seemed to quell lawmaker's concerns. He appealed to the members "to be courageous and endorse the bill."[173] Roh's arguments to the Assembly stressed the need to resolve the peninsula crisis by deploying troops to Iraq. Roh stated:

> I have reached the conclusion that assisting the United States in its time of difficulty and solidifying the Korea-U.S. relationship would be

> much more helpful in peacefully resolving the North Korean nuclear issue than driving relations to worse terms.[174]

Additionally, the deployment was framed to quell economic uneasiness. Roh stated, "Our decision to deploy forces to Iraq is contributing to clearing the anxieties of the business community, especially foreign investors, about possible discord between Seoul and Washington."[175] Further, he stated that even if the Iraq War was without justification, the deployment was necessary for upholding solidarity with the United States.[176] He acknowledged that the Iraq deployment marked a reversal of his equal partnership goals, but he noted, "it would be absurd to endanger the lives of the people in order to put the two countries' relations on an equal partnership."[177] The National Assembly eventually approved the deployment with 179 voting in favor, 68 against, and 9 abstentions, with 256 out of 270 legislators casting votes.[178]

Roh's Assembly appeal decision won support from a number of Korean editorialists, despite the uncertainty about the wisdom of the war. The conservative *Chosun Daily* said, "The president and the Assembly have acted responsibly and in a practical manner by setting aside for a moment their ideals or opinions that the war in Iraq may be unjust."[179] *JoongAng Daily*, an independent paper, determined that sending troops would help quell investor concern about the possibility of a split in the ROK-U.S. alliance. It also called for Koreans to accept the lawmakers' decision in the national interest, "Now is the time to show national maturity...further debate on this matter would be waste of the nation's time and energy."[180] A similar call came from another daily newspaper, *Dong-A*, which said the administration now had to demonstrate united leadership, while anti-war groups should respect and accept the lawmakers' decision, "We live in a democratic society where, once a decision is made by the approval of the majority, the rest should respect and carry out the decision together."[181] Notwithstanding the calls for universal support, Roh was severely criticized by his base for giving up on his ideal of an equal partnership with the United States.

While the opposition parties applauded Roh's adoption of pro-American agenda, those who supported Roh said he failed to secure a U.S. pledge to rule out any military option to end the eight-month nuclear standoff with North Korea.[182] After his May 2003 summit with President Bush in Washington, Roh's former supporters criticized his performance as a "diplomatic humiliation."[183] Young and progressive supporters posted angry remarks and attacked Roh on the internet for retreating from his campaign promises and kowtowing to the United States.[184] Roh weakened his engagement strategy with the North by linking economic assistance to positive developments in denuclearization.[185] Roh acknowledged that he sidestepped contentious issues in the summit, choosing instead to dwell on the strengths of their alliance; but these rapid policy reversals caused him to lose support in his own MDP.[186]

In September 2003, President Roh was again put to the test when the U.S. officially requested South Korea to deploy an additional brigade sized (3,000-5,000) combat force. The Bush administration made the request in several venues in Washington and Seoul on September 4-5. The government again convened an NSC meeting September 18 to discuss the timing and composition of possible ROK support. While Washington did not specify the exact number of troops it wanted South Korea to dispatch, it requested a dispatch of a unit that could form the core of a multi-national division. U.S. officials cited the 2,500-member combat unit from Poland as an example.[187] It was widely speculated that Seoul would deploy at least 5,000 troops, mostly combatants, to Mosul in northern Iraq to replace the U.S. 101st Airborne Division. Mosul at the time was one of the most dangerous spots in Iraq with numerous insurgent attacks by supporters of Saddam Hussein.[188] Public opposition in the wake of the increasing violence in Iraq forced progressives in the Blue House to seek a reduction in the number of troops who would be deployed to Iraq, despite objections from the Ministry of National Defense (MND) and Ministry of Foreign Affairs and Trade (MOFAT).

The MND and MOFAT were very supportive of efforts to increase the ROK presence in Iraq according to the U.S. request. The MND suggested dispatching 5,000 elite troops from the southern region of South Korea to minimize the disruption of forces on the peninsula. Korean Army leaders judged that small numbers of troops were not appropriate in dealing with the missions requested by the United States.[189] MOFAT agreed with the deployment as an effort to strike a decisive blow to the skeptics among the American public and opinion makers that questioned Korea's role in the ROK-U.S. alliance. Foreign Minister Yoon, along with the ROK ambassador to the United States Han Sung-joo and other adherents of the "alliance faction" argued in support of the request in light of Korea's strategic and diplomatic concerns.[190] MOFAT officials expressed concern that Korea should not be left behind when more and more nations were participating in the coalition of the willing.[191]

The Blue House and the NSC, however, did not share the optimism of the MND and MOFAT. In this instance the more progressive elements, led by NSC Vice Chief Lee Jong-seok, gained control over deployment deliberations.[192] Lee, who was deeply involved in the formation of Roh's progressive inter-Korean and foreign affairs platform, was concerned that putting Korean troops in danger would have significant negative fallout on President Roh's public opinion ratings.[193] The Blue House further noted the significant public opposition to the first deployment in their arguments to minimize the size of the deployment.[194]

Public opinion stabilized and became steady once the United Nations adopted Resolution 1551 authorizing the international community to assist Iraq stabilization and reconstruction effort. According to a poll conducted by *Hankook Ilbo* on October 23, 2003, 64.9 percent of those polled favored the idea of sending additional troops. [195] An additional survey illustrated that 73.9 percent of Koreans polled approved of the UN resolution.[196] Additionally, the Korean public urged the government to not yield to terrorist demands after the death of a Korean civilian in Baghdad. Public opinion was not universally supportive of the additional deployment. From September 23 to October 18, 2003, civic action committees organized more than twelve street demonstrations to protest Seoul's support to the Iraq conflict, which became a concern for Assembly members. A spokesperson for the Roh administration attempted to defuse critics when he stated, "the Korea-U.S. relationship, the national interest, and the recent passage of UN resolutions were all considered in making the decision."[197] Noting the civic group activity, Blue House aides sought to minimize the size of the deployment, taking into account significant public objections to the deployment. The progressives on the NSC actively managed the size, timing, and composition of the deployment in an attempt to preempt public opposition to the larger deployment.

The Blue House became sensitive to the term "combat troops" after it became clear that Washington wanted troops similar to the Polish-led multinational, light infantry division.[198] National Security Advisor Ra hinted October 1 in a radio interview that sending combat troops was unthinkable saying, "because the war in Iraq is over, we are not thinking about sending troops that might be involved in violent conflicts."[199] Lee Jong-seok, Vice Secretary-General of the NSC, ended administration discussions on troop strength when he declared that Korea would send no more than 3,000 additional troops to Iraq.[200] The NSC formally announced that Korea would support the U.S. troop request one day after the passage of UN Resolution 1551.

President Roh's decision to send no more than 3,000 additional troops to Iraq symbolized a victory for the progressive Blue House staff over the conservative ministries that favored a larger deployment.[201] The two factions inside his administration had been locked in a power struggle since the first troop deployment decision. The NSC led the charge to minimize the number of troops to be sent to Iraq and to staff the contingent mainly with non-combat soldiers, while the MND and MOFAT tried to fulfill the U.S. request for a large combat-capable force. Sources in the administration noted that the fierce opposition led by groups who had supported Roh during the presidential election campaign influenced Roh's decision making.[202] Roh felt a sense of crisis in anticipation of the upcoming 2004 general elections if he chose to side with the U.S. concerning the deployment of additional troops.[203] The cap on the troop deployment caused concerns in the MOFAT that the reduced contingent would harm ROK interests with respect to the United States. South Korean diplomats were quoted as saying the Roh administration was "naive and unrealistic" in its dealings with the United States. Others said that dealing with members of the NSC and its chief, Lee Jong-seok, was like dealing with the Taliban, as they were so radical and reactionary. This accompanied speculation that some within the administration, specifically the NSC, were North Korean sympathizers.[204] Consequently, the Korean Foreign Minister Yoon Young-kwan was forced to resign and the NSC gained greater control over South Korean foreign policy.[205]

The NSC advised President Roh to hold a vague position—while recognizing in internal discussions a 3,000-troop limit—and to repeat that he needed more time to make such an important decision. Roh presented this position to President Bush at a meeting in Bangkok on October 20.[206] In negotiations with U.S. defense officials on November 5-6, the Korean delegation could not be dislodged from the 3,000-soldier cap due to the NSC imposed limit. Roh's decisions concerning the second troop deployment were based not on alliance concerns, but rather on the predicted domestic backlash to the large Korean deployment. Once the decision regarding the troop deployment was made, the Blue House maintained strict control over the government ministries to ensure the message to the public was managed.

The Blue House secretariat coordinated with the National Assembly leadership to ensure a smoother passage of the required second authorization bill. The administration briefed details of the troop dispatch plan to the leaders of the four ruling and opposition parties on December 11 and 12 and a final decision on timing and composition was made at a December 14 meeting with Roh, Defense Minister Cho Young-kil, and Presidential National Security Adviser Ra, and the four party leaders.[207] Roh's newly formed Uri Party leadership expressed concern that the bill would splinter the young party.[208] The Uri Party, composed of the progressive lawmakers from the MDP, shared a similar agenda with the civic groups that threatened to boycott lawmakers in the upcoming April general election who supported the deployment. The Uri Party was effective at delaying the bill until it could convince a majority of its members to support the decision.[209] The conservative GNP, which by February 2004 controlled 149 seats in the 273-member parliament, publicly supported the second dispatch bill. Chough Soon-hyung, leader of the former ruling MDP, finally told his party's lawmakers during a pre-session meeting to vote for the dispatch; despite this instruction most members of the MDP voted against the measure.[210] With the leaders of the major parties supporting the deployment, the National Assembly finally scheduled a vote on the measure on February 13. The Assembly ratified the deployment plan easily by a 3 to 1 margin (155 to 50 members) with a majority of members from the Uri Party and GNP supporting the decision.[211]

Deployment of the troops was initially scheduled for late April, but it was delayed for weeks as Seoul and Washington failed to agree on where they would be located and the timeframe. The Roh government deliberately postponed the deployment in order to deploy the forces to a relatively safe area of Iraq.[212] The NSC estimated that the 30-70 casualties expected in Mosul would constitute an unbearable political setback for Roh; therefore avoiding casualties became the first priority in the deployment. At a meeting in Baghdad on March 18, the U.S. finally accepted the Korean request to change the deployment destination.[213]

The deployment was also delayed due to the March 12 impeachment of President Roh on charges that he had inappropriately backed his breakaway Uri Party in the parliamentary elections in violation of election laws.[214] These charges and the ensuing scandal caused an immediate suspension of Roh's presidency; the Prime Minster, traditionally powerless, assumed the duties of the presidency. [215] South Korea's Constitutional Court rejected the impeachment charges May 14 stating the charge of illegal electioneering "was not serious or grave enough to justify the unseating of the president."[216] No official in the government wanted to facilitate the deployment for the two months in which the Korean Constitutional Court decided on the legality of the impeachment.

In the meantime, the U.S. announced that it would deploy to Iraq a brigade of the 2nd Infantry Division that was garrisoned in Korea. Additionally, Washington informed Seoul at the 10th Future of the Alliance Talks (FOTA) on July 22, 2004, that 6,000 U.S. troops would be pulled out of South Korea by 2004, and 6,000 more by the end of

2005.[217] These deployment decisions generated speculation in Korea that the moves were punishment for the delay of the ROK troops.[218] Once the U.S. announced its decision to transfer the brigade off the peninsula, the Korean government accelerated its efforts to deploy its troops. The Korean government, with the support of the ruling Uri party, deployed the first troops in July 2004 and the main contingent in August.[219]

The continued deployment of Korean soldiers to Iraq was considered a concern for the Roh administration. Civic action groups such as the Citizen's Action against Deployment to Iraq, a coalition of 351 NGOs, proclaimed that they would work to deter any attempt to prolong the tenure of the Korean troops in Iraq.[220] Interestingly, they did not take any direct action against the Uri Party for supporting the deployment decision. In fact, due to a number of factors including the GNP's impeachment of Roh, the Uri Party gained a significant number of seats in the 2004 general election.[221] The lack of serious opposition is likely due to the preemptive drawdown of troops with the yearly mandate renewal. As discussed previously in this chapter, the Roh administration made anticipatory concessions on troop withdrawals in an attempt to disarm public opposition to the deployment. This approach seems successful, since as of May 2008, the Korean government still has approximately 650 personnel deployed to Iraq. The renewal mandates have been successful; however the opposition vote has risen over the length of the deployment.[222]

In summary, domestic politics significantly influenced the composition and timing of South Korean support to the Iraq War coalition. The Roh administration showed strong leadership in influencing the decision to deploy Korean soldier to Iraq, but this decision was somewhat influenced by resistance to the deployment in Roh's own MDP and Uri parties. The domestic structure typology predicts that decision making in South Korea would be heavily influenced by the preferences of the chief executive and this case study supports those predictions. Once President Roh publicly committed to the coalition of the willing, legislative and societal pressure failed to alter the level or composition of Korean commitment to the coalition of the willing. This is not to say, however, that public opinion had no influence over national decision making. The Roh administration frequently anticipated public attitudes and intentionally constrained its assistance to the Iraq coalition in an effort to alleviate public concerns. In this manner, the Roh administration acted like any authoritarian regime that had to balance resource extraction against domestic interests.[223] Rather than allowing public opinion form the policy, Roh managed domestic expectations so that he could commit the necessary resources to the coalition to meet Korea's foreign policy goals.

### The Role of Legitimacy

Although legitimacy arguments were raised in Roh's political circles, legitimacy arguments affected only the composition and timing of military support rather than the decision to join the Iraq War coalition. Although President Kim Dae-jung advised the Bush administration to pursue a UN mandate on Iraq, this advice was based on national concerns rather than the pursuit of international legitimacy. President Kim encouraged a UN mandate in private conversations with President Bush and encouraged a UN based multilateral action at the Asia-Europe Meeting (ASEM) in Copenhagen, however, the ROK government never attempted to withhold political, economic, or military support to the coalition based on legitimacy concerns.[224]

After the ROK government publicly committed to the coalition of the willing, a select group of National Assembly members protested the action on legitimacy grounds. A group of reformist lawmakers from the ruling and opposition parties issued a public statement opposing the government's plan to dispatch troops based on the legitimacy of the operation: "There is no grounds to participate in the war of aggression, which lacks a UN resolution, in the name of (the ROK-U.S.) alliance."[225] Ultimately, discussions in the NSC and in the National Assembly hinged on national security concerns rather than the legitimacy of the Iraq War effort. President Roh, in his address to the National Assembly, admitted that the Iraq effort was lacking a full international mandate. Roh argued that even if the Iraq War was without justification, it was nonetheless necessary for South Korea to participate for the sake of upholding solidarity with the United States.[226]

Legitimacy issues affected Korean deployments to the extent that the contribution was shaped in an effort to demonstrate that Korea was not participating in potentially illegitimate combat operations, but rather a more legitimate peacekeeping effort. The first deployment of soldiers was framed as a humanitarian effort to aid in the Iraq refugee effort. Roh made his support known for dispatching a non-combat engineering unit of 600 soldiers and approximately 100 medical personnel to support coalition forces and also to take part in postwar rehabilitation efforts.[227] After noting the public objections to the first deployment, the Roh administration ensured that the second deployment consisted of a peacekeeping rather than a combat mission. The Roh administration clearly sent the message to the public that the additional soldiers were being dispatched in order to maintain peace and public order in Iraq and not for a war against the Iraqi people. Once the stabilization operations gained the legitimacy of a UN mandate under Resolution 1551, the ROK government quickly committed to the coalition of the willing. Additionally, the government rejected a combat mission for its sizable deployment and instead negotiated for a location that nearly guaranteed that the Korean contingent would see little combat.

Unlike many countries in the international community, Korean concerns about contributing to the coalition of the willing were not based on the international legitimacy of the operation, but rather on pragmatic concerns about the influence of Korean causalities on domestic politics. This research found no evidence that the ROK government used legitimacy arguments to condition its responses to the United States. Instead, I find that deployment decisions were geared to gain leverage over U.S. policy towards the DPRK.

## Summary and Conclusions

South Korea was particularly influenced by alliance dependence on the United States. With increasing tensions between the DPRK and the United States, the Roh administration departed from its anti-American course and accepted a role in the coalition of the willing. This support sought to reduce spiraling tensions on the peninsula and to demonstrate support to its U.S. ally in the international community. Domestic structure and politics subsequently influenced the nature of support that the ROK government provided to the coalition. This research demonstrated that even Type I regimes, which have significant autonomy from the legislature, must make controversial decisions with an eye towards domestic unrest. Due to the significant influence that the Korean President has over the national government and democratic institutions, the public's main means of influencing policy is typically through organized mass protest.[228] Although the Roh administration was able to build support for the deployment in an opposition-held parliament, it also had to scale the troop contingent considering the amount of domestic unrest present. The Roh government made a series of anticipatory concessions with the public and its own party by limiting the scope and mission of the deployments. In that manner, the administration could demonstrate that it was considering the demands of society. An interesting observation, however, is that once deployment decisions were formulated within the NSC, public opinion had little effect on changing the government's decision. No decision regarding troop deployments to Iraq was modified after the public announcement of a government decision was made.

South Korea's support of the Iraq War coalition is also a case of alliance entrapment. During the transition from the Kim Dae-jung to the Roh Moo-hyun administrations, advisors sought to implement Roh's campaign goal of a more equal alliance partnership with the United States. This goal was quickly abandoned when the ROK government found that it had little influence over the confrontational U.S. policy towards the North Korean nuclear ambitions. Faced with increasing tensions and the prospect of a U.S. troop drawdown on the peninsula, the Roh administration rapidly reversed course and supported the coalition of the willing in an attempt to gain leverage within the ROK-U.S. alliance. The ROK government maintained a weak bargaining position and made numerous concessions to the United States in an effort to change U.S. policy towards the DPRK. The U.S. ultimately extracted concessions from Korea by threatening to make significant reductions and realignments to its military presence on the Korean peninsula. Korea found itself trapped between U.S. expectations for Iraq and a nuclear crisis on the peninsula.

---

[1] The size of the ROK contingent of 3,600 troops was significant, making it the third largest contingent after the United States and United Kingdom. This also marked the first time the ROK has sent combat forces overseas in nearly 40 years when ROK forces constituted the second largest contingent in Vietnam.

[2] Victor D. Cha, "Korea: A Peninsula in Crisis and Flux," in *Strategic Asia 2004–05: Confronting Terrorism in the Pursuit of Power*, ed. National Bureau of Asian Research (U.S.) (Seattle, Wash.: National Bureau of Asian Research, 2004), 148-49.

[3] "South Korean Policymakers Hold Meeting on Iraq Troop Dispatch," *Yonhap News Agency*, June 14, 2004.

[4] Seung-hwan Kim, "Yankee Go Home? A Historical View of South Korean Sentiment toward the United States, 2001-2004," in *Strategy and Sentiment: South Korean Views of the United States and the U.S.-ROK Alliance*, ed. Derek J. Mitchell (Washington D.C., Seoul: Center for Strategic and International Studies and Yonsei University, 2004).

[5] Sung-Bin Ko, "South Korea's Search for an Independent Foreign Policy," *Journal of Contemporary Asia* 36, no. 2 (2006).

[6] Gregory F. Treverton, Eric Larson, and Spencer H. Kim, "Bridging the 'Open Water' in the US-South Korea Military Alliance," *The Korean Journal of Defense Analysis* XV, no. 2 (2003).

[7] Susan Peterson, *Crisis Bargaining and the State: The Domestic Politics of International Conflict* (Ann Arbor: University of Michigan Press, 1996), 31.

See also Andrew P. Cortell and James W. Davis, "How Do International Institutions Matter? The Domestic Impact of International Rules and Norms," *International Studies Quarterly* 40, no. 4 (1996), 455-56.

[8] Byoung-kwon Sohn, "Addressing Limits of Parliamentary Democracy," *The Korea Herald*, February 12, 2008.

[9] Katharine Moon, "US-South Korean Relations," in *The Future of US-Korean Relations: The Imbalance of Power*, ed. John Feffer (New York: Routledge, 2006).

[10] Young W. Kihl, *Transforming Korean Politics: Democracy, Reform, and Culture* (Armonk, N.Y.: M.E. Sharpe, 2005), 328-29.

[11] "Korea Walking Diplomatic Tightrope over War on Iraq," *Korea Times*, September 14, 2002.

[12] United States Department of State, "Section 2207 Report on Iraq Relief and Reconstruction" (Department of State Bureau of Near Eastern Affairs, April 2008 [cited May 16, 2008]); available from http://www.state.gov/documents/organization/105341.pdf. Cha, "Korea: A Peninsula in Crisis and Flux," 148.

[13] Jeffrey R. Lord and Kristin M. Lord, "Additional Cases from the Gulf Crisis and Burden Sharing in Unprofor," in *Friends in Need: Burden Sharing in the Persian Gulf War*, ed. Andrew Bennett, Joseph Lepgold, and Danny Unger (New York: St. Martin's Press, 1997).

[14] "Korea Walking Diplomatic Tightrope over War on Iraq."

[15] "Seoul against US Moves on Iraq," *Korea Times*, September 27, 2002.

[16] Ibid.

[17] "Kim to Hold Summit with Bush," *Korea Times*, September 27, 2002.

[18] "Official Says US Requests Support If Military Action Taken against Iraq," *Yonhap News Agency*, November 21, 2002.

[19] Charles Whelan, "Armitage Heads for Seoul for Talks on Iraq, Anti-Americanism," *Agence France Presse*, December 10, 2002.

[20] Ibid.

[21] Byung-Kook Kim, "North and South Korea: Unlikely Challenger, Unlikely Mediator," in *Power and Security in Northeast Asia: Shifting Strategies*, ed. Byung-Kook Kim and Anthony Jones (Boulder, Colo.: Lynne Rienner Publishers, 2007), 223.

[22] "Seoul to Throw Support for US War on Iraq," *Korea Times*, March 11, 2003.

[23] "Faction Opposes Use of S.K. Troops in Iraq," *Korea Herald*, February 17, 2003.

[24] "Defense Ministry Reaffirms Non-Combat Troop Dispatch," *Korea Times*, February 12, 2003, "Seoul to Throw Support for US War on Iraq."

[25] "Seoul to Throw Support for US War on Iraq."

[26] Ibid.

[27] "Roh, Bush Show Signs of Reconciliation," *Korea Times*, March 15, 2003, Hyun-jin Seo, "Both Roh, Bush Score in Phone Talks," *The Korea Herald*, March 14, 2003.

[28] "Roh, Bush Show Signs of Reconciliation," Seo, "Both Roh, Bush Score in Phone Talks."

[29] Republic of Korea., "The Policy for Peace and Prosperity," ed. Ministry of Unification (2003).

[30] In-duk Kang, "Toward Peace and Prosperity: The New Government's North Korea Policy," *East Asian Review* 15, no. 1 (2003), 4.

[31] Kim, "North and South Korea: Unlikely Challenger, Unlikely Mediator."

[32] United States Department of State, "Section 2207 Report on Iraq Relief and Reconstruction," (Washington DC: Department of State Bureau of Near Eastern Affairs, 2005).

[33] "Korea Commits $200 Million to Iraq," *The Korea Herald*, October 25, 2003.

[34] "Seoul to Offer $10 Mil. for Iraqi Refugees," *Korea Times*, April 4, 2003, "Seoul to Provide $10 Mil. to Iraq for Humanitarian Assistance," *Korea Times*, April 7, 2003.

[35] Paul Knox, "October 23, 2003," *The Globe and Mail*, October 23, 2003, "Korea Commits $200 Million to Iraq."

[36] "US Respects Seoul's Decision on Troop Dispatch to Iraq: Rumsfeld," *Korea Times*, November 18, 2003.

[37] "South Korean Leader Pledges Additional Aid to Iraq in Meeting with Arab Envoys," *Yonhap News Agency*, February 17, 2004.

[38] Ibid.

[39] Troy Stangarone, *Taking a Larger Role in International Affairs: Korea's Growing Efforts in Peacekeeping Missions and Development Aid* (Korea Economic Institute, August 2007 [cited May 19, 2008]); available from http://www.keia.com/Publications/Insight/2007/august%2007.pdf.

[40] The six major donors include: Japan, ROK, UK, Sweden, Canada, and the EU. Iraq Ministry of Planning and Development, *Report on Donors' Contributions to Reconstruction Efforts up to March 2008* (The Iraqi Strategic Review Board (ISRB) International Cooperation Department, 2008 [cited May 20, 2008]); available from http://www.mop-iraq.org/mopdc/resources/pdf/DAD/DAD%20Reporte_april.pdf.

[41] Lord and Lord, "Additional Cases from the Gulf Crisis and Burden Sharing in UNPROFOR," 329-30.

[42] "Defense Ministry Reaffirms Non-Combat Troop Dispatch."

[43] Kyudok Hong, "The Impact of NGOs on South Korea's Decision to Dispatch Troops to Iraq," *Journal of International and Area Studies* 12, no. 2 (2005), 33, Kwang Sub Kwak, "The US-ROK Alliance, 1953 – 2004: Alliance Institutionalization" (Southern Illinois University Carbondale, 2006), 247-48.

[44] United States Central Command, *Coalition Countries: Republic of Korea* (U.S. Central Command, 2008 [cited May 15, 2008]); available from http://www.centcom.mil/en/finance/93.html. President Bush declared the end to combat operations and "mission accomplished" on May 1, 2003.

[45] Eric Schmitt, "Up to 30,000 Troops from a Dozen Nations to Replace Some G.I.'S in Iraq," *The New York Times*, June 19, 2003.

[46] Hong, "The Impact of NGOs on South Korea's Decision to Dispatch Troops to Iraq," 32.

[47] Chae-Jin Lee, *A Troubled Peace: U.S. Policy and the Two Koreas* (Baltimore: Johns Hopkins University Press, 2006), 269.

[48] Hong, "The Impact of NGOs on South Korea's Decision to Dispatch Troops to Iraq," 33.

[49] Lee, *A Troubled Peace: U.S. Policy and the Two Koreas*, 269-70.

[50] Hong, "The Impact of NGOs on South Korea's Decision to Dispatch Troops to Iraq," 31, Lee, *A Troubled Peace: U.S. Policy and the Two Koreas*, "U.S. Requested Dispatch of S.K. Light Infantry to Iraq: Official," *Yonhap News Agency*, September 15, 2003, Yu Wong-won, "Which Unit Will Be Dispatched to Iraq? Possibility of Dispatching Special Commando Brigade," *Choson Ilbo*, September 29, 2003.

[51] Hong, "The Impact of NGOs on South Korea's Decision to Dispatch Troops to Iraq," 31, "Over 5,000 ROK Soldiers Likely to Head to Iraq," *Korea Times*, October 20, 2003.

[52] "ROK Delays Dispatch of Troops Earmarked for Iraq," *China Daily*, March 20, 2004, "U.S. Requests Brigade-Level Combat Troop Deployment to Iraq," *Yonhap News Agency*, September 15, 2003.

[53] Balbina Y. Hwang, *South Korean Troops to Iraq: A Boost for U.S.-ROK Relations* (The Heritage Foundation, 2004 [cited May 19, 2008]); available from http://www.heritage.org/Research/AsiaandthePacific/wm427.cfm.

[54] Ibid, Kwak, "The US-ROK Alliance, 1953 – 2004: Alliance Institutionalization".

[55] Major General Eui-Don Hwang, "Republic of Korea Forces in Iraq: Peacekeeping and Reconstruction," *Military Review* LXXXV, no. 06 (2005), Dae-woong Jin, "Korean Troops Welcomed by Kurds in Iraq," *The Korea Herald*, March 19, 2006.

[56] Hwang, "Republic of Korea Forces in Iraq: Peacekeeping and Reconstruction," Dae-woong Jin, "Korean Troops Mark Two Years in Iraqi Kurdistan Town," *The Korea Herald*, February 23, 2006.

[57] Kwak, "The US-ROK Alliance, 1953 – 2004: Alliance Institutionalization", "New Commander to Take Command of Troops in Iraq," *Yonhap News Agency*, April 15, 2008, "S. Korea to Decrease Activity of Troops in Iraq," *Yonhap News Agency*, December 29, 2007.

[58] Jae-soon Chang, "South Korea Plans to Withdraw One-Third of Troops from Iraq," *Associated Press*, November 17, 2005, Al Kamen, "Coalition Members Look for an Exit," *The Washington Post*, November 17, 2005, A17, "No Friction in Alliance over Iraq Troop Cut," *Korea Times*, November 25, 2005, "South Korean Minister Seeks to Resolve Dispute with US over Iraq Troop Cut," *Yonhap News Agency*, November 24, 2005, "Talk of South Korean Troop Reduction Points to Uncertainty of Iraq Coalition Future," *Associated Press*, November 18, 2005.

[59] "US Learned of South Korean Troop Reduction from Media," *Yonhap News Agency*, November 21, 2005.

[60] Dae-woong Jin, "Korea Notifies U.S. Of Iraq Troop Pullout," *The Korea Herald*, December 6, 2006, "S. Korea's Ruling Party Will Back Troop Extension in Iraq," *Associated Press*, November 24, 2006, "S.Korea to Withdraw Iraq Troops Next Year," *United Press International*, November 30,

2006, "South Korea Appoves Extension of Troops in Iraq," *Yonhap News Agency*, December 22, 2006.

[61] The governor of Arbil hinted that his provincial government would give an oil concession to South Korean firms for the country's successful efforts to help rebuild the region. Sung-ki Jung, "S. Korea Delays Decision on Fate of Troops in Iraq," *Korea Times*, June 28, 2007. See also Dae-woong Jin, "Troop Deployment in Iraq Emerges as Key Campaign Issue," *The Korea Herald*, October 23, 2007, Sung-ki Jung, "Extension of Iraq Troop Deployment Hits Snag," *Korea Times*, May 21, 2007, Sung-ki Jung, "Think Tank Calls for Extending Zaytun Mission in Iraq," *Korea Times*, May 31, 2007.

[62] "South Korea to Extend Troop Stay in Iraq but Cut Presence by Half," *Yonhap News Agency*, October 23, 2007.

[63] Hong, "The Impact of NGOs on South Korea's Decision to Dispatch Troops to Iraq," 39, "South Korea Says Saddam's Arrest Reduces Uneasiness over Sending Troops to Iraq," *Yonhap News Agency*, December 15, 2003.

[64] The so-called "386 generation" is a reference to the 386a computer chip which became prevalent while the generation acted as pro-democracy activists in the 1980s. 386ers are those college educated Koreans in their 30s and early 40s, who went to college and fought in the pro-democracy movements in the 1980s and were born in the 1960s. According to one 386 activist, "My generation, the 386 generation, were in the streets fighting in the 80s against the military dictatorship. Now, 20 years later, we are combat-ready with our internet." Caroline Gluck, *South Korea's Web Guerillas* (BBC News, 2003 [cited May 23, 2008]); available from http://news.bbc.co.uk/2/hi/asia-pacific/2843651.stm.

[65] In May 1980, hundreds of civilians were massacred by soldiers in the south-western city of Kwangju after rising up against military rule. Although it was brutally suppressed, the Kwangju Uprising is now seen by many as a pivotal moment in the South Korean struggle for democracy in the long period of dictatorship following the Korean War. The final toll of those who lost their lives is still unknown, as it is believed the military dumped bodies in mass graves or lakes, however, estimates today range from 500 to 2,000. At the time of the Kwangju uprising, a U.S. general retained ultimate operational control over combined U.S. and South Korean forces, therefore activists hold the U.S. complicit in the massacre. Becky Branford, *Lingering Legacy of Korean Massacre* (BBC News, 2005 [cited May 23, 2008]); available from http://news.bbc.co.uk/2/hi/asia-pacific/4557315.stm.

[66] Victor D. Cha, "South Korea: Anchored or Adrift?" in *Strategic Asia 2003–04*, ed. National Bureau of Asian Research (U.S.) (Seattle, Wash.: National Bureau of Asian Research, 2003), 113-14, Norimitsu Onishi, "U.S. And South Korea Try to Redefine Their Alliance," *The New York Times*, December 26, 2003.

[67] Chung Min Lee, "Reassessing the ROK-US Alliance: Transformation Challenges and the Consequences of South Korea's Choices," *Australian Journal of International Affairs* 57, no. 2 (2003), 284.

[68] Bruce E. Bechtol, Jr., "Civil-Military Relations in the Republic of Korea: Background and Implications," *Korea Observer* 36, no. 4 (2005).

[69] Onishi, "U.S. And South Korea Try to Redefine Their Alliance."

[70] Tae-Hwan Kwak and Seung-Ho Joo, eds., *The United States and the Korean Peninsula in the 21st Century* (Aldershot, England; Burlington, Vt: Ashgate, 2006), 4, Robert Marquand, "Rethinking US Troops in S. Korea," *Christian Science Monitor*, March 10, 2003.

[71] Kim, "North and South Korea: Unlikely Challenger, Unlikely Mediator," 212-15, "Roh to Walk Diplomatic Fine Line over Nk," *Korea Times*, February 26, 2003, "Roh Trying to Mend Fences with US," *Korea Times*, March 13, 2003, Seo, "Both Roh, Bush Score in Phone Talks."

[72] The sunshine policy emphasized peaceful cooperation, seeking short-term reconciliation as a prelude to eventual Korean reunification. Eric V. Larson et al., *Ambivalent Allies? A Study of South Korean Attitudes toward the U.S.* (Santa Monica: RAND Corporation, 2004), 27, Gi-wook Shin and Paul Y Chang, "The Politics of Nationalism in US-Korean Relations," in *The Future of US-Korean Relations: The Imbalance of Power*, ed. John Feffer (New York: Routledge, 2006).

[73] The ROK stripped North Korea of the title "main enemy" in the 2004 Defense White Paper. Seung-Ho Joo, "US-ROK Relations: The Political-Diplomatic Dimension," in *The United States and the Korean Peninsula in the 21st Century*, ed. Tae-Hwan Kwak and Seung-Ho Joo (Aldershot, England; Burlington, VT: Ashgate, 2006), 52, Cheon Seongwhun, "North Korea and the ROK–U.S. Security Alliance," *Armed Forces and Society* 34, no. 1 (2007).

[74] President Kim communicated two mega messages: that his administration's goals would be peaceful co-existence, not unification; and that its policies would seek to reassure the North Korean regime of, not undermine confidence in, South Korea's good intentions. The Sunshine Policy was a new attempt, a departure from the cold war containment policy, to transform an inter-Korean zero-sum game into a nonzero-sum game for a desirable future on the Korean peninsula. Ralph A. Cossa, *U.S.-ROK: Diverging Threat Perceptions of North Korea?* (The Maureen and Mike Mansfield Foundation, 2005 [cited May 28, 2008]); available from http://www.mansfieldfdn.org/programs/program_pdfs/rok_us_cossa.pdf, Ko, "South Korea's Search for an Independent Foreign Policy," Eundak Kwon and Jae-Cheon Lim, "Crossing the River That Divides the Korean Peninsula: An Evaluation of the Sunshine Policy," *International Relations of the Asia-Pacific* 6, no. 2 (2006), Hong Soon-young, "Thawing Korea's Cold War: The Path to Peace on the Korean Peninsula," *Foreign Affairs* 78, no. 3 (1999), 10.

[75] Shin and Chang, "The Politics of Nationalism in US-Korean Relations," 47.

[76] James Brooke, "South Opposes Pressuring North Korea," *The New York Times*, January 1, 2003, Cha, "Korea: A Peninsula in Crisis and Flux," Joo, "US-ROK Relations: The Political-Diplomatic Dimension," 51, Sung-han Kim, "Anti-American Sentiment and the ROK-US Alliance," *The Korean Journal of Defense Analysis* XV, no. 2 (2003).

[77] Ralph A. Cossa, *U.S.-Korea: Summit Aftermath* (Pacific Forum, Center for Strategic and International Studies, March 16 2001 [cited June 26, 2008]); available from http://www.csis.org/media/csis/pubs/pac0111.pdf.

[78] Kwak and Joo, eds., *The United States and the Korean Peninsula in the 21st Century*, 3-4.

[79] Sook-Jong Lee, "Allying with the United States: Changing South Korean Attitudes," *The Korean Journal of Defense Analysis* XVII, no. 1 (2005), 84.

[80] Hyeong Jung Park, *Divergent Threat Perceptions on North Korea* (The Maureen and Mike Mansfield Foundation, 2005 [cited May 28, 2008]); available from http://www.mansfieldfdn.org/programs/program_pdfs/rok_us_park.pdf, Shin and Chang, "The Politics of Nationalism in US-Korean Relations."

[81] During a visit to Pyongyang in April 2002 South Korea's National Security Advisor Lim Dong-won tried to persuade Kim Jong -il to receive a special envoy from the United States. North Korea decided to resume the bilateral dialogue and Assistant Secretary of State Kelly's visit to the DPRK was the first round of the renewed talks. Christoph Bluth, "Between a Rock and an Incomprehensible Place: The United States and the Second North Korean Nuclear Crisis," *The Korean Journal of Defense Analysis* XVII, no. 2 (2005), 89.

[82] Ibid, John S. Park, "Inside Multilateralism: The Six-Party Talks," *The Washington Quarterly* 28, no. 4 (2005).

[83] North Korea demanded bilateral talks with the U.S. in an effort to establish a non-aggression pact between the two countries. The U.S. countered that the Korean War was a multilateral effort that required multilateral talks. In a *60 Minutes* interview, younger Koreans accepted that President Bush is more threatening than Kim Jong-il. See Victor D. Cha and David C. Kang, "The Korea Crisis," *Foreign Policy*, no. 136 (2003).

[84] Cha, "Korea: A Peninsula in Crisis and Flux," 141, Ralph A. Cossa, "US-DPRK Nuclear Stand-Off: Anatomy of a "Crisis"," *The Korean Journal of Defense Analysis* XV, no. 1 (2003).

[85] Kim, "Anti-American Sentiment and the ROK-US Alliance," Seongho Sheen, "Grudging Partner: South Korea," *Asian Affairs, an American Review* 30, no. 2 (2003), 98.

[86] Brooke, "South Opposes Pressuring North Korea."

[87] Lee, "Allying with the United States: Changing South Korean Attitudes," 99.

[88] The Seoul metropolitan area was already within range of thousands of North Korean chemical artillery tubes and therefore did not consider a nuclear capability a significant increase in threat.

[89] Sheen, "Grudging Partner: South Korea," 98.

[90] The National Unification Board has estimated that the cost of Korean reunification could be between $200–500 billion over 10 years. Yeon Bong Jung, "Strategy on Stilts: The U.S. Response to the North Korea Nuclear Issue," *The Korean Journal of Defense Analysis* XVII, no. 2 (2005).

[91] Kwak and Joo, eds., *The United States and the Korean Peninsula in the 21st Century*, 5, Shin and Chang, "The Politics of Nationalism in US-Korean Relations."

[92] Kim, "North and South Korea: Unlikely Challenger, Unlikely Mediator," 215-16.

[93] Katharina Coleman argues that the global norm of multilateralism provides an incentive for states to engage in tokenism, or the dispatch of token forces as part of a multilateral coalition. See Katharina P. Coleman, "The Significance of Token Forces" (paper presented at the International Studies Association Annual Convention, San Francisco, March, 2008).

[94] Glenn H. Snyder, *Alliance Politics*, Cornell Studies in Security Affairs (Ithaca, N.Y.: Cornell University Press, 1997), 181.

[95] Michael Mandelbaum, *The Nuclear Revolution: International Politics before and after Hiroshima* (New York: Cambridge University Press, 1981), 150-51.

[96] Balbina Y. Hwang, "The U.S.–Korea Alliance on the Rocks: Shaken, Not Stirred," *Heritage Lectures*, no. 970 (2006).

[97] Doug Bandow, *Time for a Korean Divorce* (National Review Online, January 6 2003 [cited June 3, 2008]); available from http://www.nationalreview.com/comment/comment-bandow010603.asp, Lee, "Reassessing the ROK-US Alliance: Transformation Challenges and the Consequences of South Korea's Choices."

[98] Ko, "South Korea's Search for an Independent Foreign Policy," 262-63, Larson et al., *Ambivalent Allies? A Study of South Korean Attitudes toward the U.S.*, 37.

[99] Kim, "North and South Korea: Unlikely Challenger, Unlikely Mediator," 213-14, Lee, "Reassessing the ROK-US Alliance: Transformation Challenges and the Consequences of South Korea's Choices," Lee, "Allying with the United States: Changing South Korean Attitudes," Shin and Chang, "The Politics of Nationalism in US-Korean Relations."

[100] Scott Snyder, "South Korea's Squeeze Play," *The Washington Quarterly* 28, no. 4 (2005), 99.

[101] Hoon Jaung, *President Roh Moo-Hyun and the New Politics of South Korea* (The Asia Society, February 2003 [cited May 30, 2008]); available from http://www.asiasociety.org/publications/update_korea2.html#election, Shin and Chang, "The Politics of Nationalism in US-Korean Relations."

[102] Howard W. French, "Reversals in U.S.-South Korea Links, and Some Jagged Fault Lines," *The New York Times*, February 11, 2003.

[103] Ibid., 17, "Roh to Walk Diplomatic Fine Line over Nk."

[104] Sang-hun Choe, "North Korea Launches Anti-Ship Missile," *Associated Press*, February 24, 2003, Howard W. French, "North Taunts Seoul with a Missile Test," *The New York Times*, February 26, 2003, Ihlwan Moon, Mark L. Clifford, and Stan Crock, "The Politics of Peril," *Business Week*, February 24, 2003, "Roh Faces Foreign Policy Challenges," *Korea Times*, March 6, 2003.

[105] Snyder, "South Korea's Squeeze Play."

[106] Kim, "North and South Korea: Unlikely Challenger, Unlikely Mediator," 213-14.

[107] On March 6, Secretary of Defense Rumsfeld noted that the South "has all the capability in the world of providing the kind of upfront deterrent that's needed" and further suggested that the American military could play a more

supportive role on the Korean peninsula by arranging its forces at an "air hub" and "sea hub," and as off-peninsul reinforcements for South Korean front-line troops. James Brooke, "Musing on an Exodus of G.I.'S, South Korea Hails U.S. Presence," *The New York Times*, March 8, 2003. Dong Shin Kim, "The ROK–U.S. Alliance: Where Is It Headed?" *Strategic Forum* (Washington DC: Institute for National Strategic Studies, National Defense University, 2003).

[108] Geoge Wehrfritz and B.J. Lee, "A Life-or-Death Issue," *Newsweek*, March 3, 2003, 38.

[109] Eric Schmitt, "North Korea Migs Intercept U.S. Jet on Spying Mission," *The New York Times*, March 4, 2003.

[110] Matt Kelley, "U.S. Repositioning Bombers near North Korea, May Send Fighter Escorts with Surveillance Planes," *Associated Press*, March 5, 2003.

[111] Don Kirk, "Seoul Makes Case for U.S. Presence; 'Trip Wire Should Remain' against North," *The International Herald Tribune*, March 7, 2003, 1, Richard Lloyd Parry, "I Urge the US: Don't Go Too Far," *The Times*, March 7, 2003, 6.

[112] Brooke, "Musing on an Exodus of G.I.'S, South Korea Hails U.S. Presence."

[113] "Expecting Trouble?" *The Economist*, March 15, 2003.

[114] Richard Spencer, "S Korea Urges US Troops to Stay," *The Daily Telegraph*, March 8, 2003.

[115] Marquand, "Rethinking US Troops in S. Korea."

[116] Yong-chin Oh, "Roh Puts Top Priority on Preventing War," *Korea Times*, March 7, 2003.

[117] Doug Struck, "Powell Makes Few Gains on Asia Tour; Secretary Unable to Win Pledges of Support on North Korea, Iraq," *The Washington Post*, February 25, 2003, A16, "U.S. Asks for Help in Iraq War," *The Korea Herald*, March 11, 2003.

[118] "U.S. Asks for Help in Iraq War."

[119] Kim, "North and South Korea: Unlikely Challenger, Unlikely Mediator," 212-13, "Roh Trying to Mend Fences with US," "South Korean President Chairs National Security Council Meeting," *Yonhap News Agency*, March 20, 2003.

[120] "Korea yet to Decide Level of Support for U.S.-Led War with Iraq," *Yonhap News Agency*, March 13, 2003.

[121] "Korea to Send Engineering Troops to Support U.S. War with Iraq," *Yonhap News Agency*, March 13, 2003, "ROK Foreign Minister on DPRK Nuclear Issue, USFK, ROK Troop Support in Iraq," *KBS Radio 1*, March 12, 2003.

[122] Howard W. French, "A Nation at War: The Asian Arena; South Korea Agrees to Send Troops to Iraq," *The New York Times*, April 3, 2003, "Roh Trying to Mend Fences with US," "South Korean President Chairs National Security Council Meeting," "South Korean President Seeks Bipartisan Support for Troop Deployment to Gulf," *Yonhap News Agency*, March 19, 2003.

[123] "Roh Tries to Soften Opposition to Troop Dispatch," *Korea Times*, March 27, 2003.

[124] French, "A Nation at War: The Asian Arena; South Korea Agrees to Send Troops to Iraq."

[125] Ibid, "South Korea's National Assembly Approves Bill on Troop Dispatch to Iraq," *Yonhap News Agency*, April 2, 2003, "South Korean President's Speech Finds across-the-Board Support at Assembly," *Yonhap News Agency*, April 2, 2003.

[126] "Seoul's Decision to Send Troops Assures US of Alliance," *Korea Times*, March 31, 2003.

[127] Kihl, *Transforming Korean Politics: Democracy, Reform, and Culture*, 328-29, Yong-chin Oh, "Is President Roh Turning Pro-United States?" *Korea Times*, March 31, 2003, "S. Korean Government, Parties Hope Troop Bill to 'Solidify' 'Alliance' with US," *Yonhap News Agency*, April 2, 2003, "Seoul's Decision to Send Troops Assures US of Alliance."

[128] In a March 13, 2003 phone conversation with Roh, Bush quelled South Korean fears of military intervention. Bush is quoted as stating that the United States would seek a peaceful solution to its nuclear standoff with North Korea. Bush also denied speculation that the United States is pursuing its military options in deliberating over the matter. In response, Roh pledged Seoul's active support for the U.S. efforts to resolve the Iraqi issue. "Roh Trying to Mend Fences with US," Seo, "Both Roh, Bush Score in Phone Talks," "USA Reiterates Support for South Korea's 'Sunshine Policy,'" *Yonhap News Agency*, March 14, 2003.

[129] Treverton, Larson, and Kim, "Bridging the 'Open Water' in the US-South Korea Military Alliance," 169.

[130] Cha, "Korea: A Peninsula in Crisis and Flux," "Divisions Deepen as Protests over Iraqi War Intensify," *Korea Times*, March 31, 2003, Ko, "South Korea's Search for an Independent Foreign Policy," "Young Rebel against Roh on Iraq War," *Korea Times*, March 28, 2003.

[131] Kim, "North and South Korea: Unlikely Challenger, Unlikely Mediator," 215-16.

[132] Doug Bandow, "The Future of the U.S.-ROK Alliance: Equality, Mutuality, and International Security," *East Asian Review* 17, no. 2 (2005), 53, Joo, "US-ROK Relations: The Political-Diplomatic Dimension," 48, James I. Matray, "Alliance of Convenience," *Donga Ilbo*, April, 2003, Jonathan D. Pollack, "US Strategies in Northeast Asia: A Revisionist Hegemon," in *Power and Security in Northeast Asia: Shifting Strategies*, ed. Byung-Kook Kim and Anthony Jones (Boulder, Colo.: Lynne Rienner Publishers, 2007), 72-73.

[133] Esther Schrader, "The World; U.S. To Realign Troops in Asia; the Pentagon Is Shifting to Smaller, More Mobile Forces to Confront New Challenges. Among the Changes, It May Seek to Base Ships Off Vietnam," *Los Angeles Times*, May 29, 2003, A1.

[134] "Korea, U.S. To Hold Second Round of Alliance Talks," *Yonhap News Agency*, June 4, 2003, Pollack, "US Strategies in Northeast Asia: A Revisionist Hegemon," 72.

[135] Moon, "US-South Korean Relations," 42.

[136] Pollack, "US Strategies in Northeast Asia: A Revisionist Hegemon."

[137] Cha, "Korea: A Peninsula in Crisis and Flux," 148.

[138] Pollack, "US Strategies in Northeast Asia: A Revisionist Hegemon."

[139] Hong, "The Impact of NGOs on South Korea's Decision to Dispatch Troops to Iraq," "US Asks ROK to Send Light Infantry Division to Iraq," *Korea Times*, September 16, 2003.

[140] Cha, "Korea: A Peninsula in Crisis and Flux," 150.

[141] Tong Kim, "Irony of Roh Moo-Hyun," *The Korea Times*, February 24, 2008.

[142] Sung Deuk Hahm and L. Christopher Plein, *After Development: Transformation of the Korean Presidency and Bureaucracy* (Washington, D.C.: Georgetown University Press, 1997), Jung In Kang, "Reflections on Recent Democratization," in *Korean Politics: Striving for Democracy and Unification*, ed. Jung In Kang, Sallie W. Yea, and Byong-Man Ahn (Elizabeth, NJ: Hollym, 2002), Kihl, *Transforming Korean Politics: Democracy, Reform, and Culture*. Instead of consolidating democracy, the Republic of Korea, may be represented as an "Organizing Democracy" where liberal principles are accepted, but democratic institutions are immature, see Andreas Schedler, "What Is Democratic Consolidation?" *Journal of Democracy* 9, no. 2 (1998).

[143] Hahm and Plein, *After Development: Transformation of the Korean Presidency and Bureaucracy*, 134.

[144] Economist Intelligence Unit, "Country Profile. South Korea," (London: The Economist, 2003), 5, Sohn, "Addressing Limits of Parliamentary Democracy."

[145] Chung Mok Chung, "A New Perspective for Korean Local Government," in *Korean Politics: Striving for Democracy and Unification*, ed. Jung In Kang, Sallie W. Yea, and Byong-Man Ahn (Elizabeth, NJ: Hollym, 2002).

[146] Byong-Man Ahn, *Elites and Political Power in South Korea* (Northampton, Mass.: Edward Elgar Publishing, 2003).

[147] Ibid, Hahm and Plein, *After Development: Transformation of the Korean Presidency and Bureaucracy*, 215, Young-jae Jin, "Lee Brings Back 'Strong Presidentialism': President-Elect Seeks to Curtail the Power of the Prime Minister and the Number of Ministries," *The Korea Herald*, January 21, 2008, David C. Kang, "The Institutional Foundations of Korean Politics," in *Understanding Korean Politics: An Introduction*, ed. Soong Hoom Kil and Chung-in Moon (Albany: State University of New York Press, 2001), Kihl, *Transforming Korean Politics: Democracy, Reform, and Culture*, Soong Hoom Kil and Chung-in Moon, eds., *Understanding Korean Politics: An Introduction, SUNY Series in Korean Studies* (Albany: State University of New York Press, 2001).

[148] Cha, "Korea: A Peninsula in Crisis and Flux," 148-49.

[149] Hong Nack Kim, "The 2000 Parliamentary Election in South Korea," *Asian Survey* 40, no. 6 (2000), 894.

[150] Kihl, *Transforming Korean Politics: Democracy, Reform, and Culture*, 16-17.

[151] Yong-chin Oh, "Roh Assures US That Troops Will Be Sent as Promised," *The Korea Times*, March 31, 2003, Yong-pae Shin, "Roh Makes Final Appeal over Troop Bill," *The Korea Herald*, April 2, 2003, "Two of

Roh's Decisions Expected to Have Major Implications," *Yonhap News Agency*, March 28, 2003.

[152] Oh, "Is President Roh Turning Pro-United States?"

[153] Chong-rok Sin, "Who Moves President Roh? Trio Quickly Rising," *Choson Ilbo*, March 26, 2003.

[154] Oh, "Is President Roh Turning Pro-United States?", "Roh Appears to Be Winning Some U.S. Hearts and Minds," *Yonhap News Agency*, April 1, 2003.

[155] "Roh Trying to Mend Fences with US."

[156] Oh, "Is President Roh Turning Pro-United States?"

[157] "Seoul to Throw Support for US War on Iraq."

[158] Hyung-jin Kim, "Roh to Meet Party Leaders on Iraq," *The Korea Herald*, March 19, 2003, "South Korean President Seeks Bipartisan Support for Troop Deployment to Gulf", "South Korean President, Parties to Discuss Cooperation in Event of Iraq War," *Yonhap News Agency*, March 18, 2003.

[159] "Gov't Fast-Tracks Troop Dispatch," *Korea Times*, March 22, 2003.

[160] Ibid.

[161] "South Korean Assembly Postpones Vote on Dispatch of Troops to Iraq," *Yonhap News Agency*, March 25, 2003.

[162] Hong, "The Impact of NGOs on South Korea's Decision to Dispatch Troops to Iraq."

[163] "Troop Dispatch Cuts President Roh's Support Group in Half," *Korea Times*, March 31, 2003.

[164] "Divisions Deepen as Protests over Iraqi War Intensify."

[165] "South Korean Assembly Postpones Vote on Dispatch of Troops to Iraq."

[166] "Roh Tries to Soften Opposition to Troop Dispatch."

[167] "Parliament Delays Vote on Non-Combat Troop Dispatch to Iraq," *Yonhap News Agency*, March 28, 2003.

[168] "Roh to Appeal to Nation for Troop Dispatch Bill Today," *Korea Times*, April 2, 2003.

[169] Hyung-jin Kim, "Assembly to Vote on Troop Dispatch Bill Amid Protests," *The Korea Herald*, March 28, 2003.

[170] "Parties Blast 'Rejection Campaigns' for Troop Dispatch to Iraq," *Korea Times*, March 31, 2003.

[171] "Roh to Appeal to Nation for Troop Dispatch Bill Today."

[172] "83.8 Percent of Koreans 'Understand' Roh's Troop Dispatch Decision," *Yonhap News Agency*, April 1, 2003.

[173] "South Korea's Nátional Assembly Approves Bill on Troop Dispatch to Iraq."

[174] "South Korean President Appeals for Support on Troops Dispatch to Iraq," *Yonhap News Agency*, April 2, 2003.

[175] "Roh Appeals to Nation to Back Troop Dispatch," *Korea Times*, April 3, 2003.

[176] Lee, *A Troubled Peace: U.S. Policy and the Two Koreas.*

[177] "Roh Vows Closer Ties with US," *Korea Times*, April 3, 2003.

[178] "South Korea's National Assembly Approves Bill on Troop Dispatch to Iraq."

[179] Patrick Goodenough, *Flood of Volunteers after South Korea Okays Troop Dispatch* (CNSNews.com, April 3 2003 [cited June 12, 2008]); available from http://www.cnsnews.com/ViewPrint.asp?Page=\ForeignBureaus\archive\200304\FOR20030403b.html.

[180] Ibid.

[181] Ibid.

[182] Jong-heon Lee, "Summit Feared to Cloud Inter-Korean Ties," *United Press International*, May 15, 2003.

[183] Jang-jin Hwang, "Roh Feels Anguish over 'Culture Clash'," *The Korea Herald*, May 24, 2003.

[184] Lee, "Summit Feared to Cloud Inter-Korean Ties," "Roh's Controversial Performance in Summit Theatrics," *Korea Times*, May 19, 2003.

[185] Jang-jin Hwang, "Roh Shifting N. Korea Strategy: Says Inter-Korean Ties to Be Linked to Progress in Nuke," *The Korea Herald*, May 17, 2003, Hyun-jin Seo, "South Flexes New Negotiation Muscle," *The Korea Herald*, May 24, 2003.

[186] Christopher Torchia, "South Korean President Says He Avoided Sensitive Issues in Bush Meeting with Bush," *The Associated Press*, May 15, 2003.

[187] "Sources Say US Requesting 5,000 South Korean Troops for Iraq Mission," *Yonhap News Agency*, September 27, 2003, "South Korean Security Council to Meet 18 September on Troops for Iraq," *Yonhap News Agency*, September 16, 2003, "US Wants Korea to Command Multinational Division in Iraq," *Korea Times*, September 19, 2003.

[188] "U.S. Wants South Korea to Send Troops to Mosul, Official Says," *Yonhap News Agency*, October 2, 2003.

[189] Hong, "The Impact of NGOs on South Korea's Decision to Dispatch Troops to Iraq," 39.

[190] Lee, *A Troubled Peace: U.S. Policy and the Two Koreas*, 269.

[191] Hong, "The Impact of NGOs on South Korea's Decision to Dispatch Troops to Iraq."

[192] Bechtol, "Civil-Military Relations in the Republic of Korea: Background and Implications," Yong-chin Oh, "Roh-Lee Combination Spells Danger," *Korea Times*, November 18, 2003.

[193] "South Korean Defense Minister Denies Number of Troops to Iraq Decided," *Yonhap News Agency*, October 28, 2003.

[194] Hong, "The Impact of NGOs on South Korea's Decision to Dispatch Troops to Iraq," 39.

[195] Ibid., 36.

[196] Lee, *A Troubled Peace: U.S. Policy and the Two Koreas*, 270.

[197] Ibid.

[198] Hong, "The Impact of NGOs on South Korea's Decision to Dispatch Troops to Iraq," 39.

[199] Ibid.

[200] Ibid., 35, Jong-heon Lee, "S.Korea May Send Fewer Troops to Iraq," *United Press International*, November 4, 2003, "Roh-Lee Combination Spells Danger," *Korea Times*, November 18, 2003. For a discussion on Jong's

influence see Bechtol, "Civil-Military Relations in the Republic of Korea: Background and Implications."

[201] "Roh-Lee Combination Spells Danger."

[202] "Progressives Prevail in Roh's Administration," *Korea Times*, November 15, 2003.

[203] Ibid.

[204] David Scofield, *Clearing the Nuclear Fog over North Korea* (Worldpress.org, January 22 2004 [cited June 27, 2008]); available from http://www.worldpress.org/Asia/1768.cfm, "South Korea to Investigate Diplomats for Questioning Policy," *Yonhap News Agency*, January 12, 2004.

[205] Bechtol, "Civil-Military Relations in the Republic of Korea: Background and Implications," 618.

[206] Hong, "The Impact of NGOs on South Korea's Decision to Dispatch Troops to Iraq," 39, Lee, *A Troubled Peace: U.S. Policy and the Two Koreas*, 269.

[207] "South Korea Plans to Dispatch 3,200 Troops to Iraq," *Choson Ilbo*, December 11, 2003.

[208] The Uri Party was formed in late 2003 from a left-leaning faction of the MDP. It gained a slim majority in the National Assembly after the April 2004 legislative elections, but lost it in subsequent by-elections.

[209] "Uri under Fire for Stalling Iraq Troop Dispatch Bill," *Korea Times*, February 11, 2004.

[210] Lee, *A Troubled Peace: U.S. Policy and the Two Koreas*, "Vote on Troop Dispatch Delayed Again," *Yonhap News Agency*, February 9, 2004, 271.

[211] Sang-mee Bak, "South Korean Self-Identity and Evolving Views of the United States," in *Strategy and Sentiment: South Korean Views of the United States and the U.S.-ROK Alliance*, ed. Derek J. Mitchell (Washington D.C., Seoul: Center for Strategic and International Studies and Yonsei University, 2004), 47, Lee, *A Troubled Peace: U.S. Policy and the Two Koreas*, 270-71.

[212] Ko, "South Korea's Search for an Independent Foreign Policy," 264-65.

[213] Hong, "The Impact of NGOs on South Korea's Decision to Dispatch Troops to Iraq," 42.

[214] *S. Korea Votes to Impeach Roh* (CNN, May 5 2004 [cited June 27, 2008]); available from http://www.cnn.com/2004/WORLD/asiapcf/03/11/skorea.roh.fighting/.

[215] For a review of the impeachment see Youngjae Lee, "Law, Politics, and Impeachment: The Impeachment of Roh Moo-Hyun from a Comparative Constitutional Perspective," *New York University Public Law and Legal Theory Working Papers*, no. 4 (2005).

[216] Anthony Faiola, "Court Rejects S. Korean President's Impeachment," *The Washington Post*, May 14, 2004, A12.

[217] Yongho Kim and Myungchul Kim, "North Korea's Risk-Taking Vis-À-Vis the U.S. Coercion in the Nuclear Quagmire," *The Korean Journal of Defense Analysis* XIX, no. 4 (2007), 62.

[218] Hong, "The Impact of NGOs on South Korea's Decision to Dispatch Troops to Iraq," "Seoul Will Send Iraq Troops," *Korea Times*, May 20, 2004.

[219] Hong, "The Impact of NGOs on South Korea's Decision to Dispatch Troops to Iraq," 43.

[220] Ibid.

[221] South Korea's ruling Uri Party (UP), formed in 2003 by defectors from the Millennium Democratic Party (MDP), captured 152 seats. The Grand National Party (GNP), won a landslide victory in its traditional stronghold in the Kyungsang provinces, including Pusan and Taegu, but lost its majority in parliament. Wonbin Cho, "The General Election in South Korea, April 2004," *Electoral Studies* 24, no. 3 (2005).

[222] The renewal votes for 2005-2007 are as follows: 2005 (110-31-17), 2006 (114-60-16), and 2007 (146-104-6). Bo-mi Lim, "South Korean National Assembly Approves Iraq Troop Reduction Plan," *Associated Press*, December 30, 2005. "South Korea Approves Extension of Troops in Iraq," *Yonhap News Agency*, December 22, 2006. Hyung-jin Kim, "South Korean Parliament Approves Iraq Troop Extension for Another Year," *Associated Press*, December 28, 2007.

[223] Michael N. Barnett and Jack S. Levy, "Domestic Sources of Alliances and Alignments: The Case of Egypt, 1962-73," *International Organization* 45, no. 3 (1991).

[224] "Seoul against US Moves on Iraq."

[225] "South Korean Assembly Postpones Vote on Dispatch of Troops to Iraq."

[226] Lee, *A Troubled Peace: U.S. Policy and the Two Koreas*, 268.

[227] Kihl, *Transforming Korean Politics: Democracy, Reform, and Culture*, 328.

[228] The recent mass protests against imported beef demonstrates that protest has become the primary means for Korean citizens to influence government decisions. For discussion on the influence of political protest on the ROK government see Jaehyun Joo, "Explaining Social Policy Adoption in South Korea: The Cases of the Medical Insurance Law and the Minimum Wage Law," *Journal of Social Policy* 28, no. 3 (1999), Aie-Rie Lee, "Down and Down We Go: Trust and Compliance in South Korea," *Social Science Quarterly* 84, no. 2 (2003).

# 3

# Germany: Non-coalition, but Cooperating

After the devastating 9/11 attacks, German Chancellor Gerhard Schröder was quick to promise *uneingeschränkte Solidarität* (unlimited solidarity) in all necessary measures against global terrorism.[1] Within a year of Schröder's unqualified declaration of support, he was also the first Western leader, however, to issue a categorical "no" to the Bush administration for participation in the Iraq War. The Schröder government not only declined to make a direct German contribution to the war in 2003, but moreover engaged in active counter-coalition-building by lobbying France and Russia to support Germany's resistance to the U.S. "adventure."[2] Germany abandoned its traditional policy of balancing between Washington and Paris, and instead created a counter-coalition with Russia and France against the United States. Germany's refusal to support the U.S. led coalition—even under a UN mandate—seriously undermined the diplomatic position of the Bush administration in building an effective coalition against Iraq. Philip Gordon and Jeremy Shapiro, in *Allies at War*, contend that Schröder's declared refusal to support the use of force against Iraq—even if authorized by the UN Security Council—was, simply put, "irresponsible." They add, "Germany's decision to stand with France in blocking NATO's preparation for the possible defense of Turkey in the context of an Iraq war was also difficult to defend."[3] The Chirac-Schröder strategy stripped the U.S.-led intervention of the legitimacy of a UN Security Council mandate and unintentionally sent false signals to Saddam Hussein on the probability of armed intervention, weakening US crisis management, and actually increasing the danger of war.[4]

Open government opposition to U.S. foreign policy measures is unusual for Germany. It is not abnormal for France to seek to counter the United States in international politicking; however, France typically uses this strategy to extract concessions from the United States before joining in on a common action.[5] Germany, in contrast, has rarely and reluctantly differed openly with the United States on major issues.[6] This pattern was shattered when Chancellor Schröder broke with U.S. policy in August 2002, and later encouraged Europe and the Security Council to break with the U.S. preferred action. Germany, with France, would consequently work together to frustrate U.S. efforts in the Security Council.

Germany's position concerning Iraq is puzzling in two dimensions. First, why did Germany stake out such an extreme foreign policy position when it could have quietly withheld support? Typically, German foreign policy rejects the notion that it would be either advisable or even promising to tackle foreign policy problems unilaterally; in this case, however, Germany's position was firm and uncoordinated.[7] As Germany was scheduled to occupy a temporary seat on the Security Council, why did it make its anti-war stance so public when it could have gained the same result through quiet diplomacy? Secondly, why did Germany cooperate with the United States in so many others aspects of the war effort while at the same time thwarting U.S. efforts diplomatically? In the area of military cooperation, for example, Germany was a much more supportive ally than NATO ally Turkey; Germany put no limitations on the use of U.S. military bases and actually supplied German soldiers to guard U.S. bases so that U.S. military forces could deploy to Iraq. This level of support contrasts directly with the assistance initially provided by Turkey, which provided very limited logistical support. This level of support contrasts greatly with German support to the NATO mission in Afghanistan. As of March 2008, some 3200 German soldiers were serving in Afghanistan, and Germany had suffered 26 fatalities.[8] Thus, why did Germany provide essential support to the U.S. war effort, while at the same time maintaining a hardened diplomatic stance against war preparations?

Two explanations of Germany's Iraq policy have emerged. One group of scholars stresses the role of the September 2002 federal elections, arguing that Schröder and the Social Democratic Party (SPD) exploited widespread German public skepticism for a military intervention in Iraq to turn the tide in their faltering electoral campaign.[9] A second group of scholars argues that ideational factors, particularly Berlin's "culture of restraint" concerning early use of military force, explains Germany's Iraq policy.[10] Unfortunately both of these arguments are underspecified and do not completely explain Germany's early stance against a military intervention in Iraq.[11]

This chapter will demonstrate that both domestic explanations, combined with a continued dependence on the United States within NATO and the greater international community, explains Germany's policy stance towards the Iraq War. Chancellor Schröder's early public opposition against military ventures in September 2001, and categorical "no" for a military intervention in Iraq policy, can be best understood by taking into account Schröder's role in preserving the SPD-Greens coalition government in the face of considerable public opposition to a foreign military intervention in Iraq. Schröder felt obliged to rule out any military participation by Germany (even before the Bush administration had committed itself to military action), as this would have spelled the likely demise of his government.[12] Germany however, complied with numerous Bush administration requests as long as they did not require parliamentary approval. Due to Schröder's weak domestic position vis-à-vis parliament and the public, Germany could only provide support only in those areas in which the executive maintained control. Schröder was motivated to participate in these areas to maintain U.S. support in NATO and other regional and international institutions.

## The Timing, Size, and Mix of Germany's Contributions

Germany was the first Western power to issue a categorical "no" to the Bush administration for participation in the Iraq War. While refusing to participate in any U.S. intervention, the Schröder government aggressively countered the Bush administration in international venues such as the United Nations Security Council and NATO.[13] Germany's refusal to support the U.S. led coalition—even under a UN mandate—seriously undermined the diplomatic position of the Bush administration in building an effective coalition against Iraq, and incited a European policy split that threatened viability of both the United Nations Security Council and NATO. Schröder's anti-war coalition ensured that the U.S. did not gain the legitimacy of a UN Security Council mandate, thereby allowing Saddam Hussein to assume that military action was unlikely.[14]

### *Political Contributions*

Germany's diplomatic response to Bush administration objectives began in the immediate aftermath of the September 11 attacks on New York and Washington. Schröder pledged Germany's "unlimited solidarity" with the United States in the fight against international terrorism. This statement surprised many in Germany, and he soon qualified his remarks by stating that there would be no participation in any foreign "adventures." He stressed that any military action within the NATO framework would require consultations between members. In his remarks to the *Bundestag* requesting a vote of solidarity with the United States, he stated:

> Naturally: Every right corresponds with a duty. But this, of course, also applies the other way around, which means information and consultation. What do we want to achieve as Germans and Europeans: unlimited solidarity with the United States in all necessary measures. Risk, including military, will be shared by Germany but she is not prepared for adventures. These are not asked for by the American administration, because of its considerate position after the attacks, and they will certainly not be asked for in the future.[15]

Schröder was asking the *Bundestag* to support NATO, but assuaged their fears that the support would be unrestricted. According to Schröder, effective alliance management required the consultation of equals.

Germany defended the NATO decision to evoke Article 5 of the NATO treaty legitimizing military action and promised support to the United States under the auspices of NATO, but endorsed a legalistic version of support, which did not necessarily commit military forces.[16] German Defense Minister Rudolf Scharping stated, "It [NATO support] does not mean we are at war." According to Scharping, the NATO treaty requires assistance, but does not specify exactly the type of assistance member states must provide.[17] Reacting to Schröder's request of solidarity and the lack of request for military support, the German parliament passed a resolution with 611 out of a possible 666 votes expressing full solidarity with the United States, only the ex-communist Party of Democratic Socialism (PDS) opposed the measure.[18]

Washington's response to NATO's Article 5 declaration suggested that Germany did not have to fear being drawn into military action. Washington was quick to rebuff a NATO led response, instead opting for a tailored military coalition that proffered a greater degree of U.S. control. The U.S. government did not initially request German military support. The German government, however, continued to prepare for a NATO intervention. With the challenges of commanding a NATO force in Kosovo fresh in American minds, NATO could not be allowed to hinder any U.S. military response in Afghanistan.[19] Deputy Secretary of Defense Paul Wolfowitz announced, "If we need collective action, we will ask for it; we don't anticipate that at the moment."[20] Secretary Rumsfeld further clarified the U.S. position by stating, "The mission determines the coalition. The coalition doesn't determine the mission."[21] German officials were alarmed by this unilateral tone. "It is safe to say that Germans after 9/11 expected that the attacks would lead to greater multilateralism," according to one German diplomat.[22] Nonetheless, to support a possible NATO role in Afghanistan, Schröder insisted on—and won—a *Bundestag* mandate in November 2001 authorizing an out of area deployment of 3,900 *Bundeswehr* troops.[23] This request reflected a decade-long trend for *Bundeswehr* participation in NATO military actions, but was met with staunch domestic opposition who questioned the role of military interventions outside Europe.[24] Schröder's coalition government was nearly toppled by the vote, and eventually required a vote of confidence for passage.[25] Although German domestic support existed for the United States in general, the government was fiercely challenged by the opposition The Left (PDS) party in *Bundestag* debates and even the SPD showed little enthusiasm to have German troops engaged in what was seen as a risky campaign.[26] The vote of no confidence is noteworthy as it marked a turning point in the German use of military force; it was the first time in post WWII history that German combat troops would be authorized to deploy combat forces outside of Europe. The deployment vote illustrated that the governing coalition remained far from united regarding Germany's role in the U.S.-led war on terror.

The Iraq War began to emerge onto the international agenda in early 2002 with President Bush's declaration of an "axis of evil" in his State of the Union address.[27] The German public and elite were critical of the declaration of "rogue states" and were uncomfortable with the idea of aggressively policing of states that harbor terrorism.[28] Bush, however, assured Schröder that there were no plans for attack and the NATO alliance partners would be informed of any military preparations.[29] Although Schröder held reservations that the United States was not adequately consulting with the NATO allies, he remained mildly supportive of U.S. objectives within a multilateral framework, while continuing to warn against ill-conceived military ventures.[30]

The annual Munich Security Conference in February 2002 became the first public forum for the Americans and Europeans to voice their opinions on future military operations regarding the war on terrorism. The American representatives clearly articulated their position: Deputy Secretary of Defense Paul Wolfowitz stated that the United States was still at war after the September 11 attacks and that the new threats meant that Washington had to act preventatively. In the words of Secretary Rumsfeld, the United States was prepared "to take the war to the enemy."[31] Senator John McCain clarified the U.S. position by mentioning that the "day of reckoning" was approaching for Iraq.[32] In contrast to the American position on Iraq, German Defense Minister

Rudolf Scharping noted that it would be naïve to think that European societies would support military action. Europe, and specifically Germany, would support military intervention only if several conditions were met: a clear mandate under international law, a clear role for the United Nations, and a multinational political and military approach.[33] Sharping's comments reflected Germany's reluctance to expand the war on terrorism to Iraq. The SPD/Green coalition government and German public were unconvinced of the connections between al-Qaeda and Iraq and skeptical of U.S. claims of Weapons of Mass Destruction (WMD) in Iraq. Throughout the spring of 2002, Germany supported U.S. policy diplomatically, but stressed the need for a UN mandate to support military operations against Iraq. At the March European Union (EU) summit in Barcelona, Schröder confirmed the German stance when he stated that Germany would only join an anti-Iraq coalition if the United Nations supported an intervention.[34]

A serious rift in German and U.S. policy developed after Bush visited Berlin in May 2002. Bush made his case against Iraq to Schröder, but gave reassurances that he would not act without consultation with the allies. It was reportedly agreed that Bush would not start preparations for war before the German elections, and Schröder would not campaign on the antiwar issue during his election campaign.[35] Both promises were soon broken. As news of an impending Iraq War began to surface in the early summer, the German government remained cautious towards U.S. policy as long as the U.S. made no concrete requests for German support. As long as there were no specific requests from Washington, a Berlin spokesperson stated, there was no need for the government to make a decision.[36] After President Bush's West Point address that made the case for preventive military action against emerging WMD threats, however, German public opinion polls showed that an overwhelming majority of Germans opposed a military intervention in Iraq.[37] An October 2002 Pew Research Center poll reported that while 75 percent of German respondents supported the removal of Saddam Hussein, only 26 percent supported the use of force.[38] Weakened by a poor economic record and facing a strong challenge in the upcoming federal elections, Schröder felt he could no longer take a cautious approach towards Iraq and embraced negative public attitudes towards the impending conflict as a defining election issue.

Immediately after the start of the German election campaign in August 2002, Schröder hardened his rhetoric against a military intervention in Iraq and explicitly stated that Germany was not going to support the U.S. policy. In an election rally in Hanover on August 5,

Schröder stated, "We must get the international inspectors into Iraq. But playing games [*Spielerei*] with war and military intervention—against that I can only warn. This will happen without us...We are not available for adventures [*Abenteuer*], and the time of checkbook diplomacy is finally at an end."[39] In an interview in the news weekly *Die Zeit*, Schröder openly criticized the Bush administration for not consulting with Germany and declared the need for a "German Way" in foreign policy. He began to use charged phrases like "reckless adventure" and emphasized that there would be no German military contribution to a war in Iraq, even though the Bush administration had not specifically asked for one. Foreign Minister Fischer was also critical of any war in Iraq, but was careful to formulate his positions diplomatically. Fischer's more nuanced position concerning Iraq, based on a UN mandate, is significant given his pacifist background as an activist in The Greens party and 1960s peace movements. Fischer believed that German support should be conditional on an international mandate. The German opposition was also critical of Schröder's stance, arguing instead for the coalition government to work out a common European position in the Iraq debate.[40] According to the opposition, Germany and Europe would be better served by a unified European position on Iraq. They were concerned that a foreign policy classified as "The German Way" would cause considerable upset in European foreign policy circles.

Instead, Schröder publicly continued to criticize U.S. policy for domestic gains. His staunch opposition to the war marked him from his challenger, CSU candidate Edmund Stoiber. *Der Spiegel* magazine later observed that the campaign marked the end of "unlimited solidarity" when Schröder became the Chancellor of Peace.[41] Schröder's position hardened in late August in reaction to Vice President Cheney's speech to the Veterans of Foreign Wars claiming the need to overthrow Saddam Hussein by military means, if necessary. Cheney stated, "old doctrines of security do not apply;" quoting Henry Kissinger he continued, "The imminence of proliferation of weapons of mass destruction, the huge dangers it involves, the rejection of a viable inspection system, and the demonstrated hostility of Saddam Hussein combine to produce an imperative for preemptive action." [42] Cheney's speech presented Schröder an ideal opportunity to escalate his opposition to U.S. policy on Iraq, and the Iraq issue became the dominant theme in the elections.[43] In an interview in the *New York Times*, Schröder stated that the arguments against a war with Iraq are so strong that he would oppose one *even if the Security Council approved* [emphasis added].[44] During the course of the national election campaign, the German position on a possible Iraq war changed from support with a UN mandate to unequivocal opposition to any military intervention even under a UN mandate. Schröder's anti-war stance isolated Germany within Europe and established a policy position from which Schröder could not retreat after the elections.[45] The anti-war rhetoric resonated well in the east where suspicion of NATO was strong, and along with a the government's competent response to a massive flood just a few days before the election, turned a 10 percentage point deficit into a SPD-Greens victory by the slimmest margin in the Federal Republic's history.[46] The governing coalition gained a narrow four-seat majority in the *Bundestag*, yet the unintended consequences of Schröder's rhetoric quickly became apparent: a weak coalition government, European isolation from U.S. foreign policy prerogatives, and a soured German-American relationship.

The resolute policy position taken by Schröder in the campaign left little room for any adaptation or modification. The day after the election, Schröder met with the left wing of his parliamentary party and told its foreign policy spokesperson, Gernot Erler, that his decision on Iraq was fundamental and unshakable. To change his approach would cost him credibility with his party and the voters, and he had no mandate to do so.[47] Schröder welcomed the late September decision by the United States to seek a UN Security Council resolution but continued to counter any U.S. policy advocating the use of force. Foreign Minister Joschka Fischer stressed that any UN resolution should not contain mechanisms to justify immediate military action in the case of Iraqi non-compliance. Fischer also re-stated Germany's earlier position that it would not participate in military intervention, even if the United Nations provided a clear mandate for that participation.[48] This position lost Germany any real leverage to influence the Bush administration into taking a more restrained approach towards Iraq. Furthermore, the stance continued to isolate Berlin among its European partners who continued to suggest a military intervention would require at least an additional UN resolution. Schröder's unilateral stance was critiqued within policy circles, "It does not say much for the prospects of a shared security and defense policy when Schröder comes out with a stance like this without any liaison," said Frank Umbach, a senior research analyst at the independent German Council on Foreign Relations.[49] Schröder was alone among NATO leaders in ruling out military action regardless if it was supported by a United Nations resolution.

At the same time that Germany refused to support military intervention, it attempted to repair diplomatic relations with the United States in a strategy of damage limitation. Schröder supported efforts in the larger war on terrorism, while also providing Iraq support that did not require a vote in the *Bundestag*. Schröder offered support to the United Nations for arms inspections in Iraq.[50] At the end of September, Foreign Minister Fischer declared that Germany could participate in a post-war UN-mandated force although it still opposed military intervention in the first instance.[51] The *Bundestag* consequently extended the mandate for the German contingent for *Operation Enduring Freedom*.[52] At the advice of U.S. Secretary of State Colin Powell, Germany expanded its military role in Afghanistan to include almost 2,000 troops and volunteered to command NATO's International Security Assistance Force (ISAF) once the force came under NATO's authority.[53] Most significantly, the federal government—in spite of concerns of several members of the governing coalition who deemed this commitment would violate international and German constitutional law—promised transit rights for German territory and air space as well as rights to the use of U.S. installations in the case of military intervention.[54] Chancellor Schröder also agreed to provide security for U.S. bases in Germany in case of war thereby making U.S. troops from the 4th Infantry Division available for deployment to Iraq.[55] Lastly, Berlin offered two Patriot missile batteries to Israel.[56] By the end of 2002, Germany was robustly supporting the war on terrorism with approximately 8,500 German troops deployed in various parts of the world, second only to United States in the effort. Politically, however, its opposition to military intervention in Iraq offset this support.

Germany was thus caught between its interest in improving relations with the United States and Schröder's uncompromising position on a war in Iraq. Foreign Minister Fischer continued to keep open the possibility that Germany might eventually lend political support to the war, and he stated: "That's something no one can predict as no one knows...which accompanying conditions the Security Council will attach. It remains certain that we will not participate militarily in an intervention."[57] Fischer's comments prompted a strong reaction in Germany. Some in the SPD and the Green parliamentary groups were worried that the government was backing away from its strong opposition to the war.[58] Using the analogy of a two-level game, Schröder had given too much for a win-set at the domestic level to have a win-set available with the United States at the international level.[59] Germany had to continue its staunch opposition to the war to maintain Schröder's credibility domestically and had to search for support in the international community to mitigate its isolation from the United States.

The natural partner to combat their perceived isolation from the United States was Germany's neighbor to the west: France, their European Union ally and traditional antagonist to the United States. By

January 2003, Germany was politically isolated by the Bush administration and unsure whether France would side with the Americans, British, Spanish, and Italians on Iraq. This position left Germany dangerously marginalized within the Western alliance. The true impact of the German anti-war position was felt by French President Jacques Chirac, pushing him towards adopting a policy of confrontation with the United States.[60] Schröder reached out to French President Chirac in a telephone conversation and agreed that they would closely coordinate their policies in the Security Council when Germany gained its rotating seat.[61] German foreign policy expert Gregor Schöllgen described Germany's role as having "had unintentionally taken on a leadership role as a counterbalance to the United States."[62] As a result, Schröder continued to court President Chirac of France to counter any U.S. military intervention. The U.S. counter-alliance solidified in a January 20 ministerial meeting in the United Nations when Foreign Minister Fischer joined French Foreign Minister Dominique de Villepin in accusing the United States of "impatience" in the confrontation with Baghdad.[63] Fischer supported the French in hinting that it would support a French veto if the United States tried to raise the issue of Iraq, particularly in anticipation of the January 27 ministerial meeting in which Hans Blix was slated to announce progress on weapons inspections. The Franco-German bloc was firmly cemented two days later when Schröder and Chirac issued a joint statement in Versailles declaring that military intervention in Iraq would be a last resort and would require a UN Security Council decision. According to a German official, "Chirac gave Schröder a great gift that day. Schröder went from being isolated to being part of a French-German-Russian bloc whose position was supported by a potential majority on the Security Council. He was no longer alone."[64]

Germany, together with France and Russia, sought an open-ended extension of the UN weapons inspections authorized under Resolution 1441. To regain momentum for the U.S.-U.K. position in the Security Council, Secretary of State Powell provided gripping testimony offering detailed evidence that argued Iraq was hiding WMD and maintaining links to al Qaeda.[65] The German-Franco-Russian axis was unmoved: the speech had little impact on their position that the inspectors should be given more time to do their work.[66] After the second report by UN inspectors Hans Blix and Director General of the IAEA Mohamed El Baradei on February 14, which showed improvement in the inspection process but a considerable lack of full co-operation on the part of Iraq, Foreign Minister Fischer declared that the inspection regime had to be improved. He advocated a strengthened verification and control mechanism so that a re-start of Iraqi weapons programs could be precluded.[67] This strategy was also pursued in the European Union, where Germany advocated a declaration that agreed that "war is not inevitable" and that "force should be used only as a last resort."[68] Berlin, however, resisted fixing a specific date for the Hussein regime to comply with Security Council demands. Instead, the German government—in a joint memorandum with France and Russia—proposed a strengthening of the inspections regime in the Security Council.[69] These measures would have taken months, if not years, to implement.[70] The anti-war bloc, now under the leadership of the French, continued to resist U.S. efforts in the Security Council. In late February, French ambassador to Washington, Jean David Levitte, urged Deputy National Security Advisor Steven Hadley not to pursue an additional Security Council resolution on Iraq. He delivered a message from Chirac, "Let's agree to disagree on Iraq, but a second resolution by the Security Council was unnecessary and would risk damaging relations further." Hadley replied that the United States did not think it needed a second UN resolution authorizing force, but that British Prime Minister Tony Blair required one for domestic political reasons. The Bush administration reasoned it had nothing to lose in attempting a second resolution. If the United States did not seek a second resolution and lost Blair, it still would not be able to win over France.[71] The United States, Great Britain, and Spain thus submitted a proposed resolution to the UN Security Council on February 24 calling for the authorization to use military force. Consequently, on March 5, France, Germany, and Russia issued a joint statement that unambiguously declared that the three states would block any attempt in the UN Security Council to use force against Iraq.[72] The draft resolution was withdrawn on March 10 when Chirac stated "whatever the circumstances, France will vote no."[73]

To counter the German-French-Russian impasse in the Security Council, British Prime Minister Tony Blair proposed changes to the proposed 18th UN resolution on March 12, which would call for Iraq to meet certain benchmarks to prove that it was disarming.[74] France, which promised to veto any new resolution and could not back down from that unequivocal guarantee, immediately rejected the Blair amendment. With the outbreak of war imminent, Schröder and Fischer underlined their commitment to solving the Iraq crisis through diplomacy. In his State of the Nation speech to the Bundestag of March 14, Schröder argued, "We must have the courage to fight for peace as long as there is a scrap of hope that war can be avoided."[75] On March 16 in a prewar council held between the United States, the United

Kingdom, and Spain, a decision was made to withdraw the additional UN resolution and present Hussein with an ultimatum to leave Iraq.[76] At the UN Security Council meeting on March 19, Fischer condemned the use of military action by stating "the Security Council had not failed" and that "Germany emphatically rejects the impending war...the policy of military intervention has no credibility."[77]

Germany was also a crucial U.S. counterweight in NATO. Belgium, supported by Germany and France, led the opposition in NATO for providing Turkey with Airborne Warning and Control System (AWACS) aircraft and Patriot anti-missile batteries. The three opposing NATO members argued that voting to deploy military aid to Turkey would amount to implicit support for military operations that were underway, and they again argued against a "rush to war."[78] The debate in NATO lasted several weeks, and a solution to deploy NATO forces was found by moving the deliberations to the Defense Planning Committee (where France was not represented).[79] At the same time, German Foreign Minister Joschka Fischer further defended the German stance against the war at the annual Munich Security Conference. U.S. Secretary of Defense Rumsfeld argued that, "Diplomacy has been exhausted," while Fischer continued to urge for caution with respect to Iraq by stating, "Why now? I am not convinced."[80] Fischer criticized the United States for its militaristic strategy to combat international terrorism since September 11, arguing instead that the more important task was to promote a Middle East peace process between the Israelis and Palestinians.

Germany's diplomatic strategy in the buildup to the Iraq War was to minimize the international consequences of an anti-war policy. According to Karsten Voigt, the coordinator for German-American cooperation and a former Member of Parliament, "The Americans were telling us that the French would leave us by ourselves, so we moved closer to France to avoid that isolation."[81] By aligning Germany with France and promoting views that enjoyed broad support within the public, Schröder broke with the basic tenets of his country's foreign policy: promoting strong rapport with the United States. As a result of Schröder's anti-war stance, the relationship with the United States was severely damaged and, on the continent, smaller EU members felt rejected by the exclusivity of the French–German relationship.[82] Central and East European political leaders argued that there was a dual standard in the EU when Chirac commented that the East and Central Europeans had missed a "great opportunity to shut up," when they wrote an open letter in support of the United States on Iraq. Their frustration was best illustrated by Hungarian writer Péter Esterházy, who stated that whereas he had once been an East European, he then became Central European, and then for a few months a new European but, even before he could get accustomed to it or reject it, he was now relegated to being a non-core European.[83] Schröder repeatedly emphasized in practically every speech he held on major foreign policy issues that alignment with France served Germany's national interests better than any other strategy.

Overall, German diplomatic opposition to U.S. planning for a military intervention in Iraq began immediately after the attacks of September 11 and remained fairly consistent. Germany's unqualified refusal for military action created a dilemma for the Schröder government when the Bush administration decided to pursue Security Council approval in September 2002. By pursuing military action under the auspices of the United Nations, the Bush administration exposed the central weakness in Schröder's premature position that German armed forces would not participate in military action in Iraq. If the UN Security Council were to decide that force would be necessary to implement its former resolutions, the Schröder government would have to change its stance domestically towards German military participation. Therefore, Germany exerted significant diplomatic effort to create a counter coalition in the Security Council and NATO, strengthening Schröder's position domestically. Germany encouraged a shift in French policy to form a common position with Russia to prevent a UN resolution authorizing force. Schröder's stance vis-à-vis a UN resolution authorizing force significantly contributed to the European Union's inability to present a unified strategy on Iraq, stripped the U.S.-led intervention of the legitimacy of a UN Security Council mandate, and unintentionally sent false signals to Saddam Hussein that an armed intervention was unlikely.[84]

After the conclusion of conventional combat operations in May 2003, Chancellor Schröder softened on a German role in Iraq by suggesting to the United States that Germany would be willing to participate economically in the reconstruction of Iraq only if there were a clear UN mandate and a strong role for the United Nations in stabilization and reconstruction operations. After the conclusion of U.S. and allied combat operations in Iraq, the Schröder government toned down its anti-war rhetoric and shifted its diplomatic goals towards stabilizing the war and sanctions-torn country as well as mending fences within the European Union and NATO. Schröder signaled that his government favored lifting sanctions against Iraq during Secretary of State Powell's visit to Berlin in mid-May 2003.[85] Germany, while willing to offer limited assistance to the U.S. reconstruction effort, urged a symbolic end to Iraq's status as an occupied country. In contrast to the sharp public criticism leveled by President Chirac, Chancellor Schroeder stressed the need to move forward.[86] Additionally, Schröder indicated a willingness to expand the German patrolled security zone in Afghanistan beyond Kabul, as long as it did not change the approved mandate in the *Bundestag*.[87]

Despite strong U.S. pressure for more substantial military contributions to the Iraqi stabilization and rehabilitation effort, through 2003 Berlin continued to resist further calls for German deployment, and instead offered to help train Iraqi police and security forces in Germany.[88] Chancellor Schröder and Foreign Minister Fischer made it clear that Germany would not contribute troops to the stabilization and reconstruction process in Iraq. This resistance, however, did not block a small role for NATO in the stabilization process. In May 2003—with German approval—NATO backed logistical support for the Polish sector in Iraq, extending the decision again in December 2003. Berlin also assured Washington that it would not block a consensus on NATO's involvement in Iraq.[89] The German government argued that the UN Security Council would have to provide an appropriate mandate and that the United Nations would have to take over much of the civilian administration in the transition period towards Iraqi self-rule before it could consider supplying forces to a stabilization force. The German government suggested that the Bush administration should consider a multilateral framework for outlining goals for an interim government, similar to the "Petersburg Process" implemented for Afghanistan.[90]

Germany continued to exert pressure on the United States for a wider multinational role in the reconstruction of Iraq. In early September, both Chancellor Schröder and President Chirac announced that their countries would not support the initial American proposal that the Security Council authorize an expanded international force under American control and financial help for Iraq. France and Germany provided a prod to the United States to give the United Nations greater authority in post-war Iraq.[91] In mid-October, Germany—after urging from Russian President Putin—agreed to UN Security Council Resolution 1511, which provided a framework for UN and international participation in the political and economic rebuilding of Iraq and the maintenance of security. The resolution authorized a multinational security force and urged states to contribute to Iraq security and reconstruction.[92] Despite U.S. pressure in the wake of Resolution 1511, Berlin remained silent on the issue of troop deployments to Iraq, while supporting the substance of the resolution.

Although Germany attempted to come together with the United States in the aftermath of conventional combat operations, U.S. policy clearly showed a preference for coalition partners. In December 2003, the Department of Defense implemented a policy barring the states that did not support the Iraq coalition. France, Germany, Russia and other coalition non-participants were blocked from $18.6 billion in U.S.-financed Iraqi reconstruction projects. Chancellor Schröder intervened personally with President Bush, who subsequently sent former Secretary of State James Baker as a special envoy to encourage German creditors to forgive Iraq debt and to promise future reconstruction contracts, even though German had been deliberately excluded from the initial $18.6 billion disbursement.[93] The Bush administration policy sought to reward those states that contributed militarily to the American effort in Iraq with lucrative contracts and funds approved for reconstruction.

Finally, in January 2004, after NATO Secretary General Jaap de Scheffer again proposed a NATO force for the reconstruction of Iraq, Chancellor Schröder floated the idea of German military support for Iraq medical evacuation missions. Schröder continued his stance that Germany would not block NATO operations in a military mission for Iraq. To placate his domestic audience, Schröder argued that such an engagement would not constitute a "military deployment" of German forces that would require *Bundestag* approval, but rather a "humanitarian action."[94] However, since *Bundestag* approval had been the crucial obstruction for the SPD-Green government ever since the September 11 attacks, the Schröder initiative met strong domestic resistance within the coalition's own party caucus.[95] Germany rescinded any offer to place troops in Iraq proper.

In February 2004, Germany began to mend fences when German Foreign Minister Fischer called for a new transatlantic Middle East initiative structured around NATO at the annual Munich Security Conference, thereby embracing the U.S. position that the status quo in the region entailed a security risk for both Europe and America.[96] Furthermore, in the wake of the March 11, 2004 Madrid train bombings, Germany privately asked Spain's new leadership to tone down its anti-U.S. rhetoric. According to a senior German official, "If we give the impression that you can plant a big bomb in Europe, cause a government to fall, and force a withdrawal of troops, then this would send the wrong signal to terrorists." Stressing a unified role in combating terrorism, the official stated, "That's not in Germany's interests, or in Europe's or in Spain's."[97]

In June 2004, NATO decided to support the training of Iraqi security forces and to build up a modest military presence in Baghdad to support the training mission. The German government continued to refuse to send troops into Iraq, focusing instead on a training mission in the United Arab Emirates.[98] Another sign of rapprochement in the German-United States relationship came in November 2004, when Germany—along with the Paris Club, 19 of the world's richest countries—wrote off 80 per cent of Iraqi debt, a move long sought by the Bush administration.[99]

Germany's foreign policy during the reconstruction phase involved approachment with the United States combined with maintaining a firm stance against military involvement in Iraq's reconstruction. Germany advocated a greater role for the UN in post war Iraq, and pressured the United States in the Security Council to accept UN sponsorship of the pursuant occupation. The Schröder government actively courted U.S. policy makers and supported U.S. efforts in the greater war on terror. By the late spring of 2003, reconciliation was under way and Germany generally supported U.S. positions concerning Iraq.

### *Military Contributions*

Despite the diplomatic maneuvering and the denial of UN sanction to the war, the Schröder government provided robust support to military efforts that did not require parliamentary approval.[100] Military planners in the Pentagon noted, "Germany is an odd category. It was quietly contributing to the U.S. effort, but opposed to the war."[101] In fact, Germany provided two types of support to enhance U.S. operations in Iraq. First, Germany shouldered a larger military burden than other NATO partners in other areas of operation. Germany provided military forces in Germany, the Horn of Africa, and Afghanistan, freeing U.S. forces for participation in Iraq. Second, it provided direct covert intelligence support for U.S. coalition operations within Iraq. Schröder did everything he could –that did not require the Bundestag-and kept it quiet to not arouse the alarm of the German domestic audience.

The German government significantly cooperated with U.S. military preparations inside Germany. More than 2,500 *Bundeswehr* soldiers were tasked to protect U.S. installations in Germany, which freed up additional U.S. Army V Corps personnel to deploy for the war.[102] Additionally, Germany provided 800 Nuclear, Biological, and Chemical (NBC) defense troops and 20-25 Fuchs chemical detection vehicles as a detachment in Kuwait that was designed to detect and clean up a potential chemical or biological weapons attack.[103] Moreover, after initially resisting the NATO approved deployment, Germany supplied the Turkish military with Patriot missiles to defend against a possible Iraqi missile attack. In the Red Sea and the Gulf of Aden, German ships guarded the sea-lanes as part of *Operation Enduring Freedom*. The operation was intended to deter movement of al Qaeda, but the Germans, in effect, were safeguarding the waterways that the United States used to build up its military forces in the Persian Gulf. According to German Rear Admiral Rolf Schmitz, "We are stabilizing the area, and that probably is an advantage for your [American] forces as well."[104] Germany expanded its military role in Afghanistan including the command of the International Security Assistance Force (ISAF) once the force came under NATO's authority. It also contributed to a new NATO Reaction Force, which was established after the Prague NATO summit in the fall 2002 to undertake counterterrorism operations.[105] With their presence in the Balkans, and within the framework of the *Operation Enduring Freedom*, a total of 10,000 German soldiers were deployed worldwide at the beginning of the Iraq war.[106] Germany's political and diplomatic opposition to the war thus did not impede its military cooperation in efforts outside Iraq.

Germany also provided direct—and controversial—support to the Iraq military effort in two significant ways. First, agents of the German intelligence service (BND) reportedly provided American war planners with Iraqi plans for the defense of Baghdad. In February 2003—one month before military operations commenced—a German liaison officer to U.S. Central Command in Qatar slipped to U.S. officials an illustration of Hussein's concentric defensive lines around the capital.[107] The illustration was identified as the Baghdad defense plan presented at a December 18, 2002 meeting of Saddam and his top commanders. The plan gave the American military an extraordinary window into Iraq's top-level deliberations, including where and how Saddam Hussein planned to deploy his most loyal troops. The *New York Times* article discussing this crucial acquisition was based largely on a classified study of Iraqi military strategy prepared in 2005 by the Pentagon's Joint Forces Command and a classified German Parliamentary report on BND support the Iraq effort.[108] In addition, the *Los Angeles Times*, as well as a German TV show and the *Süddeutsche Zeitung*, reported that German intelligence operatives provided targets for the advancing U.S. troops. In particular, two German military intelligence operatives, who stayed in a Baghdad safe house after Berlin had closed its embassy, passed the intelligence tip that Saddam Hussein and his two sons had been spotted near a chicken restaurant in Baghdad's wealthy Mansour district. Less than 45 minutes later, a B-1 bomber obliterated the site with four satellite-guided bombs, leaving a deep crater and at least a dozen dead.[109] German government spokesperson, Ulrich Wilhelm, admitted the existence of the two agents and the intelligence sharing with the U.S. officials, but claimed that the relevant data did not contain military targets, but rather dealt exclusively with the identification of institutions such as mosques, hospitals, and embassies that were to be protected.[110] The reports of intelligence sharing and the significant military cooperation inside Germany is evidence that, despite their sharp political differences over the Iraq war, Germany and the United States continued practical cooperation at a high and continuous level.

### *Financial Contributions*

Germany's financial contributions to the Iraq War and post-war reconstruction stand in stark contrast to its support to the 1991 Persian Gulf War. In the 1991 effort, Germany, even under the financial strain of reunification with the German Democratic Republic, provided approximately $11.5 billion to the Gulf coalition. Germany provided direct funding to the coalition partners to support military, technical, and logistical support. Additionally, Germany contributed to international aid through the United Nations, Red Cross, and European Community. Due to constitutional limitations on the deployment of its military forces, Germany's robust financial support for the Persian Gulf War was dubbed "checkbook diplomacy," but it reflected the strong conviction that Germany share the burden with allies that had supported Germany since World War II.[111] As Ronald Asmus, an expert on German foreign policy observed, "What was perhaps most striking in the German debate was the almost total lack of any discussion about German strategic interests in the Gulf and how they should guide policy. Instead, the terms were set by such issues as whether Germans 'owed' the United States political support in the Gulf in return for American support during the unification process."[112] Germany's financial support for the 1991 Persian Gulf War reflected its dependence on the United States for influence in Europe and NATO.

Conversely, Germany's financial support for the Iraq War reflected the anti-war stance in Germany and a renewed focus on Euro-centric interests. German contributions to Iraqi reconstruction were modest considering its support of the earlier Gulf War. Germany agreed to $2 billion in debt relief and eventually pledged $155 million to training and reconstruction accounts. This amount pales in comparison to the $11.5 billion in direct compensation for the Persian Gulf War.[113] Although Chancellor Schröder pledged financial support to the Iraq reconstruction during President Bush's late September 2003 visit, Russia, France and Germany refused to commit money at the October 25 Madrid Donors Conference.[114] Germany's tepid support reflected two major concerns with Security Council Resolution 1511, passed shortly before the donor's conference: it did not stipulate a central role for the United Nations in Iraq and it did not present a precise and binding timetable for the transfer of sovereignty to Iraqis.[115] To avoid further damage to the Security Council, Germany presented its concerns through the donor's conference rather than in a Security Council vote against the resolution.[116]

Germany's lack of investment in Iraq reconstruction was exacerbated by a directive issued by Deputy Secretary of Defense Wolfowitz that announced a list of 63 countries eligible to bid for the 26 primary Iraq reconstruction contracts worth $18.6 billion. Countries eligible to bid were identified as either coalition partners or force-contributing nations.[117] Chancellor Schröder reacted immediately with a phone call to President Bush, and Bush dispatched his personal representative, former Secretary of State, James Baker to visit Berlin to discuss Iraq reconstruction and debt restructuring.[118] At Baker's urging, Germany granted Iraq a debt relief of 80 percent of the $2.5 billion Iraq owed Germany, and engaged in various reconstruction activities.[119] Germany's total contribution towards reconstruction and training totaled $155 million.[120] This contribution to reconstruction, however, pales in comparison to Japan, for example, which pledged $3.3 billion in debt relief, $1.5 billion in grants, and $3.5 billion in loans for reconstruction.[121]

Germany's financial support to the Iraq War explicitly reflects its desire to distance itself from the conflict and U.S.-led coalition. Germany did not support reconstruction efforts with the largesse that Japan or Saudi Arabia did; rather, Germany chose to contribute through institutions such as the European Union and World Bank.

## Explaining German Contributions

Germany's behavior is somewhat puzzling since it provided much of the military support the United States required to move efficiently its forces from Europe but, at the same time, its diplomatic approach ensured that Germany would be excluded from any rewards from the United States for its permissive use of airspace and facilities located in Germany. Chancellor Schröder's early public opposition against military "adventures" in Iraq, can be best understood by understanding the domestic concerns of preserving his ruling SPD-Green coalition government in the face of the considerable opposition that had developed throughout the 1990s concerning the use of military force, particularly for non-humanitarian interventions. Chancellor Schröder felt compelled to rule out any military adventures long before the Bush administration committed itself to military action or had made a request for support, because a vote on the use of force in the *Bundestag* could well have signaled the end of his government. The domestic political structure, historical learning, and alliance dependence blocks of the burden sharing decision model best explain Germany's Janus-like stance.

### Historical Learning: From "Checkbook Diplomacy" to "Tactical Abstention"

Iraq's invasion of Kuwait in August 1990 became the first significant security challenge for Germany in the post-Cold War era. All German leaders believed the invasion itself was a blatant violation of international law, but the crisis posed a complex challenge for the newly unified Federal Republic. In response to the Iraqi aggression, President George H.W. Bush personally requested that the German government consider the deployment of troops to the Gulf; deployment, however, was stymied by political disagreements about the proper response to the Gulf crisis.[122] The notion that the *Bundeswehr* could be used for purposes other than the defense of Germany was inconceivable across the political spectrum. Most German political leaders agreed that Articles 24 and 87 of the German Basic Law essentially barred the government from sending troops to the Persian Gulf.[123] In the end, Germany's participation in the 1991 Persian Gulf War amounted to "checkbook diplomacy," which provoked embarrassing international criticism that Germany was shirking in its role as a European leader by not supplying military forces. This incident convinced leading conservative politicians that Germany's international influence and standing as a partner was indeed at stake.[124] Criticism of Germany for not supplying military forces for the Persian Gulf War led German leaders to pursue a strategy of progressively stretching the boundaries of the use of armed force through the use of increasingly taxing deployments.

In Germany, discussion of the proper role for German foreign policy focused on the tension between notions of "normalization" and "civilian power." "Normalization" meant that Germany would free itself from its post-Cold War restriction on the use of force while pursuing international interests like the other large Western powers. It would act more often out of self-interest, but it would not return to its historical *Sonderweg* (special path) and once again become an international "trouble-maker."[125] Hans Maull, noted expert in German foreign policy, in contrast, explained German foreign policy with the concept of "civilian power;" civilian power referred to Germany's nature as a strong international power that was willing to respect international law and understood the necessity of cooperation. The consequence of this "civilian" attitude was a consistent preference to employ political, rather than military, solutions through multilateral organizations to address international conflict.[126] Civilian power did not stand in a direct opposition to military power, but military power was to be used only with strong international consensus; a "civilian power" did not resort to unilateral military options. German preferences for the use of military force thus swung between concepts of "normalization" and a supra-state "civilian power" notion. German foreign policy therefore emphasized the politics of dialogue and preventive diplomacy rather than military intervention.[127] Domestically, the German public rejected the notion that it would be either advisable or even promising to tackle foreign policy problems unilaterally.[128]

Chancellor Helmut Kohl and the conservative Christian Democrat-Liberal government used the 1991 Persian Gulf War crisis as an opportunity to address the constitutionality of out of area troop deployments. The government supported a broader interpretation of the Basic Law that would allow collective security participation under NATO, the United Nations, and even European Community (EC)/Western Economic Union (WEU) sponsorship.[129] Opposition Social Democrats and Greens, in contrast, strongly resisted efforts to liberalize deployment policies and argued against military action for legal and moral reasons. Legally, the opposition parties stressed that Articles 24 and 87 barred Germany from military involvement outside of the NATO area.[130] Morally, the government opposition argued that given Germany's history, it was obliged to exercise maximum restraint in all military matters.[131] A broad consensus existed in parliament that financial and logistical support represented the limits of German military participation.

The Kohl government attempted to alter the strict interpretation of the Basic Law through repeated *Bundeswehr* deployments that set new precedents for the role of the armed forces. By early 1991, Germany was providing non-combat support to the Kurdish refugee crisis in Turkey and Iran and minesweeper support to clear the Persian Gulf, thus making the Gulf safe for commerce.[132] Other crises in the 1990s helped define Germany's use-of-force boundaries. In 1992 and 1993, German ships and aircraft helped monitor a sea-embargo of Serbia/Montenegro, a no-fly zone over Bosnia Herzegovina, while German troops provided medical and logistical support to the UN missions in Somalia and Cambodia. The Somalia crisis notably marked the first deployment of

German ground forces beyond the NATO area of operations since World War II.[133] The liberal opposition opposed these "out-of-area" deployments of troops and lodged a complaint with the Constitutional Court that the deployments violated Article 87 of the Basic Law. In July 1994, the Court ruled that out-of-area engagements of the *Bundeswehr* were constitutional if they formed part of a multinational coalition, obtained the explicit approval of a simple majority in the *Bundestag*, and served to uphold "international peace and security."[134] The court decision is of central significance in that it ratified the government deployment strategy without the need for constitutional amendment; the debate about *Bundeswehr* deployments consequently lost its legalistic argument.[135] Even with this legal mandate, however, majorities on the German left maintained moral arguments against out-of-area engagements and warned against the "militarization" of German foreign policy.[136]

After the legal argument lost vigor with the court decision, the moral argument against the use of force lost steam during the ongoing bloody war in Yugoslavia, where all non-military measures to stop ethnic cleansing proved ineffectual. In July 1995, Bosnian Serb forces overran the UN "safe area" of Srebrenica and systematically killed 8,000 Muslim men and boys. Diplomatic and economic measures failed to prevent the largest European mass-murder in post-Cold War history. The massacre split the German left, bringing elements that are more moderate closer to the conservative Christian Democrat government.[137] Fischer, then influential in the pacifist opposition Greens Party, pointed to the massacre at Srebrenica as the point at which it became clear that sometimes the use of military force was not only moral, but refusal to use force might be immoral.[138] Thus, the previous opponents to "out-of-area" deployments began to argue that Germany had a historical responsibility to resist aggression and massive human-rights violations, if necessary by threatening or using force. Respected philosopher Jürgen Habermas joined Fischer by stating that preventing Serbian ethnic cleansing clearly represented a case where using force was necessary.[139] The other major opposition party also changed its official position on the use of force outside the NATO boundaries. In June 1997 and later in December 1997, the opposition Social Democrat party changed its foreign policy stance from "humanitarian support only" to a wider interpretation allowing *Bundeswehr* support for "all kinds of military operations that have the blessing of the United Nations."[140] While it superficially appeared that German security policy had undergone a profound change, pacifism still shaped the foreign policy discourse; the German government supported a wider range of military intervention, but a robust consensus between elites on the proper use of armed forces reflected the tension between the "normalization" and "civilian power" advocates. The use of force was marked by a propensity to consider using the *Bundeswehr* in a greater range of missions, but consensus would require a strict mandate based on UN support, a multilateral framework, a clear mission statement, and a clear humanitarian dimension.[141]

In 1998, the liberal Social Democrat-Greens government replaced the conservative coalition, yet the use of force policy continued on a "normal" path. The 1999 Kosovo conflict further solidified Germany's transformation in the use of military force. The deployment of 14 fighter aircraft for *Operation Allied Force*—a NATO sponsored bombing campaign aimed at halting the ethnic cleansing in Kosovo—marked the first combat deployment in the history of the *Bundeswehr*.[142] Germany had thus officially crossed the line between peacekeeping and peace enforcement.[143] The Kosovo mission was also markedly different in that it was an offensive military operation against a sovereign state without a clear UN mandate.[144] The expanded role of the *Bundeswehr* in interventions, however, came at a cost to the governing SPD coalition. The Greens party was critical of the dominant role of the United States and the way American-style coercive diplomacy had foreclosed options other than military escalation. The *Bundestag* vote of 444-318 in favor of supporting the government position reflected the view that Germany was committing the "sin" of having consented to military action without a UN mandate.[145] In contrast, German consensus solidified when the *Bundestag*, by a vote of 505-24, endorsed the deployment of 8,000 soldiers to the UN sanctioned post-conflict Kosovo Force (KFOR) peacekeeping mission.[146]

German foreign policy through the 1990s reflected a coalition between the "normalization" and "civilian power" elements in the German government. The center-right Christian Democrats were driven by concerns about Germany's international standing and influence, while the center-left Social Democrats were influenced by the perception that Germany had an obligation to combat ethnic violence and massive human rights abuses. Thus, Germany's willingness to deploy armed forces was far from unconditional, but reflected an alignment of interests between the left and the right.

The German participation in *Operation Essential Harvest* illustrated the fragile nature of German views on the use of military force. In 2001, violence again emerged in the Balkans when ethnic Albanians clashed with the army and police of the Former Yugoslav Republic of Macedonia. Germany responded swiftly to an EU and NATO brokered ceasefire and pledged troops to a NATO-led stabilization force. Chancellor Schröder's quick commitment to NATO, however, was not fully supported within his governing coalition, and Germany's participation was secured through the support of the opposition parties.[147] The government had to live with the humiliation of significant defection from within its own ranks. The case of Macedonia demonstrated that the use of force remained a highly contested issue with factions divided between pragmatic and idealistic lines. The intervention was defended by the Social Democrats and Greens in terms of human rights and Western solidarity, however those themes ran hollow since the deployment was preventive in nature and the case for dispatching soldiers was not emotionally appealing.[148] Although future votes maintaining the Macedonian presence were widely supported, the German government was severely strained by the aftermath of September 11.

Chancellor Schröder's promise of solidarity with the United States in combating international terrorism again demonstrated the tension between idealistic and pragmatic elements of the German elite. At the U.S. request for a German military contribution, Chancellor Schröder pledged 3,900 *Bundeswehr* soldiers for the campaign against terror. After the cabinet approved the deployment plan, reservations within Schröder's own governing coalition of SPD-Greens emerged about supporting an American war on terrorism. The Berlin Greens maintained, "military campaigns against civilians and the bombing of entire countries or cities is not suited to catch terrorists."[149] When the SPD–Green government sought to gain the necessary votes for German military participation in *Operation Enduring Freedom* in the *Bundestag*, the coalition fell short by several votes because 28 members of both the SPD and the Greens threatened to vote against the bill. Subsequently, the chancellor tied the deployment issue to a vote of confidence (literally a vote of trust–*Vertrauensfrage*) in his government. By linking the deployment vote to a vote of confidence, those members disagreeing with the deployment of troops would link their vote with a vote to dissolve the government. In order to gain as much support as possible from his own coalition, the government's bill proposal also included clear restrictions on the geographic scope of the mandate for German forces in *Operation Enduring Freedom*.[150] The deployment was approved by a vote of 336 to 326—thus keeping Schröder's government intact—but significantly weakening it. Over seventy deputies voting yes added a written explanation of their vote to the record explaining that their votes were cast to support the government rather than a military intervention.[151] In the weeks after the vote, the governing SPD and

Greens held several party conferences to maintain their governing coalition since they were concerned that the party rank and file would revolt against the line taken in the parliamentary vote.

The twelve-year period timeframe between *Operation Desert Storm* and *Operation Iraqi Freedom* was one of profound change in German foreign policy concerning the use of force. At the end of the Cold War, the notion that the *Bundeswehr* could be used for anything other than the defense of NATO was unimaginable across the political spectrum and German public. German policy-makers had converged on a policy of strict abstention from military conflicts beyond Europe. The numerous conflicts in the Balkans, however, provided the newly unified nation the opportunity to expand its ability to participate with the greater collective security community. By the late 1990s, Germany seemed to have reached stasis in the relationship between force and diplomacy, between "normalization" and "civilian power." Germany progressively increased its international engagement in terms of troops deployed and military difficulty of their tasks. Germany's participation in the military operation in Kosovo in 1999—a NATO campaign launched without a UN mandate—suggested Germany's foreign policy had normalized away from its initial pacifistic tendencies. However, the use of force policy that evolved through the 1990s reflects a composite consensus of groups with quite different agendas concerning the wider use of force. Conservatives were driven by concern about Germany's standing in the international community, enhanced by participating in collective security arrangements. Liberals, on the other hand, were more driven by the moral obligation to combat ethnic violence and respond to humanitarian crises. Thus, German security and defense policy has continued as a "culture of restraint." Despite the "opening" of military policy options towards combat operations, the German priority going into Afghanistan was still clearly placed on peacekeeping and peacemaking (post-conflict reconstruction) missions, especially those that contain a humanitarian element.

## Domestic Structure and Politics

Given Germany's history of restraint and the domestic view as a "civilian power," domestic structure and politics was a guiding influence on Germany's position on the Iraq War. Chancellor Schröder's early public opposition against military "adventures" in Iraq and his subsequent Iraq policy can be best understood in the framework of German domestic structure and politics.

Germany is a federal republic, where the chancellor (*Bundeskanzler*) is the head of government. The position of chancellor is equivalent to that of a prime minister and he or she is elected by—and responsible to—the lower chamber of parliament, the *Bundestag*.[152] In the realm of foreign policy making, the most important figures in Germany are the chancellor and the foreign minister; however, due to party influences and electoral politics, foreign policy is a result of party negotiations and consensus building since the chancellor and foreign minister are traditionally from different parties and may therefore, represent different subcultures and interests.[153] Controversial issues of foreign policy are usually decided by parliamentary resolution after the appropriate debate in party and parliamentary forums. This corporate view towards policy has avoided perpetuating deep rifts in the population and the political elite over basic foreign policy issues.[154]

A further limitation for the government in the foreign policy arena is the requirement in German law for Bundestag approval of every military engagement that is not self-defense related, as well as extensions of existing military operations.[155] In its ruling of 12 July 1994, the Federal Constitutional Court confirmed that the deployment of German armed forces abroad requires the consent of the *Bundestag*.[156] This ruling ensures political discussion on the merits of any deployment and limits the chancellor's power to deploy military forces independently. Therefore, politically, the *Bundeswehr's* role in an international crisis remains a highly contested issue domestically.[157]

Germany's decentralized constitutional structure instituted under the Basic Law ensures that German governments are weak and civil society is strong. The federal government is required to compromise and to consult with the governing coalition, federal offices, individual states, and opposition parties.[158] Foreign policy is the purview of the chancellor and the foreign minister, but because each is typically their respective party's leader, policy can often be divergent. The decentralized foreign policy structure combined with a parliamentary requirement to approve military deployments marks the nation as a Type IV state in the domestic structure typology. However, the chancellor may be motivated to commandeer foreign policy since his international stature can win votes for the party at elections.[159] In the approach to the Iraq war, domestic pressures heavily shaped Schröder's Iraq policy, as is evident by the internal bureaucratic bargaining required by a weak government seeking reelection. Schröder independently charted a policy course on Iraq that played to the electorate's interests. Initially, Foreign Minister Fischer maintained a more nuanced position advocating a UN mandate, but he later accepted Schröder's hard "no" against military action in Iraq.[160] This independent role of the chancellor in foreign policy is not unusual in German history. Chancellor Konrad Adenauer, the first West German Chancellor, was simultaneously Federal Chancellor and Federal Minister for Foreign Affairs until 1955. He set a precedent by which successive chancellors have defined their own foreign policy agendas, giving rise to the notion of Germany as a "chancellor democracy" (*Kanzlerdemokratie*).[161] In this manner, German foreign policy structure for the Iraq war represented a Type II typology. Schröder, whose preferences reflected the pressure generated by a domestic election campaign and public opinion that was decidedly against a military intervention in Iraq, formulated Germany's Iraq policy.

*Role of the September 2002 National Elections.* Due to the influence of national elections and popular opinion against military intervention in Iraq, Chancellor Schröder was able to claim an extreme policy position regarding Iraq by exploiting domestic public opinion for electoral gains.[162] The German government position on the war on Iraq emerged in an *ad hoc* fashion, rather than a result of conscious strategic rethinking. An important factor was the timing of the *Bundestag* elections in 2002. Without the election campaign, Schröder might have tried to steer a policy course much closer to the United States or he might have at least have refrained from strong criticism of U.S. action and rigid anti-war positions.[163]

By the 2002 election, chancellor-candidates assumed unusually prominent roles as German campaigns began to reflect the style of American presidential campaigns. Instead of running a party-centered campaign, chancellor-candidates campaigned on personal charisma and electability. For Schröder's initial winning campaign in 1998, the SPD ran a professionally designed and organized campaign, modeled on the campaigns of Bill Clinton and Tony Blair. The SPD's campaign machine deployed advanced techniques such as demographic research, professional advertising, and consultations with political scientists to a degree previously unseen in German politics.[164] The result of the professionalization of *Bundestag* campaigns was that "wedge issues" were explored to swing voters from one party to another.

The wedge issue for the 2002 campaign was German foreign policy concerning Iraq. Until late 2001, Schröder seemed certain of a second term in office. However, domestic concerns about a sluggish economy and high unemployment eroded the early lead of Schröder's SPD in public opinion polls putting. The SPD had not kept its 1998 election promises to revive the economy and significantly reduce unemployment.

Early in the year, the opposition CDU/CSU candidate Edmund Stoiber and the Christian Democrats managed to eliminate the lead in the polls that the SPD had enjoyed by emphasizing the economic failures of the SPD-Green coalition government.[165] By midsummer, Schröder had become desperate for support and realized that he needed a broader coalition of the left.[166] Schröder's SPD and Stoiber's campaigns were nearly indistinguishable on policy grounds, therefore, Schröder needed to gain a "wedge issue" to halt his slide in the polls and distinguish his campaign from Stoiber's. To gain votes from the former East Germany, the SPD needed to appeal to two ideologically distinct sets of voters: the center-left electorate which made up their own clientele base and undecided eastern voters on the radical left who might possibly be pilfered from the Party of Democratic Socialism (PDS—formerly the East German Stalinist SED). The strategy for the SPD was to center the campaign on Schröder as a leader and to prioritize the campaign in the east, concentrating on practical issues of interest to eastern voters rather than on socialist ideals.[167] Nevertheless, all his tactics—including an attempt to paint his opponent, Edmund Stoiber of Bavaria, as a right-wing extremist—failed. Five weeks before the election, a poll by the Dimap Institute indicated that 45 per cent of voters were still undecided. Both campaign teams understood that it would be essential to win over this important undecided bloc.[168] The government's competent response to a major flood days before the election and Schröder's staunch anti-war stance reversed the favorable trend for the opposition CDU/CSU. Schröder's insistence late in the campaign that his government would not participate in, nor support, *any* military action against Iraq was a populist guarantee that appealed to the electorate in the former East Germany.[169]

The Schröder campaign polled the electorate on the Iraq issue and saw it as a wild card that could be played as a last resort. Polls had shown that eastern voters were less attached to Germany's relationship with the United States than were western voters and that they had more concerns about war and NATO.[170] The SPD party council decided on 1 August to start the final phase of the re-election campaign earlier than planned with the aim of stopping the party's slide in public opinion polls. Franz Müntefering, the party's general secretary, took the helm as election campaign manager and proposed a new campaign based on the concept of "the German Way," which was meant to focus domestically on social reform. However, before discussion of the foreign policy agenda, Chancellor Schröder left the party board meeting and gave a television interview that highlighted Iraq as a campaign issue. Asked how the SPD would try to improve its re-election chances, the chancellor repeated the central points of his party's agenda but added ominously that Germany would not participate in any "adventures."[171] Shortly thereafter, in an August 5 campaign speech in Hanover, Schröder intensified his anti-war rhetoric by stating, "pressure on Saddam Hussein, yes. We must get the international inspectors into Iraq. But playing games [*Spielerei*] with war and military intervention—against that I can only warn. This will happen without us... We are not available for adventures [*Abenteuer*], and the time of checkbook diplomacy is finally at an end."[172] With these two successive appearances, Schröder was able to commandeer German foreign policy and set the tone for the German response to Iraq. Schröder's clear rejection of German participation in a war against Iraq, even if covered by a UN resolution, evoked severe criticism from Stoiber and the CDU/CSU. The CDU/CSU and FDP (Free Democratic Party) warned against a "German separate way" and demanded instead that the government should work out a common European position in the Iraq debate.[173] CDU foreign policy expert Wolfgang Schaeuble accused the German government of "creating a bogey" and weakening the United Nations in the Iraq debate for its own electoral ends.[174] Schröder countered this assault by effectively arguing that it was the Bush administration that was weakening international institutions. In an interview with *Die Zeit*, Schröder openly criticized the Bush administration for not consulting with Germany and continued stressing the need for a "German Way." He began to use charged phrases like "reckless adventure" when referring to Bush's terrorism policy. *Der Spiegel* was later to observe, the time of "unlimited solidarity" ended in Hanover on August 5 when Schröder became the Chancellor of Peace, campaigning on a pacifist platform.[175]

By late August, it was evident that the Iraq issue was helping Schröder in the polls. After an impassioned speech by Vice President Cheney at VFW 103rd National Convention, arguing for a preemptive regime change in Iraq, the Iraq War became the dominant theme of the *Bundestag* elections.[176] Cheney's speech—which one Schröder advisor described privately as "the miracle"—presented Schröder with an ideal opportunity to escalate his opposition to U.S. policy on Iraq and gain separation from Stoiber on the Iraq issue.[177] Cheney's sharply unilateralist speech shocked the German public and supported media portrayals of the Bush administration as dismissive of its allies. It also shifted the emphasis in Iraq from controlling WMD to regime change—a new development in the eyes of Berlin.[178] In an interview with the magazine *Stern*, Schröder strengthened his anti-war position by saying that under his leadership, Germany would not participate in a military intervention in Iraq and that the coming election would not change his stance. SPD Secretary General Müntefering further stressed that the chancellor's "no" was definite, "We should not participate in any case...the United Nations will not decide."[179] At the same time, Stoiber and the CDU/CSU moved toward Schröder's policy position on Iraq; Stoiber could no longer afford to maintain a neutral policy on Iraq.[180] Whereas Stoiber had initially criticized Schröder's refusal to involve Germany in U.S. action against Iraq, after the Cheney speech, Stoiber publicly warned the Bush administration that unilateral action without consultation and a UN mandate would not be supported by Germany. Michael Glos, leader of the CSU group in the *Bundestag*, mirrored Schröder's earlier rhetoric, stating that Germany was not prepared to participate in any "adventures in Iraq."[181]

Schröder used Iraq as an embodiment for pacifist and nationalist themes, warning of the dangers of war while stressing that Germany should not be afraid to stand alone on the issue if necessary. This popular message reached multiple bases in contemporary German politics. It reinforced Germany's identity as a "civilian power," which was particularly strong among left-leaning voters. At the same time, his message embraced an acceptable face of German nationalism: the ability to stand alone against aggression. In this manner, Schröder claimed the center and left-leaning population on the Iraq issue while forcing Stoiber and the CDU/CSU to clarify the occasions they would support the use of the German military in Iraq. Ultimately, Stoiber reacted hesitatingly and awkwardly in moving his party's position to the left to gain public support.[182]

Schröder consequently won the closest election in postwar German history by only 6,000 votes. Capitalizing on the Iraq issue contained a number of positive effects for the SPD's campaign. First, it shifted attention away from domestic economic issues. Secondly, it mobilized the SPD and Green constituencies, many of whom were deeply skeptical of the use of military force and the motives of the Bush administration in Iraq and elsewhere around the world.[183] In this way, Schröder exploited popular attitudes on Iraq and the United States to gain domestic credibility. Thirdly, it also appealed to voters in eastern Germany—especially PDS supporters—who were pacifist. Lastly, Iraq allowed Schröder to take advantage of his leadership edge over Edmund Stoiber in an area where an incumbent chancellor always has the advantage over a challenger: security policy.[184] According to Friedbert Pflüger, a leading foreign policy specialist in the opposition CDU, "This time and for the first time, the government was not in danger of yielding to the street, it was fueling the street."[185] It is clear that Schröder was both shaping and responding to a broad sense of uneasiness and concern about the Bush administration as well as its policy on Iraq.

Chancellor Schröder cemented his anti-war position the day after the election. In a meeting with the left wing of his parliamentary party he told its foreign policy spokesman that his decision on Iraq was fundamental and unshakable. To change his approach would cost him all credibility with his party and the voters and he had no mandate to do so. That promise took on added weight soon after the election when he began to break his campaign promises concerning unemployment and EU Common Agricultural Policy reform and suffered a loss of public confidence in his government right at the beginning of his new term.[186] He could not afford to wobble on Iraq. The White House viewed the political faction of Schröder's party as "defiant," and this faction sought to keep the Iraq issue alive.[187]

Schröder's effective use of the Iraq crisis reflected a two-level game where the required domestic stance overruled a favorable policy vis-à-vis the United States.[188] His zealous stance contributed favorably to his reelection, but it also ensured that Germany would be unable to influence future Iraq policy. If Schröder had supported the tough U.S. stance on Iraq, he would have likely lost many SPD and Green party supporters who strongly opposed military intervention. Schröder's weak position in the government ensured that he could not embrace a policy in conflict with a majority of his base support. Alternatively, he could not have adopted a more measured policy, because the Stoiber campaign had already positioned itself as supporting intervention under a UN mandate. Schröder's self-inflicted stance of ruling out German military participation—even under a UN mandate—locked out future policy options on dealing with the United States regarding Iraq. Berlin was trapped between the possibility that the government would have to withdraw previously approved basing rights for the passage of U.S. forces stationed in Germany—thereby putting the NATO Alliance at risk—and the option of voting for a second resolution authorizing the use of force in Iraq. The government took all measures to circumvent and postpone any *Bundestag* vote on Iraq, ensuring that Schröder government would not be embarrassed by a defeat of any mandate on Iraq. As the vote for German participation in *Operation Enduring Freedom* had to be linked to a vote of confidence in the government, Schröder was relatively sure that he could not garner *Bundestag* support for any additional measures in Iraq. Therefore, he approved U.S. transit rights under the NATO treaty, which ensured that there would be no vote in the Bundestag concerning this support for the war effort.[189] Schröder's strategy after the election remained consistent: no German military personnel would be sent to Iraq.[190] After the declared end of combat operations in Iraq, Schröder stressed the importance of good transatlantic relations and expressed the wish for a greater UN role in postwar Iraq and a clear timetable for restoring Iraqi sovereignty. Schröder was ready to support Bush and Blair's plan to lift sanctions against Iraq in the UN Security Council.[191] Even after the occupation gained UN legitimacy, however, Germany maintained a hands-off policy regarding Iraq. Germany provided limited financial support to the UN-sponsored reconstruction fund and continued to reject U.S. requests for military support for Iraq stabilization. Instead, to show some level of solidarity in the general War on Terror, Berlin provided additional support to Afghanistan, providing significant military, economic, and diplomatic support to NATO's ISAF. As of March 2008, 3200 German soldiers were serving in Afghanistan, and Germany had suffered 26 fatalities.[192] Germany's contribution to ISAF marks it as the third largest participant behind the United States and Britain. The mandate issued by the *Bundestag*, however, does not allow German soldiers to take part in combat operations against the Taliban insurgency in the south and east of Afghanistan, but rather authorizes the training and arming of the Afghan army and staffing of provincial reconstruction teams.[193]

Domestic issues particularly drove Germany's position regarding the Iraq war. The SPD–Green coalition leadership steered a policy course that would preserve its parliamentary majority in the face of a blocking majority in its own ranks. As predicted by the domestic politics framework, Germany was unable to show strong support to the Iraq effort due to the influence of the legislature and polity on deployment decisions. Given the requirement for a *Bundestag* mandate, Schröder would have had to expend significant political capital—which he did not have—building a domestic coalition to pass a mandate supporting the use of force. This political maneuver had been done throughout the 1990s by the Kohl and Schröder governments, but the vote for the Afghanistan intervention demonstrated that the German people had become war weary.[194] In the Iraq case, Schröder assessed that his policy must reflect public opinion to ensure the survival of his government given the fragile state of his coalition's majority in the *Bundestag*. With just a few votes more than the opposition, the government likely would have circumvented any decision involving military assets. Such a decision would have required a formal mandate for which there was no firm majority in the coalition parties. The Schröder government proved unable to bridge the gap between its own domestic supporters and its allies for two reasons. First, leading German policy-makers were not convinced that the Iraq issue demanded a military response. Secondly, the continuing German debate on the use of force through the 1990s had a cumulative effect that shrank the government's majority with every military commitment abroad.[195]

Germany's policy concerning Iraq reflects David Auerswald's contention, in *Disarmed Democracies*, that national elections can dramatically influence a state's decision to use military force.[196] This conclusion reinforces the theories of Herbert Kitschelt and Susan Peterson who argue that leaders become more influenced by the public during election campaigns and are more likely to choose policy positions that reflect public sentiment.[197] Germany's Iraq position reflects observations from American politics that the executive will attempt to maximize the reelection chances by announcing a change in domestically unpopular commitments, even if the executive risks damaging the state's international reputation.[198] Because of Schröder's weak position going into the elections he found it necessary to capitalize on the Iraq position to build domestic support for reelection. Since the pressure for reelection was so strong, domestic considerations dominated international influences in the burden sharing model.

### Balance of Threat

Balance of threat theory predicts that when a state perceives an external threat it will form alliances or build strength internally to balance against that threat. In the burden sharing decision model, balance of threat theory predicts German lack of support for the Iraq War coalition but a greater amount of support for the greater War on Terror efforts based on German perceptions of the threat of terrorism. Specifically, Germans understood the threat of international terrorism and were generally supportive of efforts to halt the proliferation of terror organizations. However, this concern about terrorism broadly did not include Iraq since there was no proven link between the Hussein regime and al Qaeda.

The German government, in general, recognized radical Islamic terrorism as a significant security threat and regarded itself as a potential target of attack.[199] Although German citizens had not been directly targeted, they had frequently been the victims of radical Islamic terrorism. Between September 11, 2001 and January 2005, more German citizens died as victims of Islamic terrorist attacks than at the hands of the Red Army Faction, a left-wing terrorist group that operated in Germany for over thirty years.[200] In response to this threat, Germany initiated numerous domestic and international programs. Domestically, Germany adopted two major anti-terrorism packages that targeted loopholes in German law that permitted terrorists to live and raise money in Germany.[201] Internationally, Germany directly participated in five major counter terror missions as part of the global anti-terror coalition with forty percent of its 7,800 troops based abroad directly involved in counter terror operations. Germany supported a number of counter terror resolutions, most notably the UN sanctions regime targeting members or associates of al Qaeda and the Taliban. Germany also ratified the UN International Convention for the Suppression of Terrorist Bombings. Finally, Germany also contributed financially to counter terror efforts; by the end of 2004, Germany contributed $384 million for the reconstruction of Afghanistan.[202] Germany's extensive cooperation in the global fight against international terrorism reflects the threat that it perceives from terrorism.

The Schröder administration, however, remained unconvinced that a direct terrorist threat emanated from Iraq. Their first concern was that a compelling link between the Hussein regime and international terrorism had not been established. According to German leaders, there did not seem to be a connection between Iraq and the terrorist threat they had agreed to combat after September 11 and they were not convinced Iraqi WMD was a direct threat.[203] After September 11, German intelligence found no provable link between al-Qaeda and Iraq and shared these assessments with British and other intelligence services, including the CIA.[204] Without a direct link between al Qaeda and Iraq, Germany needed to be convinced that Iraqi WMD posed at threat.

Although German intelligence confirmed that Saddam was likely developing chemical and biological weapons, the government did not consider the development a direct threat to Germany. Chancellor Schröder said he had seen no new evidence indicating that the military danger from Iraq had increased and therefore perceived little urgency in dealing with Iraq. German intelligence discounted information on mobile WMD labs and Iraqi yellowcake acquisition and warned the United States that the information was not credible.[205] In the 2001 Report on Disarmament (*Abrüstungsbericht*), the threat by terrorist groups and the proliferation of WMD was emphasized and the report called for a vigorous effort in disarmament, arms control, and non-proliferation policy. However, the report did not list Iraq or its possible WMD program as a worldwide and regional proliferation concern. Instead, the report merely stated that the status of disarming Iraq had remained unchanged since the eviction of the UN Special Commission (UNSCOM) inspectors in 1998. The 2001 report downplayed any mention of WMD and instead emphasized the "difficult consensus finding process" in the UN Security Council for determining a solution to Iraqi disarmament. Though the BND assessed in a 1999 report that Iraq had reconstituted its WMD program after the expulsion of UNSCOM inspectors, by 2001 there was no sense of urgency for Iraqi disarmament measures.[206] Iraq was not pictured as an immediate threat, but rather a troubling country in the volatile Middle East. German leaders were consistent in regarding the Hussein regime as distasteful but contained, but regarded Middle East insecurity as a greater threat.

German leadership saw a military intervention in Iraq as more threatening than a contained Saddam Hussein. Foreign Minister Joschka Fischer, in an interview with *Der Spiegel,* noted that the German government saw no link between the terrorist actions of September 11 and Iraq. The German government was focused on the anti-terror fight in Afghanistan and saw regime change in Baghdad, rather than Iraqi WMD, as a more dangerous proposition; in fact, Germans found an unstable Middle East more threatening than Iraq.[207] According to Fischer, "It would be wrong if we declared a change of regime in Baghdad as top priority."[208] The Foreign Minister questioned whether the analyses of the threat justified taking on a risk of an entirely different order of magnitude and assuming responsibility for peace and stability in the region for years, perhaps even for decades—specifically through outside intervention.[209] Chancellor Schröder and Fischer warned that, "no one has a really clear idea of the political order that would follow in the Middle East" or of the effects of a war on the stability of moderate Arab states or the cohesion of the anti-terror coalition. There has been little discussion, according to Schröder, of the economic consequences, in particular the price of oil, for the rest of the world.[210] German leadership was more concerned with the regional instability that would ensue after a military intervention rather than the direct threat offered by Iraq.[211]

This lack of imminent threat from international terrorism—or Iraq writ large—explains why German domestic politics heavily influenced government decisions involving Iraq. Given that Iraq was contained, had most of its air space off limits to its own aircraft due to militarily enforced "no-fly zones," and was not in a position to pose a direct threat to its neighbors, Germans were not convinced that Iraq was a threat requiring military action, therefore domestic concerns were much more influential to German decision making.[212] Schröder simply believed that the threat constituted by Iraq was not great enough to provoke a military intervention that could weaken his government.[213]

### *Alliance Dependence*

Alliance dependence predicts that a state will support an ally that is demanding a contribution if dependence pressures outweigh fears. The trade-off between benefits and costs creates a tension between two fears, the fear of abandonment and the fear of entrapment. An alliance dependence motivation explains Germany's limited support for the Iraq coalition and also offers insight into Germany's support for the greater War on Terror. Although dependence was present, it was not nearly as pronounced as in the run-up to the 1991 Persian Gulf War. In 1991, Germany provided substantial financial support to the coalition under pressure from the United States for a contribution to the coalition. Since Germany was domestically limited to providing financial support due to disputes on the constitutionality of the use of force, the Bush administration requested a robust financial support package. President George H.W. Bush planned on a mid-September 1991 meeting between his personal envoy Secretary of State Baker and Chancellor Kohl to negotiate the German contribution. Against this background, the German government supported a European Community resolution that pledged support to Saudi Arabia Arabs but rejected support for the military buildup of the United States. Members of Congress reacted angrily to the perceived lack of German support to the U.S.-led coalition buildup.[214] Bush personally urged Kohl to contribute its "fair share" and hinted that the Americans would look very closely at how the Germans reacted. Chancellor Kohl's statement that he would support the coalition with DM 3.3 billion, almost 50 per cent dedicated directly to the U.S. military, came only four days after Bush informed Kohl that he would not be attending the October 3 ceremony marking German unification. At the same time, Secretary Baker publicly indicated that the United States was considering an additional drawdown of U.S. forces in Europe. At a time when it was still uncertain whether Russia would drawdown in the east as planned, these announcements caused concern in Germany that it would be abandoned in the face of a questionable Soviet withdrawal. In total, Germany contributed $11.5 billion to the 1991 Gulf coalition, an outstanding sum given the cost of German re-unification.[215]

After the Cold War, Germany had fewer incentives to support the United States on questions of security. During the Cold War, given its position as a frontier-state Germany relied on the United States particularly through NATO for the provision of its security. In contrast, Germany pursued a unified European security policy in the aftermath of the Cold War. Although Germany continued "dual-hatted" support for

NATO, it envisioned a European security structure that would deal with European issues. In a speech to the European Parliament in January 1999, foreign minister Fischer emphasized the importance of a European security and defense identity.[216] The issue of European security and defense cooperation was encouraged further by NATO's campaign against Serbia. The Kosovo campaign highlighted European dependence on the U.S. military. In reaction, the European Council agreed that the European Union required the ability for autonomous action backed by credible military forces. To that end, Germany was highly supportive of a European Security and Defense Policy (ESDP) and the European Rapid Reaction Force in an effort to lessen dependence on the United States in security matters and to gain more leverage over U.S. security policy.

The German leadership no longer felt as constrained by geography, history, or strategic threats and Germany's increased participation in military operations showed that Germany could take a more consultative role with the United States.[217] Germany's role in European defense policy and the Western European Union showed that Germany would forge policy to meet its interests. Germany's was "emancipated" from its role as U.S. policy agent to one of independence. Germany's unilateral recognition of Croatia and Slovenia in 1992 signified this growing independence.[218] As a result, Germany considered that its position in NATO obliged the United States to consult with it substantially before planning or implementing a military action in Iraq. Early in the preparations for war, Foreign Minister Fischer warned the Bush administration that European allies did not want to be treated like satellite states.[219] In addition, Schröder stated that he would no longer agree to the previous division of labor in international coalitions, in which Germany was not available for participation but paid, nevertheless. Germany would no longer be a country where "checkbook diplomacy replaces policy."[220] Germany saw itself as a more equal international partner due to its role in endorsing European security institutions and policy.

Once major combat operations ceased in May 2003, the United States applied political and economic pressure on Germany to punish it for its intransigence in the war build-up. Shortly after President Bush declared an end to combat operations in May 2003, the Chairman of the Joint Chiefs of Staff General Richard Myers toured Eastern European bases and stated that the United States was considering "reshuffling the military structure in Europe" by moving forces eastward.[221] He stated that the Department of Defense (DOD) strategy had shifted eastward and that a large stationing of military forces in Western Europe would no longer make strategic sense. The new strategy envisioned withdrawing the bulk of its 71,000 military personnel from Germany to the United States, while maintaining a series of smaller expeditionary bases in Eastern Europe to serve as jumping points for troops deploying to points south and east of Europe. The plans included moving a small number of U.S. forces to new bases in Poland, Bulgaria, and Romania and maintaining only the key U.S. airbase in Ramstein and a few other facilities in Germany. The outline of the proposal and its timing suggested to Germany that it was being punished for its opposition to the war in Iraq and that the states that had supported the administration were being rewarded.[222] This perception was reinforced in the fall when the DOD barred French, German, and Russian companies from competing in $18.6 billion in reconstruction contracts. According to U.S. Deputy Defense Secretary Wolfowitz, this restriction on contracts was a response to German lack of support for the war and for its failure to contribute directly to Iraq's reconstruction fund.[223]

Germany's measured response to U.S. pressure indicates that Germany had gained a more independent role in the alliance, but also demonstrated the desire of Germany to keep the NATO alliance intact. The issue of U.S. use of German military bases is illustrative. Given Schröder's staunch anti-war position, one would expect Germany to limit U.S. access to German bases and airspace. During the highly contested *Operation El Dorado Canyon* airstrikes on Libya in 1986, France and Spain denied basing and over flight rights. This restriction caused the increased operational complexity and added 1,300 miles one way to the mission.[224] In contrast, Germany allowed free use of German airbases and provided security so that U.S. forces could deploy to Iraq. After the war commenced, German policy-makers emphasized the need to look ahead and to cooperate in building a democratic Iraqi state, even as the Iraqi insurgency was escalating throughout most of 2003.[225] At the 2004 Munich Security Conference, German Foreign Minister Fischer stated, "We were not, and are still not, convinced of the validity of the reasons for war," however he continued to state that it was in the German interest for the Iraqi people—and, by extension—the Americans to succeed. Fischer continued to state that it is certainly not in Germany's interest for its major ally, the United States, to become bogged down in a quagmire.[226] Fischer's Munich speech was an explicit attempt to realign Germany with the United States. A few weeks after the Munich conference, Schröder traveled to Washington and publicly declared that the United States and Germany were still strong allies. During that meeting, Schröder proposed a wider Marshall Plan-like approach for the Muslim world, a multifaceted effort—that was first outlined by Fischer in Munich—to address the poverty and desperation that are, in the German view, at the heart of the problem. Overall, Germany resisted direct investment in Iraq, but continued to allow unrestricted access to U.S. bases in Germany, while its military forces embraced the stabilization and reconstruction of Afghanistan and the numerous NATO/UN missions in the former Yugoslavia.

Overall, Germany officially was not a member of the Iraq War coalition, but provided assistance that was critical to U.S. efforts in both Iraq and Afghanistan. Schröder would have likely caused the collapse of his government if he actively supported the invasion coalition, and his reelection hinged on open opposition to the Bush plan. However, he was able to provide significant support to U.S. forces under the guise of NATO support.[227] Schröder played a two-level game, denigrating the war to the domestic public, while at the same time allowing the United States to use critical infrastructure that directly supported the Iraq War. Even though there was a widespread view in Germany that the Iraq war was a dangerous course of action, the government did not want to infringe on its role as a critical partner of the United States. If Schröder had blocked access to German bases, he would likely have cemented the demise of the Atlantic alliance. Instead, he ceded to modest U.S. requests to insure that the United States remained in NATO and—more importantly—continued to have an influence in the alliance. Although the German–French resistance to the Iraq War marked a high point in the two countries' political alignment, Germany still needed the United States to influence the new NATO partners to the east. German and French efforts to carve out an independent defense and security role for the European Union were regarded with suspicion by Polish, Czech and Hungarian politicians and security experts who have preferred to look to the United States for their security guarantees. European Union and NATO stability still relies on the influence of the United States.[228]

Germany allowed full use of military facilities, combined with over flight rights, which ensured that American forces would be able to transit Europe through normal logistics nodes. This contribution alone ensured that the United States would not have to expend significant diplomatic and material energy developing alternate logistic plans for transiting military forces through Europe. This German contribution was crucial to U.S. strategy, but also insured that European disagreements with the United States remained a temporary annoyance rather than a permanent split.

### *Collective Action*

Germany's "checkbook diplomacy" in the 1991 Persian Gulf War was viewed by some scholars as a classic example of collective action free-riding. Germany's limitation to financial contribution was seen by some coalition partners as a method to avoid the direct costs of military action—essentially a free ride.[229] This classification, however, does not adequately represent the limitation on the German use-of-force in 1991. Germany's economic contribution was significant for the *Desert Storm* coalition, and rather than free-riding, it marked a conscious effort for Germany to robustly participate in the collective effort given its constitutional limitations.[230] In contrast, German actions in the lead up to the second Iraq War reflected the German view that the Iraq action was not a collective action. Germany did not accept Iraqi disarmament through military force as a collective good and countered U.S. attempts internationally to depict the intervention as a collective good. Schröder's position was that no evidence indicated that the military danger from Iraq had increased and therefore he did not perceive the need for a collective action. Additionally, German leadership saw a military intervention in Iraq as more threatening than a contained Saddam Hussein. Germany expended significant political capital to ensure that the intervention did not gain international legitimacy and gain the status of an accepted collective action. Schröder was the first Western leader to declare unequivocally that Germany would not support an Iraq intervention under any auspices and held that position even risking isolation internationally.[231] Evidence presented in previous sections shows that the Schröder administration assessed an Iraq intervention as a mistake. Germany was concerned with post-war stability and economic disruption in the Middle East.[232] Schröder's administration assessed the collective good as Iraqi disarmament through a UN inspections regime rather than armed intervention.

## The Role of Legitimacy

Though Germany's opposition to the Iraq War appeared to be based purely on legitimacy of the invasion and occupation, German opposition showed the tension between the legitimacy of a UN sanctioned military action and the German norm against the use of military force. As shown in the historical learning section of this chapter, German foreign policy since the end of the Cold War had been marked by a tension between the view of Germany as a "civilian power" that was a strong international power willing to respect international law and understood the necessity of cooperation and a "normal power" that was willing to use force for self-interests. Since the end of World War II, the German public maintained a preference for the "civilian power" representation of Germany in the international community. This preference against military intervention was shown in a 1982 survey where only 35 percent of the adult German population stated that they would be willing to fight for their country in the event of a war. In contrast, almost 70 percent of American and over 60 percent of British respondents were willing to fight.[233] During the 1990s, the German public supported military efforts that were aimed at peacekeeping and post-conflict stabilization rather than combat missions themselves. This preference against the use of military force was still prevalent as the Iraq War coalition was being built. An international survey, conducted by the German Marshall Fund in summer 2003, found that Germans stood out in their unwillingness to believe that some wars could be just. When asked whether, under some conditions, war is necessary to obtain justice, only 39 percent of Germans agreed, compared with 74 percent of Britons and 84 percent of Americans.[234] Clearly, due to the lessons learned from World War II, the German public maintains a high standard concerning the appropriate conditions requiring the use of military force.

By stating that Germany would not support an intervention, even if the internationally established process for lawful intervention were followed, Germany invoked its normative standard above the procedural legitimacy provided by a UN Security Council sanction. By declaring that Germany would not participate in an Iraq intervention—even with UN Security Council approval—Chancellor Schröder ordered German normative preferences above the procedural legitimacy provided by the international community through the Security Council.

Procedural legitimacy arguments reflect the viewpoint that behavior is legitimated when it is approved by legitimate international institutions.[235] Actions are collectively legitimized by the consensus built by a body of statute under multilateral endorsement.[236] According to Inis Claude, the United Nations has the ability to grant legitimacy because it has come to be regarded as the arbiter of international claims.[237] The UN gains legitimacy not through the abstract will of the international community, but rather through the process for dialog and consensus building within the Security Council.[238]

The German state officially recognizes the procedural legitimacy provided by the United Nations. In a recent speech to the United Nations General Assembly, the German Minister of State recently stated, "The UN is and remains the sole global forum of collective security. The Security Council has the central role in preserving peace and security. Security Council Resolutions also guarantee legitimacy for international peacekeeping missions; both the classic blue-helmet missions and those mandated by the Security Council and carried out by regional organizations and alliances."[239]

Schröder undermined the legitimacy provided by the UN, however, when he stated that Germany would not support a military effort in Iraq, regardless of the outcome of a Security Council vote. By rebuking the sanction provided by the UN, Schröder was discounting the legitimacy provided by the deliberation process in the United Nations. In this manner, he was placing national interest in the form of normative legitimacy above the international legitimacy provided by the Security Council process for authorizing military action. Clearly, Schröder could have taken a more nuanced position similar to France and Turkey that enhanced the legitimacy of the United Nations, but instead he issued a categorical "no," which played well with domestic audiences and ignited his reelection effort. Germany maintained this position of non-support even after the Security Council marked the occupation of Iraq legitimate with Resolution 1511. If Germany marked the UN sanction as legitimate, support for Iraqi security and reconstruction should have commenced after the Security Council urged states to participate in the multinational coalition. The German government did not significantly increase support to Iraq in the war's aftermath, instead they continued to refuse to send troops into Iraq, focusing instead on a NATO training mission in the United Arab Emirates.[240] The U.S. administration appealed for international help, but Germany committed neither significant funds nor troops even when the occupation gained UN authorization.

Unfortunately, German actions did not reflect the public's normative stance against the use of force in Iraq. If the German public thought that the Iraq effort lacked normative legitimacy, one would expect that the German government would block efforts to use German territory and resources in the Iraq War. As shown earlier, however, German support to the war effort was significant, gaining it the distinction as "non-coalition but cooperating" from the Pentagon.[241] Germany's acquiescence to significant U.S. requests that did not require parliamentary sanction undermined German legitimacy arguments. Rather than rebuking U.S. efforts, the German government streamlined and enabled U.S. logistic and intelligence support for the war effort. Interestingly, the public showed little interest in lessening German support to U.S. forces transitioning to Iraq. In effect, the government and public provided sanction to the Iraq War effort as long as German forces were not directly involved.

Germany's stance had two significant outcomes. First, it highlighted the difficulty of legitimacy arguments. The German case shows that legitimacy stems from multiple sources, and these sources may conflict in a particular circumstance. It also highlights the difficulty in separating legitimacy arguments from national interest. Was German assistance undermined by the German normative stance against armed intervention or rather its desire to distance itself from an effort where Germany saw little national and elite interest? This research suggests that Schröder's desire for reelection was a major motivator for him to fan German anti-war sentiment.

Ultimately, German policy undermined legitimacy arguments for two reasons. First, Schröder's categorical refusal to participate in an Iraq coalition, even under a UN mandate undermined the procedural legitimacy of the UN. One role of procedural legitimacy is to establish a set of rules for a state to follow so that decisions are based on deliberation and transparency. Germany undermined the process by stating that it would not participate regardless of the outcome of the process. Second, the fact that Germany did support U.S. efforts by making German bases available showed that it was not normatively against a war in Iraq, but rather against German participation.

## Summary and Conclusion

German resistance to a military intervention in Iraq and its belligerent tone in the summer and fall 2003 is best explained by domestic political considerations; however, its support of basing, overflight rights, and increased military participation in Afghanistan reflects the Schröder government's eagerness to help in areas not requiring parliamentary approval because of alliance dependence on the U. S. Germany did not perceive a direct threat from Iraq, nor did it believe that a collective action was required against Iraq. Given Chancellor Schröder's need to invoke a vote of confidence in his government, he was in a very weak position to authorize the use of force in Iraq. The German national elections of September 2002 further weakened Schröder's position in relation to the use of force in Iraq. Significant risks exist in using, or supporting the use of force, immediately before an election when the public will be focused on the conflict and base voting decisions on the outcome.[242] In Germany's case, Schröder recognized that any support of the Iraq coalition would spell disaster for the upcoming elections and that he could gain political advantage by embracing the strong sentiment against military intervention. By unilaterally declaring a "no" on Iraq, with minor consultations with the foreign policy establishment, Schröder's government reflected a Type II rather than a Type IV domestic structure. Schröder was able to commandeer the foreign policy process and imprint his preferences on German policy. Schröder was able to accomplish this feat by appealing to public attitudes concerning the use of force in Iraq. Since Schröder's stance resonated well with the public, he was able to accomplish a policy coup and develop a policy position individually, instead of through the collaborative process. The appeal to mass public opinion resulted in less coalition building and policy coordination than would normally be seen in a Type IV typology. Schröder avoided the more moderate stance that was being advocated by Joschka Fischer and the Foreign Ministry. When urged to weigh his words more carefully by his national security advisor and veteran diplomat Dieter Kastrup, Schröder responded, "I have to win the election."[243] Schröder was able to set Germany's Iraq policy unilaterally because it resonated with the electorate, especially in the former East Germany.

Being a NATO partner unwilling to completely reject the U.S. role in the alliance, Germany provided a significant amount of support to U.S. efforts in Iraq and Afghanistan as long as those efforts did not trigger a parliamentary vote. For the Iraq effort, Germany provided significant intelligence on Iraqi force disposition, allowed full use of German-based U.S. infrastructure, allowed unrestricted over flight rights, provided security forces to guard American bases, and eventually trained Iraqi security forces. In Afghanistan, Germany supported a role for NATO, commanded the ISAF, and increased the presence of its ground forces. Due to alliance dependence reasons, the German government supported U.S. objectives in areas that would not generate significant public attention.

Realist scholars argue that Germany's Iraq policy represents a parting of Germany from the Atlantic alliance and support of U.S. foreign policy concerning Europe. According to Henry Kissinger, the German confrontation with the United States without consulting other European states represented a challenge not only to the United States but also to Europe.[244] Stephen Szabo, an expert on U.S.-German relations notes that there is "a serious possibility of a deepening and more permanent rift and the emergence of a relationship based on rivalry."[245] However, Germany's burden sharing for the Iraq War reflected a belligerent rather than a parting ally. Schröder would have likely taken a more neutral stance supporting a UN mandate for Iraq if he could have won the national elections on that stance. Schröder won reelection not by leading German public opinion, but by following it at a time when anti-war sentiment had reached a peak. Instead of a reasoned move towards German independence in foreign policy, Schröder's stance was framed by domestic exigencies. On the one hand, the German government spoke out against the war vociferously, and yet on the other, made the war possible by supporting it extensively. In the end, the U.S. military employed the phrase "non-coalition but cooperating" to describe Germany's burden sharing.[246]

---

[1] Schröder's statement can be translated as either 'unlimited' or 'infinite' solidarity. In either case, the lack of qualification surprised many German observers that feared an entanglement in a wide-ranging military intervention. See Scott Erb, *German Foreign Policy: Navigating a New Era* (Boulder, Colo.: L. Rienner, 2003), 192. Schröder later qualified his statement stressing that Germany would not participate in any "adventures." See Gerhard Schröder, "Die Anschläge in Den USA [the Strikes in the USA]," (government declaration: 2001). Quoted in Tuomas Forsberg, "The Debate over German Normality: A Normal German Debate?" in *Political Thought and German Unification: A New German Ideology*, ed. Howard Williams, Colin Wight, and Norbert Kapferer (London: Macmillan, 2000), 217, Sebastian Harnisch, "German Non-Proliferation Policy and the Iraq Conflict," *German Politics* 13, no. 1 (2004).

[2] Schröder looked to coordinate his position with Russia and to use the new 'strategic partnership' with Russia that included a regular government consultation process. Anja Dalgaard-Nielsen, "The Test of Strategic Culture: Germany, Pacifism and Pre-Emptive Strikes," *Security Dialogue* 36, no. 3 (2005), 340, Graham Timmins, "Germany: Solidarity without Adventures," in *The Iraq War: Causes and Consequences*, ed. Rick Fawn and Raymond A. Hinnebusch (Boulder, Colo.: Lynne Rienner Publishers, 2006), 67.

[3] Philip H. Gordon and Jeremy Shapiro, *Allies at War: America, Europe, and the Crisis over Iraq* (New York: McGraw-Hill, 2004), 175-76.

[4] Germany's stand on Iraq in the UN Security Council allowed Saddam Hussein to assume that U.S. invasion plans were merely posturing. See "German Stand on Iraq Weakens US Crisis Management, Heightens War Risk - Paper," *Die Welt*, August 28, 2002. Saddam Hussein spent great effort gaining service contract for France and Russia to build a pro-Iraqi bloc in the Security Council and to avert support for an American war effort, see Kevin M. Woods and Joint Center for Operational Analysis (U.S.), *Iraqi Perspectives Project: A View of Operation Iraqi Freedom from Saddam's Senior Leadership* (United States Joint Forces Command, Joint Center for Operational Analysis, 2006 [cited October 11, 2007]); available from http://purl.access.gpo.gov/GPO/ LPS68139

[5] Daniel Benjamin, "Germany: A Questionable Ally," in *America and the World in the Age of Terror: A New Landscape in International Relations*, ed. Daniel Benjamin (Washington, D.C.: CSIS Press, Center for Strategic and International Studies, 2005), 53.

[6] Erb, *German Foreign Policy: Navigating a New Era*.

[7] Sebastian Bartsch, "Foreign Policy Influence and Transnational Relations of Political Parties," in *Germany's New Foreign Policy: Decision-Making in an Interdependent World*, ed. Wolf-Dieter Eberwein and Karl Kaiser (Houndmills, Basingstoke, Hampshire ; New York: Palgrave, 2001), 303.

[8] *The List: Who's Left in Afghanistan?* (Carnegie Endowment for International Peace, 2008 [cited June 25 2008]); available from http://www.foreignpolicy.com/story/cms.php?story_id=4235.

[9] See William Chandler, "Foreign and European Policy Issues in the 2002 Bundestag Elections," *German Politics and Society* 21, no. 1 (2003), Patricia Hogwood, "The Chancellor-Candidates and the Campaign," *German Politics* 13, no. 2 (2004), Stephen F. Szabo, *Parting Ways: The Crisis in German-American Relations* (Washington, D.C.: Brookings Institution Press, 2004), Martin Walker, "The Winter of Germany's Discontent," *World Policy Journal* 19, no. 4 (2002/2003).

[10] Anja Dalgaard-Nielsen, "Gulf War: The German Resistance," *Survival* 45, no. 1 (2003), Erb, *German Foreign Policy: Navigating a New Era*, Jeffrey S. Lantis, *Strategic Dilemmas and the Evolution of German Foreign Policy since Unification* (Westport, Conn.: Praeger, 2002), Kerry Anne Longhurst, *Germany and the Use of Force*, Issues in German Politics (Manchester [UK] ; New York: Manchester University Press; Palgrave, 2004), Akan Malici, "Germans as Venutians: The Culture of German Foreign Policy Behavior," *Foreign Policy Analysis* 2 (2006).

[11] See Harnisch, "German Non-Proliferation Policy and the Iraq Conflict."

[12] Ibid., 2-3.

[13] Schröder looked to coordinate his position with Russia and to use the new 'strategic partnership' with Russia that included a regular government consultation process. Dalgaard-Nielsen, "The Test of Strategic Culture: Germany, Pacifism and Pre-Emptive Strikes," 340, Timmins, "Germany: Solidarity without Adventures," 67.

[14] "German Stand on Iraq Weakens US Crisis Management, Heightens War Risk."

[15] Schröder comments to the Bundestag, September 19, 2001, quoted in Harnisch, "German Non-Proliferation Policy and the Iraq Conflict," 6.

[16] Article 5 states that any attack on a member state will be considered an attack against the entire group of members. North Atlantic Treaty Organization, *The North Atlantic Treaty* (North Atlantic Treaty Organization, April 4 1949 [cited March 10, 2008]); available from http://www.nato.int/docu/basictxt/treaty.htm. Article 5 does provide for differing levels and types of support, see Lawrence S. Kaplan, *NATO after Forty Years* (Wilmington, Del.: SR Books, 1990).

[17] Erb, *German Foreign Policy: Navigating a New Era*, 193. Timmins, "Germany: Solidarity without Adventures," 61.

[18] Erb, *German Foreign Policy: Navigating a New Era*, 193.

[19] Heiko Borchert and Mary N. Hampton, "The Lessons of Kosovo: Boon or Bust for Transatlantic Security," *Orbis* 46, no. 2 (2002).

[20] Rebecca Johnson and Micah Zenko, "All Dressed up and No Place to Go," *Parameters* (2002/3), 52.

[21] Donald Rumsfeld, *Secretary Rumsfeld Media Stakeout in Washington* (U.S. Department of Defense, 2001 [cited December 19, 2007]); available from http://www.defenselink.mil/transcripts/transcript.aspx?transcriptid=1926. Johnson and Zenko, "All Dressed up and No Place to Go," 51.

[22] Benjamin, "Germany: A Questionable Ally," 57.

[23] Ibid., 58, Dalgaard-Nielsen, "The Test of Strategic Culture: Germany, Pacifism and Pre-Emptive Strikes," 350, Erb, *German Foreign Policy: Navigating a New Era*, 193-94, Harnisch, "German Non-Proliferation Policy and the Iraq Conflict," 6, Marco Overhaus, "German Foreign Policy and the Shadow of the Past," *SAIS Review* XXV, no. 2 (2005), 30, Szabo, *Parting Ways: The Crisis in German-American Relations*, 17.

[24] Harnisch, "German Non-Proliferation Policy and the Iraq Conflict," Lantis, *Strategic Dilemmas and the Evolution of German Foreign Policy since Unification*.

[25] Schröder won the vote of confidence with 336 votes, only 2 more than the simple majority that he needed.

[26] Dalgaard-Nielsen, "Gulf War: The German Resistance," 108, Longhurst, *Germany and the Use of Force*, 84.

[27] George W. Bush, *President Delivers State of the Union Address* (The White House, 2002 [cited December 19, 2007]); available from http://www.whitehouse.gov/news/releases/2002/01/20020129-11.html.

[28] Dalgaard-Nielsen, "Gulf War: The German Resistance," Martin Gehlen, "German Skepticism About America's Intent and Goals in Iraq," *Nieman Reports* (2003), Ingrid A. Lehmann, "Exploring the Transatlantic Media Divide over Iraq: How and Why U.S. And German Media Differed in Reporting on UN Weapons Inspections in Iraq, 2002-2003," *The Harvard International Journal of Press and Politics* 10, no. 1 (2005).

[29] "German Chancellor Says Strike against Iraq Not on the Agenda," *DDP News Agency*, February 18, 2002. Peter Rudolf, "The Myth of the 'German Way': German Foreign Policy and Transatlantic Relations," *Survival* 47, no. 1 (2005), 142.

[30] Lally Weymouth, "The Importance of Having Friends: Schroder on Bush, the Terror War and His Woes at Home," *Newsweek*, February 11, 2002. Peter Ford, "United against Terror, Divided on Trade, Coalition Strains," *Christian Science Monitor*, March 8, 2002.

[31] Paul D. Wolfowitz, *Speech at the 38th Munich Conference on Security Policy* (Munich Conference on Security Policy, 2002 [cited December 19, 2007]); available from http://www.securityconference.de/konferenzen/rede.php ?menu_2002=&id=69&sprache=en&.

[32] John McCain, *From Crisis to Opportunity: American Internationalism and the New Atlantic Order* (Munich Conference on Security Policy, 2002 [cited December 19, 2007]); available from http://www.securityconference.de/ konferenzen/rede.php?menu_2002=&menu_konferenzen_archiv=&menu_2008 =&menu_konferenzen=&sprache=en&id=76&.

[33] Rudolph Scharping, *Global Security - New Challenges, New Strategies* (Munich Conference on Security Policy, 2002 [cited February 20, 2008]); available from http://www.securityconference.de/konferenzen/rede.php?menu_2002=&menu_konferenzen_archiv=&menu_2008=&menu_konferenzen=&sprache=en&id=88&. Harnisch, "German Non-Proliferation Policy and the Iraq Conflict," 8, Longhurst, *Germany and the Use of Force*, 87.

[34] *Britain 'Isolated' over Iraq* (BBC News, 2002 [cited December 10 2007]); available from http://news.bbc.co.uk/2/hi/uk_news/1876015.stm.

[35] Gordon and Shapiro, *Allies at War: America, Europe, and the Crisis over Iraq*, 109, Klaus Larres, "Mutual Incomprehension: U.S.-German Value Gaps Beyond Iraq," *The Washington Quarterly* 26, no. 2 (2003), Rudolf, "The Myth of the 'German Way': German Foreign Policy and Transatlantic Relations," 143-44, Szabo, *Parting Ways: The Crisis in German-American Relations*, 19.

[36] Quoted in Harnisch, "German Non-Proliferation Policy and the Iraq Conflict," 9.

[37] Chandler, "Foreign and European Policy Issues in the 2002 Bundestag Elections," Tuomas Forsberg, "German Foreign Policy and the War on Iraq: Anti-Americanism, Pacifism or Emancipation," *Security Dialogue* 36, no. 2 (2005), 218.

[38] Madeline Albright and Andrew Kohut, "What the World Thinks in 2002," *Pew Global Attitudes Project* (Washington DC: The Pew Research Center for the People and the Press, 2002), 3.

[39] This quote is in response to the notion that Germany provided only checkbook support in the 1991 Persian Gulf War. Quoted in Szabo, *Parting Ways: The Crisis in German-American Relations*, 23. Forsberg, "German Foreign Policy and the War on Iraq: Anti-Americanism, Pacifism or Emancipation," 218. "Gerhard Schröder Auf Anti-Amerika Kurs [Gerhard Schröder on an Anti-American Course]," *Die Tageszeitung*, August 6, 2002.

[40] "German Opposition Critical of Government Stance on Iraq," *Die Welt*, August 7, 2002.

[41] Quoted in Szabo, *Parting Ways: The Crisis in German-American Relations*, 23.

[42] Richard Cheney, *Vice President Speaks at VFW 103rd National Convention* (White House Press Office, 2002 [cited December 20, 2007]); available from http://www.whitehouse.gov/news/releases/2002/08/20020826.html.

[43] Chandler, "Foreign and European Policy Issues in the 2002 Bundestag Elections," Forsberg, "German Foreign Policy and the War on Iraq: Anti-Americanism, Pacifism or Emancipation," 218. White House, *Vice President Speaks at VFW 103rd National Convention* (White House Press Office, 2002 [cited December 3, 2007]); available from http://www.whitehouse.gov/news/releases/2002/08/20020826.html.

[44] Steven Erlanger, "German Leader's Warning: War Plan Is a Huge Mistake; Perspectives -- Sept. 11 and Beyond: Gerhard Schroder," *The New York Times*, September 5, 2002. See also Szabo, *Parting Ways: The Crisis in German-American Relations*, 26.

[45] Erlanger, "German Leader's Warning: War Plan Is a Huge Mistake; Perspectives -- Sept. 11 and Beyond: Gerhard Schroder," William Horsley, *Foreign Policy Works for Schroeder* (BBC News, 2002 [cited December 4, 2007]); available from http://news.bbc.co.uk/2/hi/europe/2261878.stm.

[46] Chandler, "Foreign and European Policy Issues in the 2002 Bundestag Elections," Dalgaard-Nielsen, "The Test of Strategic Culture: Germany, Pacifism and Pre-Emptive Strikes," 351, Hogwood, "The Chancellor-Candidates and the Campaign."

[47] Szabo, *Parting Ways: The Crisis in German-American Relations*, 34.

[48] Harnisch, "German Non-Proliferation Policy and the Iraq Conflict," 12.

[49] *Schröder's Iraq Rhetoric Alarms Western Allies* (Telegraph Media Group, 2002 [cited March 4, 2008]); available from http://www.telegraph.co.uk/news/main.jhtml?xml=/news/2002/09/15/wschr15.xml.

[50] "German Chancellor Offers Support for UN Arms Inspections in Iraq," *DDP News Agency*, September 17, 2002.

[51] Harnisch, "German Non-Proliferation Policy and the Iraq Conflict," 12.

[52] "German Parliament Approves Extension of Enduring Freedom Mandate," *DDP News Agency*, November 15, 2002.

[53] Steven Erlanger, "Rumsfeld Urges NATO to Set up Strike Force," *The New York Times*, September 25, 2002, "German Cabinet Extends Bundeswehr Mandate for Afghanistan, Macedonia," *DDP News Agency*, December 3, 2002. "German Minister Stresses Need for Ongoing Isaf Mission in Afghanistan," *DDP News Agency*, December 20, 2002, Szabo, *Parting Ways: The Crisis in German-American Relations*, 35.

[54] "German Chancellor Expected to Grant USA Use of Air Space" *Der Spiegel*, November 20, 2002, "Germany to Grant Overflight Rights to US, Allies in Case of Iraq War," *DDP News Agency*, November 22, 2002.

[55] Szabo, *Parting Ways: The Crisis in German-American Relations*, 35.

[56] "Germany, Israel to Hold Talks on Patriot Missiles," *DDP News Agency*, December 3, 2002, "Germany to Grant Overflight Rights to US, Allies in Case of Iraq War."

[57] *Die Hoffnung Wird Immer Kleiner [Hope Is Becoming Smaller All the Time]* (December 30 2002 [cited December 3, 2007]); available from http://service.spiegel.de/digas/find?DID=26024486. Quoted in Forsberg, "German Foreign Policy and the War on Iraq: Anti-Americanism, Pacifism or Emancipation," 219. Szabo, *Parting Ways: The Crisis in German-American Relations*, 37.

[58] Szabo, *Parting Ways: The Crisis in German-American Relations*, 37.

[59] Robert D. Putnam, "Diplomacy and Domestic Politics: The Logic of Two-Level Games," *International Organization* 42, no. 3 (1988).

[60] Szabo, *Parting Ways: The Crisis in German-American Relations*, 38.

[61] Ibid., 37.

[62] Quoted in Timmins, "Germany: Solidarity without Adventures," 65.

[63] Szabo, *Parting Ways: The Crisis in German-American Relations*.

[64] Quoted in James Kitfield, "Damage Control," *National Journal*, July 19, 2003.

[65] United States. White House, *U.S. Secretary of State Colin Powell Addresses the U.N. Security Council* (February 5, 2003 [cited February 21, 2008]); available from http://www.whitehouse.gov/news/releases/2003/02/20030205-1.html#17.

[66] Szabo, *Parting Ways: The Crisis in German-American Relations*, 42.

[67] Harnisch, "German Non-Proliferation Policy and the Iraq Conflict," 17-18.

[68] "Extraordinary European Council, Brussels, February 17, 2003," (Brussels: Council of the European Union, 2003).

[69] The Declaration on Iraq by Russia, Germany, and France stated, "U.N. Resolution 1441, adopted unanimously by the U.N. Security Council, provides a framework of which the potential has not yet been fully exploited." It continued, "There is still an alternative to war. The use of force can only be considered as a last resort. Russia, Germany and France are determined to ensure that everything possible is done to disarm Iraq peacefully." *Declaration by Russia, Germany and France Pronounced by Jacques Chirac, President of the Republic, During a Joint Press Briefing with Vladimir Poutine, President of the Russian Federation* (Embassy of France in the United States, February 10, 2003 [cited March 4, 2008]); available from http://www.ambafrance-us.org/news/statmnts/2003/chirac021003.asp.

[70] Harnisch, "German Non-Proliferation Policy and the Iraq Conflict," 18.

[71] Kitfield, "Damage Control." Szabo, *Parting Ways: The Crisis in German-American Relations*, 39.

[72] Timmins, "Germany: Solidarity without Adventures," 67.

[73] Elaine Sciolino, "Threats and Responses: Discord; France to Veto Resolution on Iraq War, Chirac Says," *The New York Times*, March 11, 2003.

[74] Anthony Depalma, "Threats and Responses: An Overview: March 12, 2003; Trolling for U.N. Votes (8 Enough?), Terms for Delay, Drones on Display," *The New York Times*, March 13, 2003. For text of the draft resolution see United Nations Security Council, *Spain, United Kingdom of Great Britain and Northern Ireland and United States of America: Draft Resolution. S/2003/215* (United Nations, March 7, 2003 [cited March 4, 2008]); available from http://www.un.org/News/dh/iraq/res-iraq-07mar03-en-rev.pdf.

[75] Quoted in Timmins, "Germany: Solidarity without Adventures," 67.

[76] *US, Britain and Spain Abandon Resolution* (Associated Press, 2003 [cited December 27, 2007]); available from http://www.globalpolicy.org/security/issues/iraq/attack/armtwist/2003/0317usbritspain.htm.

[77] United Nations, *Security Council Meeting Minutes, 4721st Meeting, 19 March 2003, S/Pv.4721* (2003 [cited December 27 2007]); available from http://daccessdds.un.org/doc/UNDOC/PRO/N03/286/04/PDF/N0328604.pdf.

[78] Forsberg, "German Foreign Policy and the War on Iraq: Anti-Americanism, Pacifism or Emancipation," 220, Timmins, "Germany: Solidarity without Adventures," 65-66.

[79] France pulled out of the Defense Planning Committee in 1966 over DeGaulle's belief that French nuclear weapons should not be subject to NATO oversight. As a result, France participates diplomatically in NATO discussions but not in defense planning operations. The Bush administration requested

under Article 4 of the treaty that planning begin and arms transfer for the defense of Turkey. Rebecca R. Moore, *NATO's New Mission : Projecting Stability in a Post-Cold War World* (Westport, Conn.: Praeger Security International, 2007), 95-96. Richard Bernstein and Steven R. Weisman, "Threats and Responses: Alliance; NATO Settles Rift over Aid to Turks in Case of War," *The New York Times*, February 17, 2003. Harnisch, "German Non-Proliferation Policy and the Iraq Conflict," 15.

[80] Petra Spoerle-Strohmenger, *Struggling Hard to Find Solutions to the Conflict in Iraq* (2003 [cited December 3, 2007]); available from http://www.securityconference.de/konferenzen/2003/.

[81] Richard Bernstein, "Germany Hoping for Return of Strong American Bond," *The New York Times*, March 12, 2003, A16.

[82] Kaare Dahl Martinsen, "The End of the Affair? Germany's Relationship with France," *German Politics* 14, no. 4 (2005), 413.

[83] Quoted in Ibid., 409.

[84] Throughout the fall of 2002 and spring of 2003, Saddam's public and private comments reflected his belief that the United States and United Kingdom lacked the stomach for war. Additionally, sometime in the first week of March 2003, the Russian ambassador to Iraq assured the Iraqi government that Russia, China, France and Germany would counter U.S. efforts in the Security Council giving Saddam the hope that the international community would dissuade the coalition from attacking. Woods and Joint Center for Operational Analysis (U.S.), *Iraqi Perspectives Project: A View of Operation Iraqi Freedom from Saddam's Senior Leadership.* See also Benjamin, "Germany: A Questionable Ally," 63-64, Longhurst, *Germany and the Use of Force*, 89-90.

[85] "Germany's Schroeder for Lifting Iraq Sanctions," *DDP News Agency*, May 15, 2003.

[86] Greg Hitt and Jess Bravin, "U.S., Germany Repair Iraq Rift; Bush Bid to U.N. Yet to Bear Fruit," *The Wall Street Journal*, September 25, 2003.

[87] "Germany Rejects Change of Mandate for Soldiers in Afghanistan," *DDP News Agency*, May 16, 2003.

[88] Maggie Farley and Farley Reynolds, "Bush, Schroeder End Feud; Germany Offers Aid in Iraq," *Los Angeles Times*, September 25, 2003.

[89] Overhaus, "German Foreign Policy and the Shadow of the Past," 30.

[90] Harnisch, "German Non-Proliferation Policy and the Iraq Conflict," 20.

[91] Richard Bernstein, "France and Germany Differ with U.S. On Plan for Iraq," *The New York Times*, September 5, 2003.

[92] United Nations Security Council, *Resolution 1511* (United Nations, 2003 [cited October 24, 2007]); available from http://daccessdds.un.org/doc/UNDOC/GEN/N03/563/91/PDF/N0356391.pdf.

[93] Elisabeth Bumiller, "Bush Defends Barring Nations from Iraq Deals," *The New York Times*, December 12, 2003, Harnisch, "German Non-Proliferation Policy and the Iraq Conflict," 21.

[94] "Germany Reportedly No Longer Rules out Humanitarian Commitment in Iraq," *DDP News Agency*, January 14, 2004, Karl-Heinz Kamp, *Kas Germany Update - January 2004* (Konrad-Adenauer-Stiftung, 2004 [cited

December 28, 2007]); available from http://www.kas.org.ar/Doc/Docum/Realidad%20Alemana/GermUpd_Jan04.pdf.

[95] "German Participation in NATO Iraq Mission "Premature" - Social Democrats," *Frankfurter Rundschau*, January 16, 2004.

[96] Joschka Fischer, *Speech on the 40th Munich Conference on Security Policy* (Munich Conference on Security Policy, 2004 [cited December 28, 2007]); available from http://www.securityconference.de/konferenzen/rede.php?id=123&sprache=en&.

[97] Marc Champion and Greg Jaffe, "Poland's Leader Questions U.S. Steps in Iraq; Weapons Issue Is Criticized; German Officials Try to Get Spain to Temper Rhetoric," *The Wall Street Journal*, March 19, 2004.

[98] "German Leader Expects Continuing Problems in Iraq, Skeptical on NATO Role," *DDP News Agency*, June 10, 2004, Overhaus, "German Foreign Policy and the Shadow of the Past," 31, Gerhard Schröder, "We Have a Good Relationship," *The Washington Post*, February 29, 2004.

[99] Benjamin, "Germany: A Questionable Ally," 69, Helmut Reuter, "Germany's Red Line in Its Aid to Iraq: No Troops," *Deutsche Presse-Agentur*, June 21, 2005, Martin A. Weiss, "Iraq: Paris Club Debt Relief," *CRS Report for Congress - RS21765* (Washington DC: Congressional Research Service, 2005).

[100] Rudolf, "The Myth of the 'German Way': German Foreign Policy and Transatlantic Relations," 134.

[101] Michael R. Gordon and Bernard E. Trainor, *Cobra II: The inside Story of the Invasion and Occupation of Iraq*, 1st ed. (New York: Pantheon Books, 2006), 123.

[102] "Germany's Struck to Discuss Bundeswehr Changes, Iraq at Munich Security Talks," *Welt am Sonntag*, February 1, 2004.

[103] "German Defence Ministry: Deployment of NBC Units in Kuwait Possible," *DDP News Agency*, January 9, 2002.

[104] Quoted in Gordon and Trainor, *Cobra II: The inside Story of the Invasion and Occupation of Iraq*, 123.

[105] Forsberg, "German Foreign Policy and the War on Iraq: Anti-Americanism, Pacifism or Emancipation," 224, Szabo, *Parting Ways: The Crisis in German-American Relations*, 44. Although Germany has a significant ground presence in Afghanistan, its soldiers are still restricted from participating in combat operations, see "NATO Requests German Troops for Combat Role in Afghanistan," *Deutsche Welle*, no. February 21 (2008), http://www.dw-world.de/dw/article/0,2144,3095130,00.html.

[106] "Germany's Schroeder on Postwar Iraq, EU Split, Relations with USA," *DDP News Agency*, March 28, 2003.

[107] "Germany Admits Providing Washington with Iraq Intelligence," *Deutsche Presse-Agentur*, February 24, 2006, Michael R. Gordon, "German Intelligence Gave U.S. Iraqi Defense Plan, Report Says," *The New York Times*, February 27, 2006. See also Gordon and Trainor, *Cobra II: The inside Story of the Invasion and Occupation of Iraq*, 123-24.

[108] Richard Bernstein and Michael R. Gordon, *German Help on Iraq Lasted Months* (2006 [cited December 31, 2007]); available from http://www.iht.com/articles/2006/03/02/news/germany.php.

[109] Bob Drogin, "German Spies Aided U.S. Attempt to Kill Hussein in Aerial Attack," *Los Angeles Times*, January 12, 2006.

[110] Richard Bernstein and Judy Dempsey, "Germany Denies Giving U.S. Iraq's Plan to Defend Baghdad," *The New York Times*, February 28, 2006, "German Agent Did Not Pass on Iraq Information, Says BND," *Deutsche Presse-Agentur*, March 3, 2006. Peter Schwarz, *New York Times Raises New Charges against German Intelligence* (2006 [cited December 31, 2007]); available from http://www.wsws.org/articles/2006/mar2006/nbnd-m02.shtml.

[111] Gunther Hellmann, "Absorbing Shocks and Mounting Checks: Germany and Alliance Burden Sharing in the Gulf War," in *Friends in Need: Burden Sharing in the Persian Gulf War*, ed. Andrew Bennett, Joseph Lepgold, and Danny Unger (New York: St. Martin's Press, 1997). According interpretations of German Basic Law in 1991, the government was barred from supplying troops for military operations other than self defense or NATO defense of Europe. See Historical Learning, this chapter, for a discussion on Germany's broadening interpretation of the Basic Law.

[112] Quoted in Lantis, *Strategic Dilemmas and the Evolution of German Foreign Policy since Unification*, 47-48.

[113] Michael E. O'Hanlon and Jason H. Campbell, *Tracking Variables of Reconstruction & Security in Post-Saddam Iraq, April 18, 2005* (The Brookings Institution, Saban Center for Middle East Policy, 2005 [cited September 18, 2007]); available from http://www3.brookings.edu/fp/saban/iraq/index20050418.pdf.

[114] Maggie Farley and Maura Reynolds, "Bush, Schroeder End Feud; Germany Offers Aid in Iraq," *Los Angeles Times*, September 25, 2003. "German Cabinet "Boycotting" Donors' Conference for Iraq," *Der Spiegel*, October 20, 2003.

[115] *German Daily Questions Use of Iraq Donor Conference without UN Resolution* (BBC Monitoring International Reports, 2003.

[116] Chancellor Schröder noted that the resolution was a "step in the right direction," but fell short of German requirements for full support. See "Legitimization for the US Occupation Power," *Die Welt*, October 17, 2003.

[117] Bumiller, "Bush Defends Barring Nations from Iraq Deals," Harnisch, "German Non-Proliferation Policy and the Iraq Conflict," 21.

[118] "Bush's Personal Representative to Berlin 'before Christmas' to Discuss Iraq," *DDP News Agency*, December 11, 2003.

[119] Dalgaard-Nielsen, "The Test of Strategic Culture: Germany, Pacifism and Pre-Emptive Strikes," 352. See also Nikolaus Blome and Torsten Krauel, "Gerhard and George," *Die Welt*, February 26, 2004. Craig S. Smith, "Major Creditors Agree to Cancel 80% of Iraq Debt," *The New York Times*, November 22, 2004.

[120] Jeremy M. Sharp and Christopher M. Blanchard, "Post-War Iraq: Foreign Contributions to Training, Peacekeeping, and Reconstruction," *CRS Report for Congress - RL32105* (Congressional Research Service, 2007).

[121] Subcommittee on International Organizations, Human Rights, and Oversight of the Committee on Foreign Affairs, *Economic and Military Support for the U.S. Efforts in Iraq: The Coalition of the Willing, Then and Now*, First

Session, May 9 2007, O'Hanlon and Campbell, *Tracking Variables of Reconstruction & Security in Post-Saddam Iraq, April 18, 2005.*

[122] Lantis, *Strategic Dilemmas and the Evolution of German Foreign Policy since Unification*, 21-22.

[123] Article 24, paragraph 2 stated, "For the maintenance of peace, the Federation may join a system of mutual collective security; in doing so it will consent to such limitations upon its sovereign powers as will bring about and secure a peaceful and lasting order in Europe and among the nations of the world." Article 87 stated, "The Federation shall establish Armed Forces for Defense purposes... Apart from Defense, the Armed Forces may only be used insofar as explicitly permitted by this Basic Law." See *Basic Law for the Federal Republic of Germany as Amended by the Unification Treaty of 31 August 1990 and Federal Statute of 23 September 1990* (The Constitution Society, 1993 [cited January 2, 2008]); available from http://www.constitution.org/cons/germany.txt.

[124] Dalgaard-Nielsen, "Gulf War: The German Resistance," 103, Erb, *German Foreign Policy: Navigating a New Era*, 155.

[125] Forsberg, "The Debate over German Normality: A Normal German Debate?", James A. McAdams, "Germany after Unification: Normal at Last?" *World Politics* 49, no. 2 (1997).

[126] Hanns Maull, "Germany's Foreign Policy, Post-Kosovo: Still a 'Civilian Power'?" in *Germany as a Civilian Power? The Foreign Policy of the Berlin Republic*, ed. Sebastian Harnisch and Hanns Maull (Manchester; New York: Manchester University Press; Palgrave, 2001), Henning Tewes, "How Civilian? How Much Power? Germany and the Eastern Enlargement of NATO," in *Germany as a Civilian Power? The Foreign Policy of the Berlin Republic*, ed. Sebastian Harnisch and Hanns Maull (Manchester; New York: Manchester University Press; Palgrave, 2001), Timmins, "Germany: Solidarity without Adventures," 61. Overhaus, "German Foreign Policy and the Shadow of the Past," 29, Rudolf, "The Myth of the 'German Way': German Foreign Policy and Transatlantic Relations."

[127] Judith Siwert-Probst, "Traditional Institutions of Foreign Policy," in *Germany's New Foreign Policy: Decision-Making in an Interdependent World*, ed. Wolf-Dieter Eberwein and Karl Kaiser (Houndmills, Basingstoke, Hampshire ; New York: Palgrave, 2001), 31.

[128] Bartsch, "Foreign Policy Influence and Transnational Relations of Political Parties," 303.

[129] Dalgaard-Nielsen, "Gulf War: The German Resistance," 102, Lantis, *Strategic Dilemmas and the Evolution of German Foreign Policy since Unification*, 23-24, Longhurst, *Germany and the Use of Force*, 56.

[130] Lantis, *Strategic Dilemmas and the Evolution of German Foreign Policy since Unification*, 24.

[131] Dalgaard-Nielsen, "Gulf War: The German Resistance," 102.

[132] Lantis, *Strategic Dilemmas and the Evolution of German Foreign Policy since Unification*, 46-47.

[133] Dalgaard-Nielsen, "Gulf War: The German Resistance," 103, Lantis, *Strategic Dilemmas and the Evolution of German Foreign Policy since Unification*, 54-105, Longhurst, *Germany and the Use of Force*, 59-60.

[134] Hanns Maull, "Germany and the Use of Force: Still a Civilian Power?" (paper presented at the Workshop on Force, Order and Global Governance, Washington DC, July 1-2, 1999). See also Press release issued by the Federal Constitutional Court, No. 29/94 (Karlsruhe, Germany).

[135] Longhurst, *Germany and the Use of Force*, 64-65.

[136] Dalgaard-Nielsen, "Gulf War: The German Resistance," 103.

[137] Ibid.

[138] Erb, *German Foreign Policy: Navigating a New Era*, 164.

[139] Jürgen Habermas, "Ein Abgrund Von Trauer [an Abyss of Grief]," *Der Spiegel*, August 7, 1995.

[140] Longhurst, *Germany and the Use of Force*, 67-68.

[141] Ibid., 69.

[142] Dalgaard-Nielsen, "Gulf War: The German Resistance," 104.

[143] Considerable opposition remained domestically concerning the use of ground forces in Kosovo and the ruling SPD-Greens coalition would have likely opened up deep fissures in the ruling coalition. Mary Buckley and Sally N. Cummings, *Kosovo: Perceptions of War and Its Aftermath* (London; New York: Continuum, 2001).

[144] Longhurst, *Germany and the Use of Force*, 70-71.

[145] Erb, *German Foreign Policy: Navigating a New Era*, 167-74, Rudolf, "The Myth of the 'German Way': German Foreign Policy and Transatlantic Relations," 141.

[146] Dalgaard-Nielsen, "Gulf War: The German Resistance," 104.

[147] Erb, *German Foreign Policy: Navigating a New Era*, 174-75, Longhurst, *Germany and the Use of Force*, 78-80.

[148] Dalgaard-Nielsen, "Gulf War: The German Resistance," 107.

[149] "Germany: Berlin Greens Reject Bundeswehr Participation in Afghanistan War," *DDP News Agency*, November 8, 2003.

[150] H Harnisch, "German Non-Proliferation Policy and the Iraq Conflict," 6-7.

[151] Erb, *German Foreign Policy: Navigating a New Era*, 202, Longhurst, *Germany and the Use of Force*, 86.

[152] David P. Conradt, *The German Polity*, 6th ed. (White Plains, N.Y.: Longman, 1996), 195.

[153] Malici, "Germans as Venutians: The Culture of German Foreign Policy Behavior."

[154] Joachim Krause, "The Role of the Bundestag in German Foreign Policy," in *Germany's New Foreign Policy: Decision-Making in an Interdependent World*, ed. Wolf-Dieter Eberwein and Karl Kaiser (Houndmills, Basingstoke, Hampshire; New York: Palgrave, 2001), 159.

[155] Erb, *German Foreign Policy: Navigating a New Era*, 191.

[156] Krause, "The Role of the Bundestag in German Foreign Policy," 162.

[157] Longhurst, *Germany and the Use of Force*, 79.

[158] Walker, "The Winter of Germany's Discontent," 42-43. Conradt, *The German Polity*.

[159] Bartsch, "Foreign Policy Influence and Transnational Relations of Political Parties," 196.

[160] "Election Will Not Change German Opposition to War, Says Foreign Minister," *DDP News Agency*, September 16, 2002, "German Foreign Minister Considers UN Mandate for Iraq Strike Unlikely," *DDP News Agency*, August 7, 2002.

[161] Siwert-Probst, "Traditional Institutions of Foreign Policy," 20.

[162] Weak coalition governments tend to act aggressively on foreign policy issues in order to demonstrate the government's ability to cope with policy crises and thereby attain some legitimacy domestically. See Joe D. Hagan, *Political Opposition and Foreign Policy in Comparative Perspective* (Boulder, Colo.: L. Rienner, 1993), Juliet Kaarbo and Ryan K. Beasley, "Taking It to the Extreme: The Effect of Coalition Cabinets on Foreign Policy," *Foreign Policy Analysis* 4, no. 1 (2008), Jack S. Levy, "The Diversionary Theory of War: A Critique," in *Handbook of War Studies*, ed. Manus I. Midlarsky (Boston: Unwin Hyman, 1989), Brandon C. Prins and Christopher Sprecher, "Institutional Constraints, Political Opposition, and Interstate Dispute Escalation: Evidence from Parlimentary Systems, 1946-1989," *Journal of Peace Research* 36, no. 2 (1999).

[163] Forsberg, "German Foreign Policy and the War on Iraq: Anti-Americanism, Pacifism or Emancipation," 226.

[164] Hogwood, "The Chancellor-Candidates and the Campaign."

[165] Geoffrey K. Roberts, *German Electoral Politics*, Issues in German Politics (Manchester; New York: Manchester University Press; Palgrave, 2006), 94-97.

[166] Major polling organizations showed the Christian Democratic Union (CDU)/Christian Social Union (CSU) with 38 to 40 percent and the SPD with between 33 and 36 percent in early July 2002. More alarming the SPD trailed in its power center, the state of North Rhine—Westphalia. At the end of July, just before the launch of the anti-Iraq campaign, the SPD lost another 5 points in the polls and the opposition had gained 2 points, so that the SPD was trailing the CDU/CSU by a margin of 43 to 35 percent. Szabo, *Parting Ways: The Crisis in German-American Relations*, 161-62.

[167] Hogwood, "The Chancellor-Candidates and the Campaign," 251.

[168] Ibid., 253.

[169] Roberts, *German Electoral Politics*, 95. Erb, *German Foreign Policy: Navigating a New Era*, Harnisch, "German Non-Proliferation Policy and the Iraq Conflict," 204-05.

[170] Szabo, *Parting Ways: The Crisis in German-American Relations*, 21-22.

[171] Harnisch, "German Non-Proliferation Policy and the Iraq Conflict," 10.

[172] Quoted in Szabo, *Parting Ways: The Crisis in German-American Relations*, 23. Forsberg, "German Foreign Policy and the War on Iraq: Anti-Americanism, Pacifism or Emancipation," 218, "Gerhard Schröder Auf Anti-Amerika Kurs [Gerhard Schröder on an Anti-American Course]."

[173] "German Opposition Critical of Government Stance on Iraq."

[174] "German Ministers Repeat Opposition to Military Intervention in Iraq," *DDP News Agency*, August 9, 2002.

[175] Quoted in Szabo, *Parting Ways: The Crisis in German-American Relations*, 23.

[176] Chandler, "Foreign and European Policy Issues in the 2002 Bundestag Elections," Forsberg, "German Foreign Policy and the War on Iraq: Anti-Americanism, Pacifism or Emancipation," 218. White House, *Vice President Speaks at VFW 103rd National Convention.*

[177] Walker, "The Winter of Germany's Discontent," 37.

[178] Szabo, *Parting Ways: The Crisis in German-American Relations*, 24-25.

[179] Quoted in Harnisch, "German Non-Proliferation Policy and the Iraq Conflict," 11. See also Erlanger, "German Leader's Warning: War Plan Is a Huge Mistake; Perspectives -- Sept. 11 and Beyond: Gerhard Schroder," Horsley, *Foreign Policy Works for Schroeder.*

[180] Erb, *German Foreign Policy: Navigating a New Era*, 205-06.

[181] Harnisch, "German Non-Proliferation Policy and the Iraq Conflict."

[182] Chandler, "Foreign and European Policy Issues in the 2002 Bundestag Elections," 169.

[183] Ibid.

[184] Hogwood, "The Chancellor-Candidates and the Campaign," Roberts, *German Electoral Politics.*

[185] Quoted in Szabo, *Parting Ways: The Crisis in German-American Relations*, 79-80.

[186] Chandler, "Foreign and European Policy Issues in the 2002 Bundestag Elections," Hogwood, "The Chancellor-Candidates and the Campaign."

[187] Szabo, *Parting Ways: The Crisis in German-American Relations*, 34.

[188] During an election, the accountability to the electorate is likely to overshadow foreign policy options; the executive's core reelection constituency can hold him directly responsible for foreign policy behavior. See David P. Auerswald, *Disarmed Democracies: Domestic Institutions and the Use of Force* (Ann Arbor: University of Michigan Press, 2000), 19-21, Bruce Bueno de Mesquita, *The Logic of Political Survival* (Cambridge, Mass.: MIT Press, 2003), Kurt Taylor Gaubatz, "Election Cycles and War," *Journal of Conflict Resolution* 35, no. 2 (1991), Philip G. Roeder, *Red Sunset: The Failure of Soviet Politics* (Princeton, N.J.: Princeton University Press, 1993).

[189] "German Greens Back Schroeder's Iraq Stance, Accept "Alliance Obligations"," *Welt am Sonntag*, February 24, 2003.

[190] Gerhard Schröder, "German Leader Rejects Idea of More Help for Iraq," *Der Spiegel*, November 24, 2003.

[191] Forsberg, "German Foreign Policy and the War on Iraq: Anti-Americanism, Pacifism or Emancipation," 220.

[192] *The List: Who's Left in Afghanistan?*

[193] David P. Auerswald, Stephen M. Saideman, and Michael J. Tierney, "Caveat Emptor! National Oversight and Military Operations in Afghanistan," *American Political Science Association National Meeting* (Chicago: American Political Science Association, 2007).

[194] Longhurst, *Germany and the Use of Force*, 94.

[195] Harnisch, "German Non-Proliferation Policy and the Iraq Conflict."

[196] Auerswald, *Disarmed Democracies: Domestic Institutions and the Use of Force*.

[197] Herbert P. Kitschelt, "Political Opportunity Structures and Political Protest: Anti-Nuclear Movements in Four Democracies," *British Journal of Political Science* 16, no. 1 (1986), Susan Peterson, *Crisis Bargaining and the State: The Domestic Politics of International Conflict* (Ann Arbor: University of Michigan Press, 1996).

[198] Brandice Canes-Wrone, "The Public Presidency, Personal Approval Ratings, and Policy Making," *Political Science Quarterly* 34, no. 3 (2004), David R. Mayhew, *Congress: The Electoral Connection*, 2nd ed. (New Haven: Yale University Press, 2006).

[199] Statement of the Minister of the Interior, Otto Schily, during press conference of issuing the "Verfassungschutzbericht 2003" at May 17, 2004.

[200] This statistic includes those Germans who died in the World Trade Center on 9/11, and in the terrorist bombings in recent years in Bali, Djerba/Tunisia etc. Eleven Germans are believed to have died in the World Trade Center attack. The bombing of a Tunisian synagogue in April 2002, reportedly linked to Al Qaeda, killed 21 people, including 14 Germans. See Francis T. Miko and Christian Froehlich, "Germany's Role in Fighting Terrorism: Implications for U.S. Policy" *CRS Report for Congress RL32710* (Washington DC: Congressional Research Service, The Library of Congress, 2004), 9.

[201] Ibid., 4.

[202] Ibid., 12.

[203] "German Minister Says Iraq Poses No Threat," *Die Welt*, February 19, 2003, "Germany's Fischer Unconvinced of Direct Threat from Iraq," *DDP News Agency*, February 8, 2003.

[204] Szabo, *Parting Ways: The Crisis in German-American Relations*, 45.

[205] Ibid., 45-46.

[206] "German Intelligence Says Iraq Rearming 'Massively'," *Die Welt*, February 23, 2001, Harnisch, "German Non-Proliferation Policy and the Iraq Conflict," 6.

[207] Walker, "The Winter of Germany's Discontent," 39.

[208] Joschka Fischer, "German Foreign Minister Reiterates View on Iraq, Says Peace Hopes Diminishing," *Der Spiegel*, December 30, 2002.

[209] Joschka Fischer, "Solving Mideast Conflict Should Be Priority, Not Iraq," *Frankfurter Rundschau*, September 12, 2002.

[210] Erlanger, "German Leader's Warning: War Plan Is a Huge Mistake; Perspectives -- Sept. 11 and Beyond: Gerhard Schroder."

[211] Siwert-Probst, "Traditional Institutions of Foreign Policy," 31.

[212] Erb, *German Foreign Policy: Navigating a New Era*, 204.

[213] Gerhard Schröder, "Rücktritt Wäre Flucht, Dazu Neige Ich Nicht [to Step Down Would Be an Escape, That Is Not My Inclination]," *Der Stern*, February 13, 2003.

[214] R.W. Apple, "Bonn and Tokyo Are Criticized for Not Bearing More of Gulf Cost," *The New York Times*, September 13, 1990. Hellmann, "Absorbing

Shocks and Mounting Checks: Germany and Alliance Burden Sharing in the Gulf War."

[215] Hellmann, "Absorbing Shocks and Mounting Checks: Germany and Alliance Burden Sharing in the Gulf War," 174-76.

[216] Gunther Hellmann et al., "De-Europeanization by Default? Germany's EU Policy in Defense and Asylum," *Foreign Policy Analysis* 1, no. 1 (2005).

[217] Borchert and Hampton, "The Lessons of Kosovo: Boon or Bust for Transatlantic Security," Szabo, *Parting Ways: The Crisis in German-American Relations*, 130.

[218] Beverly Crawford, "Explaining Defection from International Cooperation: Germany's Unilateral Recognition of Croatia," *World Politics* 48, no. 4 (1996).

[219] Forsberg, "German Foreign Policy and the War on Iraq: Anti-Americanism, Pacifism or Emancipation," 218.

[220] "German Chancellor Warns against War on Iraq," *DDP News Agency*, August 3, 2002.

[221] Thomas Fuller, *Romania Dangles Use of a Sea Base to Woo U.S.* (2003 [cited January 11, 2008]); available from http://www.iht.com/articles/2003/06/18/romania_ed3_.php.

[222] Szabo, *Parting Ways: The Crisis in German-American Relations*, 125.

[223] Douglas Jehl, "A Region Inflamed: The Reconstruction; Pentagon Bars Three Nations from Iraq Bids," *The New York Times*, December 10, 2003.

[224] Robert E. Venkus, *Raid on Qaddafi: The Untold Story of History's Longest Fighter Mission by the Pilot Who Directed It*, 1st ed. (New York: St. Martin's Press, 1992).

[225] Blome and Krauel, "Gerhard and George," John Vincour, "Berlin Says Europeans Need Close Bond to U.S.," *International Herald Tribune*, July 17, 2004.

[226] Richard Bernstein, "The German Question," *The New York Times*, May 2, 2004.

[227] See "Military Contributions" earlier.

[228] Martinsen, "The End of the Affair? Germany's Relationship with France," 409.

[229] Thomas U. Berger, *Cultures of Antimilitarism: National Security in Germany and Japan* (Baltimore, Md.: The Johns Hopkins University Press, 1998), 171-77.

[230] Andrew Bennett, Joseph Lepgold, and Danny Unger, eds., *Friends in Need: Burden Sharing in the Persian Gulf War*, Erb, *German Foreign Policy: Navigating a New Era.*

[231] Jonathon Steele, "Germany's Cast Iron Chancellor: Schroder Is Determined to Keep out of Any US War with Iraq," *The Guardian*, December 3, 2002, "German Official Downplays Row with USA over Iraq," *La Stampa*, September 26, 2002, Hannah Cleaver, "Stoiber Accuses 'Isolated' Schroder," *The Daily Telegraph*, September 18, 2002.

[232] Erlanger, "German Leader's Warning: War Plan Is a Huge Mistake; Perspectives -- Sept. 11 and Beyond: Gerhard Schroder."

[233] Conradt, *The German Polity*, 200.

[234] Szabo, *Parting Ways: The Crisis in German-American Relations*, 86.

[235] G. John Ikenberry, *After Victory: Institutions, Strategic Restraint, and the Rebuilding of Order after Major Wars*, Princeton Studies in International History and Politics (Princeton: Princeton University Press, 2001).

[236] Inis L. Claude, Jr., "Collective Legitimization as a Political Function of the United Nations," *International Organization* 20, no. 3 (1966), 370.

[237] Ibid., 367.

[238] Hall Gardner, *American Global Strategy and The "War on Terrorism"* (Burlington, VT: Ashgate, 2005), 176.

[239] Gernot Erler, *Political Principles of the German Engagement in International Peace Missions* (German Federal Foreign Office [Auswärtiges Amt], 2007 [cited June 25, 2008]); available from http://www.auswaertiges-amt.de/diplo/en/Infoservice/Presse/Rede/2007/070206-ErlerVN.html.

[240] Overhaus, "German Foreign Policy and the Shadow of the Past," 31.

[241] Gordon, "German Intelligence Gave U.S. Iraqi Defense Plan, Report Says."

[242] Auerswald, *Disarmed Democracies: Domestic Institutions and the Use of Force*, 19-20, Roeder, *Red Sunset: The Failure of Soviet Politics*, 25-27.

[243] Szabo, *Parting Ways: The Crisis in German-American Relations*, 23.

[244] Quoted in Rudolf, "The Myth of the 'German Way': German Foreign Policy and Transatlantic Relations."

[245] Szabo, *Parting Ways: The Crisis in German-American Relations*, 153.

[246] Gordon, "German Intelligence Gave U.S. Iraqi Defense Plan, Report Says."

# 4
# Turkey: Involuntary Defection and Eventual Rapprochement

The Bush administration's inability to win Ankara's approval for a northern front in the Iraq War significantly affected U.S. Iraq war plans and dealt a serious blow to U.S.-Turkish relations. The Turkish parliament's failure, after months of negotiations, to grant U.S. ground forces access necessary to launch a direct land assault against northern Iraq struck a blow to the Bush administration's military plan and added an additional political disappointment to the "coalition of the willing."[1] The Bush administration expected cooperation from the only NATO ally bordering Iraq and instead regarded the Turkish parliament's vote opposing vote as tantamount to betrayal.[2] Turkish commentators saw the vote as an example of democracy in action, but the result for Turkey was lost influence with the United States over Turkish vital interests regarding the Kurdish north in Iraq. This level of support contrasts sharply with Turkey's assistance to the 1991 Gulf War coalition. In that conflict, Turkish President Turgut Özal pursued active regional diplomacy to mobilize Middle Eastern support and allowed use of Turkish airbases for U.S. strikes into Iraq.[3]

General Tommy Franks, commander of U.S. Central Command (CENTCOM) and leader of the coalition military effort, considered a northern front through Turkey to be critical for military success. A coalition invasion from the north would compel Iraq to divide its attention and resources, easing the U.S. main thrust from Kuwait in the south. Lieutenant General David McKiernan, Franks' commander for the Iraq invasion, argued it was worth spending a "national blue chip" to get basing approval for a minimum force of 35,000 troops departing from Turkey for northern Iraq.[4] Taking the advice of its military commanders, the Bush administration aggressively pursued a strategy to base up to 90,000 soldiers in southern Turkey to support a northern front in Iraq. Militarily, a two-front invasion was considered essential for successful prosecution of the war.

In addition to this operational necessity, the United States needed to gain Turkish support for military action—as the only NATO ally bordering Iraq, and a secular state with a predominantly Muslim population—to help solidify international coalition-building efforts.[5] The bargaining delays from October 2002 through February 2003, and subsequent failure on March 1 of the *Türkiye Büyük Millet Meclisi* (TBMM, or Turkish Grand National Assembly) to approve the bargained use of Turkish territory, emerged as a crucial turning point in the U.S. coalition buildup for the Iraq war. Turkey accomplished with a single vote what France, Germany, Russia and other nations failed to achieve in months of UN negotiations: a change in U.S. war plans.[6]

Turkey's rejection was especially surprising to administration officials given Turkey's otherwise loyal support of U.S. military actions since the Korean War. For most of the 1990s, the basing of British and American aircraft at Incirlik Air Base to enforce the northern no fly zone over Iraq was one of the major policy anchors designed to contain Saddam Hussein.[7] At the time the United States requested support for an Iraq War, Turkey was already providing significant military support to U.S.-led efforts in Afghanistan. Turkey sent a general officer to CENTCOM Headquarters and an additional liaison team to U.S. European Command (EUCOM) Headquarters to coordinate efforts in the war on terrorism. Moreover, Turkey sent 90 Special Forces troops to Afghanistan to train the Northern Alliance, and Turkish ships in the Mediterranean and Adriatic shadowed, interdicted, and boarded vessels suspected of supporting the Taliban and al Qaeda. After the fall of the Taliban, Turkey sent 1,500 troops to join and eventually command the 5,000 person NATO International Security Assistance Force (ISAF). Finally, Turkey froze al Qaeda assets and arrested al Qaeda operatives en route from Iran to instigate terrorist attacks on Israel.[8] Turkey had proven to be a worthy supporter in the Global War on Terrorism and the United States expected little resistance to its requests to base U.S. troops from Turkish soil.

The TBMM refusal was especially surprising given that Washington and Ankara had negotiated a memorandum of agreement outlining Turkey's support in any possible military operation against Iraq, and Parliament had already approved a resolution on February 6 allowing U.S. troops to modernize Turkish ports and airfields in anticipation of the upcoming invasion.[9] Ruling Justice and Development Party (*Adalet ve Kalkınma Partisi*, AKP) leader Recep Tayyip Erdoğan had promised administration officials that he could deliver the necessary votes in

Parliament supporting the effort.[10] Unfortunately for U.S. plans, the TBMM failed to pass the resolution by a slim margin. Bush administration officials labeled the March 1 referendum as a "stab-in-the-back." U.S. Deputy Secretary of Defense Paul Wolfowitz expressed the administration's "disappointment" with harsh words claiming that the Turkish military did not show "leadership" by steering the government to support the United States in the second Iraq War.[11] Turkish commentators responded that, "We did something not even the British Parliament, the cradle of democracy, was able to do. We voted with the public, against a war."[12]

While Turkey's concerns about the Kurdish north weighed heavily in its calculations, Turkey's rejection of the U.S. plan actually limited Turkish influence over policy concerning northern Iraq and presented Turkey with a problem as to how to shape future events in that strategic area.[13] Erdoğan attempted to regain Turkish influence through multiple engagement opportunities with the United States after the war commenced, but these efforts were stifled due to external events. Erdoğan offered to resubmit the failed resolution to parliament after his government was seated, but this effort would not meet the U.S. timeline for invasion. Later in the year, when the United States requested international assistance in maintaining security in Iraq, Turkey pledged troops and passed a resolution authorizing their deployment to Iraq. Unfortunately, Kurdish elements in the fledgling Iraqi government stifled these efforts, fearing the influence of a Turkish intervention.[14] Turkey's initial rejection of the U.S. war plan was widely popular domestically, but left Turkey vulnerable to U.S. interests in the Kurdish north of Iraq.

Given Turkey's robust support of past U.S. military efforts, and its incentives to work with the U.S. to protect its interests in northern Iraq, why did the Grand National Assembly refuse a substantial aid package to remain on the sidelines of the Iraq war and thus risk U.S. condemnation? Why was the usually centrally controlled government unable to garner the support for the memorandum of understanding negotiated with the United States, especially after the United States had significantly improved Turkish infrastructure to support the war? Turkey's support in the second Iraq War stands in stark contrast to the basing support provided in the first conflict. This chapter will show that Turkish domestic politics changed significantly between the first and second Iraq Wars and especially between October 2002 and February 2003, making coalition support more difficult for a weak Justice and Development Party. Turkey's domestic structure moved from one with little accountability to the public to one highly influenced by domestic opinion. Erdoğan's inability to pass the resolution authorizing the United States to use Turkey as a staging point reflected his weakness vis-à-vis parliament and the inexperience of his administration.

## The Timing, Size, and Mix of Turkey's Contributions

Turkey's support of the coalition in the 2003 Iraq War was minimal compared to the military assistance that it provided during the 1991 Persian Gulf War. Although Turkish officials tentatively agreed to massive U.S. requests supporting the war plan, the government pursued a dual track strategy of protracted negotiations, delaying U.S. support while negotiating for a regional settlement short of war. Turkey's delay caused the United States to deploy a large number of troops through Kuwait, rather than pushing Iraqi forces from both the north and south.[15] In the end, Turkish support for the coalition was well below U.S. requests and initially reflected Ankara's desire to "keep its distance" from the conflict, however, it soon realized that it would lose influence over U.S.-Kurdish policy if it did not become a coalition partner.

In contrast, Turkey's contribution to the first Gulf War was critical to the military success of Operation Desert Storm. Although Turkey initially responded to U.S. requests with caution in 1990, it eventually became a full supporter of international efforts against the Hussein regime.[16] At considerable economic cost, Turkey terminated the flow of Iraqi oil exports through Turkish pipelines, thus enforcing UN economic sanctions against Baghdad. It deployed about 150,000 troops along its border with Iraq, causing Baghdad to divert an equivalent number of forces from the south to the north of the country. Furthermore, Turkey authorized unrestricted use of the military air base at Incirlik for raids over Iraq.[17] Finally, Turkey also provided considerable diplomatic support in the international community by robustly supporting George H.W. Bush's initiatives in the UN and regional forums. Unfortunately, economic sanctions against Iraq devastated the Turkish economy and international compensation failed to meet President Özal's war dividend promises.

Turkey's contribution to the anti-Iraq coalition of 2003 demonstrates the tension between intense external pressure for coalition support from a dominant ally and domestic pressure for non-involvement. Turkey's initial reaction to Bush administration efforts for support constituted a two-level game balancing domestic concerns for the war's economic and security impact against the desire to remain within a superpower's good graces.[18] For the fledgling government elected by a disgruntled populace in November 2002, U.S. demands for basing rights for a northern invasion route to Iraq provided a profound political burden. External factors dictated a need to support the U.S. campaign against Saddam Hussein, but domestic political pressures were definitive, with 80 to 90 percent of the Turkish public opposed to war with Iraq.[19] This level of domestic animosity is consistent with the public disapproval towards external intervention in Iraq.[20] Ankara's response was to pursue two foreign policy tracks of continuing to lobby against war on the one hand—which included regionally-based endeavors to find alternatives to it—and positioning Turkey to make the best of an unwanted situation on the other.[21]

U.S. military requests to Turkey were enormous, far more than in the first Gulf War, involving an unprecedented massive deployment of foreign soldiers to Turkish soil. Initial requests placed the number of U.S. troops at 90,000.[22] After lengthy negotiations with the Gül government and numerous revisions of the war plan, this request was eventually adjusted down to 62,000 soldiers.[23] The final request would have created a force that could advance on Baghdad from the north while a larger U.S. force based in Kuwait moved up from the south. This two-pronged assault, American officials argued, would shorten any war with Saddam Hussein, minimizing U.S. and coalition casualties.[24]

Turkish concerns throughout negotiation with the United States were twofold. First, the overthrow of Saddam might allow the Iraqi Kurds to form their own state and capture the important oil-producing centre of Kirkuk, thus re-igniting the Kurdish separatist movement within Turkey. Second, the war and trade disruption would bring a second round of economic devastation to the state. To address Turkish reservations, the U.S. government conceded to allow Turkish troops to enter a limited zone in northern Iraq to prevent a flood of refugees into Turkey, secure its border, and effectively pressure Iraqi Kurds. The United States also promised Turkey a massive financial aid package worth up to $6 billion in grants and $24 billion in loan guarantees.[25] Despite intense domestic opposition, the Turkish government negotiated a memorandum of understanding with the United States that would allow the creation of a second front. To take effect, the plan had to be ratified by the TBMM, but due to inept handling of the parliamentary vote, this measure was rejected—very late for U.S. planning for the Iraq War—by a narrow margin on March 1.[26] The agreement would have allowed for a sizable Turkish military presence in Iraq and influence over Kurdish policy in the north.[27] After the initiation of war, Ankara realized that Turkey would have limited influence over Iraq policy and rapidly approved overflight rights for U.S. military aircraft on March 20 in an attempt to recover its standing with the United States.

Turks heralded the March 1 referendum as democracy in action, as civilians made a parliamentary decision based on an evaluation of public sentiment, without military intimidation.[28] In contrast, U.S. officials expressed disappointment that the Turkish armed forces had not exercised "the strong leadership role that we would have expected," by dictating a yes vote to the Justice and Development Party.[29] In the end, Turkey provided minimal logistical support to U.S. Special Forces in northern Iraq and allowed U.S. aircraft and missiles to transit Turkish airspace. The United States was restricted in the use of Incirlik airbase and could not use that facility to mount strikes against Iraq.

By the summer of 2003, the inability to restore order and stability in Iraq well after the end of formal hostilities led to increasing calls by the United States for Turkish assistance. The U.S. government authorized the potential release of $8.5 billion in credits without openly linking it to Turkish troop deployments in Iraq. In an effort to legitimize Turkish involvement in the eyes of the public, both the government and the military stressed that Turkey's role would be a humanitarian one emphasizing the restoration of public services. The Turkish parliament, on October 8, 2003, authorized a deployment of up to 15,000 troops to Iraq.[30]

### *Political Contributions*

In contrast to the first Gulf War, Turkey's pre-war political maneuvering in 2002-2003 undermined U.S. efforts to build a regional or international coalition. Before Operation Desert Storm, however, Turkey pursued active regional diplomacy to garner military and economic support from other Middle Eastern states. Turkey provided strong diplomatic support for the first Bush administration both in international forums such as the UN and in regional diplomatic initiatives. President Özal, the Turkish president and a former prime minister, personally emphasized the need for a strong, quick response, in reaction to the Iraqi aggression in Kuwait.[31] In contrast, Ankara's reaction to the second Bush administration was quite different politically and diplomatically. Early in the negotiation process, President Ahmet Necdet Sezer, a former president of the constitutional court in Turkey, and Prime Minister Bülent Ecevit actively opposed U.S. intervention without a clear international mandate and questioned Turkey's role in a second Gulf War. They based their stance not on legitimacy issues, but rather on the desire for Turkey to avoid the economic disruption posed by a war with Iraq. As early as January 2002, the Turkish government explained at great length the adversities a war would produce.[32] Ecevit warned, "northern Iraq is a serious problem for us. It could be used as a basis for partitioning in Turkey, as well."[33] Sezer's stance from the beginning was unequivocal, "Let us not enter war. This problem is not our problem. This war is not our war. Our military and government should also be opposed to this intervention."[34] In numerous encounters with the Bush administration, Bülent Ecevit's coalition government strenuously warned Washington of Turkey's opposition to war, while at the same time negotiating Turkey's price for support if war was inevitable.[35]

Elections in 2002 marked a significant change in Turkish government when voters threw out the governing parties and elected the fledgling, anti-establishment AKP. Interim Prime Minister Gül's approach was no more supportive of U.S. interests. While Turkey agreed with the United States that Iraq should be disarmed, it stressed a peaceful resolution to the crisis and added that a Security Council resolution was required in the use of force against Iraq.[36] Gül committed his personal prestige on a political solution short of war as vigorously as Özal sought to fulfill Bush administration objectives in 1991. Gül attempted to build a regional coalition to apply diplomatic pressure to Hussein. He traveled extensively with the aim of becoming a regional influence, and "exchanging views with the regional leaders on what we, as regional countries, can do to ease the recent tension and crisis in the region, and contribute to efforts to solve the problem without war."[37] Gül emphasized a regional diplomatic plan to the exclusion of U.S. diplomatic efforts towards a forceful strategy. Gül's approach was aimed at applying diplomatic pressure on Saddam to submit to weapons inspections while forging non-aggression agreements with Iran and Kuwait.[38] While Turkey agreed in principle that Iraq should be disarmed, it saw the UN impasse on a resolution to use force as vindication of its foreign policy approach.

To delay the U.S. deployment and forestall a war in Iraq, Gül and Sezer emphasized that a Security Council Resolution in addition to Resolution 1441 was required *before* a parliamentary vote allowing use of Turkish facilities.[39] They also reiterated that a parliamentary vote was required by Article 92 of the Turkish Constitution for non-NATO military operations.[40] By tying the Article 92 vote to an additional Security Council Resolution, Turkey effectively undermined an early deployment of U.S. troops to Turkey and the two-front strategy.[41]

Once it was clear that neither Saddam nor the U.S. coalition would be satisfied through diplomacy, Gül and Sezer believed Turkey could prevent a war by dragging out basing negotiations and voting no—if necessary—on the Article 92 resolution. "We tried very hard to prevent the war," acknowledged one senior Turkish official, speaking on condition of anonymity. "Many believed it was possible."[42] This view was reinforced by French, German, and Russian resistance to U.S. plans in the Security Council and through personal encouragement by French President Jacques Chirac to Gül. According to French officials, Turkey's reticence strengthened Chirac's efforts at the United Nations to continue inspections and avoid a war.[43]

Overall, Turkey's political efforts influenced the coalition negatively and undermined U.S. international efforts to apply coercive pressure on Iraq. Turkey's negotiating strategy had two serious negative effects on the second gulf coalition. First, Prime Minister Gül's whirlwind diplomatic tour to find an honorable exit for Saddam Hussein in January through early February 2003 weakened U.S. efforts to build strong consensus in the UN that force was necessary to disarm Iraq and that regime change was necessary.[44] Secondly, this effort sent the message to the Iraqi regime that the international community would not back the U.S. coalition and that the regime could weather the diplomatic barrage.

After the resolution was rejected, Erdoğan sought to submit the authorization bill to the TBMM again to gain U.S. credibility. In an attempt to avoid another parliamentary mishap, he planned to appeal to his party's parliamentary group after forming his government. The U.S. timetable, however, did not match Erdoğan's. President Bush declared war on Iraq before another resolution could be considered. Foreign Minister Gül contacted Colin Powell to coordinate with the U.S. government for a second resolution authorizing a northern front but Powell had already remarked to Congress that, "Our proposals to the Turkish government are no longer on the table."[45]

After President Bush declared an end to combat operations in May 2003, Turkey aggressively attempted to regain Washington's favor. Ankara realized that it would need to fully participate on Iraq policy with the United States in order to influence policy on the Kurdish north.[46] The first sign that Turkish-U.S. relations were normalizing occurred when Ankara lifted the restrictions it had imposed on the use of the Incirlik Airbase by U.S. aircraft. According to the June 24 Cabinet decision, which did not require the approval of the National Assembly, U.S. aircraft serving in Iraq were authorized to use both Incirlik Airbase and Sabiha Gokcen Airport for refueling, supplies, and other business. The lifting of restrictions at Incirlik was the result of a Washington visit by Foreign Ministry Undersecretary Ugur Ziyal. U.S. officials stressed the need for Turkey to prove its strategic value to the United States and stated. "We are expecting a gesture to be made with respect to Incirlik."[47]

This early warming of relations was soon derailed by several diplomatic gaffes by the U.S. government. On July 6, in the northern Iraqi town of Suleymaniyah, U.S. soldiers and Kurdish paramilitary peshmergas captured 11 Turkish military officials suspected of planning violent activities. The Turks were transported to Baghdad initially and subjected to the same treatment as insurgents. Although eventually released, Ankara and the Turkish public were outraged by the U.S. treatment of the Turkish "allied" soldiers.[48] Turkish commentators noted that the incident reflects U.S. disdain for Turkey as a result of its failure to allow a northern front.[49] This incident coincided with U.S. requests for a Turkish brigade to support stabilization efforts in the Shiite region in southern Iraq.[50]

Despite the prisoner gaffe, Turkey was the first Islamic nation to pledge troops to assist the U.S.-led stabilization mission in Iraq. During the summer of 2003, Washington pursued a UN resolution authorizing a multinational stability mission, while at the same time requested support for a stability mission in Iraq under the auspices of the original invasion coalition. The U.S. government assured Turkey that the Iraqi Interim Government would support foreign ground forces to provide security within Iraq, and Turkey led the effort to form a regional Islamic coalition to take over security operations.[51] Turkey's goals were twofold: first, to gain influence over Iraq policy concerning an autonomous Kurdistan; and second, to broker an Islamic solution to Iraq and gain regional power status.[52] While at the same time negotiating with the U.S. government concerning military support for the stabilization of Iraq, Prime Minister Erdoğan tried to build an Islamic coalition to remove the United States from Iraq. Erdoğan told Iran and Gül told Pakistan: "Muslim countries should immediately go to Iraq in order to ensure that the United States withdraws from this country without any delay."[53] In October 2003, parliament gave Prime Minister Erdoğan permission to send troops into Iraq for up to one year, but the Iraqi Governing Council—with its members handpicked by the United States—rejected the idea and embarrassed Turkey. Iraq's Interim Governing Council responded by saying, "they do not want soldiers from neighboring countries meddling in their affairs".[54] The United States was left to build an occupying coalition from states such as South Korea and Poland that historically had no direct influence in Iraq, and Turkey was left without direct influence on Iraqi policy.

Once it was clear that Turkish ground forces would not be welcome in Iraq, Ankara pursued two policy objectives vis-à-vis Iraq. First,

Turkey supported efforts for the Iraqi government to maintain central control over Iraqi territory. In the aftermath of the failed 1991 uprisings in Iraq against Saddam Hussein the UN established no fly zones in Kurdish areas of Iraq giving those areas de facto independence. The separatist Kurdish guerrilla group, the Kurdistan Workers Party (PKK), operating from their safe haven in Iraq, launched an armed campaign in Turkey resulting in more than 30,000 deaths in their quest for independence. Turkey was concerned that a successful, independent Kurdish Autonomous region would re-ignite Kurdish dissent in Turkey. As a result of this concern, Erdoğan established "red lines" bilaterally with the Bush administration concerning the fate of Kirkuk—in northern Iraq—and the distribution of Iraqi oil revenue.[55] Ankara was critical of Iraq's January 2005 elections and argued that Kurds were being relocated to Kirkuk to skew election results. In a letter sent to UN Secretary General Kofi Annan, Gül stated that efforts to make demographic changes in Kirkuk were rapidly continuing. He wrote, "It is worrying that certain political groups have been tampering with demographics of Kirkuk, to claim supremacy of power through elections."[56] Gül noted that this was part of a larger effort to turn the elections into a referendum for independence in Northern Iraq. Prime Minister Erdoğan raised the same concerns at the World Economic Summit in Davos, "There is an issue of transferring populations. This development constitutes the first sign of a negative development for Iraq's future."[57] Secondly, Ankara pursued a strategy to eliminate the PKK as a threat. In October 2003, Ankara and Washington agreed to a joint action plan employing political, economic, and legal means to discredit the PKK. Part of the U.S. package was an $8.5 billion loan package to Turkey, contingent that Turkey would not intervene unilaterally action in Iraq.[58] Despite this package, the Bush administration was reluctant to use military force against the PKK, since Kurdish forces supported the Iraq invasion, even though the Kurdish rebels re-engaged in hostilities with Turkey in June 2004.

Turkish diplomatic efforts after the initiation of the war were largely supportive of U.S. efforts, except concerning the disposition of Kirkuk. Turkey supported the formation of a multinational peacekeeping coalition, encouraged Muslim support in the coalition to build a regional focus to rebuilding Iraq, and supported efforts to build a credible Iraqi government. Turkey actively engaged the international community supporting the interests of Turkmen and Sunni populations as a method to increase the strength and legitimacy of the Iraqi central government. Any effort to increase the Kurdish presence in Kirkuk, however, was seen as an effort to gain the oil regions of the north and eventually build an autonomous Kurdish state.

### *Economic Contributions*

Prior to the implementation of economic sanctions in 1991, Turkey was one of Iraq's major trading partners, with total trade between the two countries valued at about $3 billion per year. Despite this favorable trade relationship, Turkey aggressively implemented UN mandated sanctions in the first Gulf War to the detriment of the Turkish economy. Turkish firms reportedly reengaged with Iraq in the mid-1990s under the UN sponsored Oil for Food Program (OFFP). Oil trade grew to a value of $340 million in 2002, making Turkey Iraq's seventh-largest supplier under the UN program.[59] No additional economic sanctions were authorized by the Security Council or encouraged by the United States in the build-up to the second Gulf War.

Turkey's economic support to Iraq exists mainly in the form of business development, rather than grants or loans through the Iraq Reconstruction Fund. Turkey's unique geographic position marks it as the gateway for European support for and trade with Iraq. No other major economies border northern Iraq—with the exception of Iran—and due to the disruption of the war, significant trade flows shifted through Turkey.[60] Northern Iraq continues to be highly dependent on supplies coming from Turkey over the Habur Bridge in the east of the country, which carries 1,000 trucks a day.[61] Economic flow through Turkey supports U.S. policy in the north and allows Turkey to have some economic influence over Kurdish policy.[62] About 80 per cent of foreign investment in Kurdistan now comes from Turkey. In Dohuk, the largest city in northwestern Kurdistan, the seven largest infrastructure and investment projects are being built by Turkish construction companies. Turkish investors are also building three large housing projects, including a $400 million venture that will feature 1,800 apartments as well as a health clinic, school, gas station, and shopping center. At the construction site for a 15-story office building in central Dohuk, all of the engineers and managers are Turkish, as are dozens of laborers.[63] By May 2005, trade with northern Iraq had recovered to the point that Turkish state minister Kursat Tuzmen set an annual trade target of $10 billion.[64] Turkey did not economically support the initial coalition effort, but they subsequently contributed $50 million to the reconstruction and stabilization effort.[65]

### Military Contributions

Although the Turkish government did not allow the United States to open a northern front in the Iraq war, Turkey did provide minimal assistance to the military campaign. Turkey was the transit point for Central Intelligence Agency and Special Operations Forces that were operating in Kurdish regions before the war.[66] Turkey allowed special action teams to build a resistance effort in Kurdish regions of northern Iraq, while also maintaining surveillance on U.S. actions to ensure that a Kurdish republic was not created. The intelligence provided by the action teams allowed the U.S. military to precisely target elements of the Hussein regime.[67] Turkey allowed passage of special operations teams and U.S. diplomats to coordinate coalition support for the main Kurdish parties, the Patriotic Union of Kurdistan (PUK) and the Kurdistan Democratic Party (KDP) in an attempt to influence policy on northern Iraq.

Much like the first Gulf War, Turkey did eventually support coalition use of its airspace, but it remained short of the basing rights it provided in 1991. After the U.S. declaration of war, U.S. Secretary of State Powell coordinated with the Gül for the use of the Incirlik Air Base and an air corridor and offered $1 billion in U.S. compensation. Gül once again attempted to link the request with full military cooperation in northern Iraq. Not willing to cede influence in northern Iraq, Powell responded that the U.S. request would be only for use of Turkish airspace.[68] Turkey hurriedly passed a third motion in parliament—without the prerequisite UN mandate—opening Turkish airspace to U.S. and coalition aircraft and missiles on March 20, 2003, the first day of combat operations.[69] This rapid about face reflected the perception that Turkey had "missed the train" concerning Iraq and needed an issue to gain leverage over U.S. policy in northern Iraq.[70] Ultimately, American airplanes flew more than 4,000 sorties over Turkey into Iraq. In January 2004, Ankara expanded U.S. use of Incirlik to allow the largest rotation of troops in U.S. history. President Bush responded by noting that Turkey was "a friend and important ally."[71]

Turkey also provided logistical support to the small coalition ground presence in northern Iraq. For example, at the onset of the Iraq campaign on March 27, Turkey allowed the transit of 204 vehicles into northern Iraq to support U.S. forces that had been airlifted into the north.[72]

Turkish contributions initially could be classified as outcome 3, "no contribution in areas with public or state opposition" in the burden sharing decision model. Gül's diplomatic effort failed, and the impression that "there can be no war with Turkey" had turned out wrong. Once the government finally realized that war was inevitable, they made efforts to join the military coalition, but found that they were too late. Prime Minister Erdoğan recognized, "we missed the train."[73] U.S. forces had already redeployed south and the coalition proceeded with "Plan B." Turkey subsequently tried to join the stabilizing coalition in Iraq at U.S. urging, but was barred from joining the military coalition by Kurdish elements in the Iraqi Interim Government who feared Turkish influence in the north.[74] Overall, Turkish contribution is initially categorized as a case of a state "keeping its distance." Turkey was not free-riding on U.S. contributions, but rather, thought the effort would be contrary to its interests. Once it was clear that the U.S. would unseat the regime in Iraq, Turkey changed its strategy to support the coalition in areas that were palatable to the public. In this manner, Turkey's contribution reflected Outcome 2 on the burden sharing model, "contribution in area with public or state support," where it "reflected its preferences and paid up."

## Explaining Turkey's Contributions

Turkey's contribution to the Iraq War can be explained by the convergence of domestic politics with the elite learning experience from the first Gulf War. These factors—combined with traditional elements of Turkish foreign policy, such as noninvolvement in regional conflicts and cultivation of economic relations with Iraq—constrained Turkish support to U.S. coalition access to a northern front. The key difference between the first and second war was the lack of support by a strong leader, who could unite factions in the TBMM and government. In 2003, policy was much more constrained by the legislature and public opinion.

In 1991, President Özal seized the opportunity for Turkey to play an active role in the Gulf coalition. He saw the Iraq War as a chance to assert Turkey's geopolitical significance at a time when it was in question, considering the decline in the Soviet Union. Many observers in Turkey were less than enthusiastic about Turkish participation in the 1991 Gulf War, including senior elements of the Turkish military. President Özal, however, saw a chance for Turkey to secure a seat at the table after Baghdad's defeat.[75] Support of U.S. coalition efforts, however, directly conflicted with Turkish elite and public opinion that questioned direct Turkish involvement where no clear Turkish national interests seemed to be at stake. Özal, however, was able to force the issue through parliament on promises of the future benefits for Turkey if it supported U.S. efforts in Iraq.[76] His approach caused numerous resignations within the government, including the foreign minister, defense minister, and military chief of staff.[77] Although the resignations cannot be directly attributed to Özal's policy in the Gulf crisis, they reflect the domestic opposition Özal countered.[78] Public opinion was decidedly against intervention, with 74 percent of the public opposed to Turkish support to the war effort.[79] Özal's ability to promote an aggressive foreign policy agenda despite these high-level resignations demonstrated his autonomy vis-à-vis the bureaucracy, parliament, and society. Bureaucratic politics and domestic bargaining did not significantly influence policy decisions affecting Turkey during the 1991 Gulf War.[80]

In 2003, however, the Turkish government was more responsive to public opinion and less supportive of U.S. intervention for two reasons. First, due to a proliferation of private television and radio, the government no longer had a monopoly on the dissemination of information and the shaping of public discourse. The government and military officials had to increasingly take its case to the public for support.[81] Second, due to the November 2002 general election, the ruling AKP party had to be more responsive to electoral concerns since it won only 34 per cent of the popular vote. The previous government's coalition suffered an unprecedented loss by losing *all* of its seats in parliament.[82] The administration was vulnerable to a vote of no confidence; therefore, the prime minister and president could not afford to take positions independent of the electorate without vigorously shaping public opinion. In the second Gulf War case, the United States did not see clear leadership advocating its position in Turkish domestic areas.[83]

### *Historical Learning*

Turkey's forward leaning stance in the first Gulf War left important and somewhat divergent lessons for both sides. In the United States, the experience of 1990-91 reinforced the image of Turkey as a strategic ally, at the forefront of new security challenges emanating from the Middle East—an impression Turkish policy makers sought to reinforce with American policy audiences. In Turkey, by contrast, the first Iraq conflict and the experience of operations Provide Comfort and Northern Watch were widely viewed as the place where the "trouble" started, including widespread economic devastation, PKK insurgency, more complicated relations with Syria and Iran, and more contentious relations with Washington.[84] Özal's promises of a war dividend failed to materialize after the first Gulf War. Turkey reaped neither economic benefits, a closer relationship to the West, nor influence in U.S.-Kurdish policy. The U.S. policy supporting an independent Kurdish enclave in northern Iraq ran counter to Turkish national interests. Finally, Turkey suffered immense losses in a Kurdish insurgency that was re-ignited by the first Gulf War.[85] This experience had an immense impact on the public and the decision making elite that resulted in a policy of limited involvement.

Far from the new strategic relationship Özal had envisioned, the Gulf War and its aftermath left a legacy of resentment in relations with the United States.[86] Economic sanctions against Iraq—as a result of the first Gulf conflict—devastated the Turkish economy and the international community failed to compensate the country adequately. Iraq had previously been one of Turkey's most important trading partners and its lost trade and other earnings were estimated to have cost the Turkish economy around $2 billion (USD) per year. In 1991, this loss was compensated by special payments of around $2.2 billion (USD), mainly from Kuwait and Saudi Arabia. However, financial compensation decreased rapidly and by the mid 1990s disappeared altogether.[87]

Loss of trade and commerce with the wider Middle East was also negatively affected by the war. Sanctions on Iraq closed lucrative routes for Turkish commodities to other markets, undermining Turkey's comparative advantage supplying the Gulf countries with agricultural products. Turkish exports to the Middle East dropped from 23 percent of its overall exports just before the war to 14 percent in 1996. A fleet of more than forty thousand trucks fell idle. By 1998, the foreign ministry put the revenue and trade loss due to Iraq sanctions at more than $35 billion.[88] Objectively, Turkey would have suffered many of these costs—even if it remained neutral in the Gulf War—the episode, however, left many Turks with a sense of disappointment and suspicion regarding American policy.[89]

Turkey also did not gain increased favor in U.S. foreign aid as promised by President Özal. Turkey was a long-term, major recipient of U.S. foreign aid through FY 1998. However, the Clinton administration did not request Foreign Military Financing (FMF) or Economic Support Funds (ESF) for FY 1999, arguing that Turkey had graduated from an assistance relationship to be more like other NATO members.[90] With compensation waning, elite and public opinion became critical of the costs of participation in the first coalition and of Turkey's failure to receive sufficient compensation from the West.[91] Cem Duna, a former Turkish ambassador to the European Union reflected the common sentiment, "Last time Turkey was taken for a ride, promises were made, none of which were kept, and Turkey suffered serious losses."[92]

As the second Gulf war approached, trade with Iraq was showing signs of recovery, therefore, the government was hesitant to plunge the country again into an economic disaster. By 2002, trade with Iraq totaled $1 billion annually because of the OFFP begun in December 1996, and a black market trade in Iraqi diesel and crude oil. Even during the UN imposed trade embargo, Turkey and Iraq were looking to reach pre-Gulf War trade levels of about $2.5 billion annually. The clean sweep of government in the 2002 elections showed that the voting public did not want to see Turkey's economic growth trend reversed.[93]

The first Iraq War also adversely affected Turkey's national security interest of countering Kurdish migration and independence. The Iraqi military operation, in late March 1991, against the Kurdish uprising in northern Iraq, precipitated one of the largest refugee crises in recent history. More than a million and a half mostly Kurdish refugees fled toward Iran and Turkey.[94] In the Turkish view, however, a more serious danger than the arrival of refugees was the establishment in northern Iraq of an autonomous Kurdish area within a federation. Operation Provide Comfort and Operation Northern Watch, two U.S. coalition efforts to protect the Kurds in northern Iraq, have led to a widely shared belief in Turkey that the U.S. supports the establishment of a Kurdish state at the expense of Turkey's territorial integrity.[95] Ankara saw the emergence of Kurdish administrative organs in northern Iraq (created to fill the gap left by the withdrawal of Iraqi central authorities) as a step toward the establishment of a de facto Kurdish state. Preventing such a development has long been a cornerstone of Turkish regional policy.

Ankara is concerned about the impact that Kurdish statehood would have on Turkey's own Kurdish population.[96] The post Gulf War power vacuum in northern Iraq created an environment that enabled the PKK to find safe havens from which they prosecuted a deadly insurgency against Ankara.[97] Turkey feared the birth of a Kurdish state in northern Iraq could serve as a model for Kurdish separatists in Anatolia. Therefore, the Turkish public and government elites took a hard line against the revolutionary secessionism of the PKK. The Turkish military fought a grueling insurgency to suppress Kurdish separatism in the southeast. Despite the loss of 30,000 lives, Turkey stood firm against Kurdish claims for self-determination. In Ankara's view, the Iraqi Kurdish self-governing arrangements pose a serious challenge to Turkey's hold over its own, equally sensitive Kurdish provinces. Ankara suspects that full independence and sovereignty is the ultimate goal of Kurds on both sides of the border and any moves towards the establishment of an independent Kurdish state would threaten to unravel the entire region.[98]

Due to the 1998 Washington Agreement between the KDP and PUK, Turkey considers U.S. efforts in northern Iraq questionable. The Washington Agreement called for a commitment to a federative Kurdish political entity within a pluralistic and democratic Iraq. Turkish political leaders, especially Deputy Prime Minister Bülent Ecevit, were embarrassed that Turkey had been absent from the final rounds of the negotiation and the signing of the agreement. They had the barely concealed suspicion that the agreement would open the way to eventual establishment of a Separate Kurdish state in northern Iraq.[99] As a result, Ankara warmed relations with Baghdad announcing that relations with Baghdad would be upgraded to the ambassadorial level. On the other hand, many in the Turkish military regard U.S. actions with suspicion despite decades of alliance. In the mid 1990s, many Turks came to see the U.S. as a less-than-reliable ally, and some Americans came to see Turkey as part ally, part rogue state.[100]

In retrospect, Turkey's lessons from the first Gulf War were hardly positive. With the end of U.S. security assistance, and with economic sanctions against Iraq still in place more than a decade after the invasion of Kuwait, many Turks feel that they had little to show for their cooperation with Washington in the Gulf. Most Turks believe that the post Gulf War power vacuum in northern Iraq created an environment that enabled the PKK to find safe havens and export its war in Turkey. The military resisted Turkish involvement in the second Iraq war because it was worried the United States might allow Iraqi Kurds to establish an independent state, losing the Turkish equivalent of the Vietnam War. The military succeeded in a protracted insurgency against the PKK and did not want to see their gains reversed in an independent Kurdish region. "This was our Vietnam War," said on military official. "The military took all risks, and at a high cost in lives, they finally succeeded. It was an expensive victory, and they don't want that victory to be wasted."[101] Turkey feared that a new war would lead to a power vacuum, the partition of Iraq and the birth of a Kurdish state in the north that could serve as a model for Turkish separatists seeking their own state in southeast Turkey.[102] Believing that they did not get fair compensation either politically or economically in the first Gulf War, the political elite used diplomacy to slow U.S. efforts while the military elite argued for a larger influence in Kurdish Iraq.

### *Collective Action*

In the first Gulf War, Turkey did not pursue a strategy of "free-riding" as predicted by the collective action hypothesis. Instead, it made several key contributions to the coalition that were disproportionately high compared to its capabilities.[103] Even though the first Bush administration made public its decision to send thousands of troops to Saudi Arabia, Turkey strongly supported with the deployment of 150,000 troops along the border with Iraq, and unreservedly participated in the economic embargo.

Although Turkey appears to be a collective action "free rider," in the Iraq War case, process-tracing evidence shows little evidence that burden sharing decisions were based on the collective action hypothesis. This paper identifies one collective good for the second Iraq War case: the disarmament of Iraqi offensive weapons of mass destruction (WMD). Research shows that Turkish elites were more concerned with the impact of war on the accessibility of private goods rather than the collective good pursued by the coalition. Turkey was not concerned with Iraqi WMD, but rather with the potential for a Kurdish revolt. Emin Sirin, one of dozens of lawmakers from the ruling Justice and Development Party who voted against U.S. deployment stated, "we had real security concerns about what Iraq would look like after Saddam. They [the U.S.] never addressed those concerns."[104] The Turkish military was focused on what would happen in Northern Iraq, worrying that some sort of Kurdish state would emerge from war. They were less than enthusiastic about a war and, despite U.S. repeated commitment to Iraq's territorial integrity, were skeptical about U.S. ability to manage the Kurdish situation during and after the war.[105]

Both Iraq wars show that Turkish burden sharing decisions were not significantly influenced by collective action theory. Turkish elites in both cases were not concerned with attempting to undersupply a good already provided by a strong coalition leader. In actuality, for the second Gulf War case, Turkish elites did not consider the U.S. led action a collective good, and saw the impending war effort as a threat to more important private goods. Although Turkey's burden sharing actions on the surface appear to be a case of collective action "free-riding," it is more logically explained as a case of a state "keeping its distance."

### *Balance of Threat*

In the 1991 Gulf War, the balance of threat hypothesis had greater relevance for explaining Turkey's burden sharing decisions than the "collective goods" approach of the collective action theory. Iraq's invasion of Kuwait was seen as a security threat to neighboring Turkey.

Turkish officials reiterated their belief that the conflict could create general instability and that Iraq's hostile intentions might increase if it was rewarded for its Kuwaiti aggression.[106]

In the second Iraq War, balance of threat theory predicts that Turkey would be unlikely to support the Iraq coalition since it perceived Kurdish independence as the greater threat. An Iraq War against Hussein was dangerous since he was weak and not seen as a physical threat. However, once the Kurdish threat increased as a result of the war, Turkey tried to become more involved to shape policy concerning the Kurdish north. Indeed, Saddam Hussein had accused Turkey on a number of occasions of acting unfaithfully by assisting in the "thirty-state aggression" against Iraq in the first war. Saddam also criticized Turkey's policy of permitting use of Incirlik air base by U.S. and British to use its territory to bomb Iraq. In February 1999, Baghdad actually threatened to attack Turkey if it continued to allow the U.S. and Britain to use its territory to bomb Iraq. Hussein historically supported the PKK and actually helped PKK supporters settle into villages near the Turkish border after his offensive against Kurdish groups in 1988.[107] However, key to balance of threat theory is not only proximate capability of an adversary, but also a perception of that adversary's threatening intent.[108] In the decade after Desert Storm Ankara found Iraq diminished in both capability and intent. A weakened Iraq was not perceived as threatening democracy in Turkey. Nor were Turks, after 1991, much worried by Saddam Hussein's weapons of mass destruction. In fact, the air attacks from Operation Northern Watch in northern Iraq were thought to have removed the imminent threat to Turkish cities. Politically, a weakened unitary Iraq ruled by the secular Baathist Party suited Turkish national interests. Ankara feared the disintegration of Iraq would allow the Shia majority in the south to develop closer links with Iran, a much more dangerous rival.

More accurately, Turkey was more threatened by a resurgent Kurdish insurgency rather than a despotic Hussein. Disintegration of a centralized Iraq might well enable Iraqi Kurds to develop further the autonomy they had enjoyed in northern Iraq.[109] Turkey's military establishment was extraordinarily consistent over the previous decade that Kurdish separatism and Islamic extremism were seen as the leading security challenges for the Turkish state.[110] Ankara considered the threat posed by Saddam Hussein as manageable and considered a strengthened Kurdish federation or strengthened Iran as the significant regional security challenges.

Turkey's negotiation with the U.S. reflected this security outlook. Turkey allowed the minimal coalition military presence necessary to meet its security challenges, but attempted to block or gain regional control of any operations from the Kurdish area of Iraq. Key in negotiations with the U.S. was the requirement for a Turkish led force in northern Iraq to quell any Kurdish ambitions.[111] In the end, Turkey's concerns were not with an Iraq under Hussein, but rather the aftereffects of its disintegration. Balance of threat theory does not explain Turkish burden sharing decisions. Turkish elites and institutions had come to an accommodation with Hussein and did not feel threatened by his WMD or military capability. In contrast, Iraq cooperated with Turkish cross border raids and only threatened Turkey in response to U.S. military action from Turkish soil.

In the aftermath of the Iraq War conventional combat phase, Turkey began to be concerned with the threat of a Federated Kurdistan. The security elite were concerned that the chaos and instability in Iraq would instigate its break-up and the emergence of a Kurdish state. In contrast to the discussions before the war, the elite now argued that sending troops would block these outcomes while guaranteeing Turkey a place at the negotiating table where Iraq's future would be discussed. These officials were particularly disturbed by the prominent Kurdish presence in the U.S.-appointed Governing Council in Baghdad. The security elite scrutinized every American move and statement concerning northern Iraq and concluded that the United States was conspiring to set up a Kurdish state. Therefore, a military presence in Iraq was required to counter this danger.[112]

### *Alliance Dependence*

In the first Gulf War, alliance dependence best explained Turkish foreign policy. Turkey built a close political, military, and intelligence ties with the United States and North Atlantic Treaty Organization (NATO). Bilateral ties with the United States, and multilateral ties with NATO, were key components of Turkish defense and foreign policy throughout the Cold War. Iraq's invasion of Kuwait, and Washington's commitment to stopping this aggression, offered Turkey an opportunity to reaffirm Ankara's position and continued importance to U.S. strategic interests in the Middle East. President Özal believed that Turkey's strategic and political role would be enhanced by accommodating Washington and firmly supporting the U.S. led coalition.[113]

In the second Gulf War, alliance dependence was the trap that Turkey wanted to escape. In this case, Turkey was presented with the classic alliance security dilemma; cooperate and minimize the risk of abandonment, or defect and avoid entrapment. Turkey's foreign policy leading up to the second Gulf War is characterized as an alliance "defection."[114] Ankara pursued a weak commitment to the U.S. led coalition that was intended to maintain cordial U.S.-Turkish bilateral lateral relations while at the same time not entrapping it into a domestically objectionable military action. The bureaucracies of the foreign ministry and military general staff were convinced early that the U.S. administration had already embarked on an irreversible course over Iraq, and that Turkey's interests mandated cooperation with the United States, hence avoiding abandonment by the U.S.[115] Prime Minister Ecevit, however, pursued a strategy of defection, which increased Turkey's bargaining advantage with the U.S. while providing Ecevit domestic maneuvering room. Ecevit stressed the importance of the strategic partnership between Turkey and the United States, but instructed his bureaucrats to make no meaningful deal with the United States. In a meeting with Deputy Secretary of Defense Wolfowitz in July 2002, Ecevit stated, "The United States is Turkey's strategic ally. Turkey will consider the steps you take on this issue within the framework of its strategic partnership with the United States." However, with the organs of government he authorized "detailed negotiations" only on condition that "no commitments be made regarding American requests."[116]

Throughout negotiations for coalition support, Turkey balanced costs of alliance defection against the costs of an entrapment. As a result, Turkey negotiated for significant concessions from the U.S. to allow a northern front through Turkey. Concessions Turkey gained included an aid package of close to $6 billion in grants and up to $20 billion in loan guarantees, a new status of forces agreement covering U.S. troops, approval for a significant Turkish troop presence in northern Iraq, and guarantees of Turkish influence in northern Iraq policy.[117] However, the onerous negotiations caused considerable friction and eventually distrust between the two governments. Turkish Foreign Minister Yakis eventually demanded $92 billion from the U.S., which the U.S. countered with the final offer of $6 billion. Clearly, Turkey was attempting to gain compensation for the costs of alliance entrapment. Although Turkey had significantly raised the financial awards over the level from Desert Storm, their hardball negotiating position, while at the same time delaying U.S. military efforts, created the condition of distrust and lack of influence in U.S. policy that Turkey feared.[118]

Learning the lessons of the first Gulf War, Turkish military elite also attempted to minimize entrapment to the U.S. course of action. In meetings of the National Security Council (MGK), while recommending support of the U.S. deployment, the military also suggested that Turkey should act independently of the United States to safeguard its own interests and avoid entrapment. The military wing of the MGK stressed in deliberations that, "Turkish servicemen fight only for Turkey. They take risks only for Turkey. The Turkish military is not going to fight the Iraqi military. If there is going to be a fight then it will be between the United States and Iraq. However, in such a situation the TSK (Turkish General Staff) will take the appropriate military precautions in northern Iraq, which it deems of vital importance for Turkey."[119] Turkish elites were attempting to limit the impact of alliance dependence, but in the end, military members of the MGK recommended approving the U.S. deployment precisely because of fears of being abandoned in Kurdish policy, and tried to formulate a strategy maximizing Turkish influence in Iraqi Kurdistan. In the view of the MGK, if the operation was inevitable then a wholly negative reply could not be given to the requests of their strategic ally the United States. The military elite attempted to "show preferences and pay" by recommending support.[120]

In this context, elites in the foreign ministry and military attempted to balance alliance interests against national interests. Turkish negotiating positions were planned to ensure that the minimum acceptable support was extended to the United States while maintaining influence on Kurdish policy. The arms of government recommended supporting the U.S. coalition because of the fear of alliance abandonment. Although most elites did not want war in Iraq, they recognized that failure to support the U.S. coalition would likely cause Washington to chill its relations with Ankara.[121]

The alliance dependence hypothesis explains the action of elites in the foreign ministry and military, but as seen in the next section, their arguments were overridden by senior political elites that were more responsive to Turkish public opinion. U.S. officials were confident that Turkey's influential military, could be relied on to support the United States. After the first Gulf War, Turkey was a strong supporter of American interventionist policy in the Balkans, and also in Afghanistan.[122] However, the Bush administration failed to recognize the tremendous changes had swept Turkish society, including the political and public control over the military. These changes contributed to an alliance "involuntary defection" in that Turkey's government failed to provide support to the contingency where support was expected.

## *Domestic Structure and Politics*

Turkey's history of centralization of foreign policy and military decisions, combined with its party politics would normally mark the state as a Type I domestic structure. In a Type I structure, decision making authority is restricted to relatively few government officials and the chief executive enjoys near total autonomy from legislative scrutiny. Experience through the 1980s and 1990s reinforced the notion that it was a Type I state: Turkish political parties were oligarchies that required total allegiance from their ministers in parliament, the military controlled the debate on issues of strategic concern, and the armed forces lead the policy discussion concerning a military intervention.[123] Typically, especially during military rule between 1980 and 1983, public opinion was totally silenced. Even after the establishment of civilian government in 1983, freedom of expression remained quite limited due to the restrictions in the 1982 constitution.[124]

The elections in the late 1990s and early 2000s saw more influence by the electorate in seating and unseating governments. Party fragmentation and voter volatility began to weaken the influence of the parties, giving voters influence over party politics, especially in the area of economic policy. Elections in the 1990s saw a high degree of correlation between economic performance and electoral support. For instance, the governing Democratic Left Party-Nationalist Movement Party-Motherland Party coalition's electoral support slid from 54 percent in 1999 to only 15 percent in November 2002 because of Turkey's two-year long economic crisis.[125] These elections drastically changed the Turkish political landscape and marked the beginning of politics more influenced by the electorate.[126] For instance, the Justice and Development Party (AKP) was the first party since 1987 to gain a clear majority in Parliament. The AKP's 363 seats in the Parliament, however, did not translate into a majority in electoral support; it gained only 34 per cent of the electoral vote. Therefore, although a majority government, the AKP government did not hold a mandate representing the majority of the people. Any time AKP failed to obtain the opposition Republican People's Party's (*Cumhuriyet Halk Partisi*, CHP) cooperation for major legislation, the CHP and other opposition parties could justifiably question the government's legitimacy. The AKP's single party government was actually a weak government that needed to build a consensus in and out of the parliament in order to maintain its legitimacy.[127] Turkish policy required consensus building between numerous governmental and party elements while the unsteady parliament had the final vote on the stationing of U.S. troops on Turkish soil.

An additional factor weakening the government was the questionable status of AKP party leader Recep Tayyip Erdoğan for the position of Prime Minister. At the time of the 2002 national elections, Erdoğan was banned from public office for making pro-Islamist statements and was unable take over the premiership typically reserved for the party leader. As a result, a temporary government was established in November under his deputy, Abdullah Gül. Parliament rescinded Erdoğan's ban with a constitutional amendment passed in December 2002. He was subsequently elected in a by-election on March 9, 2003, and appointed prime minister three days later. Erdoğan's government finally won a vote of confidence in parliament on March 22, 2003.[128] During the period of U.S.-Turkish negotiations regarding support for an Iraq intervention, Turkey thus had two sitting governments and three prime ministers, with an interim government negotiating with the United States and passing the final Iraq resolution to Parliament. This change in leadership and governments caused policy towards Iraq to be formed in multiple venues under multiple leaders. President Sezer was the only senior politician to remain in office during the entire negotiation period.

Due to the national elections of 2002, Turkey acted more like a Type IV state rather than a Type I state in the domestic structure typology. In a Type IV state, national leaders' preferences are shaped by domestic pressures, and the state's policy response is the result of internal bureaucratic bargaining. Unable to act alone, individual policy makers must recognize domestic opponents who may appeal directly to the public. In the Turkish case, multiple prime ministers, combined with the weak AKP government, caused decision making to be influenced by multiple actors. Due to their inexperience and distrust of corrupt Turkish institutions, AKP officials stopped using the normal governmental policy channels and instead employed a wide variety of unofficial personal representatives as semi-authorized go-betweens formulating policy and communicating with the United States. This back channel, parallel governmental effort caused policy making and negotiation to be formed in numerous unofficial venues rather than in the centralized bureaucracy.[129] Additionally, the weak AKP government had significant challenges seating the government and dealing with fundamental internal economic, political, and party challenges.[130] The weak influence over the TBMM made it difficult for the Erdoğan government to authorize the passage of U.S. troops through Turkey. Article 92 of the Turkish constitution requires the TBMM to authorize any deployment of Turkish troops abroad, or of foreign forces on Turkish soil, except in performance of Turkey's treaty commitments to

NATO or under martial law.[131] The parliamentary elections and subsequent fractured government established the conditions that allowed numerous decision makers, including the National Assembly, to significantly influence Turkish policy on Iraq.

Previous diplomatic experience with Turkey led American policymakers to believe that Turkish political parties were oligarchies which command total allegiance from parliamentary deputies, that Turkish public opinion did not significantly affect policy, and that the military, through the National Security Council, formulated the decisions concerning national security.[132] Unfortunately for U.S. coalition building efforts, the U.S. failed to recognize three significant changes to Turkish domestic politics since the first Gulf War. First, due to successive changes of government during the U.S.-Turkish negotiating period, no consensus could be built in Turkish leadership for U.S. support. Second, the weakness of the AKP electoral base allowed fractured voting in the TBMM, which was exaggerated by the voting procedures of the March 1 referendum. This weakness was exacerbated by military uneasiness with supporting a moderately Islamic government. Finally, public opinion became much more influential in domestic politics. November 2002 elections signified a major realignment of the Turkish political landscape where political party members were fractured from their leadership, causing Turkey to act like a Type IV state rather than a Type I state. Erdoğan had to build a consensus on the referendum, but because of his weak position as party leader rather than prime minister, he was unable to adequately force a vote along party lines.

One major consideration in adding Turkey to the Iraq coalition was the instability of the government during the negotiation period. Due to successive changes of government during the U.S.-Turkish negotiating period, tough decisions on U.S. support were passed to the next government, rather than acted upon. Prime Minister Ecevit was the first to set a policy of restraint with the U.S., but his preferred policy position was a diplomatic solution that would preclude war in the region. Ecevit strongly opposed the military option in Iraq from the very outset and pressed his concerns about regional instability on President Bush during a state visit to Washington in January 2002.[133] Ecevit stressed to Bush that Turkey did not support the Hussein regime, but also underscored traditional Turkish concerns for Iraqi territorial integrity, and the importance that Kirkuk and Mosul remain outside of Kurdish influence. He hinted that an intervention would have disastrous consequences, especially for Turkey.[134] After the visit, Ecevit attempted to mediate between the United States and the Hussein regime. In a letter sent to

Hussein February 1, 2002, he emphasized the determination of the U.S. administration and asked for full cooperation with UN inspectors. Saddam's responded that the UN demands were illegal and Turkey's support of Operation Northern Watch would be referred to the UN by Iraq. This response led Ecevit to believe that Iraq would be uncooperative towards U.S. demands.[135]

In March 2002, Vice President Richard Cheney visited Ankara as part of a Middle East tour to seek support against Iraq. The principle aim of Cheney's tour was to explain Washington's intentions regarding Iraq to the countries of the region and to secure their backing as much as possible.[136] The most interesting aspect of this visit is that Cheney requested a separate meeting with the Commander of the Turkish Armed Forces (TAF) Hüseyin Kivrikoğlu. This request showed that the United States expected the armed forces to influence the deployment decision and take its historical role influencing security policy. Although the role of the armed forces was well known, it was very unusual for a visiting high administration official to request direct talks with the military. Instead of direct talks, a separate informal session was held between Ecevit, the Minister of Foreign Affairs Dem, General Kivrikoğlu, Cheney, and U.S. Ambassador Robert Pearson. In this meeting, Ecevit once again declared that Turkey was against military operations, while Cheney clearly articulated the U.S. intention to intervene in Iraq.[137]

During the summer of 2002, the Bush administration began to outline the plans for a military action with potential coalition partners. U.S. Deputy Secretary of Defense Paul Wolfowitz arrived in Istanbul on July 14, 2002, to convey President Bush's plan for regime change in Iraq and to seek the Ecevit government's support for the military operation that was then in the planning stages.[138] Wolfowitz, accompanied by U.S. Under Secretary of State for Political Affairs Marc Grossman, met with Ecevit July 16. Wolfowitz passed a message from Bush to the effect that a final decision on the issue of war had not been made, however, the United States needed to make military preparations for a strategy of military intervention in Iraq. Wolfowitz asked Ecevit to outline the extent of military cooperation that the U.S. strategic ally Turkey would offer in connection with an Iraq War. Ecevit replied, "The United States is Turkey's strategic ally. Turkey will consider the steps you take on this issue within the framework of its strategic partnership with the United States."[139] Although Ecevit was opposed to the war and insisted on the need for international legitimacy, reports suggested that Turkey's approach reflected a policy of tacit cooperation. Ecevit's establishment of a series of counter demands was seen as an indication that official bargaining has started between Turkey and the

United States on Iraq.[140] Ecevit's response to Wolfowitz was not made casually, but rather was formulated by professional diplomats within the Foreign Ministry. The view of the Foreign Ministry was that the U.S. administration had embarked on an irreversible course over Iraq and that Turkey's interests mandated cooperation with the United States. Although Turkey was not excited about a war in Iraq, it had not said "no." On the contrary, the response suggested that Turkey was open to cooperation. In the words of a senior Foreign Ministry official who attended the talks and who spoke to *Hurriyet* newspaper at the time, Ankara "did not pull down the shutters" in Wolfowitz's face.[141]

At a dinner later that night, Minister of the Treasury Kemal Dervis made an additional proposition to Wolfowitz, "If there is a military intervention in Iraq it would have the effect of a big shock on the Turkish economy. Financing mechanisms need to be established to offset the adverse effects of such a shock."[142] Thus began a two-pronged negotiating stance: Turkey should have a say in the Iraq War, but it should be compensated accordingly for any economic disruption caused by the intervention. According to press sources, Ecevit had no intention of opposing the United States; that is why he responded to Bush's request by saying that "Turkey would act as a strategic partner."[143]

The most significant result of the Wolfowitz visit is that it established a joint coordination mechanism between the two sides for cooperation on Iraq. Ecevit authorized "detailed negotiations" with the United States, but instructed his bureaucrats to make no meaningful deal with the United States without additional government approval."[144] Foreign Ministry Undersecretary Ugur Ziyal's visit to Washington in the last week of August was the first important step of the negotiation process. During that visit, Ziyal met with Wolfowitz and had a videoconference with Vice President Dick Cheney. The most important result of Ziyal's visit was that the United States signaled that it wanted to deploy troops in Turkey, to build staging areas for this purpose, and to use Turkey's ports and airports in connection with Iraq.[145] Ziyal countered that a military intervention would create great risks. It would harm not only the region but also to the United States. Additionally, he stressed that Turkey would require legitimacy and consensus by gained through a multilateral operation conducted within a UN mandate.[146]

Between September and October 2002, U.S. requests to Turkey to support the emerging coalition began to formalize, causing additional strain to the weakened Ecevit government. On September 16, the Turkish General Staff sent a note to the Prime Minister's Office requesting clarification on what responses should be given to various

American requests. The United States submitted its official requests to the Turkish government three days after this directive was issued. Rather than waiting for the election results, the United States opted to put its requests on record during this transition period.[147] The Turkish government was surprised that these requests came through military channels directly to the TAF, rather than through diplomatic channels. American military personnel were told that the decision was entirely political and could only be taken by the new government.[148]

The period of negotiations from Wolfowitz's July visit until November elections corresponded with a time of great instability in Turkish government. During the 2001-2002 timeframe economic reforms fueled growing dissatisfaction with the government. Criticism of the government focused on the advanced age and declining health of the Prime Minister.[149] Ecevit's health continued to decline, and in July 2002, two ministers who expected to be chosen as the next prime minister resigned once it was clear that Ecevit would not step down. During that same period, Devlet Bahçeli, the leader of one of the government's coalition parties declared that Turkey should hold an early parliamentary election in the coming November. Without a ruling coalition, Ecevit had to agree to an early election.[150] During the tenure of the Ecevit administration, the United States passed its request for Turkish support in multiple venues. Although Ecevit repeatedly countered that an Iraq war would cause significant problems for neighboring states, he never conferred an absolute "no" to the administration. Rather, he gave the impression of cooperation by negotiating terms of support with the Bush administration.

On November 3, 2002, Turkey held its national parliamentary elections. The results drastically changed the Turkish political landscape; the governing coalition parties were severely punished for the economic and political crises. None of the coalition parties was able to garner the minimum ten percent of the national vote necessary to win seats in parliament. The electorate had voted in a conservative Islamic party, the Justice and Development Party (AKP), which had little experience governing at the national level. The party's president, Recip Tayyip Erdoğan, was barred from taking political office due to his conviction in 1998 for making Islamic speeches; therefore, one of the other leading politicians Abdullah Gül formed the cabinet as the interim prime minister, while Erdoğan challenged the constitutionality of his ban from office.[151]

Shortly after the November elections, at the NATO Summit in Prague on November 20, President Bush met with President Sezer. The Gül government had not yet won a vote of confidence in the National

Assembly. As a result, there was not a single representative from the AKP at this high-level meeting. With the exception of President Sezer, whose views differed markedly from the AKP in many areas, the Bush team was meeting with bureaucrats and political lame ducks.[152] Bush mentioned, "A short time ago we were able to get Resolution 1441 from the UN Security Council. We consider it important that you stand by our side as we continue these efforts." Sezer countered, "That resolution does not automatically authorize you to declare war. For that reason you will have to obtain a second resolution from the Security Council." Sezer then continued, "We are strategic partners with you. Of course, we will support our strategic partner. However international legitimacy will determine the extent of our support." In one sense, the Turkish President introduced a 'criterion for Turkey's support' and was sending the message, "Do not expect much from Turkey if you cannot obtain a (second) UN resolution."[153]

In December, Wolfowitz and Grossman again arrived in Ankara to finalize plans for stationing troops in Turkey for a northern front. The timing of the December 3 visit was a sign of the importance to the Bush administration for having the new AKP government on its side for the American Iraq strategy. The purpose of the meeting was to demonstrate U.S. support for Turkey's bid to the European Union, reconfirm with the new government the deal that he previously negotiated giving U.S. full access to airbases, and to push for permission to base U.S. ground forces in Turkey.[154] In a meeting with interim Prime Minister Gül, Wolfowitz again emphasized the need for the United States to begin deploying troops and additionally offered a grant of $2 billion to offset Turkish economic losses in a probable war.[155] Gül responded by passing leadership on the issue to parliament, which was much more responsive to public opinion, to deflect U.S. attempts for basing. Gül stated, "Our government won a vote of confidence only last week, as a democratic country we will continue talks with the United States within the bounds of our laws. Although we have an absolute majority in the Assembly, it is the Assembly that has to make such decisions."[156] Then Wolfowitz asked, "Will Turkey support a northern front? We expect your government's answer on this issue as soon as possible." Gül replied, "The only gesture we can make to you at this stage is to take certain steps within the discretion of the government. In that framework, we may agree to the beginning of survey work on the (modernization of) bases. However the TBMM has to approve your requests for the later stages."[157] Wolfowitz presented Gül with a timetable for the survey work required to assess Turkish ports and airbases. Wolfowitz suggested that a 150-person Department of Defense survey team begin survey work in the third week of December. Gül accepted the surveying work and left the door open for the other stages. However, he emphasized that the TBMM would have the final say on the subsequent stages.[158] Gül's "yes" on starting surveying work was the result of a state summit held the previous weekend at the President's Cankaya Mansion. That meeting was chaired by President Sezer and was also attended by Chief of General Staff Gen. Hilmi Özkök.[159] The approval won from Gül was intended to delay full support of the United States, while at the same time allowing negotiating room for multiple options.

Ambassador Pearson arranged a separate, unofficial, meeting at his residence that night between Wolfowitz's party and Turkish leaders. On the American side, four individuals with official status—Wolfowitz, Grossman, Pearson, and a Pentagon official—attended the dinner. On the Turkish side, AKP party leader Erdoğan was accompanied by Istanbul Deputy Egemen Bagis—who served as Erdoğan's interpreter and political advisor and is sometimes referred to as the Turkish Carl Rove—Adana Deputy Omer Celik, and businessman Cuneyd Zapsu.[160] No one on the Turkish side officially represented the government. Wolfowitz delivered to Erdoğan a written message from President Bush congratulating him on his success in the elections and a verbal message inviting him to the White House on December 10. Wolfowitz left his meeting with Erdoğan with the understanding that the AKP leader and his party would support a northern front in Turkish political venues.[161]

Although acting Prime Minister, and a leader in the AKP, Gül never learned of the content of the discussions between Erdoğan and Wolfowitz. As a result, Gül's bargain and delay strategy while passing the final decision for a northern front to the TBMM was never passed to Erdoğan. Additionally, Gül did not fully know what messages were being sent through the unofficial Zapsu channel. The American side, on the other hand, was intent on attaining its goals through both Gül and Erdoğan. However, this U.S. strategy led to a full-fledged "channel inflation," where the U.S. negotiated through multiple official and unofficial channels causing misperceptions in the American government on the extent of Turkish support for the intervention.[162] One result of the November elections was that Turkish foreign policy regarding the Iraq War was fragmented. Although Interim Prime Minister Gül formulated government policy, Washington was also courting President Sezer, and AK party leader Erdoğan on Iraqi issues.

In late December 2002, the Bush administration dispensed with diplomatic niceties and exerted pressure on the Gül government for a decision regarding Iraq. On December 21, the U.S. tried to expose Turkish plans by issuing an ultimatum to Interim Prime Minister Gül for a response to U.S. requests for support. In a message sent through the U.S. Ambassador, Bush set a timeline for a Turkish decision, "We expect you to inform us of your decision on the northern front in three days."[163] Prime Minister Gül was horrified by the terse tone of Bush's message. Bush's message was intended to break Turkey's approach of taking things slowly, bargaining over everything, and demanding a formal memorandum of agreement on every issue. Gül interpreted Bush's terse message as a signal that the U.S. would not allow Hussein to remain in power.[164] Gül again responded in a typical manner on January 16, responding that, "In the light of lengthy appraisals, our government will take the necessary steps to obtain the approval of the TBMM at a time of its choosing for a mode of operation that would not deprive the United States of a northern option." Gül qualified this response by stressing the need for a response through either the UN or NATO, "There is no doubt that international legitimacy and consensus will play a determining role in the result to be achieved. NATO's support will also help this process."[165] At the end of his response, Gül asked in unequivocal terms for U.S. support of Turkish 'improvements' to UN Secretary General Kofi Annan's settlement plan for Cyprus. Again, Gül gave the impression that Turkey would eventually support U.S. efforts, but he relegated the final decision to the TBMM.

Bush replied to Gül's letter on January 22 by welcoming Gül's intention to take the matter to the TBMM, "I appreciate your support for a northern option in the event of a war in Iraq." However, he admonished that time was of the essence, "My expectation from you is that these issues be concluded in the shortest possible time." Bush did not respond to Gül's condition on the issue of international legitimacy, nor his linkage of support to the Cyprus issue.[166] Gül was especially concerned that Bush did not offer a quid pro quo on Cyprus.

Days after Bush's reply was received, Secretary of State Colin Powell continued to press the issue at a private meeting with Gül and Erdoğan at the Davos World Economic Forum. Powell sought an answer to Bush's request and asked no less than three times, "When will you go to your parliament?" Gül's response was, "no authorization has been obtained from the UN Security Council. It would be hard to pass an authorization bill through our parliament in these circumstances." Erdoğan added, "We cannot act quickly on such sensitive matters."[167] Erdoğan advocated a regional strategy that would include countries such as Egypt, Jordan, Saudi Arabia, and Gulf states. Powell replied, "We may have to act without a UN resolution." Gül left Powell with the impression that Turkey would eventually support the U.S. led invasion when he stated, "A UN resolution would make our job easier. However if there is no UN resolution we cannot remain onlookers at developments in Iraq."[168]

The fledgling AKP government spent most of January 2003 wavering over which way to move on U.S. requests for a northern option into Iraq. The first sign of serious consideration of U.S. requests emerged in the last week of January. On January 31, the MGK (National Security Council) met to advise the government on possible military measures. At the meeting, members of the General Staff's command echelon officially expressed their view that the government should take step to cooperate with the United States based on agreements reached in December. The Chief of the General Staff Gen. Özkök and force commanders individually endorsed their support for the military option. The commanders also said that the government must begin to prepare the Turkish public opinion for the military option. The goal of the commanders was to present to the public an argument that highlighted Turkish interests in northern Iraq.[169] When questioned on the political climate of the meeting, Minister of Foreign Affairs Yakis stated, "when it became clear that the invasion was inevitable and we could not prevent it, then we concluded we should participate in it and cooperate."[170]

The most contentious issue at the MGK meeting was over the question of whether the parliamentary authorization bills should be split. The General Staff and the Foreign Ministry bureaucrats favored combining the authorization bills for the modernization of the bases, the arrival of U.S. soldiers, and sending Turkish soldiers to Iraq into a single bill and submitting a single text to the TBMM. Both the General Staff and Foreign Ministry Undersecretary Ugur Ziyal presented this position to Gül before the MGK meeting. However, Gül favored splitting the authorization bills into two to strengthen Turkey's hand in its negotiations with the United States. As of the end of January, Ankara had not fully obtained the concessions it wanted from the United States on issues such as economic aid, political arrangements in northern Iraq, and the rights of Iraqi Turcoman. Nor had the UN Security Council passed a resolution authorizing the use of force. Turkey thus aimed to gain concessions by bargaining at each step of the deployment process. Since France and Germany were countering U.S. positions in the Security Council, Turkey could afford a hard bargaining stance with the U.S.[171]

Negotiations began with the U.S. on the specifics of a deployment, but the U.S. government continued to pressure Turkey for a final decision on a northern option. On February 4, Vice President Cheney called Prime Minister Gül to express his delight at the start of the negotiations for the upgrade of Turkish ports and airfields for the expected flow of U.S. forces; however, he cautioned that U.S. plans needed a decision, "President Bush must decide without delay. To do that we must be able to see ahead of us clearly. Indeed the ships that will transfer our 4th Infantry Division have already sailed. They will arrive at the Turkish coast on February 10. The President must decide by February 12 the latest whether these ships should remain near the Turkish coast or head toward the Suez Canal."[172] With these remarks, Cheney clearly implied that the United States might give up on the northern front, and set a timeline for Turkish cooperation. In a press interview on February 5, Gül stated, "All avenues of seeking peace have been exhausted. It is now beyond our hands. We will now act together with our strategic partner. We will submit the authorization bill for the modernization of bases to the Assembly tomorrow." This authorization bill was approved in the Assembly the next day by 308 votes in favor, 193 votes opposed, and nine abstentions.[173] This approval of the authorization gave the Bush administration the impression that they had reached a breakthrough with Turkey; plans for a northern option were continued.[174]

Negotiations with the U.S. on the Memorandum of Agreement for conducting the war from Turkish soil commenced on February 11 and were completed on February 22, two days before the Council of Ministers met to discuss the submission of the final authorization bill—allowing the staging of U.S. troops—to the TBMM. The negotiations were tough and acrimonious and centered on issues of Turkish autonomy within northern Iraq, and the legal status of U.S. troops in Turkey.[175] Eventually, the Turkish side gained concessions allowing Turkish troops in northern Iraq to engage the PKK while remaining under Turkish command.[176] Unfortunately, the Turkish public viewed American demands regarding the Kurdish north with suspicion, and Turkish hardball tactics continued to sour relations with the U.S.[177] Although the negotiations gained the interests of both sides, the negotiating tactics created a perception with the Turkish media, public, and ministers that Turkey did not gain a memorandum of agreement that met its national interests.

Once the memorandum of agreement was completed, the Turkish government moved to endorse the resolution in the TBMM. On February 24, the Council of Ministers met in a contentious meeting to discuss the second authorization allowing U.S. forces to stage from Turkey. Turkish law required that the cabinet send the resolution to the TBMM with unanimous consent. Interim Prime Minister Gül opened the meeting by stating, "We have to make a decision about the authorization bill related to the arrival of American troops and the dispatch of Turkish troops to Iraq. I contacted the party. The party is also concerned. Our colleagues have serious concerns." Gül continued, "My request from you is to send this bill to the TBMM (Turkish Grand National Assembly). The TBMM will have the final say."[178] Gül's reference that the TBMM would have final say reflected his desire to send the difficult decision to the Assembly without strong support from the government. Gül's comments implied that the cabinet would not take political responsibility for the authorization bill and that it would only perform a forwarding service. This prompted opposing ministers to feel that they had a free hand opposing the resolution. Gül's opening remarks were followed by six hours of intense debate where Erdoğan and the AKP party position were not directly represented. Additionally, the details of negotiations for the memorandum of understanding between Turkey and the United States were never discussed.[179] Gül's closing reflected his ambivalence towards the resolution, "Our job is to forward the authorization bill to the TBMM. As we said from the outset the TBMM has the authority to make the final decision. Let us leave the decision to the Assembly. Moreover our government will step down in ten days because of the by-election in Siirt. The new government can take up this issue." In effect, Gül was passing advocacy to Erdoğan's government, which had not yet been seated. Gül concluded by passing responsibility for the resolution to the assembly, "The TBMM is the true authority on this issue. I want an opportunity to send the authorization bill to the true authority on this issue."[180] This is odd behavior in Turkish politics in that the party usually decides positions on decisions of this magnitude before cabinet discussion. The fact that the cabinet meeting was so rancorous is an indication that there were numerous decision makers influencing the discussion rather than the typical centralized decision making. When the Council of Ministers meeting ended, it was obvious to political observers that the passage of the authorization bill in the TBMM would not be easy at all.[181]

After the November 2002 election, Ecevit passed responsibility for U.S. Iraq policy to the interim Gül government causing confusion in the political elite on who would determine Turkish policy concerning Iraq. Gül assumed the responsibilities of prime minister, including directing foreign policy, while at the same time AKP Party Leader Erdoğan, and heir to the prime minister's seat, was also negotiating policy positions concerning Turkish support of the Iraq War. During this period of negotiations, Erdoğan was meeting with U.S. representatives but he had no official influence within the government. Unfortunately, on the domestic front, the split leadership of the AKP did not project the clear advocacy on the level that was presented by Özal in the first Gulf War. By the time of the March 1 TBMM vote, the Gül government passed responsibility to Party Leader and incoming Prime Minister Erdoğan, even though he was not in an official position to influence the vote. Since the government was managing the transition of the prime minister position, it was distracted from adequately presenting policy options concerning Iraq to the cabinet and TBMM. Critical information involving the negotiations with the U.S. never was introduced into party or cabinet discussions. According to Foreign Minister Yakis, the political elite and public never gained a full understanding that there was an agreement between Turkey and the U.S. that would allow Turkey significant influence in the Kurdish north.[182] Without leader advocacy, and with deflection of decisions to parliament, the war authorization was much more dependent on public opinion. Yakis believes that the public could have been persuaded to go to war if Turkish interests were perceived to be protected by the agreement with the United States.[183] Decentralized decision making allowed the TBMM to gain more influence on the deployment issue.

Although the AKP was the first party since 1987 to secure a clear majority in parliament, the government was fairly weak because it gained only 34 percent of the popular vote while the entire TBMM represented only 46 percent of the electorate. The remaining 54 percent of the popular vote did not gain any parliamentary representation because it failed to overcome the 10% minimum threshold required by law. Representatives of all three of the veteran political parties that had previously governed the country as well as nearly all the opposition parties were totally swept out of parliament. Approximately 90 percent of the incumbent parliamentarians lost their seats. Mehmet Ali Birand, a well-regarded Turkish political commentator, commented that the election results amounted to a civilian coup.[184] Most AKP deputies had never held public office before and were new to the business of politics. Their inexperience showed in the lead up to the March 1, 2003 parliamentary vote. Turkish political observers note that AKP Party Leader Erdoğan did not properly assess his political strength and mismanaged the parliament vote.

The AKP leadership's uncertain control over its factionalized and inexperienced deputies showed that the party had merely nominal control over the voting outcome. Two dominant factions emerged within the AKP leadership. One, led by party leader Erdoğan and his closest supporters in the cabinet, argued that Turkey should support the U.S. request to protect its interests in northern Iraq. Then Foreign Minister Yasar Yakis argued it would be impossible to dissuade the

United States and argued for participation as a means of influencing U.S. policy, "We do not have the means to prevent the war. If the authorization bill does not pass we will be excluded from the postwar scenarios." Minister of National Defense Gonul and Minister of Justice Cicek also expressed strong support for the authorization bill. They argued that the passage of the authorization bill would give Turkey the means to block the establishment of a Kurdish state and to have a say in the restructuring of Iraq. The other faction, led by Erdoğan's deputy, interim Prime Minister Abdullah Gül, was both morally and strategically against the war. The Gül faction highlighted the negative consequences of Özal's support in the first Persian Gulf War and suggested that a "no" vote would keep war from Iraq since Turkey was a necessary ally. Deputy Prime Minister Yalcinbayir was among the most vocal opponents of the bill and argued that an authorization bill that would directly involve Turkey in a war could not be proposed without a second UN Security Council resolution authorizing the use of force. Minister of Public Works Ergezen approached the issue from the perspective of Islamic sensitivities, "We opposed the Gulf War in 1991. How can we facilitate the bombing of a Muslim people?"[185]

The Gül government's lack of resolve for the deployment resolution rendered doubtful its capacity to deliver a parliamentary majority. Throughout negotiations with the U.S., both the Ecevit and Gül governments passed responsibility for implementation of negotiations to parliament. Rather than press the parliament for a certain decision, as Özal did in the first Gulf War, the weak leadership of Ecevit, Gül, and eventually Erdoğan allowed the parliament to set the agenda. When the U.S. pressed Ankara for basing rights in early 2003, then party leader Erdoğan said, "If necessary we will take America's demands over Iraq to a referendum" and gave the first indications that rather than let the government take the decision on this, they might put the matter directly to the people.[186] Even the authorization bill allowing a small number of troops to survey and upgrade Turkish logistics facilities showed a high rate of defection within the AKP, unusual in Turkish politics.[187]

Due to his weak political mandate, party leader Erdoğan tolerated this high level of defection in AKP votes to avoid a permanent party split. Typically, Turkish politics parties vote in a block in the TBMM, however, voting procedures for the March 1 vote encouraged individual rather than block voting. Erdoğan was sensitive to the polarization in his party on the Iraq issue and sent a clear signal to the deputies that they would be able to individually vote "no" without repercussions. In his position as Prime Minister-elect, Erdoğan was concerned that making the resolution binding to the party ministers could permanently divide his party before he was even seated.[188] He made a rare and unusual parliamentary move by calling for a closed rather than an open parliamentary vote. This unusual closed vote allowed the parliament to cast its votes confidentially, only the vote totals were made public, therefore, deputies were not individually accountable for their votes. The most plausible explanation for the closed vote was for Erdoğan to defend against a vote of "no confidence." Political observers speculate that Prime Minister Gül, who had serious reservations with the authorization bill, used the closed vote as cover to persuade other AKP deputies to vote "no." Erdoğan allowed the closed vote because such high-profile public defection would send a signal that he was weak and therefore risk the collapse of his government.[189] The closed vote enabled AKP cabinet members to vote "no" without exposing to the public the weakness of the party leader.

In the wake of the first Gulf War, Turkish public opinion became critical of the costs of participation in the coalition and of Turkey's failure to receive sufficient compensation from the West. Many Turks regarded the Gulf War as a catalyst for Kurdish separatism and a continuing cost to Turkey in lost revenue from trade with Iraq and pipeline fees. Angry about the lack of influence in post-Desert Storm policy, public opinion turned even harder against U.S. interventions in Iraq. Numerous public opinion polls reported that the Turkish public was overwhelmingly against the use of Turkish bases and troops by the American forces, and opposed to American intervention.[190] Any government showing enthusiasm for American plans would be perceived by the electorate as flying in the face of the country's interests.[191] Public opinion influenced U.S. operations from Turkey in at least one instance prior to the Iraq war. In Feb 1998, Turkish leaders refused to allow the U.S. to use Turkish territory to attack Iraq. This decision was highly influenced by public opinion; in a poll taken during the Feb 1998 crisis, some 80 percent opposed the use of Turkish military bases for attacks against Iraq.[192]

After the rout of the 2002 general election, Turkish leaders were very reluctant to shape public opinion. Government and party leaders waited until the war was a foregone conclusion before trying to convince the public that they might benefit by cooperating in a U.S.-led war against Iraq.[193] By this time there were many demonstrations, campaigns, and numerous text messages and personal visits to parliamentarians advocating a "no" vote on the authorization bill. Despite Turkey's economic hardships at the time, 72.3 percent opposed allowing the American forces to open a second front by using Turkish territory, even if that would result in significant amounts of financial aid.[194] Because of the weakness and disorganization of the AKP, parliament members felt pressure from the grassroots constituents.

Finally, the silence of the military in the debate is noteworthy since the military typically has a strong influence in Turkish politics. The military's power is institutionalized through a variety of organizations. The most important of these is the MGK. The highest advisory body to the Turkish government, at the time it consisted of the President (chair), the chief of the General Staff and the respective chiefs of the army, navy, air force, and gendarmerie; prime minister, the minister of defense, the interior minister, and the foreign affairs minister from the civilian side. Although technically the MGK makes only "recommendations" to the Council of Ministers, its recommendations can be tantamount to orders.[195]

Developments regarded as undermining the domestic stability of the country fall within the responsibility of the military. Therefore, the General Staff should be considered not only a professional military institution but also a core element of Turkey's political system. In recent instances, the military operated independently of the government to secure its interpretation of Turkish interests in the extension of the fight against the PKK across the Turkish border into northern Iraq. In March 1998, Turkish Special Forces captured Semdin Sakik, from his refuge in northern Iraq. The military did not inform the cabinet or even Prime Minister Yilmaz of this action in advance.[196]

The fact that the military, which frequently declared its views and even interfered on large and small internal security subjects did not weigh in heavily on the authorization bill is noteworthy. The military elites were concerned that the AKP wanted to shift the political responsibility for the authorization bill onto the Turkish General Staff by presenting the issue to its rank and file as: "What could we do? We were forced to pass the bill because the military wanted it." In the hours before the vote, Erdoğan elements of the AKP looked for the MGK to rescue the authorization. Minister of Justice Cemil Cicek argued that the authorization bill could be rejected without the MGK issuing a statement of unequivocal support for the bill. President Sezer, an opponent of the bill and chair of the MGK blocked any efforts for military influence, "The MGK already expressed its views on this issue and offered its advice to the government at the end of its meeting last month. Consequently there is no need to make any additional reference to it this time." [197] According to one of the most experienced journalists covering Turkish politics, this MGK meeting was perhaps "the only one in history" that produced no advice or comment on such a strategic issue.[198]

By this time, military commanders expressed their uneasy position in the authorization bill debate. If they took the AKP position, they would be at odds with President Sezer who opposed even a vote in the TBMM on the bill without a UN Security Council resolution authorizing the use of force. Turkish military commanders were seriously preoccupied with the question of "What should we do?" prior to the authorization vote, but eventually decided to stay out of the debates on this issue.[199]

Domestic political factors influenced Turkey's burden sharing decisions much more in the second Gulf War than the first. Turkey's military and political elite was not as powerful as it was in the early 90's. In the November 2002 elections, voters rejected the previous governing parties and allowed the fledgling, anti-establishment Justice and Development Party to form a government on its own. Due to its weak popular support and fractured party elite, the AKP government was vulnerable to public opinion and needed to build consensus in and out of the TBMM in order to maintain its legitimacy as a government. In this respect, the Turkish government acted much more like a Type IV rather than the Type I government seen in the first Persian Gulf War. Decision making was decentralized between Prime Minister's Ecevit, Gül, and Erdoğan, and President Sezer. Additionally, the AKP leadership's uncertain control over its factionalized and inexperienced deputies showed that the party had merely nominal control over the voting outcome. Because of its disorganization, TBMM members were more responsive to public opinion. Public opinion constrained elite decision making due to the public fears of a fight with an Islamic neighbor along with the subsequent economic devastation. The military, which traditionally influenced decisions on national security, sat on the sidelines when its initial advice was rebuffed. The military, therefore, had its own reasons for wanting the country's new leaders to be accountable for their first major test with Washington. These domestic political factors convolved to constrain executive and state autonomy in supporting the U.S. coalition.

## The Role of Legitimacy

Turkey's burden sharing was influenced by legitimacy arguments but Turkish support to the coalition was primarily based on national interest considerations constrained by domestic politics. In the approach to the Iraq War, Turkish leadership, especially President Sezer and interim Prime Minister Gül opposed Turkish action in the absence of a UN Resolution authorizing force. Sezer, a former constitutional court judge, and Gül consistently resisted support to the U.S. effort without a supporting international resolution. Although elements in the foreign ministry and military supported U.S. efforts on the grounds that the U.S. had been a strategic partner of Turkey, the leadership stated on numerous occasions that Turkey's support would be contingent on a UN mandate. In August 2002, Foreign Ministry Undersecretary Ugur Ziyal meeting with Vice President Cheney stressed the need for a UN mandate on Iraq. In the meeting, Ziyal stressed the need for "legitimacy" and "consensus." [200] In the final deliberations before the parliamentary vote, major factions argued that Turkey should not support an illegitimate effort. In a six-hour meeting, the MGK drew a distinction between legitimacy and national interests stating, "a second UN Security Council resolution would be appropriate for the Iraq operation...However, if a second resolution is not passed but the operation is still unavoidable then Turkey will take all appropriate measures to safeguard its own interests."[201] In cabinet deliberations, President Sezer, and the Speaker of the National Assembly all insisted that the operation be based on international legitimacy.[202] These arguments were more procedural than normative. Procedural legitimacy arguments reflect the viewpoint that behavior becomes legitimate when it is approved by authorized international institutions.[203] Turkey was willing to support the invasion based on the legitimacy provided by a UN vote. Some elements in the MGK even argued that because the U.S. coalition had a wide range of nations participating, it had already gained legitimate status. Although those arguments did not convince the parliament to approve the U.S. deployment, it does show that Turkey had no normative arguments against the use of force in Iraq.

Once the war started however, and Ankara found itself isolated by the United States, legitimacy issues were weighed against state interest. In April 2003, the Turkish government agreed to support U.S. logistics needs in northern Iraq. This action brought public condemnation in the press with the argument, "what happened to international legitimacy? In that case, why did we reject the motion on foreign troop deployment on Turkish soil? Was not our aim to refrain from taking part in an illegitimate war?"[204] Additionally, in the summer of 2003, the Ankara agreed in principle to join the multinational coalition in Iraq before this was supported by either the United Nations, or the Iraqi Interim Government. Turkey agreed to this offer, after the U.S. ousted a small contingent of Turkish troops from Kirkuk. Turkey saw participation in the U.S. coalition as a means of gaining influence over policy in northern Iraq. Ankara concluded that U.S. reliance on Kurdish factions came at the expense of Turkish influence.[205] Although Turkey later withdrew this offer of support, it was withdrawn at the request of the United States, not because Turkey was concerned with the legitimacy of the occupation. Turkey was willing to support the occupation force in Iraq, even without the cover of international legitimacy, because it saw that it had lost influence with the U.S. on Iraq policy.[206] Additionally, Turkey's support for the coalition did not change due to changes in legitimacy of the occupation. Turkish policy concerning Iraq remained consistent through several milestones. Turkey did not offer additional diplomatic, economic, or military support after the UN supported the occupation under Resolution 1551 through the general elections of January 2005.

Overall, legitimacy has some influence explaining Turkey's lack of support for the initial invasion into Iraq, however, Turkey's need to influence U.S. policy on northern Iraq soon outweighed legitimacy issues in policy venues.

## Summary and Conclusions

Based on their experience in the first Gulf War coalition, Turkish elites did not consider the U.S. led action a collective good, and saw the impending war effort as a threat to more important private goods. Ankara considered the threat posed by Saddam Hussein as manageable and considered a strengthened Kurdish federation as the significant regional security challenge. Turkey's lack of support for the second Iraq War coalition reflects this security outlook. Any motivation for Ankara to cooperate with U.S. demands is best explained by alliance dependence. Early in the negotiations process, the foreign ministry and military bureaucracy advocated supporting U.S. demands strictly for alliance dependence concerns. However, public opinion and the political elite were against a military operation in Iraq. In this manner, Turkey's assistance during the initial stages of the Iraq war can be seen as an "involuntary defection" in that the government was prepared to support U.S. policy, but the public was not. Turkey's lessons from the first Gulf War were hardly positive. With the end of U.S. security assistance, and with economic sanctions against Iraq still in place more than a decade after the invasion of Kuwait, many Turks felt that they had little to show for their cooperation with Washington and Europe in the Gulf. The AKP leadership's uncertain control over its factionalized and inexperienced deputies allowed the TBMM to be swayed by public opinion rather than party loyalty. Unlike in the first Gulf War, public opinion constrained the AKP's decision making due to its increased influence as a result of the November 2002 elections. The military, which traditionally influenced decisions on national security did not significantly steer the policy debate. Once it was clear that the U.S. would go to war with Iraq, the military leaders of the MGK preferred supporting the Iraq coalition. The military argued that Turkish strategy concerning Kurdistan was best served by joining the coalition and inserting Turkish forces into northern Iraq. However, the military elected to remain publicly silent so that blame for a failed vote would fall on the AKP itself. Turkey's failure to permit U.S. troops to enter Iraq from the north resulted in the ultimate irony. Turkey avoided alliance entrapment, but America's thinly spread and relatively lightly armed forces were left with no option but to rely on Iraqi Kurds to control and eventually minister to northern Iraq. American promises to keep the Kurds out of the cities of Mosul and Kirkuk were unsupportable and the United States was left with no choice but to depend on its Kurdish allies as indispensable force generators in the north.

In contrast to the first Gulf War case, elite learning and state domestic structure best describes the change of burden sharing in the second Gulf War case. Preexisting beliefs on the influence of a military operation in Iraq informed elite decision making before the U.S. even requested support from Turkey. Since Sezer, Ecevit, and Gül saw little to gain from the U.S. operation, they had little motivation to act independent of public opinion. Erdoğan, although supportive of the United States, was not in a government position to dictate the vote. Unlike the first case, the bureaucracy was the primary constituency advocating support for U.S. requests. In contrast to Özal, however, President Sezer refused to advocate the bureaucracy's arguments to the public. The fractured Justice and Development Party was not likely to counter public opinion on the heels of the devastating general election that put it into power. Although U.S. financial incentives where massive, the chief executive and government were too weak to provide more than token support to the U.S. coalition.

Analysis of the second Gulf War suggests that Turkey's dominant burden sharing strategy was to provide the least amount of support necessary to avoid abandonment by U.S. in the future. Based on this model, U.S. policy makers should have been concerned that Turkish support for a northern front was not a "slam-dunk." In this case, leaders' preferences except for party leader Erdoğan's were aligned with public opinion until war was inevitable. The burden sharing decision model suggests that U.S. strategy would have been better satisfied vis-à-vis Turkey if it had identified the threat of Kurdish independence perceived within Turkey. If U.S. policymakers had given Turkey a significant voice on policy decisions regarding northern Iraq, Turkey would have been less likely to feel threatened by an Iraq intervention. Unfortunately, this position was not reached until late in the negotiations with the U.S., and was never sufficiently presented to the Council of Ministers and the TBMM, resulting in a "no" vote.

---

[1] The Turkish Grand National Assembly (TBMM) voted 264 – 251 on a measure that would have authorized as many as 62,000 American troops to stage an invasion of Iraq from Turkish soil. Under Turkish parliamentary rules, however, a majority of Members of Parliament (MPs) present in the chamber needed to vote "yes" for the measure to pass. Since there were 19 abstentions, the measure failed by three votes.

[2] Rajan Menon and S. Enders Wimbush, "The US and Turkey: End of an Alliance?" *Survival* 49, no. 2 (2007).

[3] Sabri Sayari, "Between Allies and Neighbors: Turkey's Burden Sharing Policy in the Gulf Conflict," in *Friends in Need: Burden Sharing in the Persian Gulf War*, ed. Andrew Bennett, Joseph Lepgold, and Danny Unger (New York: St. Martin's Press, 1997), 198-201.

[4] Gordon and Trainor, *Cobra II: The inside Story of the Invasion and Occupation of Iraq*, 111, Bob Woodward, *Plan of Attack* (New York: Simon & Schuster, 2004), 123, Michael DeLong and Noah Lukeman, *Inside CENTCOM: The Unvarnished Truth About the Wars in Afghanistan and Iraq* (Washington, D.C.: Regnery Pub., 2004), 79-80.

[5] One of the largest weaknesses of the coalition building effort for the U.S. was the inability to garner basing rights from the nearest NATO ally.

[6] Bob Kemper, "White House Tells Turkey That Rebuff Could Be Costly," *Chicago Tribune*, March 4, 2003, 1, 5.

[7] Henri J. Barkey, "Turkey and Iraq: The Perils (and Prospects) of Proximity," *Iraq and Its Neighbors* (Washington DC: United States Institute of Peace, 2005), 16.

[8] Carol Migdalovitz, "Turkey: Issues for U.S. Policy," *Report for Congress RL31429* (Washington, DC: Congressional Research Service, 2002).

[9] The final memorandum of agreement was never signed since Ankara wanted an approved resolution before signing the agreement. "Ankara Steps up Iraq Diplomacy Ahead of Holiday," *Turkish Daily News*, February 8, 2003, Serpil Cevikcan, "Eighty Thousand Turkish Soldiers Will Be Deployed in Northern Iraq," *Milliyet*, February 8, 2003, 16, Gareth Winrow, "Turkey: Recalcitrant Ally," in *The Iraq War: Causes and Consequences*, ed. Rick Fawn and Raymond A. Hinnebusch (Boulder, Colo.: Lynne Rienner Publishers, 2006), 197.

[10] Morton I. Abramowitz, "What's up with Turkey?" *Wall Street Journal*, March 25, 2003, Sadat Ergin, "Tough Decision," *Hurriyet* December 13, 2002, David E. Sanger, "Turk Offers Partial Support on Iraq in Meeting with Bush," *The New York Times*, December 11, 2002.

[11] *Turkish - US Relations 2003* (Anatolia.com Inc., Office of the Prime Minister, Directorate of Press and Information, 2003 [cited January 11, 2007]); available from http://www.turkishpress.com/specials/2003/yir/usa.asp.

[12] Phillip P. Pan, "Turkish Vote on Troops Shows Surprises of Democracy," *The Washington Post*, March 6, 2003.

[13] Barkey, "Turkey and Iraq: The Perils (and Prospects) of Proximity," 2.

[14] Deniz Arslan, "Diplomatic Sources: Turkey to Reassess Sending Troops to Iraq after Gul Returns," *Anatolia*, July 28, 2003, Ugar Ergan, Turan Yilmaz, and Umit Cetin, "National Assembly Will Make the Final Decision," *Hurriyet*, August 13, 2003.

[15] Secretary of Defense Rumsfeld argued that the lack of a northern front directly affected to the ensuing insurgency. According to Rumsfeld, had the 4th Infantry Division been allowed transit through Turkey, there would have been many more troops on the ground and the insurgency might not have gained momentum. See Thom Shanker, "Rumsfeld Faults Turkey for Barring Use of Its Land in '03 to Open Northern Front in Iraq," *The New York Times*, March 21, 2005.

[16] Sayari, "Between Allies and Neighbors: Turkey's Burden Sharing Policy in the Gulf Conflict."

[17] F. Stephen Larrabee, Ian O. Lesser, and Center for Middle East Public Policy (Rand Corporation), *Turkish Foreign Policy in an Age of Uncertainty* (Santa Monica, CA: Rand, 2003), 166, Helen Chapin Metz, *The Middle East* (Government Printing Office for the Library of Congress, 1995 [cited February 25, 2008]); available from http://countrystudies.us/turkey/73.htm.

[18] For a discussion of two-level games in international politics see Putnam, "Diplomacy and Domestic Politics: The Logic of Two-Level Games."

[19] Turkish public opinion against an Iraq intervention fluctuated between 90 percent in January 2002 and 80 percent in May 2003. Christopher Brewin, "Turkey: Democratic Legitimacy," in *The Iraq War and Democratic Politics*, ed. Alex Danchev and John MacMillan (London ; New York: Routledge, 2005), 96, Nasuh Uslu et al., "Turkish Public Opinion toward the United States in the Context of the Iraq Question," *Middle East Review of International Affairs* 9, no. 3 (2005).

[20] Newspaper polls showed that 74 percent of those surveyed opposed Turkey's entry into the 1991 Persian Gulf War. Clyde Haberman, "War in the Gulf: Turkey's Role in Air Assault Sets Off Fear of Retaliation," *The New York TImes*, January 20, 1991.

[21] Bill Park, "Strategic Location, Political Dislocation: Turkey, the United States, and Northern Iraq," *Middle East Review of International Affairs* 7, no. 2 (2003), 14.

[22] Woodward, *Plan of Attack*, 324-25. Gordon and Trainor, *Cobra II: The inside Story of the Invasion and Occupation of Iraq*.

[23] Abramowitz, "What's up with Turkey?" A13.

[24] Richard Boudreaux, "Showdown with Iraq; News Analysis; the Reasons Turkey Rejected U.S.; Ultimatums and Other Perceived Insensitivities May Have Doomed Access for Ground Forces," *Los Angeles Times*, March 3, 2003, A1.

[25] Bradley Graham and Peter Slevin, "U.S. Won't Sweeten Aid Offer to Turkey; $6 Billion Offer for Access Is Final, Bush Tells Ankara," *The Washington Post*, February 20, 2003, Ilene R Prusher, "Turkey Seeks Assurances from US; Ankara Wants $30 Billion from Washington to Cover Potential Damages from an Attack by Iraq," *Christian Science Monitor*, February 18, 2003.

[26] Barkey, "Turkey and Iraq: The Perils (and Prospects) of Proximity," 17, James E Kapsis, "The Failure of U.S. - Turkish Pre-Iraq War Negotiations: An Overconfident United States, Political Mismanagement, and Conflicted Military," *Middle East Review of International Affairs* 10, no. 3 (2006).

[27] Sadat Ergin, "The United States Backed Down When Turkey Broke the Talks," *Hurriyet*, September 23, 2003.

[28] Pan, "Turkish Vote on Troops Shows Surprises of Democracy."

[29] Gerry J. Gilmore, *Disappointed Wolfowitz Still Supports U.S.-Turkish Defense Ties* (American Forces Press Service, 2003 [cited February 28, 2008]); available from http://www.defenselink.mil/news/newsarticle.aspx?id=29012.

[30] Kemal Kirişçi, "Between Europe and the Middle East: The Transformation of Turkish Policy," *Middle East Review of International Affairs* 8, no. 1 (2004), 44-45.

[31] Sabri Sayari, "Between Allies and Neighbors: Turkey's Burden Sharing Policy in the Gulf Conflict," 197-99.

[32] During his visit to Washington in Jan 2002, Prime Minister Ecevit argued against military intervention due to the impact on Turkey of a war. Sadat Ergin, "Do Not Worry, the Turks Will Not Let Us Down," *Hurriyet*, September 17, 2003.

[33] Jim Lehrer, *Newsmaker: Bulent Ecevit* (MacNeil/Lehrer Productions, January 17, 2002 [cited April 28, 2008]); available from http://www.pbs.org/newshour/bb/middle_east/jan-june02/ecevit_1-17.html.

[34] Fatih Erturk, "Baykal: President Sezer Is Opposed to War," *Sabah*, January 19, 2003.

[35] Park, "Strategic Location, Political Dislocation: Turkey, the United States, and Northern Iraq," 11, Bill Parks, "Bridgehead or Bridge?" *The World Today* 58, no. 10 (2002).

[36] "Turkey, US Agree on Deterrent Policy against, Territorial Integrity of Iraq" *Anatolia*, December 3, 2002.

[37] "Turkey's Gul Says Syria, Turkey to Exert Efforts for Peaceful Solution to Iraq" *Anatolia*, January 4, 2003.

[38] Fikret Bila, "Gul: Saddam Should Cease to Be a Threat," *Milliyet*, January 16, 2003, 14.

[39] "Turkey, US Agree on Deterrent Policy against, Territorial Integrity of Iraq."

[40] Karl Vivk, "After Calls on Turkey, U.S. Put on Hold," *Washington Post*, January 8, 2003.

[41] Sami Kohen, "Before the Decision Is Final..." *Milliyet* December 5, 2002.

[42] Glenn Kessler and Phillip P. Pan, "Missteps with Turkey Prove Costly; Diplomatic Debacle Denied U.S. A Strong Northern Thrust in Iraq," *The Washington Post*, March 28, 2003.

[43] Ibid.

[44] Sadat Ergin, "We Can Open a Northern Front but a UN Resolution Is Needed," *Hurriyet*, September 21, 2003.

[45] Sadat Ergin, "Looks Like We Missed That Train," *Hurriyet*, September 25, 2003.

[46] Yasemin Congar, "The Mending Has Begun," *Milliyet*, June 23, 2003.

[47] Asli Aydintasbas, "New Lease of Life with United States," *Sabah*, June 25, 2003.

[48] Dexter Filkins, "Turkey Says U.S. Has Detained Some of Its Soldiers in North Iraq," *The New York Times*, July 6, 2003.

[49] Fikret Bila, "Turkish-US Relations," *Milliyet*, July 21, 2003, Guneri Civaoglu, "Compensation for Hurt Pride," *Milliyet*, July 24, 2003.

[50] Arslan, "Diplomatic Sources: Turkey to Reassess Sending Troops to Iraq after Gul Returns," Derya Sazak, "Raid in Northern Iraq," *Milliyet*, July 6, 2003.

[51] Ergan, Yilmaz, and Cetin, "National Assembly Will Make the Final Decision," 22.

[52] Barkey, "Turkey and Iraq: The Perils (and Prospects) of Proximity," Winrow, "Turkey: Recalcitrant Ally," 204.

[53] Utku Cakir Ozer, "Muslim Countries Should Come for the United States to Leave," *Milliyet*, August 23, 2003.

[54] Barkey, "Turkey and Iraq: The Perils (and Prospects) of Proximity," 12, Susan Sachs, "Turkey Begins to Think Twice About Sending Troops to Iraq," *The New York Times*, October 24, 2003, A12, Jeremy M. Sharp and Christopher M. Blanchard, "Post-War Iraq: A Table and Chronology of Foreign Contributions," *CRS Report for Congress* (Washington DC: Congressional Research Service, 2005).

[55] Barkey, "Turkey and Iraq: The Perils (and Prospects) of Proximity," 17, Derya Sazak, "One Step Ahead," *Milliyet*, January 29, 2004, 19.

[56] "FM Gul's Letter to Annan on Iraq " *Anatolia*, January 27, 2005.

[57] "Erdogan: Developments in Kirkuk Are Not Positive," *Anatolia*, January 27, 2005.

[58] The package was approved by Congress in April 2003 and signed in Dubai in September 2003. Turkish officials eventually turned down the package in March 2005 due to the restrictions placed on the grant/loan. "Turkish US Envoy Explains Work under Way for More Appropriate Conditions for Loan," *Anatolia*, February 17, 2004, Winrow, "Turkey: Recalcitrant Ally," 200.

[59] Vivian C. Jones, "Iraq's Trade with the World: Data and Analysis," *CRS Report for Congress* (Washington D.C.: Congressional Research Service, 2004), 19.

[60] Ayla Ogus and Can Erbil, "The Effects of Instability on Turkey's Bilateral Trade with Iraq," *Turkish Policy Quarterly* 4, no. 4 (2005).

[61] Barkey, "Turkey and Iraq: The Perils (and Prospects) of Proximity."

[62] In November 2007, Turkey imposed economic sanctions on the Kurdistan Regional Government in an effort to stop cross-border operations of the PKK. See Patrick Cockburn, *Turkey Imposes Sanctions on Iraqi Kurdistan in Bid to Halt PKK* (Independent.co.uk, 2007 [cited February 29, 2008]); available from http://www.independent.co.uk/news/europe/turkey-imposes-sanctions-on-iraqi-kurdistan-in-bid-to-halt-pkk-398680.html.

[63] Richard A. Oppel, Jr., "Turkish-Bred Prosperity Makes War Less Likely in Iraqi Kurdistan," *The New York Times*, November 7, 2007.

[64] Winrow, "Turkey: Recalcitrant Ally," 205.

[65] Sharp and Blanchard, "Post-War Iraq: A Table and Chronology of Foreign Contributions," 21.

[66] Woodward, *Plan of Attack*, 139-44.

[67] Ibid. Gordon and Trainor, *Cobra II: The inside Story of the Invasion and Occupation of Iraq*.

[68] Ergin, "Looks Like We Missed That Train."

[69] "Turkey Says Current Cooperation with US Reflects US Preferences on War Plans " *Anatolia*, March 29, 2003.

[70] Turkey initially delayed opening its airspace to U.S. warplanes despite parliamentary approval for the overflights, insisting the United States agree to its demands to move troops into northern Iraq. The resolution passed by parliament would also allow Turkey to move its own forces into northern Iraq. James C. Helicke, "Turkey Agrees to U.S. Overflights for Iraq War," *Associated Press Worldstream*, March 21, 2003. See also Ergin, "Looks Like We Missed That Train," Suzan Fraser, "Turkey's Parliament Allows U.S. To Use Airspace for Iraq War," *Associated Press*, March 20, 2003, "US, Turkey Split over Airspace," *Herald Sun*, March 22, 2003.

[71] Winrow, "Turkey: Recalcitrant Ally," 204.

[72] Soner Cagaptay, *U.S.-Turkish Military Cooperation in Iraq: The Next Step* (The Washington Institute for Near East Policy, August 13, 2003 [cited November 2, 2006]); available from http://www.washingtoninstitute.org/templateC06.php?CID=393.

[73] Ergin, "Looks Like We Missed That Train."

[74] Jihan al-Husayni, "Mas'ud Barzani: The Turkish Forces' Entry into Iraq Will Lead to Large Dangers. We Will Deal with the Americans as Occupation Forces If They Do Not Withdraw after Drafting a Constitution, Electing a Parliament, and Forming a Government," *Al-Sharq al-Awsat* October 16, 2003.

[75] Larrabee, Lesser, and Center for Middle East Public Policy (Rand Corporation), *Turkish Foreign Policy in an Age of Uncertainty*, 166. William M. Hale, *Turkish Foreign Policy, 1774-2000* (London; Portland: Frank Cass, 2000).

[76] Hale, *Turkish Foreign Policy, 1774-2000*, 220, Heinz Kramer, *A Changing Turkey: The Challenge to Europe and the United States* (Washington, D.C.: Brookings Institution Press, 2000), 119.

[77] Torumtay's resignation, the first of any Chief of General Staff, underscored his opposition to direct involvement in the first Iraq war, see Sayari, "Between Allies and Neighbors: Turkey's Burden Sharing Policy in the Gulf Conflict," 211.

[78] Hale, *Turkish Foreign Policy, 1774-2000*, 220-21.

[79] Haberman, "War in the Gulf: Turkey's Role in Air Assault Sets Off Fear of Retaliation."

[80] Sayari, "Between Allies and Neighbors: Turkey's Burden Sharing Policy in the Gulf Conflict," 211.

[81] Morton I. Abramowitz, "Dateline Ankara: Turkey after Ozal," *Foreign Policy*, no. 91 (1993), 170-71.

[82] Carkoglu, "Turkey's November 2002 Elections: A New Beginning?" 32.

[83] In a review of newspaper articles in *Hurriyet* and *Milliyet*, from October 2002 through March 1, 2003, there were no articles or editorials written by prominent Turkish politicians supporting the U.S. position concerning regime change in Iraq.

[84] Ian O. Lesser, *Off Autopilot: The Future of Turkish-US Relations* (Colombia International Affairs Online, Winter (Volume 4, Number 4) 2005 [cited November 14 2006]); available from http://www.ciaonet.org/olj/tpq/vol4-4/vol4-4c.html.

[85] Larrabee, Lesser, and Center for Middle East Public Policy (Rand Corporation), *Turkish Foreign Policy in an Age of Uncertainty*, 166, Metz, *The Middle East.*

[86] Larrabee, Lesser, and Center for Middle East Public Policy (Rand Corporation), *Turkish Foreign Policy in an Age of Uncertainty*, 166.

[87] Hale, *Turkish Foreign Policy, 1774-2000*, 225. Abramowitz, "Dateline Ankara: Turkey after Ozal," 178.

[88] Kemal Kirişçi, "Turkey and the Muslim Middle East," in *Turkey's New World : Changing Dynamics in Turkish Foreign Policy*, ed. Alan Makovsky and Sabri Sayari (Washington, DC: Washington Institute for Near East Policy, 2000), 43-44.

[89] Larrabee, Lesser, and Center for Middle East Public Policy (Rand Corporation), *Turkish Foreign Policy in an Age of Uncertainty*, 166.

[90] Migdalovitz, "Turkey: Issues for U.S. Policy," CRS-17, 18.

[91] Larrabee, Lesser, and Center for Middle East Public Policy (Rand Corporation), *Turkish Foreign Policy in an Age of Uncertainty*, 34.

[92] Paul Salopek, "Cabinet Supports U.S. Use of Turkish Bases; Parliament Gets Final Say on Issue," *Chicago Tribune*, Febraury 25, 2003, 6.

[93] Migdalovitz, "Turkey: Issues for U.S. Policy," CRS-10.

[94] Kirişçi, "Turkey and the Muslim Middle East," 43.

[95] William Hale, "Turkey, the Middle East and the Gulf Crisis," *International Affairs (Royal Institute of International Affairs 1944-)* 68, no. 4 (1992), 689, Kirişçi, "Turkey and the Muslim Middle East," 55, Robins, *Suits and Uniforms: Turkish Foreign Policy since the Cold War.*

[96] Brewin, "Turkey: Democratic Legitimacy," 102-03.

[97] Migdalovitz, "Turkey: Issues for U.S. Policy," CRS-9.

[98] Park, "Strategic Location, Political Dislocation: Turkey, the United States, and Northern Iraq," 13.

[99] Kramer, *A Changing Turkey : The Challenge to Europe and the United States*, 123-24.

[100] Lesser, *Off Autopilot: The Future of Turkish-US Relations.*

[101] Kessler and Pan, "Missteps with Turkey Prove Costly; Diplomatic Debacle Denied U.S. A Strong Northern Thrust in Iraq."

[102] Migdalovitz, "Turkey: Issues for U.S. Policy," CRS-9.

[103] Sayari, "Between Allies and Neighbors: Turkey's Burden Sharing Policy in the Gulf Conflict," 204.

[104] Boudreaux, "Showdown with Iraq; News Analysis; the Reasons Turkey Rejected U.S.; Ultimatums and Other Perceived Insensitivities May Have Doomed Access for Ground Forces," A1.

[105] Abramowitz, "What's up with Turkey?" A13.

[106] Sayari, "Between Allies and Neighbors: Turkey's Burden Sharing Policy in the Gulf Conflict," 205.

[107] Kirişçi, "Turkey and the Muslim Middle East," 45.

[108] Walt, *The Origins of Alliances*.

[109] Brewin, "Turkey: Democratic Legitimacy," 99-100.

[110] Larrabee, Lesser, and Center for Middle East Public Policy (Rand Corporation), *Turkish Foreign Policy in an Age of Uncertainty*, 36-37.

[111] Keith B. Richburg and Peter Slevin, "Turks near Deal Giving U.S. Access to Bases; Aid Pact Would Open Northern Front in War," *The Washington Post*, February 22, 2003, A01, Ugar Ergan, "Turkomans Being Armed as Well," *Hurriyet*, February 25, 2003.

[112] Kirişçi, "Between Europe and the Middle East: The Transformation of Turkish Policy," 44-45.

[113] Sayari, "Between Allies and Neighbors: Turkey's Burden Sharing Policy in the Gulf Conflict," 205-08.

[114] Although Turkey did not openly defect from the U.S. led coalition, it pursued a foreign policy strategy that weakened the U.S. international position and supported the military effort to the minimum, meeting Snyder's definition of a 'defection.' Snyder, "The Security Dilemma in Alliance Politics," 466.

[115] Ergin, "Do Not Worry, the Turks Will Not Let Us Down."

[116] Sadat Ergin, "Ecevit Allowed CIA Teams and U-2 Planes," *Hurriyet*, September 18, 2003.

[117] Prusher, "Turkey Seeks Assurances from US; Ankara Wants $30 Billion from Washington to Cover Potential Damages from an Attack by Iraq," 06. Graham and Slevin, "U.S. Won't Sweeten Aid Offer to Turkey; $6 Billion Offer for Access Is Final, Bush Tells Ankara."

[118] Kessler and Pan, "Missteps with Turkey Prove Costly; Diplomatic Debacle Denied U.S. A Strong Northern Thrust in Iraq."

[119] Sadat Ergin, "The Authorization Bill Split the AKP," *Hurriyet*, September 24, 2003.

[120] Fikret Bila, "We Will Enter Iraq Not for USA but for Turkey," *Milliyet*, February 2, 2003.

[121] Metehan Demir, "War Scenarios at the MGK," *Hurriyet*, January 30, 2003.

[122] Larrabee, Lesser, and Center for Middle East Public Policy (Rand Corporation), *Turkish Foreign Policy in an Age of Uncertainty*, 166.

[123] Salmoni, *Strategic Partners or Estranged Allies: Turkey, the United States, and Operation Iraqi Freedom*.

[124] Aydin, "Determinants of Turkish Foreign Policy, and Turkey's European Vocation."

[125] The largest incumbent coalition partner, the Democratic Left Party, saw its support dwindle to only 1.2% of the electorate, marking the most significant drop in Turkish political history. Carkoglu, "Turkey's November 2002 Elections: A New Beginning?" 30, 35.

[126] Aydin, "Determinants of Turkish Foreign Policy, and Turkey's European Vocation."

[127] Carkoglu, "Turkey's November 2002 Elections: A New Beginning?" 34.

[128] "Turkey: Country Profile 2003," *Country Profiles* (London: The Economist Intelligence Unit, 2003), 4.

[129] Salmoni, *Strategic Partners or Estranged Allies: Turkey, the United States, and Operation Iraqi Freedom.*

[130] Fikret Bila, "Harmony," *Milliyet*, July 28, 2003, 14.

[131] Republic of Turkey, *The Constitution of the Republic of Turkey* (2001 [cited April 1, 2008]); available from http://www.anayasa.gov.tr/images/loaded/pdf_dosyalari/THE_CONSTITUTION_OF_THE_REPUBLIC_OF_TURKEY.pdf.

[132] Salmoni, *Strategic Partners or Estranged Allies: Turkey, the United States, and Operation Iraqi Freedom.*

[133] Ergin, "Do Not Worry, the Turks Will Not Let Us Down."

[134] Murat Yetkin, *Tezkere: Irak Krizinin Gerçek Öyküsü* (Istanbul: Remzi Kitabevi, 2004). Quoted in Ozdamar and Taydas, "Foreign Policy, Public Opinion and the Iraq War: The Turkish Case."

[135] Ozdamar and Taydas, "Foreign Policy, Public Opinion and the Iraq War: The Turkish Case," 30.

[136] Sami Kohen, "The Number One Threat," *Milliyet*, March 14, 2002.

[137] Fikret Bila, *Sivil Darbe Girisimi Ve Ankara'da Irak Savaslari* (Ankara: Ümit Yayncilik, 2003), 44. Quoted in Ozdamar and Taydas, "Foreign Policy, Public Opinion and the Iraq War: The Turkish Case," 24.

[138] Sadat Ergin, "Ecevit This Time Yielding to United States," *Hurriyet*, July 18, 2002.

[139] Ergin, "Do Not Worry, the Turks Will Not Let Us Down."

[140] Ecevit outlined four conditions for Turkish support: (1) No Kurdish state in Northern Iraq, (2) Turkish economic losses should be compensated, (3) the new regime should be acceptable to the people of Iraq, and (4) Mosul and Kirkuk could not be left to the Kurds. See Ugar Ergan, "Four Conditions by Turkey in Exchange for Saddam," *Hurriyet*, July 17, 2002.

[141] Ergin, "Do Not Worry, the Turks Will Not Let Us Down."

[142] Ergin, "Ecevit Allowed CIA Teams and U-2 Planes."

[143] Ibid.

[144] Ibid.

[145] Ibid, Sami Kohen, "To Hit or Not to Hit," *Milliyet*, August 31, 2002, 18, Bila, *Sivil Darbe Girisimi Ve Ankara'da Irak Savaslari*, 44.

[146] Kohen, "To Hit or Not to Hit."

[147] Ergin, "Ecevit Allowed CIA Teams and U-2 Planes."

[148] Yetkin, *Tezkere: Irak Krizinin Gerçek Öyküsü*. Cited in Ozdamar and Taydas, "Foreign Policy, Public Opinion and the Iraq War: The Turkish Case," 31.

[149] Bila, *Sivil Darbe Girisimi Ve Ankara'da Irak Savaslari*. Cited in Ozdamar and Taydas, "Foreign Policy, Public Opinion and the Iraq War: The Turkish Case," 23.

[150] Ertugrul Ozkok, "Has Ecevit's Illness Saved Saddam?" *Hurriyet*, June 15, 2002, 25, Derya Sazak, "Ecevit's Health," *Milliyet*, May 5, 2002, Carkoglu, "Turkey's November 2002 Elections: A New Beginning?"

[151] Soner Cagaptay, "November 2002 Elections and Turkey's New Political Era," *Middle East Review of International Affairs* 6, no. 4 (2002), Carkoglu, "Turkey's November 2002 Elections: A New Beginning?"

[152] Kapsis, "The Failure of U.S. - Turkish Pre-Iraq War Negotiations: An Overconfident United States, Political Mismanagement, and Conflicted Military."

[153] Sadat Ergin, "You Have Three Days; Otherwise There Will Be Consequences," *Hurriyet*, September 20, 2003.

[154] Stephen F. Hayes, "Wolfowitz Talks Turkey," *The Weekly Standard*, December 16, 2002.

[155] Sadat Ergin, "The Bargaining Begins," *Hurriyet*, September 19, 2003.

[156] Ibid.

[157] Ibid.

[158] Ibid., Yetkin, *Tezkere: Irak Krizinin Gerçek Öyküsü* Cited in Ozdamar and Taydas, "Foreign Policy, Public Opinion and the Iraq War: The Turkish Case," 31.

[159] Ergin, "The Bargaining Begins."

[160] Hayes, "Wolfowitz Talks Turkey."

[161] Ergin, "The Bargaining Begins."

[162] Ibid.

[163] Ergin, "You Have Three Days; Otherwise There Will Be Consequences."

[164] Ibid.

[165] Ergin, "We Can Open a Northern Front but a UN Resolution Is Needed."

[166] Ibid.

[167] Ibid.

[168] Ibid.

[169] Bila, "We Will Enter Iraq Not for USA but for Turkey," Sadat Ergin, "We Thought There Were Troops on the Ships; Turns out There Were Not Any," *Hurriyet*, September 22, 2003.

[170] Ozdamar interview with Yasar Yakis, March 7, 2008. Quoted in Ozdamar and Taydas, "Foreign Policy, Public Opinion and the Iraq War: The Turkish Case," 31-32.

[171] Bila, "We Will Enter Iraq Not for USA but for Turkey," Ergin, "We Thought There Were Troops on the Ships; Turns out There Were Not Any."

[172] Ergin, "The Authorization Bill Split the AKP."

[173] Ibid.

[174] Gordon and Trainor, *Cobra II: The inside Story of the Invasion and Occupation of Iraq*, 111-15.

[175] Cevikcan, "Eighty Thousand Turkish Soldiers Will Be Deployed in Northern Iraq," Derya Sazak, "Future of Region Not Clear for the United States," *Milliyet*, February 10, 2003.

[176] Deniz Bolukbasi, *I Mart Vakasi: Tezkere Krizi Ve Sonrasi* (Istanbul: Dogan Egmont Yayincilik ve Yapimcilik Tic, 2008). Cited in Ozdamar and Taydas, "Foreign Policy, Public Opinion and the Iraq War: The Turkish Case," 32-33.

[177] Yan Feng, "Behind the Bargaining between US and Turkey," *Xinhua Domestic Service* February 22, 2002, Ilene R Prusher, *Interview with Christian Amanpour* (CNN, 2003 [cited April 3, 2008]); available from http://transcripts.cnn.com/TRANSCRIPTS/0303/07/i_c.01.html, Samil Tayyar, "Bush's Hands Are Tied," *Sabah*, February 21, 2003.

[178] Ergin, "The Authorization Bill Split the AKP."

[179] Ozdamar and Taydas, "Foreign Policy, Public Opinion and the Iraq War: The Turkish Case," 35.

[180] Ergin, "The Authorization Bill Split the AKP."

[181] Ibid.

[182] Ozdamar and Taydas, "Foreign Policy, Public Opinion and the Iraq War: The Turkish Case," 46.

[183] Ibid.

[184] George E. Gruen, "Turkey's "Political Earthquake:" Significance for the United States and the Region," *American Foreign Policy Interests* 25 (2003).

[185] Ergin, "The Authorization Bill Split the AKP." See also Kapsis, "The Failure of U.S. - Turkish Pre-Iraq War Negotiations: An Overconfident United States, Political Mismanagement, and Conflicted Military."

[186] Ergin, "Tough Decision."

[187] Ergin, "We Thought There Were Troops on the Ships; Turns out There Were Not Any."

[188] Ozdamar and Taydas, "Foreign Policy, Public Opinion and the Iraq War: The Turkish Case," 38.

[189] Kapsis, "The Failure of U.S. - Turkish Pre-Iraq War Negotiations: An Overconfident United States, Political Mismanagement, and Conflicted Military," 39.

[190] In March 2003, an Ankara research center reported that Turks were 94% against the use of Turkish bases and troops by the American forces, and 87% opposed to American intervention see Brewin, "Turkey: Democratic Legitimacy," 96. See also Uslu et al., "Turkish Public Opinion toward the United States in the Context of the Iraq Question."

[191] Nicholas Birch, "As Turkey Reels, Hurdles Loom for EU Bid, Iraq Attack," *Christian Science Monitor*, July 12, 2002, 07.

[192] Kirişçi, "Turkey and the Muslim Middle East," 55.

[193] Phillip P. Pan, "Turkey Rejects U.S. Use of Bases; Vote Could Alter Troop Deployment," *The Washington Post*, March 2, 2003.

[194] For a comprehensive review of Turkish public opinion towards the Iraq War see Uslu et al., "Turkish Public Opinion toward the United States in the Context of the Iraq Question."

[195] Jenkins, *Context and Circumstance: The Turkish Military and Politics*, Karaosmanoglu, "The Evolution of the National Security Culture and the Military in Turkey," Kramer, *A Changing Turkey: The Challenge to Europe and the United States*, 34.

[196] Kramer, *A Changing Turkey: The Challenge to Europe and the United States*, 33.

[197] Ergin, "Looks Like We Missed That Train."

[198] Yetkin, *Tezkere: Irak Krizinin Gerçek Öyküsü.* Cited in Ozdamar and Taydas, "Foreign Policy, Public Opinion and the Iraq War: The Turkish Case," 36.

[199] Ergin, "Looks Like We Missed That Train."

[200] Kohen, "To Hit or Not to Hit," 18.

[201] Bila, "We Will Enter Iraq Not for USA but for Turkey."

[202] Sukru Kucuksahin, "Signs of a Lasting Political MOU," *Hurriet*, March 6, 2003, 17.

[203] Ikenberry, *After Victory: Institutions, Strategic Restraint, and the Rebuilding of Order after Major Wars*.

[204] Mehmet Tezkan, "What Happened to International Legitimacy?" *Sabah*, April 4, 2003.

[205] Barkey, "Turkey and Iraq: The Perils (and Prospects) of Proximity," 17.

[206] Ibid., 18-19.

# 5
# Putting the Pieces Together

The evolution of the Iraq War coalition from the initial invasion through the post-war stability and reconstruction operations highlights the transitory nature of coalitions that are not bound by formal alliance agreements. "Coalitions of the willing" or "coalitions of choice" present an interesting challenge to the participating states since by definition, threat perceptions are low—participation is voluntary rather than a matter of survival. The participants of the Iraq conflict had to weigh the demands of the U.S. and international environment against domestic pressures in many cases to remain on the sidelines. State executives were forced to employ foreign policy strategies that balanced these competing demands. Ad hoc coalition leaders must convince participants that the military adventure is worth the domestic costs. In the Iraq War, the U.S. initiated the action with a limited coalition but soon found the need to increase the level of international participation bringing partners into the coalition through a variety of private and public incentives. The Bush administration found itself with multiple "two level" bargaining problems where concessions were offered to placate domestic publics of potential participants.

The ad hoc nature of the coalition highlights the differences between coalition and alliance participation. The NATO alliance has developed an accepted process for assessing burdens on member states. Although compliance with burden assessments is somewhat questionable, NATO maintains a formalized process to adjudicate defense burdens.[1] NATO's Defense Planning Committee and Defense Review Committee oversee the force planning process and coordinate national defense plans towards NATO Force Goals. Allied defense planning is reviewed annually and given direction by NATO Ministers of Defense in an Annual Defense Review. The Annual Defense Review assesses the contribution of member countries in relation to their respective capabilities and constraints in the context of the Force Goals assigned to them. Specific defense planning targets for each member country are developed based on this ministerial level guidance. Member states implement agreed defense planning procedures, which provide the methodology for determining and reporting on the forces levels necessary to implement Force Goals. The NATO international staff monitors and assesses countries' actions in response to the required forces and capabilities placed on them by this force planning process and reports to the Defense Planning Committee on state compliance.[2] NATO's highly institutionalized process insures that states have a forum for addressing defense burden targets. Although states attempt to "burden-shift" within the NATO force planning process, a governing process exists for addressing defense burden issues.

Ad hoc coalitions, on the other hand, have no equivalent process for establishing defense burdens for a particular operation. In contrast to the highly institutionalized process seen in NATO, ad hoc coalition burdens are determined as a result of a bilateral bargaining process with the coalition initiator. Rather than addressing burdens within a committee structure, burdens are determined individually on a case-by-case basis.

States form coalitions to address a particular crisis, with no expectation of broader cooperation in other areas or continued partnership once the immediate situation is resolved. States are free to join and exit at will; therefore, coalitions are far less restrictive or inhibiting than alliances.[3] Since coalitions tend to be in response to an already ongoing crisis, potential allies have significant leverage against the coalition initiator to extract concessions for their support. Potential coalition partners have significant bargaining leverage over the coalition leader due to the short timeframe generally available for coalition building. Turkey was able to gain significant concessions from the U.S.—although never executed—because of the perceived imperative for a Turkish front for the initial invasion. Relative bargaining power turns on perceptions of comparative dependence and intensity of interest in the bargaining situation. For instance, South Korea provided significant material support to the coalition since it was highly dependent on influencing U.S. policy towards North Korea. A coalition, in most instances, will need to be assembled quickly since it is in response to an existing crisis, therefore, a bargainer who wants an agreement soon will be at a disadvantage in dealing with someone who has a temporal advantage.[4] For instance, the U.S. provided significant financial support to Poland to expedite its significant contribution to the coalition at a time when there was still disagreement in the international community regarding the legitimacy of the intervention.

The burden sharing decisions of South Korea, Germany, and Turkey illustrated the influence of domestic pressures on international decisions. Although state executives certainly influence domestic opinion, they were limited by the constraints of domestic structure. The influence of the public was shaped by the centralization of the government and the influence of the legislature on foreign policy decisions. As highlighted in the foreign policy literature—but often overlooked in the broader international relations canon—states present a myriad of responses to the international environment based on the opportunities and constraints provided by the domestic environment. State decisions to commit resources to an ad hoc security coalition are influenced by the ability of the government to extract resources from the society. The domestic structure typology of the burden sharing model provided an excellent framework for analyzing the influence of domestic politics on state foreign policy decisions, with limitations. National elections significantly affected the domestic structure and increased the influence of society over the executive.

Due to the lack of threat from Iraq for most coalition partners, their burden sharing outcomes were most influenced by alliance dependence pressures and the ability of executives to influence the government to overcome domestic pressure to abstain from the coalition.

## Domestic Influence on "Coalitions of Choice"

The three case studies, each representing a different cell in the domestic structure typology, highlight the influence of differing domestic structure on burden sharing outcomes. When controlling for external factors, domestic structure—in the form of the relationship between the state executive and legislature—significantly influences a given state's burden sharing behavior. Executive authority and parliamentary accountability appreciably affects the ability of a state to contribute military forces to an international coalition, especially in instances where threat or collective action pressures are low. States with strong executive power in the area of military oversight are less constrained in providing military forces, while states with considerable parliamentary influence are likely to show a significantly lower level of commitment.

The Republic of Korea represented a weak Type I domestic structure in the typology, in which decision making authority was restricted to relatively few government officials and the chief executive enjoyed near autonomy from legislative scrutiny. The chief executive maintains significant influence over foreign policy and is relatively free from legislative oversight in a Type I structure.[5] The political culture of

Korea, though substantially democratized in the past two decades, still favors strong executive leadership in which the President sets the tone and agenda for the National Assembly.[6] Although executive prerogatives usually gain traction in the National Assembly, the introduction of civic groups and an opposition legislature made the government a weak Type I state.[7] The Korean president enjoys significant influence over the legislature, especially in the area of foreign policy. In addition, the assembly members are relatively independent from society and reflect the interests of their party rather than their constituents. In a Type I state, the beliefs of the chief executive are expected to dominate policy decisions and therefore his or her preferences should have significant influence over executive decision making.

In the case of South Korea, the use of the domestic structure typology to determine the influence of public opinion on government decisions was a useful tool in explaining state behavior, once President Roh's preferences were known. Using the rhetoric of Roh's presidential campaign, one would predict that Roh preferred a loosening of the ROK-U.S. alliance relationship. However, since actors and structures are mutually constituted, exogenous factors can dramatically alter an actor's preferences and the structures where those preferences are translated into action. State behavior and foreign policy preferences must thus be examined within an intersubjective social context.[8] In this particular case, the North Korean nuclear crisis dramatically reordered Roh's preferences concerning the ROK relationship with the United States.[9] A pragmatic politician, Roh navigated a political middle course that reflected the need for the ROK to address the crisis on the peninsula by pursuing a more conservative agenda with the United States. Roh ideally sought an equitable alliance relationship with the United States, but against the backdrop of the North Korean nuclear crisis, Roh was forced to make more realistic policy decisions, including supporting the coalition of the willing. Roh realized that resolving the North Korean nuclear crisis was the most critical foreign policy challenge facing his presidency.

South Korea's Iraq policy was developed and implemented by a few close advisors that were loyal to Roh and sensitive to his alliance dependence concerns. Roh was able to drastically change his administration's policy towards the ROK-U.S. alliance and provide a significant number of soldiers to the coalition of the willing, despite significant domestic opposition. Once President Roh publicly committed to the coalition of the willing, legislative and societal pressure failed to alter the level or composition of Korean commitment to the coalition of the willing. The Roh administration set the public and legislative agenda, influenced key lawmakers to insure a positive vote in the National Assembly, and eventually gained legislative support for the first significant off peninsula deployment since the Vietnam War.

Although President Roh maintained significant control over the National Assembly, he still needed to formulate policy that reflected the dominant domestic preference against the Iraq deployment. The Roh administration frequently anticipated public attitudes and intentionally constrained its assistance to the Iraq coalition in an effort to alleviate public concerns. When determining the configuration of the fall 2003 deployment request, the Blue House and the National Security Council (NSC), led by Vice Chief Lee Jong-seok, were concerned that putting Korean troops in danger would have significant negative repercussions on President Roh's public opinion ratings.[10] Therefore, the NSC made anticipatory concessions that limited the scope of the deployment to safer areas in Iraq to ensure passage in the National Assembly and to disarm public opposition. The Blue House further noted the significant public opposition to the first deployment in their arguments to minimize the size of the deployment. In addition, the Roh administration made anticipatory concessions on troop withdrawals in an attempt to disarm public opposition to the deployment. This approach seems successful since, as of May 2008, the Korean government still had approximately 650 personnel deployed to Iraq. A Type I configuration does not imply that domestic attitudes are totally ignored, but rather that similar to an authoritarian regime, the administration needed to balance external needs against the level of domestic unrest.[11] Rather than allowing public opinion form the policy, Roh managed domestic expectations so that he could commit the necessary resources to the coalition to meet Korea's foreign policy goals.

The German case study proved surprising because the 2002 national elections changed the existing state structure, and allowed Germany to act as a Type II state rather than a Type IV state. German foreign policy decision making is typically decentralized due to Germany's federal arrangement in which numerous state and federal level bureaucratic offices influence foreign policy outcomes. Germany's decentralized constitutional structure instituted under the Basic Law ensures that German governments are weak and civil society is strong. The federal government is required to compromise and to consult with the governing coalition, federal offices, individual states, and opposition parties.[12] Foreign policy is the purview of the chancellor and the foreign minister but, because each is typically their respective party's leader, policy can often be divergent. To that end, a Type II state has a more centralized policy machinery than a Type IV state, but still must reflect public and legislative pressures. Due to the national elections, incumbent Chancellor Schröder was able to commandeer the foreign policy process and imprint his preferences on German policy by appealing directly to public attitudes concerning the use of force in Iraq.

The Schröder administration issued a categorical "no" to participation in the coalition of the willing and actively engaged in counter-coalition-building against the recommendations of the Foreign Office and Defense Ministry. Germany's refusal to support the U.S.-led coalition—even under a UN mandate—was unusual given the German government bureaucracy's preference to address unfavorable U.S. policies unobtrusively. As Schröder vocalized Germany's opposition to the war as a means to appeal to the public in the general election, he was able to accomplish a policy coup and develop Germany's Iraq policy position individually, rather than through the typical collaborative process that characterizes German foreign policy. The appeal to mass public opinion resulted in less elite coalition building and policy coordination than would normally be seen in a Type IV typology.

Domestic issues particularly drove Germany's position regarding the Iraq war. Schröder, leading the Social Democrat–Green coalition, steered a policy course that would preserve the coalition's parliamentary majority. As predicted by the domestic politics framework, Germany was unable to show strong support to the Iraq effort due to the influence of the legislature and polity on deployment decisions. Given the requirement for a *Bundestag* mandate, Schröder would have had to expend significant political capital—which he did not have—building a domestic coalition to pass a mandate supporting the use of force. Helmut Kohl, as well as Schröder, had performed this political maneuver throughout the 1990s, but the vote for the earlier Afghanistan intervention demonstrated that the German people had become war weary. In the Iraq case, Schröder assessed that his policy must reflect public opinion to ensure the survival of his government given the fragile state of his coalition's majority in the *Bundestag*. Such a decision would have required a formal mandate for which there was no firm majority in the coalition parties. The Schröder government proved unable to bridge the gap between its own domestic supporters and its international allies for two significant reasons. First, leading German policy-makers were not convinced that the Iraq issue demanded a military response. Secondly, the continuing German debate on the use of force through the 1990s had the cumulative effect of shrinking the government's majority with every military commitment abroad.

The strong role of the *Bundestag* in approving German military deployments ensured that the domestic constituency would influence Germany's role in the Iraq War coalition. Ultimately, the German government provided only the support that could be garnered without a *Bundestag* mandate. As a NATO partner unwilling to completely reject the U.S. role in the alliance, Germany provided a significant amount of support to U.S. efforts in Iraq and Afghanistan as long as those efforts did not necessitate a parliamentary vote. For the Iraq effort, Germany provided significant intelligence on Iraqi force disposition, allowed full use of German-based U.S. infrastructure, allowed unrestricted over flight rights, provided security forces to guard American bases, and eventually trained Iraqi security forces.

Although Turkey reflected Type I tendencies in the 1991 Persian Gulf War, in which its foreign policy was forged in a highly centralized manner without societal input, the country evolved into a Type IV state during the buildup to the Iraq War. Chronic inflation combined with persistent problems with the insurgent Kurdistan Workers Party generated a public unease with the centrally controlled authoritarian government. As a result, Turkish press and political activists gained access to the government throughout the late 1990s. The November 2002 elections, which ushered in a new ruling party, signified a major realignment of the Turkish political landscape. Members of parliament were fractured from their party leadership and held more accountable by their constituents.

A Type IV structure exists when the foreign policy decision process is composed of a number of different offices that share the responsibility for foreign policy decision making and when the legislature performs a significant oversight function. In this type of state, national leaders' preferences are shaped by domestic pressures and the state's policy response is the result of internal bureaucratic bargaining. Unable to act alone, individual policy makers must recognize domestic opponents who may appeal directly to the public. Interest groups, political parties, the media, and public opinion shape the policy-making process because the foreign policy executive is responsible to the legislature and, indirectly, to the public. Because of the many actors formulating policy, even the most powerful leaders must build a coalition of support for their preferred policy.

The Turkish government was more responsive to public opinion and less supportive of U.S. intervention in 2003 than in 1991. The United States had hoped to use Turkey to attack Iraq from the north, but the National Assembly refused to grant access to Turkish bases after weeks of wrangling over financial compensation and arrangements for sending

Turkish troops into northern Iraq. This stalemate between the government and the legislature occurred for two reasons. First, due to a proliferation of private television and radio, the government no longer had a monopoly on the dissemination of information and the shaping of public discourse. The government and military officials had to increasingly appeal to the public for support. Secondly, as a result to the November 2002 general election in which the ruling AKP party won only 34 per cent of the popular vote, it needed to be more responsive to electoral concerns.

Due to its weak popular support and splintered party elite, the AKP government was vulnerable to public opinion and needed to build consensus in and out of the National Assembly in order to garner support for a mandate allowing U.S. troops to operate from Turkish soil. After the rout of the Republican People's Party in the November 2002 general election—in which the government's coalition suffered an unprecedented set back by losing all of its seats—Turkish leaders were very reluctant to manipulate public opinion that was decidedly against an Iraq intervention. Government and party leaders waited until the war was a foregone conclusion before trying to convince the public that Turkey might benefit by cooperating in a U.S.-led war against Iraq. The AKP party leader Recep Tayyip Erdoğan could not immediately assume the Prime Minister position due to previous Islamic activity that excluded him from political office. While this issue was raised in the constitutional court, the AKP deputy Abdullah Gül assumed the office of Prime Minister. Being vulnerable to a vote of no confidence, the interim prime minister and president could not afford to take positions independent of the electorate. Due to his weak political mandate, party leader, and incoming Prime Minister, Erdoğan tolerated a high level of defection in AKP voting on the Iraq War resolution to avoid a permanent party split. Typically, Turkish politics parties vote in a bloc in the National Assembly, however, voting procedures for the March 1 vote encouraged individual rather than block voting. Erdoğan was sensitive to the polarization in his party on the Iraq issue and sent a clear signal to the deputies that they would be able to individually vote "no" without repercussions. In his position as Prime Minister Elect, Erdoğan was concerned that making the resolution binding to the party ministers could permanently divide his party before he was even seated.[13] He further made a rare parliamentary move by calling for a closed rather than an open parliamentary vote. This unusual closed vote allowed the parliament to cast its votes confidentially; only the vote totals were made public, therefore, deputies were not individually accountable for their votes. The most plausible explanation for the closed vote was for

Erdoğan to defend against a vote of "no confidence" and because such high-profile public defection would send a signal that he was weak and therefore risk the collapse of his government.[14] Political observers speculate that the outgoing Prime Minister, Abdullah Gül, who had serious reservations with the authorization bill, used the closed vote as cover to persuade other AKP deputies to vote "no." The closed vote enabled AKP cabinet members to vote "no" to a Turkish mandate without exposing to the public the weakness of the party leader.

The military, which traditionally influenced decisions on national security, remained detached from decision making once its initial advice was rebuffed. The military, concerned that the newly elected Islamic administration would blame it for a poor outcome, remained aloof so that the country's new leaders would be held accountable for their first major test with Washington.

These domestic political factors merged to constrain executive and state autonomy in supporting the U.S. coalition. In this manner, Turkey's failure to pass legislation allowing U.S. access to Turkey for a northern front in its war with Iraq can be seen as an "involuntary defection" in that the government was prepared to support U.S. policy, but domestic concerns translated through the National Assembly resulted in an outcome where Turkey kept its distance from the intervention.

Ultimately, state domestic structure was an important indicator of a state's likelihood to provide material support to the Iraq War coalition. As predicted by the burden sharing decision model, South Korea, the Type I state, provided significant levels of military support compared to the states that had more legislative influence over military deployment issues. South Korean President Roh was able to influence party politics in the unicameral legislature in order to support his desired deployment configuration. Although disagreement existed in his core constituency, he was able to build a voting bloc that would pass the deployment mandate.

The influence of a strong executive contrasts sharply with the Type IV example of Turkey. Incoming Prime Minister Erdoğan of Turkey, on the other hand, was supportive of U.S. efforts to use Turkey as a staging area for the Iraq War, but was unable to garner the necessary legislative support through typical party discipline. Since Erdoğan had to overcome legal issues to claim his position as Prime Minister, he maintained a very weak position vis-à-vis the legislature. He was unable to build enough support in the National Assembly to approve the memorandum of agreement that had been negotiated between Turkey and the United States. Erdoğan's semi-official government position allowed other government members such as Interim Prime Minister Abdullah Gül and President Sezer to influence decision making. Eventually, Erdoğan's measure supporting the U.S. was narrowly defeated in the legislature; Turkey would not allow U.S. troops to transit into Iraq. Once Erdoğan consolidated power and the Turkish public sensed the increased threat of Kurdish independence in Iraq, the government was able to convince the legislature became more supportive of measures supporting the Iraq War coalition.

Germany's support to the Iraq War coalition was also significantly influenced by domestic structure and politics. Germany was not expected by the Bush administration to substantially support the Iraq War coalition due to its history of using force only within a NATO context and overwhelming negative public reaction to U.S. Iraq policy. However, Germany's vociferous international opposition to the effort was unexpected. Chancellor Gerhard Schröder, by exploiting public attitudes for domestic political gain, ensured that a positive public reaction to any German effort in Iraq could not be supported. Since government institutions are decentralized, and policy is highly influenced by the legislature, the government was both unable and unwilling to overcome the negative view of the war constructed by Schröder. Unlike Korea, in which the government maintains significant influence over the press and the legislature, Germany was unable to build public support for German participation in the coalition.

It is important to emphasize that domestic political structure is highly dependent on issue area. A Type I state for security issues may well be a Type II state for economic issues. In South Korea, for example, the executive has significantly more influence over foreign policy than he has over economic policy. Thus, an examination of the policy-making apparatus for a particular issue area is necessary to determine the state structure for analysis.

### *Influence of State Structure on Military Deployments*

The observation that state domestic structure is an important indicator of material and diplomatic support to the coalition of the willing seems to hold when looking beyond these three case studies. States in which the executive maintained significant decision making control over, or independent from, the legislature showed a greater propensity for a high level of commitment to the coalition. The major contributor states all possessed a state structure in which the executive maintains considerable authority to deploy military forces without the consent of parliament.[15] The United Kingdom and Poland, the two largest contributors to the coalition after the United States, are states with parliaments that possess weak war powers. According to a study by the University of Düsseldorf, the United Kingdom's degree of parliamentary war powers are noted as deficient, meaning that there is no parliamentary action or debate required for the use of military force.[16] The same study designates Poland's parliamentary war powers as basic, meaning that only deployment notification is required to parliament. Conversely, states where the legislature exerts a significant influence over decision making showed a greater likelihood for no war involvement, or involvement with a very low level of commitment. Only one EU nation with comprehensive parliamentary oversight, Lithuania, provided military support to the coalition. In this case, Lithuania's military assistance can be attributed to its desire to achieve integration into Western structures, particularly the EU and NATO.[17] Ultimately, a high level of parliamentary influence over decision making in the EU was highly associated with a low degree of war involvement in Iraq.

### *Limitations of Structural Approaches: The Influence of National Elections*

State structure was an important indicator of material and diplomatic support to the coalition of the willing, however, national elections may significantly alter the influence of society over the executive. Studies of American politics suggest that the president is likely to try to maximize the chances of reelection by not committing to domestically unpopular commitments, even if this damages the state's reputation in the international community.[18] This observation has been generalized into the international community. In his quantitative study on the influence of election cycles on war propensity, Kurt Gaubatz finds that election cycle timing significantly influences a state's conflict behavior. His research suggests that democratic states tend to commit to more wars early in the election cycle and significantly fewer wars late in the cycle. Although he is careful to assign causality, he proposes that executives are unwilling to take domestically unpopular positions until safely beyond an election.[19] Atsugi Tago finds that leaders are eight times more likely to terminate a state's contribution to a coalition during an election month rather than a non-election month.[20] These research programs suggest that the electorate influence over the executive drastically increases during national elections. Considering the influence of society during elections, states are predicted to show qualities of a Type II or Type IV state during an election cycle. National leaders are unlikely to make unpopular decisions while trying to gain reelection, and assembly members are more likely to be responsive to constituent concerns during election periods that affect them.

All three case studies experience national elections during the period leading to the Iraq war and all three displayed some divergence from nominal state typology during the election period. Turkey's change was considerable. Turkey, which is typically considered a centralized-autonomous Type I state, behaved as a Type IV state due to the instability caused by national elections. Voters rejected the establishment parties and instead elected an inexperienced, anti-establishment AKP to form a government. Due to its weak popular support and fractured party elite, the AKP government was vulnerable to public opinion. Due to the uncertainty of Party Leader Erdoğan's eligibility for the Prime Minister position, the government functioned in a weak and uncoordinated manner for a number of months. During this period, the government was unable to mount a campaign supporting the Iraq War coalition and the newly elected assembly members felt more influenced by their constituencies than the party leadership. The result of this arrangement is that the Gül/Erdoğan government was unable to override public opinion, which a Type I state would normally be able to do.

Germany also underwent structural changes during the election. Chancellor Schröder was able to use the Iraq War as a wedge issue in the national elections and, in the process, centralized the policy making process concerning the Iraq War. Although this marked a change in regime type from a Type IV to a Type II, the foreign policy result was only marginally changed. Germany was unlikely to make a contribution to the coalition due to the unpopularity of the Iraq War and the necessity of garnering a *Bundestag* mandate; therefore, Germany would be expected to provide nearly the same level of support as a Type II or Type IV state. The visible difference was that Schröder was able to personalize Germany's foreign policy and present an anti-war position more extreme than what would have likely been formulated through the policy coordination process.

Finally, South Korean national and assembly elections influenced Korean decision making, but the tradition of strong presidentialism prevailed. President Roh formulated policy with an eye to domestic concerns, but once Korea's burden sharing decisions were announced, the government was able to deflect legislative and public opposition. Although elections did not change the regime type in this case, they did allow the public more influence over policy than would be typically afforded in the Korean domestic structure.

This research confirms the conclusions of Atusugi Tago in "When are Democratic Friends Unreliable?" and David Auerswald in *Disarmed Democracies* that the coalition leader is reluctant to commit to the use of force during periods of national elections if the conflict is unpopular with the public.[21] A political leader must expend a great deal of political capital to deploy forces to combat and may be unwilling to do so when faced with a public that is opposed to the intervention. Since an election is a period of heightened accountability for an executive, a failed coercive diplomacy runs the risk of severe penalty from the public. National elections represent a period of structural instability in which the electorate, and hence society, has a larger measure of authority over the executive. The heightened accountability of the executive, or in many cases the legislature, during a national election may make support to a coalition prohibitively costly. Therefore, one can expect lower levels of commitment when a leader, or his party, is subject to elections unless the military action is supported by the public.

Structural predictions are hazardous in the aftermath of national elections. One cannot adequately predict the domestic structure until the government has sufficient time to consolidate and become comfortable in its role. In the case of Turkey, the AKP could not begin to consolidate power until Prime Minister Erdoğan gained approval by the constitutional court won a follow on by-election. During Turkey's transition period, government function was highly decentralized and the party apparatus was ineffective in controlling assembly votes. Once approved as prime minister, Erdoğan consolidated power and gained influence over his party's assembly members, making Turkey once again reflect a Type I rather than a Type IV categorization. Since structural category can drastically alter predictions, one must be careful in assessing government structure during and immediately after national elections.

### *Policy Implications of Domestic Structure*

State domestic structure significantly influences the ability of the executive to execute military force policy options. An executive that is autonomous from the legislature retains significant freedom to employ military options while those that answer to the legislature must gain legislative approval to utilize military courses of action. This observation has immediate policy implications for two NATO partners of the United States.

The German *Bundestag* maintains significant control over government use-of-force decisions. Germany's coalition government has recently struggled with an effort by conservative politicians, encouraged by Chancellor Merkel, to drop some of its post-World War II inhibitions and constitutional constraints about robust security measures, including the use of military force abroad and at home. The conservative CDU has proposed a plan for Germany's parliament to cede greater discretion over troop deployments to the executive branch by creating a new National Security Council based in the chancellor's office.[22] The CDU paper suggests that the National Security Council should have the authority to approve military responses to crisis situations without waiting for parliamentary approval.[23] The Social Democrats and other opposition parties roundly criticized the idea of creating a National Security Council that would be based in the chancellery. If the German National Security Council were approved, it would likely provide the chancellery with considerable institutional influence over foreign policy.[24]

In contrast, the British House of Lords has suggested that the prime minister's war powers may have gained too much autonomy from parliamentary oversight. The United Kingdom is currently considering limiting the prime minister's authority for deploying military forces. Historically, British constitutional arrangements for deploying armed forces have been an unconstrained instrument of foreign policy. Additionally, the United Kingdom's courts have taken the view that the exercise of the deployment power is neither justifiable nor subject to review in domestic courts. As a consequence, not only is the exercise of the power immune from judicial review, but such actions are legal as a matter of domestic law.[25] Currently, Parliament has no formal role in approving deployments, although governments have usually kept Parliament informed about the decision to use force and the progress of military campaigns.[26] As a response, the House of Lords Select Committee on the Constitution has recommended a parliamentary convention to determine the role Parliament should play in making decisions to deploy force or forces outside the United Kingdom to war, intervention in an existing conflict, or to environments where there is a risk that the forces will be engaged in conflict.[27] The government responded that it is imperative that the executive have the authority to "take decisions flexibly and quickly using prerogative powers" in order to meet security demands and that existing parliamentary oversight is adequate.[28]

## The Influence of Legitimacy on Burden Sharing Decisions

Concerns about international legitimacy play an integral role in burden sharing decisions. This efficiency advantage was noted by Hans Morgenthau in *Politics Among Nations*, "Power exercised with moral or legal authority must be distinguished from naked power... legitimate power has a better chance to influence the will of its objects than equivalent illegitimate power."[29] Additionally, Morgenthau affirms the legitimacy that international organizations, such as the UN, confer on a military effort, "Power exercised in self-defense or in the name of the United Nations has a better chance to succeed than equivalent power exercised by an 'aggressor' nation or in violation of international law."[30] Legitimacy may be either normative or procedural and thus reflect a different source of authority. Procedural legitimacy arguments represent the viewpoint that behavior is legitimated when it is approved by legitimate international institutions.[31] Actions are collectively legitimized by the consensus built by a body of statute under multilateral endorsement.[32] On the other hand, normative legitimacy reflects the publicly held belief that an action is morally right or wrong. This research found each state had legitimacy concerns; however, these concerns were an incomplete indicator of state action within the Iraq War coalition. Domestic structure and the influence of society on the elements of government were important intervening variables affecting the influence of legitimacy concerns on coalition participation.

For South Korea, concerns regarding the legitimacy of the Iraq effort did not influence the decision to support the coalition, but did affect the composition and timing of the assistance offered. The initial decision to join the Iraq War coalition was not based on the international legitimacy of the operation, but rather on pragmatic concerns regarding U.S. policy towards North Korea. President Roh, in his first speech to the National Assembly, noted that the Iraq effort lacked legitimacy but was nevertheless in Korea's national interest to support the coalition. Once Korea committed to the coalition efforts, however, legitimacy issues affected the composition of the deployment. The Korean contribution was framed as a humanitarian effort, rather than as participation in potentially illegitimate combat operations. Korea's first deployment of soldiers consisted of a non-combat engineering unit of 600 soldiers and approximately 100 medical personnel to support coalition forces whose mission was to assist in controlling refugee flows and participate in postwar rehabilitation efforts. After noting the public objections to the first deployment, the Roh administration ensured that the second deployment of 3,000 soldiers comprised a peacekeeping rather than a combat mission. The Roh administration clearly sent the message to the public that the additional soldiers were dispatched in order to maintain peace and public order in Iraq and not for a war against the Iraqi people. The Roh administration rejected the U.S. request for a combat role for its sizable deployment and instead negotiated for a mission and location that in effect guaranteed that the Korean contingent would see little combat. To that end, the ROK decision to support the Iraq War coalition was not largely influenced by legitimacy concerns; however, once committed, the Roh administration balanced legitimacy concerns with the demands of national interest. Due to the ROK's Type I structure, Roh was able to overcome the public's legitimacy concerns and commit to the Iraq intervention, however, because he did not maintain a majority in the National Assembly, he had to formulate a pragmatic policy looking forward to the national elections. The public's concerns for the legitimacy of the Iraq effort influenced elite decision making, causing the Korean National Security Council to make anticipatory concessions in order to gain votes in the next assembly election.

German concerns with the Iraq War coalition exposed the difficulty in assessing legitimacy claims. German opposition illustrated the tension between normative and procedural legitimacy concerns. In the German case, these concerns conflicted, causing the government to take a foreign policy course based on German national interests. By stating that Germany would not support an intervention, even if sanctioned by the internationally established process for lawful intervention, Germany invoked its normative standard concerning the use of military force above the procedural legitimacy standard provided by a UN Security Council. By rebuking the procedural authority provided by the UN Security Council process, Schröder discounted the legitimacy provided by the United Nations in the same manner that the Bush administration discounted the legitimacy provided in its push for war. In this manner, both Schröder and Bush placed national interest above the international legitimacy provided by a Security Council resolution.

Interestingly, Germany's acquiescence to significant U.S. requests that did not require parliamentary sanction undermined German normative legitimacy arguments. Because Germany was a Type II state, Schröder could commit to the coalition in areas that did not require parliamentary support. Rather than rebuking U.S. efforts, the German government streamlined and enabled U.S. logistic and intelligence support for the war effort. The public showed little interest in lessening German support to U.S. forces transitioning to Iraq. In effect, the government and public provided sanction to the Iraq War effort as long as German forces were not directly involved. German support to the war effort was significant, gaining it the distinction as "non-coalition but cooperating."

Turkey's burden sharing was influenced by legitimacy arguments, but Turkish support to the coalition was primarily based on national interest considerations constrained by domestic politics. In the approach to the Iraq War, both President Sezer, a former constitutional court judge, and Prime Minister Gül consistently resisted contributing to the U.S. effort without a supporting international resolution. However, national interest also influenced Turkish decision making. The National Security Council drew a distinction between legitimacy and national interests stating, "a second UN Security Council resolution would be appropriate for the Iraq operation... However, if a second resolution is not passed but the operation is still unavoidable then Turkey will take all appropriate measures to safeguard its own interests." The Council approved a U.S. deployment through Turkey, but the parliament later failed to pass the authorization for Turkish participation. Once again, the Turkish case illustrated that the government took legitimacy concerns into account, but then formulated policy based on national interest. Because Turkey was a Type IV structure, domestic concerns on the legitimacy of the effort were able to override government decisions.

Legitimacy concerns were a necessary but not sufficient indicator of support to the coalition of the willing. Such concerns are transmitted to the decision making elite through public opinion. Domestic structure, especially the influence of society on the government, affects the ability of legitimacy concerns to sway government policy. In all cases, the decision making elite addressed the issue of the legitimacy of the Iraq War. In states where the leadership was autonomous from society, legitimacy concerns had a less significant effect than in states where the public had more influence over decision making. The burden sharing decision model accounts for the effect by incorporating public opinion and domestic structure.

## Implications

The war in Iraq highlights the fact that even hegemonic states will seek to share burdens across the international community for military operations. Since nations are increasingly employing military force as part of ad hoc or hybrid coalition structures, the results of the this research are important. As is evidenced in Afghanistan, burden sharing in a particular military operation is of acute interest to participating nations. Immense friction has developed in NATO over the burdens being shared in NATO's International Security Assistance Force in Afghanistan. Germany has been soundly critiqued for not providing forces to the restive areas of Afghanistan. Although on paper the German participation appears robust, the *Bundestag* mandate allows its forces to only participate in stability and reconstruction missions surrounding Kabul rather than combat missions against the Taliban and Al-Qaeda. This mandate has fomented considerable angst among NATO partners, particularly Canada and the UK who have suffered heavier causalities carrying the combat burden.[33] According to a 2007 report concerning burden sharing in Afghanistan, the coalition's internal cohesion is becoming increasingly stressed due to this burden sharing inequality. The willingness to share risks has become a key alliance issue. National caveats, which limit participation in risky mission areas, put the fundamental principle of alliance solidarity at risk.[34] The burden sharing decision model is an important tool that informs government decision makers on the influences that determine burden sharing outcomes.

This investigation of state burden sharing provides an important tool for informing the policy community on the influence of international, domestic, and cognitive factors in forming burden sharing decisions. Using the model and methodology presented here, policy makers may make predictions on expected burden sharing outcomes and also determine the factors which most influence burden sharing decisions in a particular state. For example, the U.S. government should have engaged the Turkish public as well as the government in an attempt to sell Turkish participation as a matter of national interest. Since the government was disorganized, there was no body to present national interest arguments to the public and assembly. One critique of U.S. diplomacy towards Turkey is that the State Department did not take an aggressive role in explaining to the Turkish public how a U.S intervention would meet Turkish national interests.[35] Additionally, the burden sharing model suggests that U.S. requests would be difficult for Turkey to implement. Since domestic structure had drastically changed since the 1991 Persian Gulf War, and immediate threat had greatly diminished, Turkey would not be expected to provide a level of burden sharing greater than in 1991.

In a similar fashion, the model also informs the policy community and institutionalist research program on how structures of incentives, disincentives, rules, and norms affect states' international and domestic behavior. States may manipulate international factors such as alliance dependence as a means to gain a greater share of support from a particular state. U.S. threats to reduce U.S. troop levels had significant influence on the decision making of the South Korean government. By threatening to adjust troop levels, the Bush administration forced the ROK government to assess its indigenous capability against the North Korean threat. By doing this, the U.S. was able to illustrate to the ROK government that its anti-U.S. rhetoric was unsupportable. South Korea was not able to risk a major U.S. reduction of forces on the peninsula. Similar drawdown threats towards Germany had a much smaller influence on its burden sharing outcome. Since Germany is less dependent on the United States for security, it was less influenced by alliance dependence issues. Although the planned drawdown of U.S. forces in Europe was alarming, it did not significantly influence German burden sharing outcomes.

## Concluding Thoughts

Several factors influence the proliferation of military action within coalitions as opposed to alliances. The United Nations Security Council has become more active in collective security and peacekeeping operations. Since the end of the Cold War, Russia and China have approved numerous operations that would have previously garnered a veto.[36] These United Nations authorized security missions are typically implemented through ad hoc coalitions since the UN maintains no standing security agreement. Second, the United States has fought only two military actions since World War II as a member of a standing military alliance. Rather, it chooses to engage in military action unilaterally or as a member of a coalition.[37] The termination of Cold War alignments and alliances will continue to contribute to a less rigid and more dynamic structure of international security favoring coalition versus alliance military action. "Coalitions of the willing" will need to be formed to answer to security dilemmas not anticipated by formal alliance structures. When a sense of urgency combines with sufficient international support for undertaking joint military action, coalitions are more likely than alliances to distribute costs among military members and to politically provide a sense of legitimacy and common purpose for a given action.[38] With this in mind, a more detailed understanding of coalition burden sharing is a significant and timely endeavor.

[1] Wallace J. Thies, *Friendly Rivals: Bargaining and Burden-Shifting in NATO* (Armon, NY: M.E. Sharp, 2002).

[2] North Atlantic Treaty Organization, *NATO Handbook* (Brussels: NATO Office of Information and Press, 2001), 149-51.

[3] Andrew J. Pierre, *Coalitions Building and Maintenance: The Gulf War, Kosovo, Afghanistan, and the War on Terrorism* (Washington, DC: Georgetown University, Institute for the Study of Diplomacy, 2002).

[4] Glenn H. Snyder, *Alliance Politics*, Cornell Studies in Security Affairs (Ithaca, N.Y.: Cornell University Press, 1997), 75.

[5] Susan Peterson, *Crisis Bargaining and the State: The Domestic Politics of International Conflict* (Ann Arbor: University of Michigan Press, 1996), 31. See also Andrew P. Cortell and James W. Davis, "How Do International Institutions Matter? The Domestic Impact of International Rules and Norms," *International Studies Quarterly* 40, no. 4 (1996), 455-56.

[6] Byoung-kwon Sohn, "Addressing Limits of Parliamentary Democracy," *The Korea Herald*, February 12, 2008.

[7] Katharine Moon, "US-South Korean Relations," in *The Future of US-Korean Relations: The Imbalance of Power*, ed. John Feffer (New York: Routledge, 2006).

[8] Ted Hopf, "The Promise of Constructivism in International Relations Theory," *International Security* 23, no. 1 (1998), 171-72.

[9] According to Andrew Moravcsik, states seek to realize their distinctive preferences under varying constraints imposed by the preferences of other states in the international system. Andrew Moravcsik, "Taking Preferences Seriously: A Liberal Theory of International Politics," *International Organization* 51, no. 4 (1997).

[10] "South Korean Defense Minister Denies Number of Troops to Iraq Decided," *Yonhap News Agency*, October 28, 2003.

[11] Michael N. Barnett and Jack S. Levy, "Domestic Sources of Alliances and Alignments: The Case of Egypt, 1962-73," *International Organization* 45, no. 3 (1991).

[12] Martin Walker, "The Winter of Germany's Discontent," *World Policy Journal* 19, no. 4 (2002/2003), 42-43. David P. Conradt, *The German Polity*, 6th ed. (White Plains, N.Y.: Longman, 1996).

[13] Ozgur Ozdamar and Zeynep Taydas, "Foreign Policy, Public Opinion and the Iraq War: The Turkish Case," International Studies Association Annual Convention (San Francisco: International Studies Association, 2008), 38.

[14] James E Kapsis, "The Failure of U.S.-Turkish Pre-Iraq War Negotiations: An Overconfident United States, Political Mismanagement, and Conflicted Military," *Middle East Review of International Affairs* 10, no. 3 (2006), 39.

[15] Although the U.S. and Great Britain were not required to gain legislative approval, both President Bus and Prime Minister Blair sought the support of their respective legislatures before engaging in armed conflict. This move for a vote by the legislative arms reflects the fact that public opinion supported the intervention in both the U.S. and U.K. See EOS Gallup Europe., "International Crisis Survey 21st- 27th of January 2003."

[16] Sandra Dieterich, Hartwig Hummel, and Stefan Marschall, "Parliamentary War Powers and European Participation in the Iraq War 2003: Bridging the Divide between Parliamentary Studies and International Relations" (paper presented at the 49th International ISA Convention, San Francisco, 26-29 March, 2008).

[17] Ibid, *Lithuania: Country Profile 2004*, Country Profiles (London: The Economist Intelligence Unit, 2004), 15-16.

[18] Brandice Canes-Wrone, "The Public Presidency, Personal Approval Ratings, and Policy Making," *Political Science Quarterly* 34, no. 3 (2004), David R. Mayhew, *Congress: The Electoral Connection*, 2nd ed. (New Haven: Yale University Press, 2006).

[19] Kurt Taylor Gaubatz, "Election Cycles and War," *Journal of Conflict Resolution* 35, no. 2 (1991).

[20] Atsushi Tago, "When Are Democratic Friends Unreliable? The Unilateral Withdrawal of Troops from the 'Coalition of the Willing'" (paper presented at the Annual Meeting of the American Political Science Association, Chicago, August 30-September 2, 2007).

[21] Tago finds that levels of commitment to a coalition are drastically reduced during election periods, while Auerswald suggests that executives will be reluctant to make threats and enter into armed conflict during election periods. David P. Auerswald, *Disarmed Democracies: Domestic Institutions and the Use of Force* (Ann Arbor: University of Michigan Press, 2000), Tago, "When Are Democratic Friends Unreliable? The Unilateral Withdrawal of Troops from the 'Coalition of the Willing'".

[22] Marcus Walker and McKinnon. John D., "Germany Considers Expanding Role of the Military in Security," *Wall Street Journal*, June 11, 2008, 8.

[23] "Germany's Security Strategy: Thinking the Unthinkable," *The Economist*, May 8, 2008.

[24] Judy Dempsey, "Germany Hopes to Focus on 'National Interests'," *International Herald Tribune*, May 5, 2008.

[25] House of Lords. United Kingdom, "Hl Paper 236-I Waging War: Parliament's Role and Responsibility," *15th Report of Session 2005–06*, ed. Select Committee on the Constitution (London: House of Lords, 2006), 9.

[26] Ibid.

[27] Ibid., 42.

[28] Secretary of State for Constitutional Affairs and Lord Chancellor. United Kingdom, "Government Response to the House of Lords Constitution Committee's Report Fifteenth Report of Session 2005-06: Waging War: Parliament's Role and Responsibility," (London: 2006).

[29] Hans Joachim Morgenthau and Kenneth W. Thompson, *Politics Among Nations: The Struggle for Power and Peace*, Brief ed. (New York: McGraw-Hill, 1993), 32.

[30] Ibid.

[31] G. John Ikenberry, *After Victory: Institutions, Strategic Restraint, and the Rebuilding of Order after Major Wars*, Princeton Studies in International History and Politics (Princeton: Princeton University Press, 2001).

[32] Inis L. Claude, Jr., "Collective Legitimization as a Political Function of the United Nations," *International Organization* 20, no. 3 (1966), 370.

[33] Stephen M. Saideman, David P. Auerswald, and Michael J. Tierney, "Caveat Emptor: Efforts to Control Contributions to Multilateral Military Interventions" (paper presented at the Annual Meeting of the American Political Science Association, Chicago, August 29 - September 2, 2007).

[34] Timo Noetzel and Sibylle Scheipers, "Coalition Warfare in Afghanistan: Burden-Sharing or Disunity?" *Asia and International Security Programmes*, (London: Chatham House, 2007).

[35] Bill Park, "Strategic Location, Political Dislocation: Turkey, the United States, and Northern Iraq," *Middle East Review of International Affairs* 7, no. 2 (2003), Michael Rubin, "A Comedy of Errors: American-Turkish Diplomacy and the Iraq War," (*Colombia International Affairs Online*, Spring (Volume 4, Number 1) 2005 [cited November 14, 2006]); available from http://www.ciaonet.org/olj/tpq/vol4-1/.

[36] The number of United Nations (U.N.) peacekeeping operations has increased by more than 400% since the end of the Cold War. Since 1948 there have been 61 U.N. authorized peacekeeping operations,47 have been authorized since 1998. United Nations Department of Peacekeeping Operations, "United Nations Peacekeeping Factsheet" (United Nations, 2007 [cited October 1, 2007]); available from http://www.un.org/Depts/dpko/factsheet.pdf. See also Bruce M. Russett, *What Price Vigilance? The Burdens of National Defense* (New Haven: Yale University Press, 1970), 322.

[37] The U.S. participated with alliance partners in Bosnia and Kosovo, however, even these actions were somewhat ad hoc since Article V of the North Atlantic Treaty was not activated. Participation by NATO states was voluntary for these military actions. Terry J. Pudas, "Preparing Future Coalition Commanders," *Joint Forces Quarterly*, no. 3 (1993/1994). In non-Article V operations no one can know with certainty the extent to which NATO members ultimately will contribute, see David P. Auerswald, "Explaining Wars of Choice: An Integrated Decision Model of NATO Policy in Kosovo," *International Studies Quarterly* 48, no. 3 (2004). U.S. participation in Afghanistan is separate from NATO stabilization operations.

[38] Pierre, *Coalitions Building and Maintenance: The Gulf War, Kosovo, Afghanistan, and the War on Terrorism*, 13-14.

# Bibliography


"83.8 Percent of Koreans 'Understand' Roh's Troop Dispatch Decision." *Yonhap News Agency*, April 1, 2003.

Abramowitz, Morton I. "Dateline Ankara: Turkey after Ozal." *Foreign Policy*, no. 91 (1993): 164-81.

———. "What's up with Turkey?" *Wall Street Journal*, March 25, 2003, 16.

Ahn, Byong-Man. *Elites and Political Power in South Korea*. Northampton, Mass.: Edward Elgar Publishing, 2003.

al-Husayni, Jihan "Mas'ud Barzani: The Turkish Forces' Entry into Iraq Will Lead to Large Dangers. We Will Deal with the Americans as Occupation Forces If They Do Not Withdraw after Drafting a Constitution, Electing a Parliament, and Forming a Government." *Al-Sharq al-Awsat* October 16, 2003, 3.

Albright, Madeline, and Andrew Kohut. "What the World Thinks in 2002." In *Pew Global Attitudes Project*, 79. Washington DC: The Pew Research Center for the People and the Press, 2002.

"Ankara Steps up Iraq Diplomacy Ahead of Holiday." *Turkish Daily News*, February 8, 2003.

Apple, R.W. "Bonn and Tokyo Are Criticized for Not Bearing More of Gulf Cost." *The New York Times*, September 13, 1990, A1.

Arslan, Deniz. "Diplomatic Sources: Turkey to Reassess Sending Troops to Iraq after Gul Returns." *Anatolia*, July 28, 2003.

Auerswald, David P. *Disarmed Democracies: Domestic Institutions and the Use of Force*. Ann Arbor: University of Michigan Press, 2000.

———. "Explaining Wars of Choice: An Integrated Decision Model of NATO Policy in Kosovo." *International Studies Quarterly* 48, no. 3 (2004): 631–62.

Auerswald, David P., Stephen M. Saideman, and Michael J. Tierney. "Caveat Emptor! National Oversight and Military Operations in Afghanistan." Presented to American Political Science Association National Meeting. Chicago: American Political Science Association, 2007.

Aydin, Mustafa. "Determinants of Turkish Foreign Policy, and Turkey's European Vocation." *The Review of International Affairs* 3, no. 2 (2003): 306-31.

Aydintasbas, Asli. "New Lease of Life with United States." *Sabah*, June 25, 2003.

Bak, Sang-mee. "South Korean Self-Identity and Evolving Views of the United States." In *Strategy and Sentiment: South Korean Views of the United States and the U.S.-ROK Alliance*, edited by Derek J. Mitchell, Washington D.C., Seoul: Center for Strategic and International Studies and Yonsei University, 2004.

Baldwin, David A. "Thinking About Threats." *The Journal of Conflict Resolution* 15, no. 1 (1971): 71-78.

Bandow, Doug. "The Future of the U.S.-ROK Alliance: Equality, Mutuality, and International Security." *East Asian Review* 17, no. 2 (2005): 46-68.

———. 2003. Time for a Korean Divorce. National Review Online, http://www.nationalreview.com/comment/comment-bandow010603.asp. (accessed June 3, 2008).

Barkey, Henri J. "Turkey and Iraq: The Perils (and Prospects) of Proximity." In *Iraq and Its Neighbors*, 23. Washington DC: United States Institute of Peace, 2005.

Barnett, Michael N., and Jack S. Levy. "Domestic Sources of Alliances and Alignments: The Case of Egypt, 1962-73." *International Organization* 45, no. 3 (1991): 369-95.

Bartsch, Sebastian. "Foreign Policy Influence and Transnational Relations of Political Parties." In *Germany's New Foreign Policy: Decision-Making in an Interdependent World*, edited by Wolf-Dieter Eberwein and Karl Kaiser, 189-219. Houndmills, Basingstoke, Hampshire; New York: Palgrave, 2001.

Basic Law for the Federal Republic of Germany as Amended by the Unification Treaty of 31 August 1990 and Federal Statute of 23 September 1990. *National Constitutions*, The Constitution Society, http://www.constitution.org/cons/germany.txt. (accessed January 2, 2008).

Bechtol, Bruce E., Jr. "Civil-Military Relations in the Republic of Korea: Background and Implications." *Korea Observer* 36, no. 4 (2005): 603-30.

Benjamin, Daniel. "Germany: A Questionable Ally." In *America and the World in the Age of Terror: A New Landscape in International Relations*, edited by Daniel Benjamin, 53-77. Washington, D.C.: CSIS Press, Center for Strategic and International Studies, 2005.

Bennett, Andrew, Joseph Lepgold, and Danny Unger, eds. *Friends in Need: Burden Sharing in the Persian Gulf War*. 1st ed. New York: St. Martin's Press, 1997.

Berger, Thomas U. *Cultures of Antimilitarism: National Security in Germany and Japan*. Baltimore, Md.: The Johns Hopkins University Press, 1998.

Bernstein, Richard. "France and Germany Differ with U.S. on Plan for Iraq." *The New York Times*, September 5, 2003, A9.

———. "The German Question." *The New York Times*, May 2, 2004.

———. "Germany Hoping for Return of Strong American Bond." *The New York Times*, March 12, 2003, A16.

Bernstein, Richard, and Judy Dempsey. "Germany Denies Giving U.S. Iraq's Plan to Defend Baghdad." *The New York Times*, February 28, 2006, A6.

Bernstein, Richard, and Michael R. Gordon. 2006. German Help on Iraq Lasted Months. *International Herald Tribune*, http://www.iht.com/articles/2006/03/02/news/germany.php. (accessed December 31, 2007).

Bernstein, Richard, and Steven R. Weisman. "Threats and Responses: Alliance; NATO Settles Rift over Aid to Turks in Case of War." *The New York Times*, February 17, 2003.

Bila, Fikret. "Gul: Saddam Should Cease to Be a Threat." *Milliyet*, January 16, 2003, 14.

———. "Harmony." *Milliyet*, July 28, 2003, 14.

———. "Turkish-US Relations." *Milliyet*, July 21, 2003.

———. "We Will Enter Iraq Not for USA but for Turkey." *Milliyet*, February 2, 2003.

Birch, Nicholas. "As Turkey Reels, Hurdles Loom for EU Bid, Iraq Attack." *Christian Science Monitor*, July 12, 2002, 07.

Blome, Nikolaus, and Torsten Krauel. "Gerhard and George." *Die Welt*, February 26, 2004.

Bluth, Christoph. "Between a Rock and an Incomprehensible Place: The United States and the Second North Korean Nuclear Crisis." *The Korean Journal of Defense Analysis* XVII, no. 2 (2005): 87-109.

Borchert, Heiko, and Mary N. Hampton. "The Lessons of Kosovo: Boon or Bust for Transatlantic Security." *Orbis* 46, no. 2 (2002): 369-89.

Boudreaux, Richard. "Showdown with Iraq; News Analysis; the Reasons Turkey Rejected U.S.; Ultimatums and Other Perceived Insensitivities May Have Doomed Access for Ground Forces." *Los Angeles Times*, March 3, 2003, 1.

Branford, Becky. 2005. Lingering Legacy of Korean Massacre. BBC News, http://news.bbc.co.uk/2/hi/asia-pacific/4557315.stm. (accessed May 23, 2008).

Brewin, Christopher. "Turkey: Democratic Legitimacy." In *The Iraq War and Democratic Politics*, edited by Alex Danchev and John MacMillan, 96-113. London ; New York: Routledge, 2005.

Britain 'Isolated' over Iraq. 2002. BBC News, http://news.bbc.co.uk/2/hi/uk_news/1876015.stm. (accessed December 10, 2007).

Brooke, James. "Musing on an Exodus of G.I.'S, South Korea Hails U.S. Presence." *The New York Times*, March 8, 2003, 11.

———. "South Opposes Pressuring North Korea." *The New York Times*, January 1, 2003.

Buckley, Mary, and Sally N. Cummings. *Kosovo : Perceptions of War and Its Aftermath*. London ; New York: Continuum, 2001.

Bueno de Mesquita, Bruce. *The Logic of Political Survival*. Cambridge, Mass.: MIT Press, 2003.

Bumiller, Elisabeth. "Bush Defends Barring Nations from Iraq Deals." *The New York Times*, December 12, 2003, A1.

"Bush's Personal Representative to Berlin 'before Christmas' to Discuss Iraq." *DDP News Agency*, December 11, 2003.

Bush, George W. 2002. President Delivers State of the Union Address. *White House Press Releases*, ed. Office of the Press Secretary. The White House, http://www.whitehouse.gov/news/releases/2002/01/20020129-11.html. (accessed December 19, 2007).

Cagaptay, Soner. "November 2002 Elections and Turkey's New Political Era." *Middle East Review of International Affairs* 6, no. 4 (2002): 42-48.

———. 2003. U.S.-Turkish Military Cooperation in Iraq: The Next Step. The Washington Institute for Near East Policy, http://www.washingtoninstitute.org/templateC06.php?CID=393. (accessed November 2, 2006).

Canes-Wrone, Brandice. "The Public Presidency, Personal Approval Ratings, and Policy Making." *Political Science Quarterly* 34, no. 3 (2004): 477-92.

Carkoglu, Ali. "Turkey's November 2002 Elections: A New Beginning?" *Middle East Review of International Affairs* 6, no. 4 (2002): 30-48.

Cevikcan, Serpil. "Eighty Thousand Turkish Soldiers Will Be Deployed in Northern Iraq." *Milliyet*, February 8, 2003, 16.

Cha, Victor D. "Abandonment, Entrapment, and Neoclassical Realism in Asia: The United States, Japan, and Korea." *International Studies Quarterly* 44, no. 2 (2000): 261-91.

———. "Korea: A Peninsula in Crisis and Flux." In *Strategic Asia 2004–05: Confronting Terrorism in the Pursuit of Power*, edited by National Bureau of Asian Research (U.S.), 139-61. Seattle, Wash.: National Bureau of Asian Research, 2004.

———. "South Korea: Anchored or Adrift?" In *Strategic Asia 2003–04*, edited by National Bureau of Asian Research (U.S.), 109-30. Seattle, Wash.: National Bureau of Asian Research, 2003.

Cha, Victor D., and David C. Kang. "The Korea Crisis." *Foreign Policy*, no. 136 (2003): 20-24, 26, 28.

Champion, Marc, and Greg Jaffe. "Poland's Leader Questions U.S. Steps in Iraq; Weapons Issue Is Criticized; German Officials Try to Get Spain to Temper Rhetoric." *The Wall Street Journal*, March 19, 2004, A12.

Chandler, William. "Foreign and European Policy Issues in the 2002 Bundestag Elections." *German Politics and Society* 21, no. 1 (2003): 161-77.

Chang, Jae-soon. "South Korea Plans to Withdraw One-Third of Troops from Iraq." *Associated Press*, November 17, 2005.

Cheney, Richard. 2002. Vice President Speaks at VFW 103rd National Convention. White House Press Office, http://www.whitehouse.gov/news/releases/2002/08/20020826.html. (accessed December 20, 2007).

Cho, Wonbin "The General Election in South Korea, April 2004." *Electoral Studies* 24, no. 3 (2005): 525-30.

Choe, Sang-hun. "North Korea Launches Anti-Ship Missile." *Associated Press*, February 24, 2003.

Chung, Chung Mok. "A New Perspective for Korean Local Government." In *Korean Politics: Striving for Democracy and Unification*, edited by Jung In Kang, Sallie W. Yea and Byong-Man Ahn, xv, 671 p. Elizabeth, NJ: Hollym, 2002.

Civaoglu, Guneri. "Compensation for Hurt Pride." *Milliyet*, July 24, 2003.

Claude, Inis L., Jr. "Collective Legitimization as a Political Function of the United Nations." *International Organization* 20, no. 3 (1966): 367-79.

Cleaver, Hannah. "Stoiber Accuses 'Isolated' Schroder." *The Daily Telegraph*, September 18, 2002.

Cockburn, Patrick. 2007. Turkey Imposes Sanctions on Iraqi Kurdistan in Bid to Halt PKK. *The Independent*, Independent.co.uk, http://www.independent.co.uk/news/europe/turkey-imposes-sanctions-on-iraqi-kurdistan-in-bid-to-halt-pkk-398680.html. (accessed February 29, 2008).

Cohen, Raymond. *Threat Perception in International Crisis*. Madison: University of Wisconsin Press, 1979.

Coleman, Katharina P.. "The Significance of Token Forces." Paper presented at the International Studies Association Annual Convention, San Francisco, March, 2008.

Congar, Yasemin. "The Mending Has Begun." *Milliyet*, June 23, 2003.

Conradt, David P. *The German Polity*. 6th ed. White Plains, N.Y.: Longman, 1996.

Cooper, Scott. "State-Centric Balance-of-Threat Theory: Explaining the Misunderstood Gulf Cooperation Council." *Security Studies* 13, no. 2 (2003/4): 306-49.

Cortell, Andrew P., and James W. Davis. "How Do International Institutions Matter? The Domestic Impact of International Rules and Norms." *International Studies Quarterly* 40, no. 4 (1996): 451-78.

Cossa, Ralph A. 2001. U.S.-Korea: Summit Aftermath. *PacNet*, Pacific Forum, Center for Strategic and International Studies, http://www.csis.org/media/csis/pubs/pac0111.pdf. (accessed June 26, 2008).

———. 2005. U.S.-ROK: Diverging Threat Perceptions of North Korea? *Forging New U.S.-ROK Political Relationships*, The Maureen and Mike Mansfield Foundation, http://www.mansfieldfdn.org/programs/program_pdfs/rok_us_cossa.pdf. (accessed May 28, 2008).

———. "US-DPRK Nuclear Stand-Off: Anatomy of a "Crisis"." *The Korean Journal of Defense Analysis* XV, no. 1 (2003): 7-31.

Crawford, Beverly. "Explaining Defection from International Cooperation: Germany's Unilateral Recognition of Croatia." *World Politics* 48, no. 4 (1996): 482-521.

Dalgaard-Nielsen, Anja. "Gulf War: The German Resistance." *Survival* 45, no. 1 (2003): 99-116.

———. "The Test of Strategic Culture: Germany, Pacifism and Pre-Emptive Strikes." *Security Dialogue* 36, no. 3 (2005): 339-59.

"Declaration by Russia, Germany and France Pronounced by Jacques Chirac, President of the Republic," During a Joint Press Briefing with Vladimir Poutine, President of the Russian Federation. 2003. Embassy of France in the United States, http://www.ambafrance-us.org/news/statmnts/2003/chirac021003.asp. (accessed March 4, 2008).

"Defense Ministry Reaffirms Non-Combat Troop Dispatch." *Korea Times*, February 12, 2003.

DeLong, Michael, and Noah Lukeman. *Inside CENTCOM: The Unvarnished Truth About the Wars in Afghanistan and Iraq*. Washington, D.C.: Regnery Pub., 2004.

Demir, Metehan. "War Scenarios at the MGK." *Hurriyet*, January 30, 2003.

Dempsey, Judy. "Germany Hopes to Focus on 'National Interests'." *International Herald Tribune*, May 5, 2008.

Depalma, Anthony. "Threats and Responses: An Overview: March 12, 2003; Trolling for U.N. Votes (8 Enough?), Terms for Delay, Drones on Display." *The New York Times*, March 13, 2003.

Die Hoffnung Wird Immer Kleiner [Hope Is Becoming Smaller All the Time]. 2002. *Der Spiegel*, http://service.spiegel.de/digas/find?DID=26024486. (accessed December 3, 2007).

Dieterich, Sandra, Hartwig Hummel, and Stefan Marschall. "Parliamentary War Powers and European Participation in the Iraq War 2003: Bridging the Divide between Parliamentary Studies and International Relations." Paper presented at the 49th International ISA Convention, San Francisco, 26-29 March, 2008.

"Divisions Deepen as Protests over Iraqi War Intensify." *Korea Times*, March 31, 2003.

Drogin, Bob. "German Spies Aided U.S. Attempt to Kill Hussein in Aerial Attack." *Los Angeles Times*, January 12, 2006, A3.

Subcommittee on International Organizations, Human Rights, and Oversight of the Committee on Foreign Affairs. "Economic and Military Support for the U.S. Efforts in Iraq: The Coalition of the Willing, Then and Now, First Session," May 9, 2007.

Economist Intelligence Unit. "Country Profile. South Korea." London: The Economist, 2003.

"Election Will Not Change German Opposition to War, Says Foreign Minister." *DDP News Agency*, September 16, 2002.

EOS Gallup Europe. "International Crisis Survey 21st- 27th of January 2003." 2003.

Erb, Scott. *German Foreign Policy: Navigating a New Era*. Boulder, Colo.: L. Rienner, 2003.

"Erdogan: Developments in Kirkuk Are Not Positive." *Anatolia*, January 27, 2005.

Ergan, Ugar. "Four Conditions by Turkey in Exchange for Saddam." *Hurriyet*, July 17, 2002.

———. "Turkomans Being Armed as Well." *Hurriyet*, February 25, 2003.

Ergan, Ugar, Turan Yilmaz, and Umit Cetin. "National Assembly Will Make the Final Decision." *Hurriyet*, August 13, 2003, 22.

Ergin, Sadat. "The Authorization Bill Split the AKP." *Hurriyet*, September 24, 2003.

———. "The Bargaining Begins." *Hurriyet*, September 19, 2003.

———. "Do Not Worry, the Turks Will Not Let Us Down." *Hurriyet*, September 17, 2003.

———. "Ecevit Allowed CIA Teams and U-2 Planes." *Hurriyet*, September 18, 2003.

———. "Ecevit This Time Yielding to United States." *Hurriyet*, July 18, 2002.

———. "Looks Like We Missed That Train." *Hurriyet*, September 25, 2003.

———. "Tough Decision." *Hurriyet* December 13, 2002.

———. "The United States Backed Down When Turkey Broke the Talks." *Hurriyet*, September 23, 2003.

———. "We Can Open a Northern Front but a UN Resolution Is Needed." *Hurriyet*, September 21, 2003.

———. "We Thought There Were Troops on the Ships; Turns out There Were Not Any." *Hurriyet*, September 22, 2003.

———. "You Have Three Days; Otherwise There Will Be Consequences." *Hurriyet*, September 20, 2003.

Erlanger, Steven. "German Leader's Warning: War Plan Is a Huge Mistake; Perspectives -- Sept. 11 and Beyond: Gerhard Schroder." *The New York Times*, September 5, 2002, A-1.

———. "Rumsfeld Urges NATO to Set up Strike Force." *The New York Times*, September 25, 2002.

Erler, Gernot. 2007. Political Principles of the German Engagement in International Peace Missions. German Federal Foreign Office [Auswärtiges Amt], http://www.auswaertiges-amt.de/diplo/en/Infoservice/Presse/Rede/2007/070206-ErlerVN.html. (accessed June 25, 2008).

Erturk, Fatih. "Baykal: President Sezer Is Opposed to War." *Sabah*, January 19, 2003.

Evans, Ambrose. 2003. Ten Eastern European States to Join in War. *Telegraph.co.uk*, http://www.telegraph.co.uk/news/main.jhtml?xml=/news/

2003/02/06/weur06.xml&sSheet=/news/2003/02/06/ixnewstop.html. (accessed September 21, 2007).
"Expecting Trouble?" *The Economist*, March 15, 2003.
"Extraordinary European Council, Brussels, 17 February 2003." Brussels: Council of the European Union, 2003.
"Faction Opposes Use of S.K. Troops in Iraq." *Korea Herald*, February 17, 2003.
Faiola, Anthony. "Court Rejects S. Korean President's Impeachment." *The Washington Post*, May 14, 2004, A12.
Farley, Maggie, and Maura Reynolds. "Bush, Schroeder End Feud; Germany Offers Aid in Iraq." *Los Angeles Times*, September 25, 2003, A1.
Fawn, Rick. "The Iraq War: Unfolding and Unfinished." In *The Iraq War: Causes and Consequences*, edited by Rick Fawn and Raymond A. Hinnebusch, ix, 357 p. Boulder, Colo.: Lynne Rienner Publishers, 2006.
Feng, Yan. "Behind the Bargaining between US and Turkey." *Xinhua Domestic Service* February 22, 2002.
Filkins, Dexter. "Turkey Says U.S. Has Detained Some of Its Soldiers in North Iraq." *The New York Times*, July 6, 2003, 1,6.
Fischer, Joschka. "German Foreign Minister Reiterates View on Iraq, Says Peace Hopes Diminishing." *Der Spiegel*, December 30, 2002.
———. "Solving Mideast Conflict Should Be Priority, Not Iraq." *Frankfurter Rundschau*, September 12, 2002.
———. 2004. Speech on the 40th Munich Conference on Security Policy. Munich Conference on Security Policy, http://www.securityconference.de/konferenzen/rede.php?id=123&sprache=en&. (accessed December 28, 2007).
"FM Gul's Letter to Annan on Iraq " *Anatolia*, January 27, 2005.
Ford, Peter. "United against Terror, Divided on Trade, Coalition Strains." *Christian Science Monitor*, March 8, 2002.
Forsberg, Tuomas. "The Debate over German Normality: A Normal German Debate?" In *Political Thought and German Unification: A New German Ideology*, edited by Howard Williams, Colin Wight and Norbert Kapferer, 139–55. London: Macmillan, 2000.
———. "German Foreign Policy and the War on Iraq: Anti-Americanism, Pacifism or Emancipation." *Security Dialogue* 36, no. 2 (2005): 213-31.
Foyle, Douglas C. "Public Opinion and Foreign Policy: Elite Beliefs as a Mediating Variable." *International Studies Quarterly* 41, no. 1 (1997): 141-69.
Fraser, Suzan. "Turkey's Parliament Allows U.S. To Use Airspace for Iraq War." *Associated Press*, March 20, 2003.
French, Howard W. "A Nation at War: The Asian Arena; South Korea Agrees to Send Troops to Iraq." *The New York Times*, April 3, 2003.
———. "North Taunts Seoul with a Missile Test." *The New York Times*, February 26, 2003.
———. "Reversals in U.S.-South Korea Links, and Some Jagged Fault Lines." *The New York Times*, February 11, 2003, 17.
Fuller, Thomas. 2003. Romania Dangles Use of a Sea Base to Woo U.S. *International Herald Tribune*, http://www.iht.com/articles/2003/06/18/romania_ed3_.php. (accessed January 11, 2008).

Gaddis, John Lewis. *Strategies of Containment: A Critical Appraisal of Postwar American National Security Policy*. New York: Oxford University Press, 1982.

Gardner, Hall. *American Global Strategy and The "War on Terrorism"*. Burlington, VT: Ashgate, 2005.

Gaubatz, Kurt Taylor. "Election Cycles and War." *Journal of Conflict Resolution* 35, no. 2 (1991): 212-44.

Gause, F. Gregory, III. "Balancing What? Threat Perception and Alliance Choice in the Gulf." *Security Studies* 13, no. 2 (2003/4): 273-305.

Gehlen, Martin. "German Skepticism About America's Intent and Goals in Iraq." *Nieman Reports* (2003).

"Gerhard Schröder Auf Anti-Amerika Kurs [Gerhard Schröder on an Anti-American Course]." *Die Tageszeitung*, August 6, 2002.

"German Agent Did Not Pass on Iraq Information, Says BND." *Deutsche Presse-Agentur*, March 3, 2006.

"German Cabinet "Boycotting" Donors' Conference for Iraq." *Der Spiegel*, October 20, 2003.

"German Cabinet Extends Bundeswehr Mandate for Afghanistan, Macedonia." *DDP News Agency*, December 3, 2002.

"German Chancellor Expected to Grant USA Use of Air Space " *Der Spiegel*, November 20, 2002.

"German Chancellor Offers Support for UN Arms Inspections in Iraq." *DDP News Agency*, September 17, 2002.

"German Chancellor Says Strike against Iraq Not on the Agenda." *DDP News Agency*, February 18, 2002.

"German Chancellor Warns against War on Iraq." *DDP News Agency*, August 3, 2002.

"German Defence Ministry: Deployment of NBC Units in Kuwait Possible." *DDP News Agency*, January 9, 2002.

"German Foreign Minister Considers UN Mandate for Iraq Strike Unlikely." *DDP News Agency*, August 7, 2002.

"German Greens Back Schroeder's Iraq Stance, Accept "Alliance Obligations"." *Welt am Sonntag*, February 24, 2003.

"German Intelligence Says Iraq Rearming "Massively"." *Die Welt*, February 23, 2001.

"German Leader Expects Continuing Problems in Iraq, Skeptical on NATO Role." *DDP News Agency*, June 10, 2004.

"German Minister Says Iraq Poses No Threat." *Die Welt*, February 19, 2003.

"German Minister Stresses Need for Ongoing ISAF Mission in Afghanistan." *DDP News Agency*, December 20, 2002.

"German Ministers Repeat Opposition to Military Intervention in Iraq." *DDP News Agency*, August 9, 2002.

"German Official Downplays Row with USA over Iraq." *La Stampa*, September 26, 2002.

"German Opposition Critical of Government Stance on Iraq." *Die Welt*, August 7, 2002.

"German Parliament Approves Extension of Enduring Freedom Mandate." *DDP News Agency*, November 15, 2002.

"German Participation in NATO Iraq Mission "Premature" - Social Democrats." *Frankfurter Rundschau*, January 16, 2004.

"German Stand on Iraq Weakens US Crisis Management, Heightens War Risk - Paper." *Die Welt*, August 28, 2002.

"Germany's Fischer Unconvinced of Direct Threat from Iraq." *DDP News Agency*, February 8, 2003.

"Germany's Schroeder for Lifting Iraq Sanctions." *DDP News Agency*, May 15, 2003.

"Germany's Schroeder on Postwar Iraq, EU Split, Relations with USA." *DDP News Agency*, March 28, 2003.

"Germany's Security Strategy: Thinking the Unthinkable." *The Economist*, May 8, 2008.

"Germany's Struck to Discuss Bundeswehr Changes, Iraq at Munich Security Talks." *Welt am Sonntag*, February 1, 2004.

"Germany Admits Providing Washington with Iraq Intelligence." *Deutsche Presse-Agentur*, February 24, 2006.

"Germany Rejects Change of Mandate for Soldiers in Afghanistan." *DDP News Agency*, May 16, 2003.

"Germany Reportedly No Longer Rules out Humanitarian Commitment in Iraq." *DDP News Agency*, January 14, 2004.

"Germany to Grant Overflight Rights to US, Allies in Case of Iraq War." *DDP News Agency*, November 22, 2002.

"Germany, Israel to Hold Talks on Patriot Missiles." *DDP News Agency*, December 3, 2002.

"Germany: Berlin Greens Reject Bundeswehr Participation in Afghanistan War." *DDP News Agency*, November 8, 2003.

Gilmore, Gerry J. 2003. Disappointed Wolfowitz Still Supports U.S.-Turkish Defense Ties. American Forces Press Service, http://www.defenselink.mil/news/newsarticle.aspx?id=29012. (accessed February 28, 2008).

Ginsberg, Benjamin. *The Captive Public: How Mass Opinion Promotes State Power*. New York: Basic Books, 1986.

Gluck, Caroline. 2003. South Korea's Web Guerillas. BBC News, http://news.bbc.co.uk/2/hi/asia-pacific/2843651.stm. (accessed May 23, 2008).

Goodenough, Patrick. 2003. Flood of Volunteers after South Korea Okays Troop Dispatch. CNSNews.com, http://www.cnsnews.com/ViewPrint.asp?Page=\ForeignBureaus\archive\200304\FOR20030403b.html. (accessed June 12, 2008).

Gordon, Michael R. "German Intelligence Gave U.S. Iraqi Defense Plan, Report Says." *The New York Times*, February 27, 2006, A1.

Gordon, Michael R., and Bernard E. Trainor. *Cobra II: The inside Story of the Invasion and Occupation of Iraq*. 1st ed. New York: Pantheon Books, 2006.

Gordon, Philip H., and Jeremy Shapiro. *Allies at War: America, Europe, and the Crisis over Iraq*. New York: McGraw-Hill, 2004.

"Gov't Fast-Tracks Troop Dispatch." *Korea Times*, March 22, 2003.

Graham, Bradley, and Peter Slevin. "U.S. Won't Sweeten Aid Offer to Turkey; $6 Billion Offer for Access Is Final, Bush Tells Ankara." *The Washington Post*, February 20, 2003, 31.

Gruen, George E. "Turkey's "Political Earthquake:" Significance for the United States and the Region." *American Foreign Policy Interests* 25 (2003): 87-97.

Haberman, Clyde. "War in the Gulf: Turkey's Role in Air Assault Sets Off Fear of Retaliation." *The New York TImes*, January 20, 1991.

Habermas, Jürgen. "Ein Abgrund Von Trauer [an Abyss of Grief]." *Der Spiegel*, August 7, 1995, 32-33.

Hagan, Joe D. "Domestlc Political Explanations in the Analysis of Foreign Policy." In *Foreign Policy Analysis: Continuity and Change in Its Second Generation*, edited by Laura Neack, Jeanne A. K. Hey and Patrick Jude Haney, 117-43. Englewood Cliffs, N.J.: Prentice Hall, 1995.

———. *Political Opposition and Foreign Policy in Comparative Perspective*. Boulder, Colo.: L. Rienner, 1993.

Hahm, Sung Deuk, and L. Christopher Plein. *After Development: Transformation of the Korean Presidency and Bureaucracy*. Washington, D.C.: Georgetown University Press, 1997.

Hale, William. "Turkey, the Middle East and the Gulf Crisis." *International Affairs (Royal Institute of International Affairs 1944-)* 68, no. 4 (1992): 679-92.

Hale, William M. *Turkish Foreign Policy, 1774-2000*. London ; Portland, OR: Frank Cass, 2000.

Hardin, Russell. *Collective Action*. Baltimore: Johns Hopkins University Press, 1982.

Harnisch, Sebastian. "German Non-Proliferation Policy and the Iraq Conflict." *German Politics* 13, no. 1 (2004): 1-34.

Hayes, Stephen F. "Wolfowitz Talks Turkey." *The Weekly Standard*, December 16, 2002, 9-11.

Helicke, James C. "Turkey Agrees to U.S. Overflights for Iraq War." *Associated Press Worldstream*, March 21, 2003.

Hellmann, Gunther. "Absorbing Shocks and Mounting Checks: Germany and Alliance Burden Sharing in the Gulf War." In *Friends in Need: Burden Sharing in the Persian Gulf War*, edited by Andrew Bennett, Joseph Lepgold and Danny Unger, 165-94. New York: St. Martin's Press, 1997.

Hellmann, Gunther, Rainer Baumann, Monika Bosche, and Benjamin Herborth. "De-Europeanization by Default? Germany's EU Policy in Defense and Asylum." *Foreign Policy Analysis* 1, no. 1 (2005): 143-64.

Herman, Edward S., and Noam Chomsky. *Manufacturing Consent: The Political Economy of the Mass Media*. New York: Pantheon Books, 2002.

Hermann, Tamar. "Grassroots Activism as a Factor in Foreign Policy-Making." In *The Limits of State Autonomy: Societal Groups and Foreign Policy Formulation*, edited by David Skidmore and Valerie M. Hudson, 127-47. Boulder: Westview Press, 1993.

Hitt, Greg , and Jess Bravin. "U.S., Germany Repair Iraq Rift; Bush Bid to U.N. Yet to Bear Fruit." *The Wall Street Journal*, September 25, 2003, A4.

Hogwood, Patricia. "The Chancellor-Candidates and the Campaign." *German Politics* 13, no. 2 (2004): 243–67.

Holsti, Ole R. *Public Opinion and American Foreign Policy*, Analytical Perspectives on Politics. Ann Arbor: University of Michigan Press, 1996.

Hong, Kyudok. "The Impact of NGOs on South Korea's Decision to Dispatch Troops to Iraq." *Journal of International and Area Studies* 12, no. 2 (2005): 31-46.

Hopf, Ted. "The Promise of Constructivism in International Relations Theory." *International Security* 23, no. 1 (1998): 171-200.

Horsley, William. 2002. Foreign Policy Works for Schroeder. BBC News, http://news.bbc.co.uk/2/hi/europe/2261878.stm. (accessed December 4, 2007).

Howorth, Jolyon. "France: Defender of International Legitimacy." In *The Iraq War: Causes and Consequences*, edited by Rick Fawn and Raymond A. Hinnebusch, 49-59. Boulder, Colo.: Lynne Rienner Publishers, 2006.

Hwang, Balbina Y. 2004. South Korean Troops to Iraq: A Boost for U.S.-ROK Relations. *Web Memo*, The Heritage Foundation, http://www.heritage.org/Research/AsiaandthePacific/wm427.cfm. (accessed May 19, 2008).

———. "The U.S.–Korea Alliance on the Rocks: Shaken, Not Stirred." *Heritage Lectures*, no. 970 (2006).

Hwang, Jang-jin. "Roh Feels Anguish over 'Culture Clash'." *The Korea Herald*, May 24, 2003.

———. "Roh Shifting N. Korea Strategy: Says Inter-Korean Ties to Be Linked to Progress in Nuke." *The Korea Herald*, May 17, 2003.

Hwang, Major General Eui-Don. "Republic of Korea Forces in Iraq: Peacekeeping and Reconstruction." *Military Review* LXXXV, no. 06 (2005): 27-31.

Ikenberry, G. John. *After Victory: Institutions, Strategic Restraint, and the Rebuilding of Order after Major Wars*, Princeton Studies in International History and Politics. Princeton: Princeton University Press, 2001.

International Institute for Strategic Studies. *The Military Balance*, London: Routledge, 2002.

Iraq Ministry of Planning and Development. 2008. Report on Donors' Contributions to Reconstruction Efforts up to March 2008 The Iraqi Strategic Review Board (ISRB) International Cooperation Department, http://www.mop-iraq.org/mopdc/resources/pdf/DAD/DAD%20Reporte_april.pdf. (accessed May 20, 2008).

Jacobs, Lawrence R., and Robert Y. Shapiro. "Studying Substantive Democracy." *PS: Political Science and Politics* 27, no. 1 (1994): 9-17.

Jaung, Hoon 2003. President Roh Moo-Hyun and the New Politics of South Korea. The Asia Society, http://www.asiasociety.org/publications/update_korea2.html#election. (accessed May 30, 2008).

Jehl, Douglas. "A Region Inflamed: The Reconstruction; Pentagon Bars Three Nations from Iraq Bids." *The New York Times*, December 10, 2003.

Jenkins, Gareth. *Context and Circumstance: The Turkish Military and Politics*. Oxford ; New York: Oxford University Press for the International Institute for Strategic Studies, 2001.

Jervis, Robert. *Perception and Misperception in International Politics*. Princeton, N.J.: Princeton University Press, 1976.

Jin, Dae-woong. "Korea Notifies U.S. Of Iraq Troop Pullout." *The Korea Herald*, December 6, 2006.

———. "Korean Troops Mark Two Years in Iraqi Kurdistan Town." *The Korea Herald*, February 23, 2006.

———. "Korean Troops Welcomed by Kurds in Iraq." *The Korea Herald*, March 19, 2006.

———. "Troop Deployment in Iraq Emerges as Key Campaign Issue." *The Korea Herald*, October 23, 2007.

Jin, Young-jae. "Lee Brings Back 'Strong Presidentialism': President-Elect Seeks to Curtail the Power of the Prime Minister and the Number of Ministries." *The Korea Herald*, January 21, 2008.

Johnson, Rebecca, and Micah Zenko. "All Dressed up and No Place to Go." *Parameters* (2002/3): 48-63.

Jones, Vivian C. "Iraq's Trade with the World: Data and Analysis." In *CRS Report for Congress*, 47. Washington D.C.: Congressional Research Service, 2004.

Joo, Jaehyun. "Explaining Social Policy Adoption in South Korea: The Cases of the Medical Insurance Law and the Minimum Wage Law." *Journal of Social Policy* 28, no. 3 (1999): 387-412.

Joo, Seung-Ho. "US-ROK Relations: The Political-Diplomatic Dimension." In *The United States and the Korean Peninsula in the 21st Century*, edited by Tae-Hwan Kwak and Seung-Ho Joo, 39-60. Aldershot, England ; Burlington, VT: Ashgate, 2006.

Jung, Sung-ki. "Extension of Iraq Troop Deployment Hits Snag." *Korea Times*, May 21, 2007.

———. "S. Korea Delays Decision on Fate of Troops in Iraq." *Korea Times*, June 28, 2007.

———. "Think Tank Calls for Extending Zaytun Mission in Iraq." *Korea Times*, May 31, 2007.

Jung, Yeon Bong. "Strategy on Stilts: The U.S. Response to the North Korea Nuclear Issue." *The Korean Journal of Defense Analysis* XVII, no. 2 (2005): 63-86.

Kaarbo, Juliet, and Ryan K. Beasley. "Taking It to the Extreme: The Effect of Coalition Cabinets on Foreign Policy." *Foreign Policy Analysis* 4, no. 1 (2008): 67-81.

Kamen, Al. "Coalition Members Look for an Exit." *The Washington Post*, November 17, 2005, A17.

Kamp, Karl-Heinz. 2004. Kas Germany Update - January 2004 *Current Issues in German Politics No. 14*, Konrad-Adenauer-Stiftung, http://www.kas.org.ar/Doc/Docum/Realidad%20Alemana/GermUpd_Jan04.pdf. (accessed December 28, 2007).

Kang, David C. "The Institutional Foundations of Korean Politics." In *Understanding Korean Politics: An Introduction*, edited by Soong Hoom Kil and Chung-in Moon, 71-106. Albany: State University of New York Press, 2001.

Kang, In-duk. "Toward Peace and Prosperity: The New Government's North Korea Policy." *East Asian Review* 15, no. 1 (2003): 3-18.

Kang, Jung In. "Reflections on Recent Democratization." In *Korean Politics: Striving for Democracy and Unification*, edited by Jung In Kang, Sallie W. Yea and Byong-Man Ahn, Elizabeth, NJ: Hollym, 2002.

Kaplan, Lawrence S. *NATO after Forty Years*. Wilmington, Del.: SR Books, 1990.

Kapsis, James E. "The Failure of U.S.-Turkish Pre-Iraq War Negotiations: An Overconfident United States, Political Mismanagement, and Conflicted Military." *Middle East Review of International Affairs* 10, no. 3 (2006): 33-45.

Karaosmanoglu, Ali. "The Evolution of the National Security Culture and the Military in Turkey." *Journal of International Affairs* 54, no. 1 (2000): 199-216.

Kelley, Matt. "U.S. Repositioning Bombers near North Korea, May Send Fighter Escorts with Surveillance Planes." *Associated Press*, March 5, 2003.

Kemper, Bob. "White House Tells Turkey That Rebuff Could Be Costly." *Chicago Tribune*, March 4, 2003.

Kessler, Glenn, and Phillip P. Pan. "Missteps with Turkey Prove Costly; Diplomatic Debacle Denied U.S. A Strong Northern Thrust in Iraq." *The Washington Post*, March 28, 2003, 1.

Khong, Yuen Foong. *Analogies at War: Korea, Munich, Dien Bien Phu, and the Vietnam Decisions of 1965*. Princeton, N.J.: Princeton University Press, 1992.

Kihl, Young W. *Transforming Korean Politics: Democracy, Reform, and Culture*. Armonk, N.Y.: M.E. Sharpe, 2005.

Kil, Soong Hoom, and Chung-in Moon, eds. *Understanding Korean Politics: An Introduction, SUNY Series in Korean Studies*. Albany: State University of New York Press, 2001.

Kim, Byung-Kook. "North and South Korea: Unlikely Challenger, Unlikely Mediator." In *Power and Security in Northeast Asia: Shifting Strategies*, edited by Byung-Kook Kim and Anthony Jones, 197-224. Boulder, Colo.: Lynne Rienner Publishers, 2007.

Kim, Dong Shin. "The ROK–U.S. Alliance: Where Is It Headed?" In *Strategic Forum*. Washington DC: Institute for National Strategic Studies, National Defense University, 2003.

Kim, Hong Nack. "The 2000 Parliamentary Election in South Korea." *Asian Survey* 40, no. 6 (2000): 894-913.

Kim, Hyung-jin. "Assembly to Vote on Troop Dispatch Bill Amid Protests." *The Korea Herald*, March 28, 2003.

———. "Roh to Meet Party Leaders on Iraq." *The Korea Herald*, March 19, 2003.

———. "South Korean Parliament Approves Iraq Troop Extension for Another Year." *Associated Press*, December 28, 2007.

Kim, Seung-hwan. "Yankee Go Home? A Historical View of South Korean Sentiment toward the United States, 2001-2004." In *Strategy and Sentiment: South Korean Views of the United States and the U.S.-ROK Alliance*, edited by Derek J. Mitchell, 24-35. Washington D.C., Seoul: Center for Strategic and International Studies and Yonsei University, 2004.

Kim, Sung-han. "Anti-American Sentiment and the ROK-US Alliance." *The Korean Journal of Defense Analysis* XV, no. 2 (2003): 105-30.

"Kim to Hold Summit with Bush." *Korea Times*, September 27, 2002.

Kim, Tong. "Irony of Roh Moo-Hyun." *The Korea Times*, February 24, 2008.

Kim, Yongho, and Myungchul Kim. "North Korea's Risk-Taking Vis-á-Vis the U.S. Coercion in the Nuclear Quagmire." *The Korean Journal of Defense Analysis* XIX, no. 4 (2007): 51-69.

Kirişçi, Kemal. "Between Europe and the Middle East: The Transformation of Turkish Policy." *Middle East Review of International Affairs* 8, no. 1 (2004): 39-51.

———. "Turkey and the Muslim Middle East." In *Turkey's New World : Changing Dynamics in Turkish Foreign Policy*, edited by Alan Makovsky and Sabri Sayari. Washington, DC: Washington Institute for Near East Policy, 2000.

Kirk, Don. "Seoul Makes Case for U.S. Presence; 'Trip Wire Should Remain' against North." *The International Herald Tribune*, March 7, 2003, 1.

Kitfield, James. "Damage Control." *National Journal*, July 19, 2003, 2336-42.

Kitschelt, Herbert P. "Political Opportunity Structures and Political Protest: Anti-Nuclear Movements in Four Democracies." *British Journal of Political Science* 16, no. 1 (1986): 57-85.

Knorr, Klaus. "Threat Perception." In *Historical Dimensions of National Security Problems*, edited by Klaus Knorr, 78-119. Lawrence: University Press of Kansas, 1976.

Knox, Paul. "October 23, 2003." *The Globe and Mail*, October 23, 2003.

Ko, Sung-Bin. "South Korea's Search for an Independent Foreign Policy." *Journal of Contemporary Asia* 36, no. 2 (2006): 258-73.

Kohen, Sami. "Before the Decision Is Final..." *Milliyet* December 5, 2002, FBIS-NES-2002-1205

———. "The Number One Threat." *Milliyet*, March 14, 2002.

———. "To Hit or Not to Hit." *Milliyet*, August 31, 2002, 18.

"Korea Commits $200 Million to Iraq." *The Korea Herald*, October 25, 2003.

"Korea to Send Engineering Troops to Support U.S. War with Iraq." *Yonhap News Agency*, March 13, 2003.

"Korea Walking Diplomatic Tightrope over War on Iraq." *Korea Times*, September 14, 2002.

"Korea yet to Decide Level of Support for U.S.-Led War with Iraq." *Yonhap News Agency*, March 13, 2003.

"Korea, U.S. To Hold Second Round of Alliance Talks." *Yonhap News Agency*, June 4, 2003.

Kramer, Heinz. *A Changing Turkey : The Challenge to Europe and the United States*. Washington, D.C.: Brookings Institution Press, 2000.

Krause, Joachim. "The Role of the Bundestag in German Foreign Policy." In *Germany's New Foreign Policy: Decision-Making in an Interdependent World*, edited by Wolf-Dieter Eberwein and Karl Kaiser, 157-72. Houndmills, Basingstoke, Hampshire ; New York: Palgrave, 2001.

Kucuksahin, Sukru. "Signs of a Lasting Political MoU." *Hurriet*, March 6, 2003, 17.

Kwak, Kwang Sub. "The US-ROK Alliance, 1953 – 2004: Alliance Institutionalization." Southern Illinois University Carbondale, 2006.

Kwak, Tae-Hwan, and Seung-Ho Joo, eds. *The United States and the Korean Peninsula in the 21st Century*. Aldershot, England ; Burlington, VT: Ashgate, 2006.

Kwon, Eundak, and Jae-Cheon Lim. "Crossing the River That Divides the Korean Peninsula: An Evaluation of the Sunshine Policy." *International Relations of the Asia-Pacific* 6, no. 2 (2006): 129-56.

Lantis, Jeffrey S. *Strategic Dilemmas and the Evolution of German Foreign Policy since Unification*. Westport, Conn.: Praeger, 2002.

Larrabee, F. Stephen, Ian O. Lesser, and Center for Middle East Public Policy (Rand Corporation). *Turkish Foreign Policy in an Age of Uncertainty*. Santa Monica, CA: Rand, 2003.

Larres, Klaus. "Mutual Incomprehension: U.S.-German Value Gaps Beyond Iraq." *The Washington Quarterly* 26, no. 2 (2003): 23-42.

Larson, Eric V., Norman D. Levin, Seonhae Baik, and Bogdan Savych. *Ambivalent Allies? A Study of South Korean Attitudes toward the U.S.* Santa Monica: RAND Corporation, 2004.

Lee, Aie-Rie. "Down and Down We Go: Trust and Compliance in South Korea." *Social Science Quarterly* 84, no. 2 (2003): 329–43.

Lee, Chae-Jin. *A Troubled Peace: U.S. Policy and the Two Koreas*. Baltimore: Johns Hopkins University Press, 2006.

Lee, Chung Min. "Reassessing the ROK-US Alliance: Transformation Challenges and the Consequences of South Korea's Choices." *Australian Journal of International Affairs* 57, no. 2 (2003): 281-307.

Lee, Jong-heon. "S.Korea May Send Fewer Troops to Iraq." *United Press International*, November 4, 2003.

———. "Summit Feared to Cloud Inter-Korean Ties." *United Press International*, May 15, 2003.

Lee, Sook-Jong. "Allying with the United States: Changing South Korean Attitudes." *The Korean Journal of Defense Analysis* XVII, no. 1 (2005): 81-104.

Lee, Youngjae. "Law, Politics, and Impeachment: The Impeachment of Roh Moo-Hyun from a Comparative Constitutional Perspective." *New York University Public Law and Legal Theory Working Papers*, no. 4 (2005).

"Legitimization for the US Occupation Power." *Die Welt*, October 17, 2003.

Lehmann, Ingrid A. "Exploring the Transatlantic Media Divide over Iraq: How and Why U.S. And German Media Differed in Reporting on UN Weapons Inspections in Iraq, 2002-2003." *The Harvard International Journal of Press and Politics* 10, no. 1 (2005): 63-89.

Lehrer, Jim. 2002. Newsmaker: Bulent Ecevit. *NewsHour with Jim Lehrer Transcript*, MacNeil/Lehrer Productions, http://www.pbs.org/newshour/bb/middle_east/jan-june02/ecevit_1-17.html. (accessed April 28, 2008).

Lesser, Ian O. 2005. Off Autopilot: The Future of Turkish-US Relations. *Turkish Policy Quarterly*, Colombia International Affairs Online, http://www.ciaonet.org/olj/tpq/vol4-4/vol4-4c.html. (accessed November 14, 2006).

Levy, Jack S. "The Diversionary Theory of War: A Critique." In *Handbook of War Studies*, edited by Manus I. Midlarsky. Boston: Unwin Hyman, 1989.

Lim, Bo-mi. "South Korean National Assembly Approves Iraq Troop Reduction Plan." *Associated Press*, December 30, 2005.

The List: Who's Left in Afghanistan? 2008. *Foreign Policy*, Carnegie Endowment for International Peace, http://www.foreignpolicy.com/story/cms.php?story_id=4235. (accessed June 25, 2008).

*Lithuania: Country Profile 2004*. Country Profiles. London: The Economist Intelligence Unit, 2004.

Longhurst, Kerry Anne. *Germany and the Use of Force*, Issues in German Politics. Manchester [UK] ; New York: Manchester University Press; Palgrave, 2004.

Lord, Jeffrey R., and Kristin M. Lord. "Additional Cases from the Gulf Crisis and Burden Sharing in Unprofor." In *Friends in Need: Burden Sharing in the Persian Gulf War*, edited by Andrew Bennett, Joseph Lepgold and Danny Unger, 362 p. New York: St. Martin's Press, 1997.

Malici, Akan. "Germans as Venutians: The Culture of German Foreign Policy Behavior." *Foreign Policy Analysis* 2 (2006): 37-62.

Mandelbaum, Michael. *The Nuclear Revolution: International Politics before and after Hiroshima*. New York: Cambridge University Press, 1981.

Marquand, Robert. "Rethinking US Troops in S. Korea." *Christian Science Monitor*, March 10, 2003.

Martinsen, Kaare Dahl. "The End of the Affair? Germany's Relationship with France." *German Politics* 14, no. 4 (2005): 401-16.

Matray, James I. . "Alliance of Convenience." *Donga Ilbo*, April, 2003.

Maull, Hanns. "Germany's Foreign Policy, Post-Kosovo: Still a 'Civilian Power'?" In *Germany as a Civilian Power? The Foreign Policy of the Berlin Republic*, edited by Sebastian Harnisch and Hanns Maull, 106-27. Manchester; New York: Manchester University Press; Palgrave, 2001.

———. "Germany and the Use of Force: Still a Civilian Power?" Paper presented at the Workshop on Force, Order and Global Governance, Washington DC, July 1-2, 1999.

Mayhew, David R. *Congress: The Electoral Connection*. 2nd ed. New Haven: Yale University Press, 2006.

McAdams, James A. "Germany after Unification: Normal at Last?" *World Politics* 49, no. 2 (1997): 282–308.

McCain, John. 2002. From Crisis to Opportunity: American Internationalism and the New Atlantic Order. Munich Conference on Security Policy, http://www.securityconference.de/konferenzen/rede.php?menu_2002=&menu_konferenzen_archiv=&menu_2008=&menu_konferenzen=&sprache=en&id=76&. (accessed December 19, 2007).

Menon, Rajan, and S. Enders Wimbush. "The US and Turkey: End of an Alliance?" *Survival* 49, no. 2 (2007): 129-44.

Metz, Helen Chapin. 1995. The Middle East. *Turkey: A Country Study*, Government Printing Office for the Library of Congress, http://countrystudies.us/turkey/73.htm. (accessed February 25, 2008).

Migdalovitz, Carol. "Turkey: Issues for U.S. Policy." In *Report for Congress RL31429*. Washington, DC: Congressional Research Service, 2002.

Miko, Francis T., and Christian Froehlich. "Germany's Role in Fighting Terrorism: Implications for U.S. Policy." In *CRS Report for Congress RL32710*, 22. Washington DC: Congressional Research Service, The Library of Congress, 2004.

Miller, Warren E., and Donald E. Stokes. "Constituency Influence in Congress." *American Political Science Review* 57, no. 1 (1963): 45-56.

Moon, Ihlwan, Mark L. Clifford, and Stan Crock. "The Politics of Peril." *Business Week*, February 24, 2003.

Moon, Katharine. "US-South Korean Relations." In *The Future of US-Korean Relations: The Imbalance of Power*, edited by John Feffer, 29-44. New York: Routledge, 2006.

Moore, Rebecca R. *NATO's New Mission : Projecting Stability in a Post-Cold War World*. Westport, Conn.: Praeger Security International, 2007.

Moravcsik, Andrew. "Taking Preferences Seriously: A Liberal Theory of International Politics." *International Organization* 51, no. 4 (1997): 513-53.

Morgenthau, Hans Joachim, and Kenneth W. Thompson. *Politics Among Nations: The Struggle for Power and Peace*. Brief ed. New York: McGraw-Hill, 1993.

Mueller, John E. *War, Presidents, and Public Opinion*. Lanham, MD: University Press of America, 1985.

"NATO Requests German Troops for Combat Role in Afghanistan." Review of Reviewed Item. *Deutsche Welle*, no. February 21 (2008), http://www.dw-world.de/dw/article/0,2144,3095130,00.html.

Neustadt, Richard E., and Ernest R. May. *Thinking in Time: The Uses of History for Decision-Makers*. New York: Free Press; Collier Macmillan, 1986.

"New Commander to Take Command of Troops in Iraq." *Yonhap News Agency*, April 15, 2008.

"No Friction in Alliance over Iraq Troop Cut." *Korea Times*, November 25, 2005.

Noetzel, Timo, and Sibylle Scheipers. "Coalition Warfare in Afghanistan: Burden-Sharing or Disunity?" In *Asia and International Security Programmes*, 8. London: Chatham House, 2007.

North Atlantic Treaty Organization. *NATO Handbook*. Brussels: NATO Office of Information and Press, 2001.

———. 1949. The North Atlantic Treaty. North Atlantic Treaty Organization, http://www.nato.int/docu/basictxt/treaty.htm. (accessed March 10, 2008).

O'Hanlon, Michael E., and Jason H. Campbell. 2005. Tracking Variables of Reconstruction & Security in Post-Saddam Iraq, April 18, 2005. *Iraq Index*, ed. Michael E. O'Hanlon. The Brookings Institution, Saban Center for Middle East Policy, http://www3.brookings.edu/fp/saban/iraq/index20050418.pdf. (accessed September 18, 2007).

"Official Says US Requests Support if Military Action Taken against Iraq." *Yonhap News Agency*, November 21, 2002.

Ogus, Ayla, and Can Erbil. "The Effects of Instability on Turkey's Bilateral Trade with Iraq." *Turkish Policy Quarterly* 4, no. 4 (2005).

Oh, Yong-chin. "Is President Roh Turning Pro-United States?" *Korea Times*, March 31, 2003.

———. "Roh-Lee Combination Spells Danger." *Korea Times*, November 18, 2003.

———. "Roh Assures US That Troops Will Be Sent as Promised." *The Korea Times*, March 31, 2003.

———. "Roh Puts Top Priority on Preventing War." *Korea Times*, March 7, 2003.

Olson, Mancur. *The Logic of Collective Action; Public Goods and the Theory of Groups*, Harvard Economic Studies, V. 124. Cambridge, Mass.,: Harvard University Press, 1965.

Onishi, Norimitsu. "U.S. And South Korea Try to Redefine Their Alliance." *The New York Times*, December 26, 2003.

Oppel, Richard A., Jr. "Turkish-Bred Prosperity Makes War Less Likely in Iraqi Kurdistan." *The New York Times*, November 7, 2007.

"Over 5,000 ROK Soldiers Likely to Head to Iraq." *Korea Times*, October 20, 2003.

Overhaus, Marco. "German Foreign Policy and the Shadow of the Past." *SAIS Review* XXV, no. 2 (2005): 27-41.

Ozdamar, Ozgur, and Zeynep Taydas. "Foreign Policy, Public Opinion and the Iraq War: The Turkish Case." Presented to the International Studies Association Annual Convention. San Francisco: 2008.

Ozer, Utku Cakir. "Muslim Countries Should Come for the United States to Leave." *Milliyet*, August 23, 2003.

Ozkok, Ertugrul. "Has Ecevit's Illness Saved Saddam?" *Hurriyet*, June 15, 2002, 25.

Page, Benjamin I., and Robert Y. Shapiro. "Effects of Public Opinion on Policy." *American Political Science Review* 77, no. 1 (1983): 175-90.

Pan, Phillip P. "Turkey Rejects U.S. Use of Bases; Vote Could Alter Troop Deployment." *The Washington Post*, March 2, 2003, 01.

———. "Turkish Vote on Troops Shows Surprises of Democracy." *The Washington Post*, March 6, 2003, A18.

Park, Bill. "Strategic Location, Political Dislocation: Turkey, the United States, and Northern Iraq." *Middle East Review of International Affairs* 7, no. 2 (2003): 11-23.

Park, Hyeong Jung. 2005. Divergent Threat Perceptions on North Korea. *Forging New U.S.-ROK Political Relationships*, The Maureen and Mike Mansfield Foundation, http://www.mansfieldfdn.org/programs/program_pdfs/rok_us_park.pdf. (accessed May 28, 2008).

Park, John S. "Inside Multilateralism: The Six-Party Talks." *The Washington Quarterly* 28, no. 4 (2005): 75-91.

Parks, Bill. "Bridgehead or Bridge?" *The World Today* 58, no. 10 (2002): 7-9.

"Parliament Delays Vote on Non-Combat Troop Dispatch to Iraq." *Yonhap News Agency*, March 28, 2003.

Parry, Richard Lloyd. "I Urge the US: Don't Go Too Far." *The Times*, March 7, 2003, 6.

"Parties Blast 'Rejection Campaigns' for Troop Dispatch to Iraq." *Korea Times*, March 31, 2003.

Pauly, Robert J., and Tom Lansford. *Strategic Preemption: U.S. Foreign Policy and the Second Iraq War*. Burlington, VT: Ashgate Pub., 2004.

Peterson, Susan. *Crisis Bargaining and the State: The Domestic Politics of International Conflict*. Ann Arbor: University of Michigan Press, 1996.

Pierre, Andrew J. *Coalitions Building and Maintenance: The Gulf War, Kosovo, Afghanistan, and the War on Terrorism*. Washington, DC: Georgetown University, Institute for the Study of Diplomacy, 2002.

Pollack, Jonathan D. "US Strategies in Northeast Asia: A Revisionist Hegemon." In *Power and Security in Northeast Asia: Shifting Strategies*, edited by Byung-Kook Kim and Anthony Jones, 55-98. Boulder, Colo.: Lynne Rienner Publishers, 2007.

Prins, Brandon C., and Christopher Sprecher. "Institutional Constraints, Political Opposition, and Interstate Dispute Escalation: Evidence from Parlimentary Systems, 1946-1989." *Journal of Peace Research* 36, no. 2 (1999): 271-87.

"Progressives Prevail in Roh's Administration." *Korea Times*, November 15, 2003.

Prusher, Ilene R. 2003. Interview with Christian Amanpour. *International Correspondents*, CNN, http://transcripts.cnn.com/TRANSCRIPTS/0303/07/i_c.01.html. (accessed April 3, 2008).

———. "Turkey Seeks Assurances from US ; Ankara Wants $30 Billion from Washington to Cover Potential Damages from an Attack by Iraq." *Christian Science Monitor*, February 18, 2003, 06.

Pudas, Terry J. "Preparing Future Coalition Commanders." *Joint Forces Quarterly*, no. 3 (1993/1994): 40-46.

Putnam, Robert D. "Diplomacy and Domestic Politics: The Logic of Two-Level Games." *International Organization* 42, no. 3 (1988): 427-60.

Record, Jeffrey. *The Specter of Munich: Reconsidering the Lessons of Appeasing Hitler*. 1st ed. Washington, D.C.: Potomac Books, 2007.

Reiter, Dan. *Crucible of Beliefs: Learning, Alliances, and World Wars*, Cornell Studies in Security Affairs. Ithaca, N.Y.: Cornell University Press, 1996.

Republic of Korea. "The Policy for Peace and Prosperity." edited by Ministry of Unification, 28, 2003.

Republic of Turkey, . 2001. The Constitution of the Republic of Turkey. http://www.anayasa.gov.tr/images/loaded/pdf_dosyalari/THE_CONSTITUTION_OF_THE_REPUBLIC_OF_TURKEY.pdf. (accessed April 1, 2008).

Reuter, Helmut. "Germany's Red Line in Its Aid to Iraq: No Troops." *Deutsche Presse-Agentur*, June 21, 2005.

Richburg, Keith B., and Peter Slevin. "Turks near Deal Giving U.S. Access to Bases; Aid Pact Would Open Northern Front in War:." *The Washington Post*, February 22, 2003, 01.

Risse-Kappen, Thomas. "Public Opinion, Domestic Structure, and Foreign Policy in Liberal Democracies." *World Politics* 43, no. 4 (1991): 479-512.

Roberts, Geoffrey K. *German Electoral Politics*, Issues in German Politics. Manchester; New York: Manchester University Press; Palgrave, 2006.

Robins, Philip. *Suits and Uniforms: Turkish Foreign Policy since the Cold War*. Seattle, Wash.: University of Washington Press, 2003.

Roeder, Philip G. *Red Sunset: The Failure of Soviet Politics*. Princeton, N.J.: Princeton University Press, 1993.

"Roh's Controversial Performance in Summit Theatrics." *Korea Times*, May 19, 2003.

"Roh-Lee Combination Spells Danger." *Korea Times*, November 18, 2003.

"Roh Appeals to Nation to Back Troop Dispatch." *Korea Times*, April 3, 2003.

"Roh Appears to Be Winning Some U.S. Hearts and Minds." *Yonhap News Agency*, April 1, 2003.

"Roh Faces Foreign Policy Challenges." *Korea Times*, March 6, 2003.

"Roh to Appeal to Nation for Troop Dispatch Bill Today." *Korea Times*, April 2, 2003.

"Roh to Walk Diplomatic Fine Line over Nk." *Korea Times*, February 26, 2003.

"Roh Tries to Soften Opposition to Troop Dispatch." *Korea Times*, March 27, 2003.

"Roh Trying to Mend Fences with US." *Korea Times*, March 13, 2003.

"Roh Vows Closer Ties with US." *Korea Times*, April 3, 2003.

"Roh, Bush Show Signs of Reconciliation." *Korea Times*, March 15, 2003.

"ROK Delays Dispatch of Troops Earmarked for Iraq." *China Daily*, March 20, 2004.

"ROK Foreign Minister on DPRK Nuclear Issue, USFK, ROK Troop Support in Iraq." *KBS Radio 1*, March 12, 2003.

Rosati, Jerel A. "A Cognitive Approach to the Study of Foreign Policy." In *Foreign Policy Analysis: Continuity and Change in Its Second Generation*, edited by Laura Neack, Jeanne A. K. Hey and Patrick Jude Haney, 49-70. Englewood Cliffs, N.J.: Prentice Hall, 1995.

Rosenau, James N. *Public Opinion and Foreign Policy; an Operational Formulation*. New York,: Random House, 1961.

Rubin, Michael. 2005. A Comedy of Errors: American-Turkish Diplomacy and the Iraq War. *Turkish Policy Quarterly*, Colombia International Affairs Online, http://www.ciaonet.org/olj/tpq/vol4-1/. (accessed November 14, 2006).

Rudolf, Peter. "The Myth of the 'German Way': German Foreign Policy and Transatlantic Relations." *Survival* 47, no. 1 (2005): 133-52.

Rumsfeld, Donald. 2001. Secretary Rumsfeld Media Stakeout in Washington. *News Transcript*, ed. Defense Link News. U.S. Department of Defense, http://www.defenselink.mil/transcripts/transcript.aspx?transcriptid=1926. (accessed December 19, 2007).

Russett, Bruce M. *What Price Vigilance? The Burdens of National Defense*. New Haven,: Yale University Press, 1970.

Russett, Bruce M., and Harvey Starr. *World Politics: The Menu for Choice*. 3rd ed. New York: W.H. Freeman, 1989.

"S. Korea's Ruling Party Will Back Troop Extension in Iraq." *Associated Press*, November 24, 2006.

"S. Korea to Decrease Activity of Troops in Iraq." *Yonhap News Agency*, December 29, 2007.

S. Korea Votes to Impeach Roh. 2004. CNN, http://www.cnn.com/2004/WORLD/asiapcf/03/11/skorea.roh.fighting/. (accessed June 27, 2008).

"S. Korean Government, Parties Hope Troop Bill to 'Solidify' 'Alliance' with US." *Yonhap News Agency*, April 2, 2003.

"S.Korea to Withdraw Iraq Troops Next Year." *United Press International*, November 30, 2006.

Sachs, Susan. "Turkey Begins to Think Twice About Sending Troops to Iraq." *The New York Times*, October 24, 2003, A12.

Saideman, Stephen M., David P. Auerswald, and Michael J. Tierney. "Caveat Emptor: Efforts to Control Contributions to Multilateral Military Interventions." Paper presented at the Annual Meeting of the American Political Science Association, Chicago, August 29 - September 2, 2007.

Salmoni, Barak A. 2003. Strategic Partners or Estranged Allies: Turkey, the United States, and Operation Iraqi Freedom. *Strategic Insights*, Center for Contemporary Conflict, Naval Postgraduate School, http://www.ccc.nps.navy.mil/si/july03/middleEast.asp. (accessed November 10, 2006).

Salopek, Paul. "Cabinet Supports U.S. Use of Turkish Bases; Parliament Gets Final Say on Issue." *Chicago Tribune*, Febraury 25, 2003, 6.

Sanger, David E. "Turk Offers Partial Support on Iraq in Meeting with Bush." *The New York Times*, December 11, 2002, A21.

Sayari, Sabri. "Between Allies and Neighbors: Turkey's Burden Sharing Policy in the Gulf Conflict." In *Friends in Need : Burden Sharing in the Persian Gulf War*, edited by Andrew Bennett, Joseph Lepgold and Danny Unger, 197-217. New York: St. Martin's Press, 1997.

Sazak, Derya. "Ecevit's Health." *Milliyet*, May 5, 2002.

———. "Future of Region Not Clear for the United States." *Milliyet*, February 10, 2003, FBIS-NES-2003-0211

———. "One Step Ahead." *Milliyet*, January 29, 2004, 19.

———. "Raid in Northern Iraq." *Milliyet*, July 6, 2003.

Scharping, Rudolph. 2002. Global Security - New Challenges, New Strategies. Munich Conference on Security Policy, http://www.securityconference.de/konferenzen/rede.php?menu_2002=&menu_konferenzen_archiv=&menu_2008=&menu_konferenzen=&sprache=en&id=88&. (accessed February 20, 2008).

Schedler, Andreas "What Is Democratic Consolidation?" *Journal of Democracy* 9, no. 2 (1998): 91-107.

Schmitt, Eric. "North Korea Mig's Intercept U.S. Jet on Spying Mission." *The New York Times*, March 4, 2003.

———. "Up to 30,000 Troops from a Dozen Nations to Replace Some G.I.'S in Iraq." *The New York Times*, June 19, 2003.

Schrader, Esther. "The World; U.S. To Realign Troops in Asia; the Pentagon Is Shifting to Smaller, More Mobile Forces to Confront New Challenges. Among the Changes, It May Seek to Base Ships Off Vietnam." *Los Angeles Times*, May 29, 2003, 1.

Schröder's Iraq Rhetoric Alarms Western Allies. 2002. Telegraph Media Group, http://www.telegraph.co.uk/news/main.jhtml?xml=/news/2002/09/15/wschr15.xml. (accessed March 4, 2008).

Schröder, Gerhard. "Die Anschläge in Den USA [the Strikes in the USA]." government declaration, 2001.

———. "German Leader Rejects Idea of More Help for Iraq." *Der Spiegel*, November 24, 2003, 33-36.

———. "Rücktritt Wäre Flucht, Dazu Neige Ich Nicht [to Step Down Would Be an Escape, That Is Not My Inclination]." *Der Stern*, February 13, 2003.

———. "We Have a Good Relationship." *The Washington Post*, February 29, 2004, B07.

Schwarz, Peter. 2006. New York Times Raises New Charges against German Intelligence. *World Socialist Web Site*, http://www.wsws.org/articles/2006/mar2006/nbnd-m02.shtml. (accessed December 31, 2007).

Sciolino, Elaine. "Threats and Responses: Discord; France to Veto Resolution on Iraq War, Chirac Says." *The New York Times*, March 11, 2003.

Scofield, David. 2004. Clearing the Nuclear Fog over North Korea. Worldpress.org, http://www.worldpress.org/Asia/1768.cfm. (accessed June 27, 2008).

Seo, Hyun-jin. "South Flexes New Negotiation Muscle." *The Korea Herald*, May 24, 2003.

Seo, Hyun-jin "Both Roh, Bush Score in Phone Talks." *The Korea Herald*, March 14, 2003.

Seongwhun, Cheon "North Korea and the ROK–U.S. Security Alliance." *Armed Forces and Society* 34, no. 1 (2007): 4-21.

"Seoul's Decision to Send Troops Assures US of Alliance." *Korea Times*, March 31, 2003.

"Seoul against US Moves on Iraq." *Korea Times*, September 27, 2002.

"Seoul to Offer $10 Mil. For Iraqi Refugees." *Korea Times*, April 4, 2003.

"Seoul to Provide $10 Mil. To Iraq for Humanitarian Assistance." *Korea Times*, April 7, 2003.

"Seoul to Throw Support for US War on Iraq." *Korea Times*, March 11, 2003.

"Seoul Will Send Iraq Troops." *Korea Times*, May 20, 2004.

Shanker, Thom. "Rumsfeld Faults Turkey for Barring Use of Its Land in '03 to Open Northern Front in Iraq." *The New York Times*, March 21, 2005.

Sharp, Jeremy M., and Christopher M. Blanchard. "Post-War Iraq: A Table and Chronology of Foreign Contributions." *CRS Report for Congress*, 23. Washington DC: Congressional Research Service, 2005.

———. "Post-War Iraq: Foreign Contributions to Training, Peacekeeping, and Reconstruction." *CRS Report for Congress - RL32105*: Congressional Research Service, 2007.

Sheen, Seongho. "Grudging Partner: South Korea." *Asian Affairs, an American Review* 30, no. 2 (2003): 96-103.

Shin, Gi-wook, and Paul Y Chang. "The Politics of Nationalism in US-Korean Relations." In *The Future of US-Korean Relations: The Imbalance of Power*, edited by John Feffer, 45-63. New York: Routledge, 2006.

Shin, Yong-pae. "Roh Makes Final Appeal over Troop Bill." *The Korea Herald*, April 2, 2003.

Sin, Chong-rok. "Who Moves President Roh? Trio Quickly Rising." *Choson Ilbo*, March 26, 2003.

Siwert-Probst, Judith. "Traditional Institutions of Foreign Policy." In *Germany's New Foreign Policy: Decision-Making in an Interdependent World*, edited by Wolf-Dieter Eberwein and Karl Kaiser, 19-37. Houndmills, Basingstoke, Hampshire ; New York: Palgrave, 2001.

Smith, Craig S. "Major Creditors Agree to Cancel 80% of Iraq Debt." *The New York Times*, November 22, 2004, A1.

Snyder, Glenn H. *Alliance Politics*, Cornell Studies in Security Affairs. Ithaca, N.Y.: Cornell University Press, 1997.

———. "The Security Dilemma in Alliance Politics." *World Politics* 36, no. 4 (1984): 461-95.

Snyder, Scott. "South Korea's Squeeze Play." *The Washington Quarterly* 28, no. 4 (2005): 93-106.

Sohn, Byoung-kwon. "Addressing Limits of Parliamentary Democracy." *The Korea Herald*, February 12, 2008.

Soon-young, Hong. "Thawing Korea's Cold War: The Path to Peace on the Korean Peninsula." *Foreign Affairs* 78, no. 3 (1999).

"Sources Say US Requesting 5,000 South Korean Troops for Iraq Mission." *Yonhap News Agency*, September 27, 2003.

"South Korea's National Assembly Approves Bill on Troop Dispatch to Iraq." *Yonhap News Agency*, April 2, 2003.

"South Korea Approves Extension of Troops in Iraq." *Yonhap News Agency*, December 22, 2006.

"South Korea Plans to Dispatch 3,200 Troops to Iraq." *Choson Ilbo*, December 11, 2003.

"South Korea Says Saddam's Arrest Reduces Uneasiness over Sending Troops to Iraq." *Yonhap News Agency*, December 15, 2003.

"South Korea to Extend Troop Stay in Iraq but Cut Presence by Half." *Yonhap News Agency*, October 23, 2007.

"South Korea to Investigate Diplomats for Questioning Policy." *Yonhap News Agency*, January 12, 2004.

"South Korean Assembly Postpones Vote on Dispatch of Troops to Iraq." *Yonhap News Agency*, March 25, 2003.

"South Korean Defense Minister Denies Number of Troops to Iraq Decided." *Yonhap News Agency*, October 28, 2003.

"South Korean Leader Pledges Additional Aid to Iraq in Meeting with Arab Envoys." *Yonhap News Agency*, February 17, 2004.

"South Korean Minister Seeks to Resolve Dispute with US over Iraq Troop Cut." *Yonhap News Agency*, November 24, 2005.

"South Korean Policymakers Hold Meeting on Iraq Troop Dispatch." *Yonhap News Agency*, June 14, 2004.

"South Korean President's Speech Finds across-the-Board Support at Assembly." *Yonhap News Agency*, April 2, 2003.

"South Korean President Appeals for Support on Troops Dispatch to Iraq." *Yonhap News Agency*, April 2, 2003.

"South Korean President Chairs National Security Council Meeting." *Yonhap News Agency*, March 20, 2003.

"South Korean President Seeks Bipartisan Support for Troop Deployment to Gulf." *Yonhap News Agency*, March 19, 2003.

"South Korean President, Parties to Discuss Cooperation in Event of Iraq War." *Yonhap News Agency*, March 18, 2003.

"South Korean Security Council to Meet 18 September on Troops for Iraq." *Yonhap News Agency*, September 16, 2003.

Special Inspector General for Iraq Reconstruction. "Section 2--Iraq Reconstruction: Funding Sources and Uses." 80. Arlington, Virginia: SIGIR, 2009.

Spencer, Richard. "S Korea Urges US Troops to Stay." *The Daily Telegraph*, March 8, 2003.

Spoerle-Strohmenger, Petra. 2003. Struggling Hard to Find Solutions to the Conflict in Iraq. *39th Munich Conference on Security Policy*, ed. Munich Conference on Security Policy. http://www.securityconference.de/konferenzen/2003/. (accessed December 3, 2007).

Sprowls, George. "States and War Coalitions: A Study of the Gulf War." Dissertation, West Virginia University, 1998.

Stangarone, Troy. 2007. Taking a Larger Role in International Affairs: Korea's Growing Efforts in Peacekeeping Missions and Development Aid. *Korea Insight*, Korea Economic Institute, http://www.keia.com/Publications/Insight/2007/august%2007.pdf. (accessed May 19, 2008).

Steele, Jonathon. "Germany's Cast Iron Chancellor: Schroder Is Determined to Keep out of Any US War with Iraq." *The Guardian*, December 3, 2002.

Steinberg, Gerald. *The American Political Science Review* 92, no. 3 (1998): 743-44.

Struck, Doug. "Powell Makes Few Gains on Asia Tour; Secretary Unable to Win Pledges of Support on North Korea, Iraq." *The Washington Post*, February 25, 2003, 16.

Szabo, Stephen F. *Parting Ways: The Crisis in German-American Relations*. Washington, D.C.: Brookings Institution Press, 2004.

Tago, Atsushi. "When Are Democratic Friends Unreliable? The Unilateral Withdrawal of Troops from the 'Coalition of the Willing'." Paper presented at the Annual Meeting of the American Political Science Association, Chicago, August 30-September 2, 2007.

"Talk of South Korean Troop Reduction Points to Uncertainty of Iraq Coalition Future." *Associated Press*, November 18, 2005.

Tayyar, Samil. "Bush's Hands Are Tied." *Sabah*, February 21, 2003.
Tewes, Henning. "How Civilian? How Much Power? Germany and the Eastern Enlargement of NATO." In *Germany as a Civilian Power? The Foreign Policy of the Berlin Republic*, edited by Sebastian Harnisch and Hanns Maull, 10-25. Manchester; New York: Manchester University Press; Palgrave, 2001.
Tezkan, Mehmet. "What Happened to International Legitimacy?" *Sabah*, April 4, 2003.
Thies, Wallace J. *Friendly Rivals: Bargaining and Burden-Shifting in NATO*. Armon, NY: M.E. Sharp, 2002.
Timmins, Graham. "Germany: Solidarity without Adventures." In *The Iraq War: Causes and Consequences*, edited by Rick Fawn and Raymond A. Hinnebusch, ix, 357 p. Boulder, Colo.: Lynne Rienner Publishers, 2006.
Torchia, Christopher. "South Korean President Says He Avoided Sensitive Issues in Bush Meeting with Bush." *The Associated Press*, May 15, 2003.
Treverton, Gregory F., Eric Larson, and Spencer H. Kim. "Bridging the 'Open Water' in the US-South Korea Military Alliance." *The Korean Journal of Defense Analysis* XV, no. 2 (2003): 153-76.
"Troop Dispatch Cuts President Roh's Support Group in Half." *Korea Times*, March 31, 2003.
"Turkey's Gul Says Syria, Turkey to Exert Efforts for Peaceful Solution to Iraq " *Anatolia*, January 4, 2003.
"Turkey Says Current Cooperation with US Reflects US Preferences on War Plans " *Anatolia*, March 29, 2003.
"Turkey, US Agree on Deterrent Policy against, Territorial Integrity of Iraq " *Anatolia*, December 3, 2002.
"Turkey: Country Profile 2003." In *Country Profiles*. London: The Economist Intelligence Unit, 2003.
Turkish-US Relations 2003. 2003. Anatolia.com Inc., Office of the Prime Minister, Directorate of Press and Information, http://www.turkishpress.com/specials/2003/yir/usa.asp. (accessed January 11, 2007).
"Turkish US Envoy Explains Work under Way for More Appropriate Conditions for Loan." *Anatolia*, February 17, 2004.
"Two of Roh's Decisions Expected to Have Major Implications." *Yonhap News Agency*, March 28, 2003.
"U.S. Asks for Help in Iraq War." *The Korea Herald*, March 11, 2003.
"U.S. Requested Dispatch of S.K. Light Infantry to Iraq: Official." *Yonhap News Agency*, September 15, 2003.
"U.S. Requests Brigade-Level Combat Troop Deployment to Iraq." *Yonhap News Agency*, September 15, 2003.
"U.S. Wants South Korea to Send Troops to Mosul, Official Says." *Yonhap News Agency*, October 2, 2003.
United Kingdom, House of Lords. "Hl Paper 236-I Waging War: Parliament's Role and Responsibility." In *15th Report of Session 2005–06*, edited by Select Committee on the Constitution, 61. London: House of Lords, 2006.
United Kingdom, Secretary of State for Constitutional Affairs and Lord Chancellor. "Government Response to the House of Lords Constitution Committee's Report Fifteenth Report of Session 2005-06: Waging War: Parliament's Role and Responsibility." 6. London, 2006.

United Nations. 2003. Security Council Meeting Minutes, 4721st Meeting, 19 March 2003, S/Pv.4721. *Meetings Conducted/Actions Taken by the Security Council in 2003*, http://daccessdds.un.org/doc/UNDOC/PRO/N03/286/04/PDF/N0328604.pdf?OpenElement. (accessed December 27, 2007).

United Nations Department of Peacekeeping Operations. 2007. United Nations Peacekeeping Factsheet. United Nations, http://www.un.org/Depts/dpko/factsheet.pdf. (accessed October 1, 2007).

United Nations Security Council, . 2003. Spain, United Kingdom of Great Britain and Northern Ireland and United States of America: Draft Resolution. S/2003/215. United Nations, http://www.un.org/News/dh/iraq/res-iraq-07mar03-en-rev.pdf. (accessed March 4, 2008).

United Nations Security Council. 2002. Resolution 1441. United Nations, http://daccessdds.un.org/doc/UNDOC/GEN/N02/682/26/PDF/N0268226.pdf. (accessed October 12, 2007).

———. 2003. Resolution 1472. United Nations, http://daccessdds.un.org/doc/UNDOC/GEN/N03/563/91/PDF/N0330209.pdf. (accessed May 10, 2009).

———. 2003. Resolution 1511. United Nations, http://daccessdds.un.org/doc/UNDOC/GEN/N03/563/91/PDF/N0356391.pdf. (accessed October 24, 2007).

United Nations. 1945. Chapter VII: Action with Respect to Threats to the Peace, Breaches of the Peace, and Acts of Aggression. United Nations, http://www.un.org/en/documents/charter/chapter7.shtml. (accessed June 4, 2009).

United States Central Command. 2008. Coalition Countries: Republic of Korea. U.S. Central Command, http://www.centcom.mil/en/finance/93.html. (accessed May 15, 2008).

United States Department of State. "Section 2207 Report on Iraq Relief and Reconstruction." Washington DC: Department of State Bureau of Near Eastern Affairs, 2005.

———. 2008. "Section 2207 Report on Iraq Relief and Reconstruction." Department of State Bureau of Near Eastern Affairs, http://www.state.gov/documents/organization/105341.pdf. (accessed May 16, 2008).

United States. White House. 2003. U.S. Secretary of State Colin Powell Addresses the U.N. Security Council http://www.whitehouse.gov/news/releases/2003/02/20030205-1.html#17. (accessed February 21, 2008).

"Uri under Fire for Stalling Iraq Troop Dispatch Bill." *Korea Times*, February 11, 2004.

"US Asks ROK to Send Light Infantry Division to Iraq." *Korea Times*, September 16, 2003.

"US Learned of South Korean Troop Reduction from Media." *Yonhap News Agency*, November 21, 2005.

"US Respects Seoul's Decision on Troop Dispatch to Iraq: Rumsfeld." *Korea Times*, November 18, 2003.

"US Wants Korea to Command Multinational Division in Iraq." *Korea Times*, September 19, 2003.

US, Britain and Spain Abandon Resolution. 2003. Associated Press, http://www.globalpolicy.org/security/issues/iraq/attack/armtwist/2003/0317usbritspain.htm. (accessed December 27, 2007).

"US, Turkey Split over Airspace." *Herald Sun*, March 22, 2003.

"USA Reiterates Support for South Korea's "Sunshine Policy"." *Yonhap News Agency*, March 14, 2003.

Uslu, Nasuh, Metin Toprak, Ibrahim Dalmis, and Ertan Aydin. "Turkish Public Opinion toward the United States in the Context of the Iraq Question." *Middle East Review of International Affairs* 9, no. 3 (2005): 75-107.

Van Belle, Douglas. "Domestic Imperatives and Rational Models of Foreign Policy Decision Making." In *The Limits of State Autonomy: Societal Groups and Foreign Policy Formulation*, edited by David Skidmore and Valerie M. Hudson, 151-83. Boulder: Westview Press, 1993.

Venkus, Robert E. *Raid on Qaddafi: The Untold Story of History's Longest Fighter Mission by the Pilot Who Directed It.* 1st ed. New York: St. Martin's Press, 1992.

Vincour, John. "Berlin Says Europeans Need Close Bond to U.S." *International Herald Tribune*, July 17, 2004.

Vivk, Karl. "After Calls on Turkey, U.S. Put on Hold." *Washington Post*, January 8, 2003, 14.

"Vote on Troop Dispatch Delayed Again." *Yonhap News Agency*, February 9, 2004.

Walker, Marcus, and McKinnon. John D. "Germany Considers Expanding Role of the Military in Security." *Wall Street Journal*, June 11, 2008.

Walker, Martin. "The Winter of Germany's Discontent." *World Policy Journal* 19, no. 4 (2002/2003): 37-48.

Walt, Stephen M. *The Origins of Alliances*, Cornell Studies in Security Affairs. Ithaca: Cornell University Press, 1987.

Wehrfritz, Geoge, and B.J. Lee. "A Life-or-Death Issue." *Newsweek*, March 3, 2003.

Weiss, Martin A. "Iraq: Paris Club Debt Relief." *CRS Report for Congress - RS21765*. Washington DC: Congressional Research Service, 2005.

Weitsman, Patricia A. *Dangerous Alliances: Proponents of Peace, Weapons of War*. Stanford, Calif.: Stanford University Press, 2004.

Weymouth, Lally. "The Importance of Having Friends: Schroder on Bush, the Terror War and His Woes at Home." *Newsweek*, February 11, 2002.

Whelan, Charles. "Armitage Heads for Seoul for Talks on Iraq, Anti-Americanism." *Agence France Presse*, December 10, 2002.

White House. 2002. Vice President Speaks at VFW 103rd National Convention. White House Press Office, http://www.whitehouse.gov/news/releases/2002/08/20020826.html. (accessed December 3, 2007).

Winrow, Gareth. "Turkey: Recalcitrant Ally." In *The Iraq War: Causes and Consequences*, edited by Rick Fawn and Raymond A. Hinnebusch, 197-208. Boulder, Colo.: Lynne Rienner Publishers, 2006.

Wolfowitz, Paul D. 2002. Speech at the 38th Munich Conference on Security Policy. Munich Conference on Security Policy, http://www.security conference.de/konferenzen/rede.php?menu_2002=&id=69&sprache=en&. (accessed December 19, 2007).

Wong-won, Yu. "Which Unit Will Be Dispatched to Iraq? Possibility of Dispatching Special Commando Brigade." *Choson Ilbo*, September 29, 2003.

Woods, Kevin, James Lacey, and Williamson Murray. "Saddam's Delusions: The View from the Inside." *Foreign Affairs* 85, no. 3 (2006).

Woods, Kevin M., and Joint Center for Operational Analysis (U.S.). 2006. *Iraqi Perspectives Project: A View of Operation Iraqi Freedom from Saddam's Senior Leadership.* United States Joint Forces Command, Joint Center for Operational Analysis, http://purl.access.gpo.gov/GPO/LPS68139 (accessed October 11, 2007).

Woodward, Bob. *Plan of Attack.* New York: Simon & Schuster, 2004.

"Young Rebel against Roh on Iraq War." *Korea Times*, March 28, 2003.

# Index

# About the Book

Why do states join ad hoc military coalitions? What motivated South Korea to contribute significantly to the Iraq War "coalition of the willing," while such steadfast allies as Turkey and Germany resisted US pressure to become burden-sharing partners? Drawing on his extensive examination of South Korean, German, and Turkish politics in the approach to and during the Iraq War, Daniel Baltrusaitis offers an in-depth analysis of how domestic political dynamics critically influence a state's level of material and diplomatic support to "coalitions of choice."

**Daniel F. Baltrusaitis** is assistant professor of international security studies at the US Air War College. His analysis of US Air Force doctrine in *Centralized Control with Decentralized Execution: Never Divide the Fleet* received the Douhet-Mitchell Award for visionary research.

